ON BECKETT

On Beckett

ESSAYS
AND
CRITICISM

EDITED
AND WITH
AN INTRODUCTION
BY
S. E. GONTARSKI

GROVE PRESS, INC., NEW YORK

First Grove Press Edition 1986
First Printing 1986
ISBN: 0-394-55354-3
Library of Congress Catalog Card Number: 86-227

First Evergreen Edition 1986
First Printing 1986
ISBN: 0-394-62231-6
Library of Congress Catalog Card Number: 86-227

Library of Congress Cataloging-in-Publication Data

Main entry under title:
On Beckett: Essays and Criticism

   1. Beckett, Samuel, 1906-   Criticism and
   Interpretation—Addresses, essays, lectures.
I. Gontarski, S. E.   II. Beckett, Samuel, 1906-
PR6003.E282Z814   1986   848'.91409   86-227
ISBN 0-394-55354-3
ISBN 0-394-62231-6 (pbk.)

Designed by Abe Lerner
Printed in the United States of America
Grove Press, Inc., 920 Broadway, New York, N.Y. 10010

                                              5 4 3 2 1

For Laura

SITTING PRETTILY BETWEEN
THE VIVALDI A MINOR AND
THE BACH DOUBLE

ACKNOWLEDGMENTS

The contributors to this volume have been cheerfully cooperative in the face of requests for editorial changes to be made under difficult deadlines and have earned my gratitude. In particular I should like to thank James Knowlson and John Pilling, only coincidentally my predecessors at the editorial helm of the *Journal of Beckett Studies*, for doing double duty as critics and translators. For released time to complete this volume, I am grateful to the Department of English at the Georgia Institute of Technology, its head, A. D. Van Nostrand, and the dean of the College of Sciences and Liberal Studies, Lester A. Karlovitz. At Grove Press this manuscript has been in the very capable hands of my editor, John Oakes, whom I thank warmly for his enthusiasm and the care he has lavished on this project.

Quotations from Beckett's works throughout are to the most recent Grove Press editions except where otherwise noted.

For permission to reprint the essays, I thank the following:

Walter D. Asmus, "Beckett Directs *Godot*," *Theatre Quarterly*, 5 (19, 20, September, November 1975): 19-26.

Walter D. Asmus, "Rehearsal Notes for the German Premiere of Beckett's *That Time* and *Footfalls* at the Schiller-Theater Werkstatt, Berlin," *Journal of Beckett Studies*, no. 2 (Summer 1977): 82-95.

Pierre Astier, "Beckett's *Ohio Impromptu*: A view from the Isle of Swans," *Modern Drama*, 25 (September 1982): 331-41.

Georges Bataille, "Molloy's Silence," *Critique*, 7 (May 1951): 387-96.

Maurice Blanchot, "Where Now? Who Now?" *Evergreen Review*, 2 (7, Winter 1959): 222-29.

Herbert Blau, "Notes from the Underground: *Waiting for Godot* and *Endgame*," *The Impossible Theater: A Manifesto* (New York: The Macmillan Co., 1964).

Acknowledgments

"Dialogue: Roger Blin and Tom Bishop," *Cahiers de L'Herne: Samuel Beckett* (Paris: Editions de l'Herne, 1976), 141-46.

Victor Bockris, ed., "Burroughs with Beckett in Berlin," *With William Burroughs: A Report from the Bunker* (New York: Seaver Books, 1981), 209-14. Reprinted with permission of Seaver Books.

Enoch Brater, "Light, Sound, Movement, and Action in Beckett's *Rockaby*," *Modern Drama*, 25 (September 1982): 342-48.

Ruby Cohn, "Beckett Directs: *Endgame* and *Krapp's Last Tape*," *Just Play: Beckett's Theater* (Princeton: Princeton University Press, 1980), 249-70.

J. E. Dearlove, "The Voice and Its Words: *How It Is*," *Accommodating the Chaos: Samuel Beckett's Nonrelational Art* (Durham, N.C.: Duke University Press, 1982), 85-106. Copyright Duke University Press.

Martin Esslin, "Samuel Beckett and the Art of Radio," *Mediations: Essays on Brecht, Beckett, and the Media* (New York: Grove Press, Inc., 1982), 125-54.

S. E. Gontarski, "Literary Allusions in *Happy Days*," *Beckett's Happy Days: A Manuscript Study* (Columbus: The Ohio State University Library Publications, 1977), 59-73.

S. E. Gontarski, "*Quad* and *Catastrophe*," *The Intent of Undoing in Samuel Beckett's Dramatic Texts* (Bloomington: Indiana University Press, 1985), 179-82.

Lawrence E. Harvey, "*Watt*," *Samuel Beckett: Poet and Critic* (Princeton: Princeton University Press, 1970), 348-84. Reprinted by permission of Princeton University Press.

Wolfgang Iser, "When Is the End Not the End? The Idea of Fiction in Beckett," *The Implied Reader: Patterns of Communication in Prose Fiction from Bunyan to Beckett* (Baltimore: Johns Hopkins University Press, 1974), 257-73.

James Knowlson, "*Footfalls*," *Frescoes of the Skull: The Later Prose and Drama of Samuel Beckett* (New York: Grove Press, Inc., 1980), 220-28.

Acknowledgments

Paul Lawley, "Counterpoint, Absence, and the Medium in Beckett's *Not I*," *Modern Drama*, 26 (4, December 1983): 407-13.

Eric P. Levy, "*Mercier and Camier*: Narration, Dante, and the Couple," *Beckett and the Voice of Species: A Study of the Prose Fiction* (Totowa, NJ: Barnes & Noble Books, 1980), 39-53.

"MacGowran on Beckett," Interview by Richard Toscan, *Theatre Quarterly*, 3 (11, July-September 1973): 15-22.

Dougald McMillan, "Samuel Beckett and the Visual Arts: The Embarrassment of Allegory," *Samuel Beckett: A Collection of Criticism*, Ruby Cohn, ed. (New York: McGraw-Hill Book Co., 1975), 121-35.

Dougald McMillan, "*Worstward Ho*," *Irish Literary Supplement*, 3 (2, Fall 1984): 39.

Marjorie Perloff, "Between Verse and Prose: Beckett and the New Poetry," *Critical Inquiry*, 9 (2, December 1982): 415-34.

John Pilling, "Shards of Ends and Odds in Prose: From *Fizzles* to *The Lost Ones*," *Frescoes of the Skull: The Later Prose and Drama of Samuel Beckett* (New York: Grove Press, Inc., 1980), 132-35, 144-49.

Rubin Rabinovitz, "*Murphy* and the Uses of Repetition," *The Development of Samuel Beckett's Fiction* (Urbana: University of Illinois Press, 1984), 71-103.

Alan Schneider, "Working with Beckett," *Samuel Beckett: The Art of Rhetoric*, Edouard Morot-Sir, Howard Harper, and Dougald McMillan, eds. (Chapel Hill: North Carolina Studies in the Romance Languages and Literatures, 1976), 271-89. Reprinted with permission of the publisher.

Richard W. Seaver, "Beckett and *Merlin*," *Samuel Beckett: I Can't Go On, I'll Go On* (New York: Grove Press, Inc., 1976), x-xviii, xxiii-xxv.

*   *   *

Harcourt Brace Jovanovich, Inc., "The Hollow Men" by T. S. Eliot. From *Collected Poems 1909-1962* by T. S. Eliot, copyright 1936 by Harcourt Brace Jovanovich, Inc.; copyright © 1963, 1964 by T.S. Eliot. Reprinted by permission of the publisher.

CONTENTS

Contents

THE STAGE

Contents

CODA

INTRODUCTION

Crritics and Crriticism: "Getting Known"

> Vladimir: *Sewer-rat!*
> Estragon: *Curate!*
> Vladimir: *Cretin!*
> Estragon (*with finality*): *Crritic!*

On 13 April 1986 Samuel Barclay Beckett marked his eightieth birthday, an event commemorated by international festivals, performances, and publications unprecedented in an author's lifetime. Such attention was neither sought nor particularly welcomed by Beckett, but it is fully the measure of his impact on the literature and culture of the latter half of the twentieth century—on that period now regularly called postmodern. With his eye on an academic career, Beckett began publishing in the twilight of the twenties with a pair of essays finally more polemical than critical—a defense of James Joyce's *Finnegans Wake* with its quirky, temporal punctuation, "Dante ...Bruno . Vico .. Joyce" (1929), and the commissioned monograph *Proust* (1931)—and a long, arcane poem, *Whoroscope* (1930), written within and simultaneously beyond the modernist tradition of *The Waste Land* and *Hugh Selwyn Mauberley*.

However, Beckett's work garnered little critical attention until the trilogy began to appear just after mid-century.[1] By then Beckett had completed an additional six prose works (three in English and the French trilogy), a volume of poems, *Echo's Bones and Other Precipitates* (1935), two full-length plays (one of which, *Eleuthéria*, he offered to Roger Blin along with *Godot* for production but subsequently withdrew), and an assortment of reviews as acidic and polemical as the early essays.[2]

Publication in these years, however, usually lagged behind composition, and in 1951, at age forty-five, having been publishing for more than two decades, Beckett was little known outside a small circle of

I

avant-garde artists. It is a memory he doubtless tapped for one of Krapp's birthday memoirs: "Seventeen copies sold, of which eleven at trade price to free circulating libraries beyond the seas. Getting known."[3]

As the century turned its midpoint, however, Beckett's critical reputation turned as well. By the early 1950s his French work began to appear from Les Editions de Minuit: *Molloy* and *Malone Meurt* in 1951, *En attendant Godot* in 1952, and *L'Innommable* in 1953. This work began to generate notice from the likes of Jean Anouilh, Alain Robbe-Grillet, and Maurice Blanchot, among others. The earliest serious assessment was a longish review from the novelist and disaffected surrealist Georges Bataille, which appeared in the literary journal *Critique* in 1951 (here reprinted in a fresh translation by John Pilling). That early enthusiasm for Beckett's French work is further reflected in Maurice Blanchot's analysis of *The Unnamable*, "Where Now? Who Now?" and in Richard Seaver's memoir "Beckett and *Merlin*." (*Merlin* not only published excerpts from *Watt* and *Molloy*, but also printed Seaver's own critical analysis, "Samuel Beckett: An Introduction," in the autumn of 1952.)

Interest in the United States followed as translations of the French work began to appear from Grove Press: *Waiting for Godot* in 1954, *Molloy* (jointly with Olympia Press, Paris) in 1955, *Malone Dies* in 1956, and *The Unnamable* and *Endgame* in 1958. The work quickly caught the attention of the American academic community. Edith Kern, for instance, published her "Drama Stripped for Inaction: Beckett's *Godot*" in the winter of 1954-55. The Irish-American critic Vivian Mercier produced a series of essays and reviews of Beckett's work in 1955 for *New Republic*, *Hudson Review*, *New Statesman*, and *The Nation*. Ruby Cohn edited the first special issue of a journal devoted to Beckett's work, *Perspective*, in the autumn of 1959, completed the first doctoral dissertation on Beckett's work at Washington University, St. Louis, the following year, and published it two years later with Rutgers University Press as *Samuel Beckett: The Comic Gamut*.

The first book to appear in English on Beckett's work, however, was Hugh Kenner's perceptive *Samuel Beckett: A Critical Study*, published by Grove Press in 1961 and by John Calder in 1962. Kenner, who had caused a critical stir in 1956 with his revised dissertation, *Dublin's Joyce*, first came across Beckett's name in an essay by Mercier (the polymath to whom Kenner's book is dedicated), "Dublin under the Joyces." The essay sent him to the Yale library to ferret out *Murphy*. Regrettably, not every member of that first generation of critics—that group which Ruby Cohn calls Becketteers—can be represented in this volume and still retain a substantial emphasis on the post-1961 work, but assuredly all subsequent analysts of Beckett's art stand on their critical shoulders.

In the "Personal Foreword" to *Back to Beckett* (1973), Ruby Cohn recalls an editorial rebuke to her early efforts to publish criticism about Samuel Beckett's work: "We like your criticism, but we don't feel your author merits publishing space." The rejection seemed confirmation of Beckett's self-deprecating comment to Richard Seaver: "No one's interested in this . . . this rubbish." By 1967, however, writing the introduction to his *festschrift, Beckett at 60*, John Calder (publisher of Beckett's poetry and prose in England) could claim, "More books have been written on Christ, Napoleon and Wagner, in that order, than anyone else. I predict that by 2000 A.D. Beckett may well rank fourth if the present flood of literature keeps up."

Calder's comments may seem wildly extravagant, a publisher's fantasy; yet the hyperbole does capture the growing interest in Beckett's art. Since Beckett was awarded the Nobel Prize in 1969, the critical waters have risen substantially. When Raymond Federman's and John Fletcher's monumental *Samuel Beckett, His Works and His Critics: An Essay in Bibliography* appeared in 1970, it covered critical material up to 1966 (1968 for books) and cited some 580 articles and 31 books; yet it already needed a supplement.[4] By 1976, when Tom Bishop and Raymond Federman edited the Beckett number of *Cahiers de L'Herne*, they estimated that sixty-odd books and five thousand articles on Beckett were in print. The progression continues geometrically.

Yet despite the staggering amount of analysis of Beckett's work already in print, it has yet to receive *thorough* critical scrutiny. Part of the function of this introduction is not only to survey what has been done also to suggest some of what needs doing. Beckett's translations, for example, particularly those of other writers, remain neglected. In the 1930s Beckett thought to earn something like a living from translation and, in spurts, did an astonishing amount of it, even tackling the untranslatable "Anna Livia Plurabelle" episode of *Finnegans Wake*, for which, as Richard Seaver notes, he received almost no credit. His contribution to the surrealist number of *This Quarter* (September 1932) was so substantial, for example, that general editor

3

Edward Titus could say, "We cannot refrain from singling out Mr. Samuel Beckett's work for special acknowledgment. His rendering of the [Paul] Éluard and [André] Breton poems in particular is characterizable only in superlatives."

The single most neglected work in the Beckett canon is doubtless the volume of Mexican verse he translated in 1950 under a UNESCO commission. Beckett translated more than one hundred poems by some thirty-five Mexican poets selected by Octavio Paz, and the volume was published as *Anthology of Mexican Poetry* by Indiana University Press in 1958, after annoying delays. Although Beckett "loathed" the work and inscribed the presentation copy to friend Con Leventhal, "*Cette vieille foutaise alimentaire*," his achievement received some early praise. James Schuyler called the translations a "Horowitz performance of linguistic gift and skill."⁵ Yet the volume languishes, along with the translations for *This Quarter* and *transition* and his translation of Robert Pinget's *La manivelle*, published as *The Old Tune* (*Evergreen Review* 5 [March-April 1961]: 47-60), in critical obscurity.

Admittedly, Beckett's translations are not praised without qualification when they do receive notice. Reviewing several texts including *Collected Poems in English and French* (1977) and Beckett's translation of Rimbaud's *Le Bateau ivre* (1932), once thought lost in the files of *This Quarter*, Richard Coe finds Beckett's translations at best uneven, principally because "Beckett as a 'poet' is playing about on the surface of language. It is a hit-and-miss business. Sometimes it works, sometimes it does not."⁶ In an essay entitled "Beckett's English," Coe makes his point even more strongly: "Now, it is generally assumed that Beckett is a superlative translator from the French, whether his own or anyone else's. It is true that he *can* be.... On the other hand, there are some efforts that had best been left unpublished. Rimbaud's *Bateau ivre* is one of these."⁷

While Coe's 1964 monograph *Beckett*, from Oliver and Boyd in England and Grove Press in the United States, remains a useful introduction to some of the philosophical underpinnings of Beckett's early and middle fiction, Coe seems preoccupied with the "ideas" in Beckett's work at the expense of its lyric and formal features. (It is precisely such a traditional critical quest for meaning that Wolfgang Iser addresses when he analyzes "The Idea of Fiction in Beckett.") But despite the limitations of Coe's criticism, he does skewer a salient point about Beckett's art: Even as a translator Beckett thinks as a poet. Marjorie

Perloff concurs as she analyzes Beckett's late prose, particularly *Ill Seen Ill Said*, as does Enoch Brater as he examines the late drama and calls *Rockaby* a "performance poem." It is a point, furthermore, evident to any reader of Beckett's letters. The ten-line poem embedded in the radio play *Words and Music* provides an example. Except for its lineation, it is almost indistinguishable from the play's prose:

> Then down the little way
> Through the trash
> Towards where
> All dark no begging
> No giving no words
> No sense no need
> Through the scum
> Down a little way
> To whence one glimpse
> Of that wellhead.[8]

Despite the skepticism about communication apparent in almost any of Beckett's works—indeed, because of that skepticism—Beckett remains a wordsmith, the most profound Joycean legacy in his art. In a 1937 letter to friend Axel Kaun, the 31-year-old Beckett outlined his antimodernist aesthetics in characteristically paradoxical terms: "To bore one hole after another in [language], until what lurks behind it—be it something or nothing—begins to seep through. I cannot imagine a higher goal for a writer today."[9] Beckett's "literature of the unword," however, is always attained through words, through immaculately used language. Within the generic and experimental diversity of his art, the connecting thread is its poetic, almost always lyric quality, even when language is turned against itself. Whatever Beckett is writing, fiction, drama, teleplays, criticism, translations, or even letters, he is foremost a poet.

The essays in this volume have been selected with an eye toward representing the range of Beckett's work and the historical and ideological breadth of the criticism that engages it. The selections have further been designed to invite continuous reading, to comment on and develop each other so that the volume as a whole reads more like a unified book—as much as such is possible given the diversity of hands at work—than a random collection of essays.

The Preliminaries section acts as an overture and is designed to introduce several fundamental, interrelated issues, as well as three distinct critical approaches. Richard Seaver's memoir not only evokes the shock of his own discovery of Beckett and his work but also offers an insightful vignette about working with Beckett on the translation of "La Fin." Dougald McMillan details the extent to which the visual arts and Dante (especially editions with the Botticelli illustrations) inform Beckett's art. Dante was a passion Beckett shared with Joyce, and their mutual admiration for the Florentine was at least one of the reasons Beckett was selected by Joyce to write the essay "Dante ... Bruno . Vico .. Joyce."

That rich texture of literary and visual allusions in Beckett's work is developed in many of the volume's essays, particularly in Rubin Rabinovitz's analysis of *Murphy*, Eric P. Levy's study of *Mercier and Camier*, and my own look at *Happy Days*. Although most of the critics herein analyze or at least mention Beckett's use of Dante, a thorough study that does for Beckett's art as a whole what Levy has done for *Mercier and Camier* has yet to be undertaken.[10]

Wolfgang Iser brings a more theoretical perspective to Beckett's work, yet still manages to focus on particular texts. The whole of his book *The Implied Reader*, for instance, engages Wayne Booth's argument in *The Rhetoric of Fiction* for an "implied author," and the analysis of ends and ending anthologized here takes issue with Frank Kermode's very influential study *The Sense of an Ending*. Iser discusses how Beckett anticipates and subverts our sense of ends and counters his audience's attempts, its *need*, to project meaning. Iser's phenomenological approach draws attention to the role of the reader and spectator in Beckett's art, and he examines how Beckett "draws the spectator into the play."

The early criticism of Bataille and Blanchot is significant because it anticipates much of the upheaval of post-structuralist literary theory, particularly Bataille's polysemous and oxymoronic view of "language as possibility, as ruleless game," and Blanchot's devaluation or dissolution of the author. Bataille is also keen to sense in 1951 that contradiction is the very signature of Beckett's work. Yet that early momentum, that theoretical and narratological interest in Beckett's art, has not been sustained (partly no doubt because Beckett deconstructs his own texts so thoroughly that deconstructive analyses, at any rate, often seem merely redundant), and so Iser's work is particularly welcome. With Blanchot, Iser shares an interest in the question of how we deal with the human tendency to impose order on texts. The role

6

of the reader or spectator in the phenomenological process of reading (interpreted broadly to include painting, sculpture, and theater as well as books among its objects), in the process of constructing meaning generally, is a perspective surprisingly little analyzed in a body of work itself so concerned with the phenomenon of perception.

The section called The Page takes up many of the issues sounded in Preliminaries but focuses on particular works of fiction. Rubin Rabinovitz's remarkably detailed analysis of the patterns of repetition in *Murphy* highlights Beckett's strongly formalist aesthetics even in so early a work. Already at work in *Murphy* is the recurrent, cyclic structure so evident in the two acts of *Godot*, the two parts of *Molloy* and *Play*, a structure that culminates in Beckett's most geometric work, *Quad*. The corresponding tendency toward poetic repetition so obvious in a play like *Rockaby* is also an essential aesthetic component of *Murphy*, Beckett's first full novel.

Lawrence Harvey, in addition to providing some biographical details for the composition of *Watt*, succinctly isolates a "principal theme of the novel: the need to know and the difficulty and indeed impossibility of knowing." The theme is pervasive throughout Beckett's work and is as psychological as epistemological; that is, the emphasis is as strongly on *need* as on *know*. Need (or desire) suggests a deficiency, an incompleteness of self, the necessity of another, a "lost one"—a dualism Beckett has contemplated in print, often in Cartesian terms, for more than half a century. In classroom lectures at Trinity College, Dublin, in 1931, Beckett referred to the cyclic pattern and unrequited nature of desire in Racine's *Andromaque* as follows: "A loves B, and B loves C, and C loves D. The great pagan tiger of sexuality chasing its tail in outer darkness." Murphy desires Celia and yet needs to find tranquillity in the microcosm; Mercier and Camier, or finally the narrator, need a purpose, a direction to their lives, and so they undertake a directionless journey.

In *Watt* the need is more epistemological, in *Company* more aesthetic, but Beckett's protagonists—deteriorating, fragmented, or disembodied—are all moved by needs often ill understood. The extratextual parallel is the reader who needs to order texts, as Blanchot suggests of *The Unnamable*. Even the godhead Mr. Knott is not exempt: "Mr. Knott, needing nothing if not, one, not to need, and two, a witness to his not needing."[11] Moreover, subject-object relationships are in such flux in Beckett's world that attainment or satisfaction, that is, com-

7

pleteness, is beyond question. Listen to the twenty-five-year-old Beckett ostensibly discussing Proust: "The aspirations of yesterday were valid for yesterday's ego, not for to-day's. We are disappointed at the nullity of what we are pleased to call attainment."[12]

In her introductory taxonomy of Beckett's fiction, J. E. Dearlove sees *How It Is* less as the culmination of Beckett's French period than as the anticipation of those late prose works (say, after 1961) which focus on "the celebration of the artificiality of structure itself." Beckett's "later works embrace the imagination without lamenting its dissociation from material reality"; in Beckett's words, from *Fizzles*, "Closed Space. All needed to be known for say is known."[13] In "Shards of Ends and Odds in Prose: From *Fizzles* to *The Lost Ones*," John Pilling continues the emphasis on Beckett's almost hermetic fictional structures, on "the way his imagination [has been] working in the 1960s and 1970s," and in the most successful or more complete of these minimal pieces, "Beckett is well on the way . . . to constructing a paradise that need not necessarily be lost, the paradise of the imagination." At least "up to a point," as the narrator of *Company* might add.

The 1980s saw Beckett produce a series of remarkable (and for him longer) prose works: *Company* (1980), *Ill Seen Ill Said* (1981), and *Worstward Ho* (1983). *Company*, in many respects the most accessible of these texts, is divided between a series of more or less autobiographical vignettes in the second person and the fictive musings of a hypothesizing voice in the third person. Almost all the incidents that the second person iterates are potentially painful. They suggest a loveless childhood in which the boy was rebuked or derided by his parents for his comments on the perception of the sky[14] or for his report of being able to see the mountains of Wales from his "nook in the gorse"[15] in the Wicklow Hills. There is the lovelessness of parents "stooping over cradle,"[16] the lack of parental concern for a child in such desperate need of attention that he throws himself from "the top of a great fir,"[17] or the embarrassment of the child's being on exhibition, standing naked at "the tip of the high board" before the "many eyes" of his father's cronies as he is urged to "be a brave boy" and dive into the Irish Sea.[18] The child in these "memories" seems never to have been the boy his parents wanted. He was busy, even in those days, developing the light of his imagination, one of the work's dominant metaphors.

The second-person voice also recounts some embarrassing and naïve incidents: a boy who believes he can play God by intervening in the life of an ill hedgehog;[19] a child who can look out a summer-house window to see that "all without is rosy";[20] or a young adult who believes that his path (literal and metaphorical) is straight, "a beeline,"[21] and looks back one morning to see the pattern in the fresh snow, "withershins."[22] The incident is wryly comic even as it also suggests the plight of man living the pattern of the sinistral spiral of Dante's hell. Even the sensual moments are painful. The erotic episode of his feeling the "fringe of her long black hair"[23] is intimately connected to the story of the lover's pregnancy, with its pun about her being late. The episode's concluding line hints at the disastrous end to the love affair, "all dead still."[24]

When I was preparing a stage version of *Company* with Beckett in the fall of 1984 (it opened at the Los Angeles Actors' Theatre in February of 1985), Beckett discussed the contrapuntal, fugal nature of these two voices. The third-person voice, he noted, was "erecting a series of hypotheses, each of which is false." The second-person voice was "trying to create a history, a past for the third person." The third person resists the intrusions of the second person for numerous reasons. The memories are, of course, painful, for the most part, but "he" also resists the simplified notion that a sum of memories (or stories) will add up to a history, a life. And even if the second-person voice recounts incidents from the past more or less accurately, memories are not historical but fictive: selected, reordered, reemphasized versions of past incidents. Philosophically, the separation of the voices allows for the dramatization of a phenomenological theme. In order to be perceived, the voice needs to be separated from the perceiver, and so the "you" voice must always be something other than the perceiver—a split that results in another form of Beckettian dualism. Memories themselves can never be part of an essential self, can never add up to a life, for as Jean-Paul Sartre notes, being-for-itself "is always something other than what can be said about it."

In "Between Verse and Prose: Beckett and the New Poetry," Marjorie Perloff looks at the new, hybrid, unlineated poetry, or what she calls the "odd prose-verse ambiguity," of *Ill Seen Ill Said*. Perloff calls the hybrid form at times "the associative monologue," a term she borrows from Northrop Frye, or "free prose" and discusses the (almost veiled) impact of this form on such poets as John Ashbery and Robert Creeley and on such performance poets as John Cage and David Antin. Finally, in his review of *Worstward Ho*, Dougald McMillan discusses

Beckett's "progression into a new territory," further along toward the worst, a desire or need itself never to be attained. If Beckett's art is, as he claims, an art of failure, in *Worstward Ho* he is still heading worster, still failing better, still trying to rupture language with language. This series of three progressively tighter, progressively denser, progressively less referential imaginative constructs or hermetic structures may very well constitute a second trilogy, a trilogy not of the failure to say the self and cease, but of the failure to realize a perfectly imagined, self-sufficient structure.

The focus shifts somewhat in The Stage section to accommodate performance, and the emphasis in this section—and even in this portion of the introduction—is on working with as well as on Beckett. The late Jack MacGowran, who had worked closely with Beckett on numerous productions and for whom Beckett wrote the teleplay *Eh Joe*, brings an actor's perspective to Beckett's work. He views drama on a direct, physical level, and his insights can be refreshingly naïve. In his dialogue with Tom Bishop, Roger Blin discusses his direction of three major early works, *Waiting for Godot, Endgame*, and *Happy Days*.

Alan Schneider, who had worked more closely on more Beckett productions than any other director, surveys his working relationship with Beckett through 1976. I was among the lucky few who worked closely enough with Schneider to know how attuned he was to the Beckettian text. I produced *Ohio Impromptu*, a play Beckett wrote for me in 1981 (the details are discussed by Pierre Astier in "Beckett's *Ohio Impromptu*: A View from the Isle of Swans"), and throughout rehearsals Schneider's sensitivity to and respect for Beckett's work was always evident. As the producer I worried a good deal about that production: Not only was I concerned about the difficult working conditions of rehearsing a play in New York for a theater space at Ohio State University that Schneider had never seen, on which another set was being built, with a university less than sensitive to the problems of staging a professional production, but I also worried a good deal about the interpersonal, the working relationship between actor and director. David Warrilow, whom I had asked to play the Reader, wrote in June of 1980 that he was very interested in the role, but "I have never met Alan Schneider and have never seen his work." Schneider had likewise neither met Warrilow nor seen his work.

I had for a time counted among my triumphs as a producer the union of these two artists; each had considerable experience with Beckett's work, but neither had worked with the other. Theatrically, they were a study in contrast: Schneider had directed the major modern playwrights on and off Broadway, had worked with all the major regional theaters in this country, and had taught at a number of universities; Warrilow had done most of his work in the artistically communal environment of Mabou Mines and was not accustomed to being "directed." And yet come together they did, artistically, but not finally through my efforts. It was the text, Beckett's art, that generated the rapport, and that production, with Rand Mitchell as Listener, went on to play throughout the world. It was clear to each of us working on *Ohio Impromptu* that Schneider heard Beckett's cadences and saw Beckett's austere, fearful symmetries in his mind's ears and eyes.

In "Working with Beckett," Schneider further outlines his directorial philosophy, his dedication to realizing a stage production as close to the author's wishes as he could make it. It is a self-effacing directorial style echoing that of Roger Blin. They both, as Tom Bishop suggests, serve the text. Quite a different view of directing is offered by Herbert Blau in "Notes from the Underground: *Waiting for Godot* and *Endgame*," an excerpt from *The Impossible Theater*. Blau's respect for the text is mediated by an equal respect for the selves—and even the souls—of the participants. With Jules Irving, Blau was co-founder and co-director of The Actor's Workshop of San Francisco, whose 1957 production of *Godot* played San Quentin prison (an account of which appears in the opening chapter of Martin Esslin's influential study *The Theatre of the Absurd*). One of the inmates at the time was Rick Cluchey, who went on, with the help of Alan Mandell of the Actor's Workshop, to form the San Quentin Drama Workshop, a group Beckett directed in Berlin in 1977 (see Ruby Cohn's account in "Beckett Directs: *Endgame* and *Krapp's Last Tape*") and in London in 1980 and 1984. Mandell has continued his association with that group, playing Nagg in their Beckett-directed *Endgame*, and with Beckett's work in general, playing the Figure, the sole role, in my own Los Angeles Actors' Theatre production of *Company* in 1985. Of late Blau's work has been more concerned with the theory of theater than with its practice. That is a duality with hierarchical implication with which he would doubtless take issue, but he is at least, as he says, now writing from within theory rather than from within the theater.

Walter D. Asmus has assisted Beckett at the Schiller-Theater in Berlin, and has subsequently recreated Beckett's *Godot* in the United

States (in English and German). In 1984, with the San Quentin Drama Workshop, Asmus took *Godot*, based on the Schiller production, on an Australian tour. The notes published here were compiled during rehearsals of *Godot*, which Beckett directed at the Schiller-Theater in 1975 (and contain Beckett's invaluable analysis of Lucky's speech) and during rehearsals of *That Time* and *Footfalls*, once again at the Schiller, the following year.

The excerpt from Ruby Cohn's indispensable *Just Play* details Beckett's directing career through the 1977 San Quentin Drama Workshop production of *Krapp's Last Tape* at Berlin's Akademie der Kunste and gives the lie to the impression that Beckett emerged full-blown in his first official role as a director with his 1967 production of *Endgame* at the Schiller. Beckett has taken an active interest in the production of his plays from the first, as Roger Blin confirms, attending rehearsals, suggesting changes, and in some cases doing more directing than the credited director. By the time Beckett officially staged a play, he had served nearly a fifteen-year theatrical apprenticeship. Moreover, Cohn also calls attention to Beckett's staging of Robert Pinget's *Hypothèse* with Pierre Chabert, the only play by another author Beckett has ever directed (although he claimed no credit for the work).

With Beckett such an active force in the production of his own work, changing his plays with each new production, questions about the finality of texts inevitably arise. Which version of Beckett's work— current production or published text, annotated copy on deposit in a university library or original publication—is most authoritative; which represents the author's most complete thinking on the subject? And what is, or should be, the relationship between the author's treatment of his work and productions by subsequent directors? Are Beckett's productions designed to be paradigms for future directors to follow? Certainly Beckett would be the first to say no, suggesting in rehearsals of *Endgame* in 1967 that his was only one of many possible *Endgames*.

Yet there are evidently limits to a director's prerogatives, boundaries to a work beyond which a production becomes something other than the author's work. Beckett attempted in 1984 first to stop, then to disassociate himself from the American Repertory Theater's production of *Endgame* directed by JoAnne Akalaitis (herself an alumna of Herbert Blau's Actor's Workshop and the Mabou Mines). Beckett's reluctance to allow substantial deviations in the play should have come as little surprise. His views on the matter were clear as early as 1962, when he said, "*within the limits of the specified text* the producer has plenty of scope for interpretation" (emphasis added).[25] Such problems of production have barely been touched by critics. A start will be made in 1987, however, when Grove Press, in conjunction with England's Faber and Faber, plans to issue *The Theatrical Notebooks of Samuel Beckett* and all the changes Beckett made in production will be identified. Critics and directors will at least have easy access to Beckett's plans for staging his own works. Whether they follow his lead—whether they should follow his lead—is quite another matter.[26]

James Knowlson discusses the composition and productions of *Footfalls*, offering an analysis that builds on Walter Asmus's rehearsal notes. And both Paul Lawley in "Counterpoint, Absence, and the Medium in Beckett's *Not I*" and Enoch Brater in "Light, Sound, Movement, and Action is *Rockaby*" share not only a penchant for serial titles but an interest in production details for their analyses. Martin Esslin, doubtless the most informed source on the subject, details Beckett's relationship with the British Broadcasting Corporation.

The section ends with my aperçu of two very recent plays, *Quad* and *Catastrophe*, and with an amendment to the fabled Beckettian nihilism. What Beckett continues to insist on as he enters his ninth decade, if only through his persistent productivity, is that within the detritus of western civilization, in the gloaming of the twentieth century, amid the remains of our culture, art remains worthy of human effort and attention.

The volume ends with a coda, a vestigial tail (or tale) that suggests that despite efforts to the contrary, discourse remains fictive. Susan Sontag, Allen Ginsberg, and William Burroughs visited Beckett briefly in Berlin and their recollections form a concatenation of misreadings. As Burroughs says, "Everyone has a completely different story." The conversation seems almost a conspiracy of validation for the antiempirical, antiepistemological themes Beckett has been exploring for more than half a century. With Watt they could agree that *nothing* had *happened*.

Paris, 1986

NOTES

1. For an excellent sense of the early reception of Beckett's work see Lawrence Graver and Raymond Federman, eds., *Samuel Beckett: The Critical Heritage* (London: Routledge & Kegan Paul, 1979).

2. These have been collected in Ruby Cohn, ed., *Disjecta: Miscellaneous Writings and a Dramatic Fragment* (New York: Grove Press, 1984).

3. Samuel Beckett, "Krapp's Last Tape," *The Collected Shorter Plays of Samuel Beckett* (New York: Grove Press, 1984), 62.

4. Shortly after the publication of the bibliography, the University of California Press approached J. C. C. Mays to compile a supplement that would update and correct the original volume. By 1976 Mays abandoned the project as unworkable without resetting the entire volume, since even the system of decimal numeration that Federman and Fletcher designed to allow for the volume's expansion was already insufficient to accommodate the post-Nobel Prize critical surge. See J. C. C. Mays, "Beckett Bibliography: A Revised Edition of Federman and Fletcher, or Not?" *The Beckett Circle / Le Cercle de Beckett: Newsletter of the Samuel Beckett Society*, 1 (2, Fall 1978).

5. James Schuyler, review, *Evergreen Review* 2 (7, Winter 1959): 221.

6. Richard Coe, review, *The Times* (London) *Literary Supplement*, 15 July 1977.

7. Morris Beja, S. E. Gontarski, and Pierre Astier, eds., *Samuel Beckett: Humanistic Perspectives* (Columbus: Ohio State University Press, 1983), 37.

8. Samuel Beckett, "Words and Music," *The Collected Shorter Plays of Samuel Beckett* (New York: Grove Press, 1984), 133-34.

9. Cohn, *Disjecta*, 170-73.

10. This is not to say that excellent studies of Beckett and Dante are not in print. See particularly Walter A. Strauss, "Dante's Belacqua and Beckett's Tramps," *Comparative Literature*, 2 (Summer 1959): 250-61; John Fletcher, "The Debt to Dante," *Samuel Beckett's Art* (London: Chatto and Windus, 1967), 106-20; and Michael J. Robinson, "From Purgatory to Inferno: Beckett and Dante Revisited," *Journal of Beckett Studies* (5, Autumn 1979), 69-82.

11. Samuel Beckett, *Watt* (New York: Grove Press, 1959), 202-3.

12. Samuel Beckett, *Proust* (New York: Grove Press, 1970), 3.

13. Samuel Beckett, *Fizzles* (New York: Grove Press, 1976), 37.

14. Samuel Beckett, *Company* (New York: Grove Press, 1980), 10-11.

15. Ibid., 25.

16. Ibid., 47.

17. Ibid., 21-22.

18. Ibid., 18.

19. Ibid., 29-31.

20. Ibid., 39.

21. Ibid., 35.

22. Ibid., 38.

23. Ibid., 48.

24. Ibid., 42.

25. Charles Marowitz, "Paris Log," *Encore* (March 1962), 45. The problem of textual deviation has been with Beckett from the first. As early as 9 January 1953, writing to Roger Blin about the incomplete fall of Estragon's trousers, Beckett noted: "Soyez seulement assez gentil de le rétablir comme c'est indiqué dans le texte..." (Only be kind enough to restore it as the text indicates...).

26. For an overview of the problems of performance changes see James Knowl-

son, "State of Play: Performance Changes and Beckett Scholarship," *Journal of Beckett Studies* (10), 109-20. For an assessment of the ART controversy see Martin Garbus and Gerald E. Singleton, "Playwright-Director Conflict: Whose Play Is It Anyway?" *New York Law Journal*, 192 (123, 28 December 1984); reprinted in *The Beckett Circle / Le Cercle de Beckett: Newsletter of the Samuel Beckett Society* 6 (2, Spring 1985).

PRELIMINARIES

RICHARD W. SEAVER

Beckett and
"Merlin"

The early fifties found me in Paris, fresh out of college, in search of I'm not sure what gods or ghosts but convinced they could be discovered only in that magic city. I had found quarters, if that term can be applied to an abandoned warehouse, on the rue du Sabot, a tiny street directly behind St.-Germain-des-Prés. The owner was a Swiss dealer in primitive art. In return for my tending the shop a few hours a week, he gave me free lodging in an empty ground-floor warehouse at the end of the courtyard. I mention the geography because this *dépôt*— which, my Swiss landlord proudly informed me, had once been a banana-drying shed—was destined to become the headquarters of the magazine- and book-publishing enterprise known to history as *Merlin* and also because it was a scant fifty yards from the offices of the most daring and perceptive French publisher of the time, Les Editions de Minuit.

There were two routes from my warehouse-home to the bright cafés of St.-Germain-des-Prés, one by the rue du Dragon, the other by the rue Bernard-Palissy, and since I took at least two trips to St.-Germain every day and always tried to avoid taking the same route twice in a row, it happened, almost inevitably, that I passed number 7 of the latter street at least once a day. Number 7, a *bordel* until the puritanical wrath of a famous female Gallic zealot of the period, Marthe Robert, caused these dens of iniquity to close in 1948, now housed Les Editions de Minuit. The grilled peephole was still on the thick wooden door. To the right of the door was a tiny display window set into the wall, which in times past had housed God knows what bawdy come-ons. Now, in the winter of 1951-52, it housed two works, whose blue titles stared out at me each day as I passed: *Molloy* and *Malone meurt*. Closer scrutiny revealed the name of the author: Samuel Beckett. I passed that window several times before I made the connection. I was then very deeply into Joyce and remembered that it was Beckett who, twenty-odd years before, had contributed the opening essay to that collection of twelve odes to the Master, *Our Examination Round His Factification for Incamination of Work in Progress*. It was Beckett, too, I recalled, who had with French writer Alfred Péron translated the "Anna Livia Plurabelle" episode of *Finnegans Wake* into French.[1] What was this Irishman, whom I had also heard referred to as "Joyce's secretary," doing writing in French? Or were the Minuit books translations from novels Beckett had written in English? If so, I had never heard of them.

Finally, curiosity won out over avarice: One morning, on my trek to St.-Germain-des-Prés, I went into number 7 and bought both books. Later that day I opened *Molloy* and began to read: *"Je suis dans la chambre de ma mère. C'est moi qui y vis maintenant. Je ne sais pas comment j'y suis arrivé...."* Before nightfall I had finished *Molloy*. I will not say I understood all I had read, but if there is such a thing as a shock of discovery, I experienced it that day. The simplicity, the beauty, yes, and the terror of the words shook me as little had before or has since. And the man's vision of the world, his painfully honest portrayal thereof, his anti-illusionist stance. And the humor; God, the humor.... I waited a day or two, then reread *Molloy*, tempted to plunge into *Malone* but resisting the temptation, as one resists the seductive sweet. The second reading was more exciting than the first. I went on to *Malone*. Full worthy of the first. Two stunning works. Miracles.

The following morning I walked over again to number 7 and asked an employee if Minuit had published any more works by Beckett. "Who?" was the answer. "Samuel Beckett," I said. "The man who wrote *Molloy* and *Malone Dies*." I motioned to the back of the display case in which the two masterpieces were still standing. The man shrugged and gestured me upstairs.

In a second-floor office I repeated my question to a lady at a type-writer. "I don't think so," she said, "but let me check." She picked up an antiquated telephone and dialed. The person she called, I later learned, was Jérôme Lindon, owner and editor of Minuit, a man I would soon meet and come to admire beyond measure. "No," the secretary informed me, "although another work is in preparation.[2] But," she went on, "there *is* another Beckett novel available from another publisher, Bordas, which I believe is still in print. It is called *Murphy*." Murphy, Molloy, Malone. . . . Decidedly, Beckett had a thing about M's.

I thanked her, went outside, and bicycled directly over to Bordas, a stone's throw away on the rue de Tournon. Not only was *Murphy* still in print (it had been published in French, in Beckett's own translation, five years before, in 1947), but by the look of the stock in the back of the shop (Bordas was primarily a bookseller who published occasional works himself), the original printing was all but intact. (According to A. Alvarez[3] ninety-five copies had been sold by 1951.) I presume, from the delighted reaction of the clerk to my request, that my copy was ninety-six. I took my new treasure home and read it that same night. The comedy was fully as strong as in *Molloy* and *Malone*, the sense of the grotesque, the unfailing gift for dialogue, but the magic fusion of comedy and tragedy, of form and content, had not, I felt, yet wholly occurred. It would await *L'Innommable*.

While waiting, I was informed by a Parisian actress friend that the French radio was scheduled to record part of an as yet unproduced Beckett play. I went to the taping. Rumor had it that Beckett would be present. In all, there were about a dozen of us in the studio, including the actors; like Godot, however, Beckett did not come. Instead he sent a note of apology, which Roger Blin, who was not only to direct but to perform in the original stage production of *Waiting for Godot* the following year, read prior to the taping. I do not know whether that note still exists in any form, but I remember the gist of it clearly: After apologizing for his absence, Beckett went on to say that since he knew little or nothing about the theater anyway, he could not see how his presence would add anything to the occasion. Blin, a remarkable actor, was plagued offstage with a pronounced stutter and had considerable difficulty reading Beckett's note. Thus it was with a certain trepidation that the hardy handful of Beckett fans and friends gathered in the RTF studios watched as the taping began. For Blin was playing Lucky, and though I do not think any of us present had read the as yet unpublished play, we had heard that Lucky's part contained a tongue-twisting monologue that would tax the talent of the most accomplished actor. When Blin, for the first time anywhere in the world, at least publicly, launched into the French original of these lines:

Given the existence as uttered forth in the public
works of Puncher and Wattmann of a personal
God quaquaquaqua with white beard
quaquaquaqua outside time without extension...[4]

there was incredible tension in the room. But on-mike, as on stage, Blin was a professional, and as such he delivered the monologue beautifully, without the least hitch.

Over the next month or so I uncovered two other Beckett pieces, both short stories or, to be more exact, one complete story and a portion of another. The latter, called "Suite," had appeared in Sartre's *Les temps modernes* half a dozen years before, in 1946. Not unusual for France in those days, the offices of the magazine still had copies of the issue. I read it with the same pleasure with which I had consumed *Molloy*. And yet it seemed strangely incomplete. Still, with Beckett, I reasoned, his ideas of "complete" or "incomplete" doubtless had little to do with those with which I had been inculcated. It was only later that I learned, from Beckett himself, that my first reaction had not been all that wrong: "Suite" represented only the first part of the story "La Fin." In sending it to *Les temps modernes*, Beckett rightly or wrongly assumed that at some later date the magazine would publish the rest of the work. But when he sent it on, Simone de Beauvoir returned it with a note indicating it was not the magazine's policy to publish sequels. She, or Sartre, had presumably thought that what Beckett had sent them first was the complete work. Or perhaps they thought Beckett was putting them on, testing their ability to tell a part from a whole. I'm not sure Beckett ever forgave the pair for their myopia. In any event, the story was not published in its entirety till the following year, in *Merlin*, in my translation. Well, sort of my translation. About which more later.

The second story, also extraordinary, was called "L'Expulsé," which had been published in *Fontaine*, an influential literary periodical of the time, in 1947.

Until *En attendant Godot* was published later in 1952, these comprised the Beckett *oeuvres complètes* on which I could lay my hands. While I talked, apparently obsessively, about it to all who would listen, I also decided that I would try to write a critical essay imparting my "discovery" to the world. A magazine called *Points*, published sporadically by Sinbad Vail, the son of Peggy Guggenheim, operated out of a top-floor sublet in the same building that housed Les Editions de

Minuit. It was for this magazine, for want of a better outlet, that I decided to write the piece. But before I had finished it a new English-language magazine had sprung up, as literary mushrooms had been doing for decades in the fertile Paris soil: *Merlin*, run by an impressively serious, craggy-featured young Scotsman, Alexander Trocchi. I met Trocchi, liked him, and talked to him at length about Beckett. "Stop talking, mon, and put it on paper!" he said at last. "There's a deadline next Thursday!" Within a week I had put my notes into shape and written the piece, which appeared in the second issue of *Merlin*.

I sent a copy of the magazine to Mr. Beckett, whose address on the rue des Favorites I had managed to pilfer. Silence. But then one day Jérôme Lindon, to whom I had also sent the issue, let it slip that Beckett had in hiding a work, in English, written during the war and never published: *Watt*. By then I was an editor of *Merlin*, and wrote Beckett asking if we could see the work with a view toward publishing an extract in the magazine. More silence. But I had rather expected that.

We had all but given up, when one rainy afternoon, at the rue du Sabot banana-drying *dépôt*, a knock came at the door and a tall, gaunt figure in a raincoat handed in a manuscript in a black imitation-leather binding and left almost without a word. That night, half a dozen of us—Trocchi; Jane Lougee, *Merlin*'s publisher; English poet Christopher Logue and South African Patrick Bowles; a Canadian writer, Charles Hatcher; and I—sat up half the night and read *Watt* aloud, taking turns till our voices gave out. If it took many more hours than it should have, it was because we kept pausing to wait for the laughter to subside.

We never had a real editorial discussion about which section we would use in the issue: Beckett had seen to that. He had specified which section we could use: Mr. Knott's inventory of the possibilities of his attire ("As for his feet, sometimes he wore on each a sock, or on the one a sock and on the other a stocking, or a boot, or a shoe, or a slipper, or a sock and boot, or a sock and shoe, or a sock and slipper ... or nothing at all....")[5] and the possible stations of the furniture in his room ("Thus it was not rare to find, on the Sunday, the tallboy on its feet by the fire, and the dressing-table on its head by the bed, and the night-stool on its face by the door, and the washstand on its back by the window; and, on the Monday, the tallboy on its back by the bed...." etc.[6]). I suspect Beckett was testing the artistic fiber of *Merlin* in so specifying, for, taken out of context, that passage might well have been considered boring or pedantic, waggish or wearily experimental-for-experimental's-sake, by any literary review less dedicated to berating and attacking the Philistines without mercy. When, years later, I confronted Beckett with this accusation, he responded with a broad, bad-boy grin.

At any rate, we published the designated extract of *Watt* in our next issue. I will not say the reaction was worldwide, but we received several angry letters and cancellation of five percent of our subscribers (i.e., five cancellations). Avant garde, all right, the letters said, but let's keep some sense of proportion, let's draw the line somewhere! We knew we were on the right track. Thereafter, virtually every issue of *Merlin* contained something by Beckett. And when, in the autumn of 1953, having lost relatively little money on the magazine, we determined we would expand and see if we could lose more money more quickly by publishing books, the first book we chose to publish was, of course, *Watt*.

In July 1953, Beckett wrote to his old friend and former literary agent, George Reavey, who since the war had been living in New York, to bring him up-to-date on his literary activities. After detailing those works which by then were out in French, he went on:

> ...Also, (tiens-toi bien) our old misery, *Watt*, with the Merlin juveniles here in Paris who are beginning a publishing business.

Earlier that year an agreement—I do not recall whether there was ever an actual formal contract—was reached with Mr. Beckett,[7] an advance of 50,000 francs ($100) duly paid, and we were ready to go into production. As is always the case with Beckett manuscripts, *Watt* was in impeccable condition. Although we proofread it, we found virtually nothing even to query, much less change. Two months later, Beckett would write again to Reavey noting that "Watt is just out in an awful magenta cover from the Merlin Press." A full-page ad for the book appeared on the back cover of the spring-summer 1953 issue of *Merlin*, although I suspect the book had not then appeared. The fall issue ran a further ad, detailing the printing:

> *Watt* (a novel) by SAMUEL BECKETT
> Ordinary Edition (*1100 numbered copies*) 850 fr.
> Special Edition (*25 signed copies of a de luxe paper*) 2,500 fr.

As to the awful color of the cover page, I can only assume there was a special on magenta. The book was typeset and printed at the Imprimerie Richard in Paris, and despite all the author's care in typescript, the "Printer Richard," who was touted to us as especially good because of his knowledge of English, managed to infiltrate so many typos that no matter how carefully we tried, we could never eliminate them all. If Beckett despaired of the garish color of the cover, I can only guess at the depths of his depression as he perused page after page of his printed work, replete with misspellings such as "scatch" for "scratch" (page 50),[8] "nenomena" for "phenomena" (page 79), and several dozen more. Not to mention a dropped word here and there, and a line set half a paragraph beyond where it appeared in manuscript.[9] His only consolation, perhaps, was the memory that Joyce, too, had suffered the same indignity at the hands of French printers with *Ulysses*, and survived.

Up to this point, despite a brief glimpse in the misty Paris dusk, none of us had ever met Beckett. We had tried to trap him into a meeting through the ploy of needing his presence to sign the tip sheets of the twenty-five-copy limited edition of *Watt* during the summer, but he had eluded that one by having the sheets sent over to him via Les Editions de Minuit. If, from all this, anyone is under the impression that Beckett was being coy, let me reassure that insofar as that term can imply false shyness, nothing could be further from the truth. Beckett is a very private person, shy to a fault and, at least in those days, uncomfortable with strangers. And since despite our efforts in his behalf we were still "strangers," Beckett preferred to deal with us from afar.

In the mid-fifties, when I was working with Beckett over a translation—from French to English—of his short story "La Fin," I noted his increasing despair not only at our seeming inability to transpose the story from one language to another but at what seemed to Beckett to be the painful inadequacy of the original. Beckett had once told me how hard it was for him to translate his own work and how much time it took him. In my youthful exuberance—and ignorance—I suggested that, if it would give him more time to devote to creative work, I would attempt to translate something, essentially to save him time. *Molloy* seemed the most likely candidate, for hard on our publication of *Watt* we next wanted to bring out *Molloy*. I began work on a draft but had

not progressed far before the financial pressures on *Merlin* became such
that I landed a job that paid me enough not only to live on but to
finance a couple of issues of the magazine. The hitch was that it took
me out of Paris for six months, so I passed the task on to Patrick
Bowles. Later, however, when I was back in Paris, Beckett suggested
I try my hand at "The End." For weeks I labored over the text, which
when I had read it in the French had struck me as beautifully simple.
But the more I worked the more I realized how deceptive that initial
impression had been. When I had finally completed the translation I
informed Beckett, who suggested that we meet to go over it. We met
at Le Dôme at Montparnasse, ensconced ourselves at an isolated table
near the back, and began to work. Or rather: Beckett began to read.
After a few minutes of perusing first my translation, then the original,
his wire-framed glasses pushed up into the thick shock of hair above—
the better to see, no doubt—he shook his head. My heart sank. Clearly,
the translation was inadequate. "You can't translate that," he said,
fingering the original with utter disdain. "It makes no sense." Again
he squinted at the two texts. Several more minutes of ruminations and
cross-checking produced a more optimistic report. "That's good," he
murmured. "Those first three sentences read very nicely indeed." The
opening passage to which he referred went, in my translation:

> They dressed me and gave me money. I knew what the money was to be
> used for, it was for my travelling expenses. When it was gone, they said,
> I would have to get some more, if I wanted to go on travelling.

"What do you think of the word *clothed*," Beckett said, "instead of
dressed? 'They *clothed* me and gave me money.' Do you like the ring
of it better?"

Yes, clearly: *clothed* was the better word.

"In the next sentence," he said, "you're literally right. In French I
spelled it out, said 'traveling expenses' all right. But maybe we can
make it a bit tighter here, just say something like, 'It was to get me
going' or 'It was to get me started.' Do you like either of them at all?"

On we went, phrase by phrase, Beckett praising my translation as
prelude to shaping it to what he really wanted, reworking here a word,
there a whole sentence, chipping away, tightening, shortening, always
finding the better word if one existed, exchanging the ordinary for the
poetic, until the work sang. Never, I am sure, to his satisfaction, but

26

certainly to my ear. Under Beckett's tireless wand that opening passage soon became:

> They clothed me and gave me money. I knew what the money was for, it was to get me started. When it was gone I would have to get more, if I wanted to go on.[10]

During those long but edifying sessions, there were low moments and high, but for Beckett, faced with going back over a text he had left behind some years before, from which he had progressed to other levels and other considerations, it was too often painful. Finally, in response to one particularly long moment of despair, I blurted, "But Mr. Beckett! You're crazy! Don't you realize who you are? Why... you're a thousand times more important than... than Albert Camus, for example!" Searching for superlatives, I had grasped at this French writer who, at least at the time, was world famous. Camus had not yet won the Nobel Prize, but he was clearly headed for it, and readers and critics alike clamored for each new work, a response in total contrast to the virtual silence that greeted, and had always greeted, each new Beckett publication.

At that youthfully enthusiastic but obviously outlandish declaration, Beckett gazed compassionately across the table, his gaunt, hawklike features mirroring a response midway between disbelief and pity. "You don't know what you're saying, Dick." He shook his head sadly. "No one's interested in this... this rubbish." And he gestured contemptuously toward the untidy pile of manuscript pages on the table beside him.

NOTES

1. When the translation finally appeared, in the May 1931 issue of *La nouvelle revue française*, credit for the translation went to a "committee" composed of Beckett, Alfred Péron, Ivan Goll, Eugene Jolas, Paul-L. Leon, Adrienne Monnier, and Philippe Soupault, in collaboration with the author. The truth of the matter seems to be that Beckett did most of it, that Alfred Péron went over Beckett's draft. But Joyce, who enjoyed the devotion, submitted their text to the scrutiny of the "committee," which argued over it endlessly and did, finally, make numerous changes.
2. *L'Innommable*, published in 1953.
3. *Samuel Beckett* (New York: The Viking Press, 1973), 1.

4. Samuel Beckett, *Waiting for Godot* (New York: Grove Press, 1956), 29.

5. Samuel Beckett, *Watt* (New York: Grove Press, 1959), 200.

6. Ibid., 204-5.

7. For years after we first met, we "*Merlin* juveniles," who were mostly in our early or middle twenties, always called him "Mr. Beckett." It was not merely the age difference that accounted for it: There was a certain formality about the man, an awesome presence that overwhelmed even his own constant self-derogation, that prevented the first-name intimacy. Nor was it peculiar to us: in the reverse situation twenty years earlier, when Beckett-the-younger-man was involved with Joyce, both men apparently referred to each other inevitably as "Mr. Joyce" and "Mr. Beckett."

8. Page numbers in parentheses refer to original *Merlin* edition.

9. When Grove Press, which became Beckett's American publisher a short while later, printed the American edition of *Watt* in 1959, it decided, as young, struggling publishers often do, to offset the Paris edition rather than reset from "scatch." Though Beckett and Grove combined managed to eliminate most of the original misprints, a few still crept through. But at least the magenta cover was not perpetuated.

10. Samuel Beckett, "The End," *Stories and Texts for Nothing* (New York: Grove Press, 1967), 47.

DOUGALD McMILLAN

Samuel Beckett and the Visual Arts: The Embarrassment of Allegory

Samuel Beckett is a man acutely aware of the visual arts and actively involved with them. One of his earliest fictional characters, Belacqua, is familiar enough with the National Gallery of Ireland to complain of how its paintings are displayed; he also knows the Dublin Municipal Gallery, formerly located in Charlemont House, and he is quite conscious of the architectural similarities between Dublin's Pearse Street and Florence. After Beckett left Dublin, he remained close friends with the Irish painter Jack Yeats—whose paintings he reviewed, admired, and hung in his apartment. Thomas McGreevy, the poet, art critic, and director of the National Gallery of Ireland, also remained a close contact in Dublin.

Beckett's travels during the extended *Wanderjahre* 1930-37 seem often to have been dominated by his interest in art. To Lawrence Harvey he described his path through Germany in 1936 as "from museum to museum." The three notebooks of this trip are primarily records of paintings and music that impressed him. He recalls the kindness of Willi Grohmann, a director of the Zwinger Gallery, and he recalls the Nazi destruction of works of "decadent" art.

Some measure of the kind of artistic education Beckett provided for himself in his wanderings can be gained through his allusions in the fiction. Through them his path can be traced to the National Gallery of England, the British Museum, the Louvre, the Prado, the Schatzkammer, Albertina, and the *Kunsthistorisches* museum in Vienna, the Pinacoteca in Milan, the Uffizi and Santa Croce in Florence, the Sistine Chapel in Rome, the Bishop's Palace in Würzburg, the *Stadtsgalerie* in Dresden, and the Campanella in Pisa—to name the most prominent.

29

He also visited less well known collections or churches, such as those at Kassel, Chantilly, Hamburg, and Padua.

The breadth of his knowledge extends from ancient Chaldean to modern art. His essays and allusions indicate far more than a passing familiarity with schools of art ranging from the Norwich school of English landscape painting to the German postexpressionist movement. His knowledge encompasses a variety of genres ranging from traditional oil painting, sculpture, and engraving to surrealist collage and modern tapestry design. His concern for the visual extends to film, to fonts of type, and to figures that illustrate the principles of gestalt psychology.

Since settling in Paris, Beckett has been involved with the artists of the city. His "La peinture des van Velde ou le monde et le pantalon," an exceptionally well-informed assessment of the situation of modern art criticism as well as modern painting, was evoked by an exhibition in 1945 at the Galérie Maeght. It was published in the influential *Cahiers d'Art*. His condensation of that article, "Peintres de l'empêchement," appeared in the equally respected art journal *Derrière le Miroir*. His poem "Bon bon il est un pays," a comment on art as a self-contained world, was written at the request of Geer van Velde to accompany a painting in an exhibition. Not used for that occasion, it later accompanied an exhibition of the works of Avigdor Arikha, the Israeli artist and friend of Beckett. His "Hommage à Jack B. Yeats" was written as part of a symposium occasioned by Yeats's 1954 exhibition in Paris. Beckett also provided a short text in appreciation of the works of Henri Hayden for a 1952 exhibit. Even when he was forced by the Nazis to leave Paris and go into hiding in Roussillon, Beckett kept Jack Yeats's painting *Morning*, and it was partly his interest in art that helped establish his friendship with Henri Hayden during this period.

Later Beckett was to become involved in collaborative efforts with artists. In 1972 a section from *The Lost Ones* was chosen for illustration by Avigdor Arikha, who had previously illustrated *Stories and Texts for Nothing*. The result is a magnificent limited-folio edition entitled *The North*. Beckett provided an unpublished text, "Still" for another limited-folio edition illustrated with three engravings and three preliminary studies by the English engraver Stanley William Hayter. This edition was published by M'Arte Edizione of Milan in 1974. And Beckett prepared a set of texts to accompany paintings by the American artist Jasper Johns for a book brought out by the Petersborough Press in 1975.

Beckett's most important critical statements have come in his essays on painting. In "Le monde et le pantalon," "Peintres de l'empêchement," and the "Three Dialogues" with Georges Duthuit, we find general observations on modes of criticism, on traditions of modern art, and on problems of the modern artist. In his essays on Denis Devlin and Rilke, the achievements and failures of Braque, Kandinsky, and Rodin define the position of the poet as well as that of the modern painter. And many critics have applied the dialogues with Duthuit to Beckett's own work.

Whether he is dealing with the visual arts or with literature, Beckett's concern is to define the changing relationship between the artist and the "occasion" of his art—the persistent need of the artist to express, even in the face of subject matter resistant to expression and an inadequate medium. In writing about the predicament of the modern artist faced with fundamental questions of representation, Beckett has implicitly defined his own position. He does not see himself in the narrow confines of a purely literary or theatrical tradition; rather he views himself in terms applicable to all artistic fields in this century. Beckett's criticism of art as well as of literature represents a significant body of commentary pertinent to his own work and that of his contemporaries—as much commentary as we have from Wallace Stevens or James Joyce, for example, and more than we have from many other modern writers.

Beckett's involvement with art is not merely the product of a superb education or a superficial interest. He seems personally preoccupied with art and the visual. If he reads about Descartes, he retains an awareness of the Hals portrait, which appears in *Whoroscope*. He reads of the sigmoid "line of beauty" in Hogarth's *The Analysis of Beauty* and assimilates it to the curving line of the Dublin shoreline in "Serena III." He frequents Mt. Geneviève in Paris, and details of the church St. Étienne du Mont appear in "The Calmative." From the Sorbonne he retains the impression not of scholars but of the frescoes of Puvis de Chevannes, to which he alludes in "Sanies II." He lived in the 15th arrondissement, and the undistinguished municipal bust of M. Ducroix from the rue Brancion appears in *The Unnamable*. He walks in Hyde Park, and *Murphy* is filled with accounts of not only Jacob Epstein's controversial sculpture *Rima* but also George Watt's *Physical Energy* and the statue of Queen Victoria. Murphy looks at the floor and sees in the linoleum pattern a resemblance to a Braque painting. Beckett discusses the problems of the modern writer with Tom Driver and makes his point by contrasting the Madeleine and Chartres cathedrals. Where art is a part of his environment, Beckett perceives it consciously; where the environment suggests art, Beckett is aware of the connection.

Beckett's work, the fiction in particular, is pervaded by an awareness of visual forms and techniques and allusions to works of art. Beckett was quite conscious of this aspect of his work, sometimes found it embarrassing, and struggled openly with it in the poems and novels.

Beckett's fiction reveals the most pervasive influence of the visual arts. His Belacqua derives from Dante's description in canto 4 of the *Purgatorio*, which invites illustration. In the edition illustrated by Sandro Botticelli, to whom Beckett refers several times in the early fiction and poetry, Belacqua seated in a fetal position in the lea of his rock becomes an emblem of embryonic recoil from life and wearisome ascent. Throughout his works Beckett presents his characters in this emblematic posture and uses references to works of art to reinforce its suggestions. Murphy, for example, who is so reluctant to leave his rocking chair and his solipsistic interior world, "recruits himself" before the Harpy Tomb in the British Museum, which depicts the dead as a seated figure enticed by young girls to rejoin the living.[1] Macmann on his park bench, aware of but not part of the crowd he observes, is fixed by comparing his posture to that of the seated statue of the Colossus of Memnon at Thebes.

The rich surface of references to works of art in *More Pricks than Kicks* and the published parts of "A Dream of Fair to Middling Women" is not just visual characterization. It is part of a conscious aesthetic strategy. In *Echo's Bones*, Beckett wrote of the old wound of Belacqua's life that seemed never to heal. He had tried everything, we are told, including fresh air, irony, and "great art." In the story "Yellow," Belacqua ransacks his mind for a suitable engine of destruction to deal with painful thoughts. His solution is to admit them and then to "obliterate the bastards,"[2] "perforate his adversary" with laughter (page 163). He might also have wept, "it came to the same thing in the end" (page 163), but "weeping in this charnel house would be misconstrued" (page 164). In Beckett's early work, his deliberate use of art is a tactic to place the painful experience depicted in the poems of *Echo's Bones* in an ironic perspective and thus "obliterate" it. Even in *Echo's Bones* Belacqua's metamorphosis from a realistic character in "Enueg I" to a comic caricature in "Malacoda" is represented as part of a work of art. He is the *imago*, the butterfly, in a floral painting by Jan van Huysum.

As the title suggests, *More Pricks* is the account of one who sets out to oppose the world and ends up suffering from it. Through the allusions to paintings, sculptures, and architectural forms, the protagonist Belacqua becomes a comic martyr—a veritable calendar of sainthood and martyrdom: St. Paul, St. John, St. George, and St. Peter. He sets out to "kick against the pricks" as did the biblical St. Paul, but he is more like the St. Paul of Rubens's *Conversion of St. Paul*, who, blinded by God and menaced by the hooves of his own horse, can only throw up a hand to ward off further harm. As Belacqua says in "Yellow," he will return to the sanctuary of his own mind "and not wait till he was *kicked* into it by the world" (page 161 emphasis added).

Belacqua thinks of himself as "an easy going St. George at the court of Mildendo" and even has a lady with a Pisanello face like that of the finely profiled Princess of Trebizond rescued by the lance-wielding St. George in Pisanello's painting in Verona. But in spite of Belacqua's determination to "perforate his adversary," his marriage to Lucy is a docile capitulation to domesticity that leaves him frustratedly throttling snapdragons in his garden at twilight. His second marriage, to Thelma bboggs of 55 North Great St. George Street, is a further capitulation. Neither Pisanello's St. George, nor Uccello's, nor any of the other lance wielders is applicable, but rather Hogarth's etching *The Court of Mildendo*, in which Gulliver is tied down and pricked with little darts to suffer a humiliating rectal infusion.

Belacqua's fate is summed up with a reference to Velasquez's *The Surrender of Breda*, which Beckett calls *The Lances*. Like Pisanello's painting of St. George and Rubens's of St. Paul, the painting is centered on the great rump of a horse. On either side the lances of opposing armies are arranged in rows. In the center, one of the commanders hands a single key to the other. The reference underscores Belacqua's final defeat. "The body was between them on the bed like the keys between the nations in Velasquez's 'Lances,' like the water between Buda and Pest, and so on hyphen of reality."[3] The lances are in the hands of the others; he is a passive victim. For Belacqua it is more pricks than kicks. Even in death he cannot escape. Smeraldina, who is called Belacqua's "spiritual equivalent," and Hairy, who gains new life from Belacqua's death, are living components of Belacqua, and their relationship will perpetuate the relationship of Smeraldina and Belacqua. He becomes the intermediary between them, the keys to the kingdom. "Peter, on this rock..."

For Belacqua, whose life is a struggle to evade women, marriage is the principal martyrdom. As his bride approaches in "What a Misfortune," "Belacqua's heart made a hopeless dash against the wall of the box, the church suddenly cruciform cage, the bulldogs of heaven holding the chancel...."[4] "Ecce," hisses Hairy at this point (page 138). Again the whole visual tradition—Christian architecture and the *Ecce Homo*—is called into ironic juxtaposition with Belacqua's fate.

Compared to the psychological novels of Joyce and Proust, this art of displacement and obliteration makes these characters seem like "puppets." The many references to Rodin, Dürer, Epstein, Della Robbia, Velasquez, Tommaso, Uccello, and "the master of tired eyes," Paul Henry, and to annunciations and madonnas, serve to assure us that the author is aware of just how artificial his characters are. This technique is one of the most salient aspects of *More Pricks Than Kicks*. Belacqua in his characteristic posture is described in "A Wet Night" as "the central leaf on the main triptych his feet on a round so high that his knees topped the curb of the counter...."[5] He appears later in the story framed in a doorway in tableau. And lest we should miss it, the point is made quite explicitly in "Love and Lethe," where Ruby Tough is described as resembling "Magdeline* in the Perugino Pietà in the National Gallery in Dublin, always bearing in mind that the hair of our heroine is black and not ginger." The note expands the reference:

> The figure, owing to the glittering vitrine behind which the canvas cowers, can only be apprehended in sections. Patience, however, and retentive memory have been known to elicit a total statement approximating to the intention of the painter.[6]

In *Murphy* and *Watt* the visual arts become the vehicle for more serious commentary. The central issue of *Murphy*—the conflict between love and solipsism—is presented as a problem of visual perception in terms of figures of gestalt psychology, and its effects are presented by references to painting. "All life is figure and ground," says Neary at the beginning of the novel, "the face, or system of faces, against the big blooming buzzing confusion" (page 4). His beloved Miss Dwyer is "the one closed figure in the waste without form, and void" (page

5). But once attained, Miss Dwyer "became one with the ground against which she had figured so prettily" (page 48). Neary's pursuit of the closed figure now centers on Murphy. For Neary the transformation of figure into ground is a loss. For Murphy it is at first a relief, "ground mercifully free of figure" (page 245). Ultimately, however, the loss inherent in exclusion of others from perception becomes apparent to Murphy too. Having seen himself as "a speck in Mr. Endon's unseen" (page 252), Murphy himself is unable to evoke a mental picture of Celia or any other living creature. He sees instead only the confusion of partial images "evoking nothing... reeled upward off a spool level with his throat" (page 252). Murphy concludes that this reeling confusion "should be stopped, whenever possible, before the deeper coils were reached" (page 252). The alternative to seeing "nothing" is "naught"—zero, the closed figure. The alternative to chaos is a perception of the face and a return to Celia. But Murphy does not embrace this alternative; he continues on into chaos. The only organized image in Murphy's mind is one depicting his sense of loss, pain, and terror: "the clenched fists and rigid upturned face of the child in a Giovanni Bellini Circumcision, waiting to feel the knife. He saw eyeballs being scraped first any eyeballs, then Mr. Endon's (page 251)." The bulging terrified eyes of the children in Bellini's paintings, such as this one in the National Gallery of England, show the emotional effect of what has been presented in the more abstract terms of figure and ground. Irony is still present, but referring to the Bellini painting is a serious way of suggesting the terror that lies beneath the comic surface of the novel.

Beckett deals directly with paintings as allegorical expression in *Watt*. There he presents us with a series of pictures and openly invites us to contemplate their significance as commentary on the human predicament. Watt, "in search of rest, [thinks] of the possible relations between such series as these, the series of dogs, the series of men, the series of pictures...."[7]

When we are first shown Watt's room, a color reproduction on his wall is referred to but not described. Attention is focused instead on the fine view from his window of the race course. Later, though, in the waiting room, a large colored print of the horse Joss emerges from the wall. It is a picture of a poor old horse, shown in the light of an impending storm or night, contemplating without appetite the sparse grass overrun with cockles. "The horse seemed hardly able to stand. Let alone run" (page 238). The allegory is clear enough. Picture one of the human condition, in Watt's view.

The second picture is the one that hangs in the upstairs room of Erskine, the servant with access to the master, Mr. Knott. It is of a black circle on a white background broken at its lowest point. Appearing to recede in the background is a blue dot. There is an illusion of movement in space and time and the possibility for the two forms to exist in the future or to have existed in the past on the same plane. Watt wonders what the artist intended to represent. Among the nearly limitless possibilities that can relate a center and a circle, one—"the thought that it was perhaps this, a circle and a centre not its centre in search of a centre and its circle respectively, in boundless space, in endless time" (page 129)—fills him with tears. Thus, the sense of incompleteness familiar in our visual experience extends to other parts of life as well.

The third picture is evoked when Watt is cut by the brambles and barbed wire fence that separate his garden from that of the narrator, Sam.

> His face was bloody his hands also and thorns were in his scalp. (His resemblance, at the moment, to the Christ believed by Bosch, then hanging in Trafalgar Square was so striking I remarked it.) And at the same instant I suddenly felt I was standing before a great mirror in which my garden was reflected and my fence. . . . (page 159)

The circular crown of thorns prominent in the Bosch *Scourging of Christ* in the National Gallery of England recalls the circular form of the race course seen from Watt's window, the unclosed circle of the painting in Erskine's room, and the echo of that pattern formed by the barbed wire fences as they bulge out to holes positioned opposite each other. The relationship of the series of pictures is first of all visual. They all present circularity. Through the painting by Bosch the implications of circularity in human existence are suggested.

The portrait in the addenda presents an ironic allegory of the artist himself. The progression of Watt's perception of Joss had been from the general to the particular. "Watt identified, first the field, then the horse, and then thanks to an inscription of great   ?   , the horse Joss" (page 236). The portrait of the artist in the addenda is the last picture in the novel, and it is the most particular. The identity of the artist is the last detail to be discerned, and indeed it remains a question whether his identity is discernible at all.

Already in "A Casket of Pralinen for the Daughter of a Dissipated Mandarin," a poem published in *European Caravan* in 1932, Beckett reacted against stylized presentation of experience in terms of art. There he presented himself as Judas from a postexpressionist *Last Supper* and compared himself with Andrea Mantegna's *Cristo Morto* in the Pinacoteca in Milan, which he called a "butchery stout foreshortened Saviour." But at the center of the poem is a denial of this mode of presentation.

> Oh I am ashamed
> of all clumsy artistry
> I am ashamed of presuming
> to arrange words
> of everything but the ingenuous fibres
> that suffer honestly.

The parody of his own techniques in the portrait of the artist at the end of *Watt* reflects a similar sense of embarrassment at the disparity between direct presentation of "honest" suffering and dependence on allegory and art.

In the imaginary painting at the end of *Watt*, the artist is shown nude, seated at a piano with his genitals covered by a piece of stave paper. The idea of self-revelation is parodied by the combination of the nudity of the man, depicted in such naturalistic detail that muscles are described in anatomical terms and the dirt on his toenails is noticed, with the purely artificial and conventional sheet of music covering his genitals. The ludicrous attitude of the seated figure is an ironic treatment of the emblematic use of posture. One hand is on the piano, the other held to his ear to detect receding tones. His bare feet are one atop the other as in a crucifix. His expression is of a man "about to be delivered...of a particularly hard stool" (page 251). (Compare Belacqua's retreat to the toilet in "Sedendo et Quiesciendo" and, later, Lucky's dance in *Waiting for Godot.*)

The use of detail in allegorical fashion is also ridiculed. "The significant detail" (page 251) of the painting, we are told, "would have done credit to Heem" (page 250). Jan de Heem's *Fruit Piece with Skull, Crucifix, and Serpent* in the National Gallery of Ireland is typical of the combination of exacting fidelity to the natural object with symbolic meaning attached to the naturalistic details. (The catalog of the National Gallery even contains an explanation of the symbols in de Heem's work.)

The attempt to transfer the techniques of one artistic medium to another is a source of irony in the painting. The fictitious painter is referred to as "Black Velvet O'Connery" (page 247), recalling Jan "Velvet" Brueghel, who attempted to render all five senses visually in a series of allegorical paintings called *The Senses*. The attempt to achieve a cumulative effect of color is parodied by salient repetitions of "red," "red," "red." In a mockery of attempts to evoke auditory perception by visual means, Watt has no trouble identifying the chord in the painting as "C major in its second inversion" (page 250). The prominence of the sheet of music is a comic representation of the centrality of music in a nonmusical medium. (Beckett had relied heavily on musical terminology in developing his aesthetic theories in "Dream," and music as transcendent experience had been important in *Echo's Bones* and *More Pricks than Kicks*.) The assimilation of sculpture to literary ends and the general confusion of one medium with another are made comic by Beckett's calling the figure in the painting a "bust" just after his breast has been described in detail.

But the most important question is whether the artist is revealed by the technique. He is not. Art Conn O'Connery, as the name implies, is a trick—a fictitious creation made up from bits and scraps of an artistic tradition. His connections with de Heem and Brueghel have been pointed out. His other components are to be found chiefly in the representations of the Irish school in the National Gallery of Ireland. The name is taken partly from James Arthur O'Connor, whose six oils make him one of the major representatives of the school. In part it comes from Rodrick O'Connor, whose single painting, *Portrait of the Artist*, the gallery acquired in 1929. Probably (although it is uncertain how Beckett would have known of it since it was not acquired until 1951) the painting and the name owe something to Conn O'Donnell's *Portrait of Art O'Neill Harpist*, which depicts a blind harpist who is very nearly a caricature of the Homeric poet.

O'Connery is out of the "great Chinnery-Slattery tradition" (page 247). The well-known Dublin artist George Chinnery had, like Beckett in "Dream," made a *Portrait of a Mandarin*, a large painting that dominates his section of the National Gallery. John Slattery's one painting in the Dublin museum is *Portrait of William Carelton Novelist*. The addenda also associate O'Connery with "the Master of the Leopards-town Halflengths" (page 247). The Leopardstown racetrack, visible from the window of Beckett's birthplace in Foxrock, frequently provided subject matter for Beckett's friend Jack B. Yeats. Beckett shared with Yeats the tendency displayed in *Watt* to see in horses analogs to the human situation.

In the trilogy Beckett moves to rid the novels of the surrogates who suffer for him and the trappings of art that accompany them. Although it contains relatively few direct allusions to specific works of art, *Molloy* nevertheless reflects the influence of the visual arts. Molloy assures us that although he is "far from being an artist or an aesthete"[8] he sees in a way "inordinately formal" (page 50), and at another point he confesses to a "mania for symmetry" (page 85). On their "unreal journey" he and Moran move about a circle divided into quadrants, each associated with a stylized landscape of "plain," "mountain," "city," and "sea." The horizon is "burning with phosphorous and sulphur" (page 27), and the sun is "a living tongue of flame darting toward the zenith" (page 65). This grid of iconographic space owes more to the world of Gothic art than to real Ireland or the landscapes of literary allegory as in Spenser and Bunyan.

Over this grid are laid pastoral details that cause Moran to exclaim, "What a pastoral land" (page 158), and to compare the concentration of perspective in one scene to that in a "painting by an old master" (page 153). Molloy does not share Moran's enthusiasm for visual technique. "I apologize for all these details, in a moment we will go faster, much faster. And perhaps relapse again into a wealth of filthy circumstance. But which in its turn will give way to vast frescoes, dashed off with loathing. Homo mensura cannot do without staffage" (page 63). Whatever embarrassment they may cause, these artificial details are an unavoidable part of the thought process producing the work. In "Le monde et le pantalon" Beckett had made a similar excuse for staffage as an unavoidable aspect of Claude Lorrain's painting.

The conflict between direct experience and artificial expression is also presented in the contrast between Molloy and Moran. Again Beckett depends upon allusions to art to undercut his dependence on it. Molloy, the primary actor whose homeward journey is undertaken alone and reluctantly as a result of compelling inner motivation, is depicted in the familiar posture of the Belacqua figure. Moran, the observer who leaves home so eagerly to execute the command to write a report on Molloy, tries the Belacqua posture briefly but rejects it. He prefers to imagine himself in the posture of Rodin's *Thinker* and his Ugolino from *Gates of Hell*. His attitude is undercut by making the popular statue into a joke. Moran sits atop a milestone "eyes fixed on the earth as on a chess board, coldly hatching... plans for the next day, for the day after, creating time to come" (page 125).

Moran's facile attachment to the world is further ridiculed by a reference to Rodin's sculpture *The Burgesses of Calais*, in which six downtrodden citizens, linked together by a bronze rope, trudge in a weary circle. Moran would like to bind his son to him with a rope but fears that his son might untie himself and he would be left trailing one end behind him "like a burgess of Calais." This image of one of the burgesses detached from the others, trailing his bronze rope behind him, is preposterous. Like Rodin, whom Beckett had disparaged in "Smeraldina's Billet Doux" and his review of Rilke's *Poems*, Moran is too eager to insert himself in allegory, while masquerading as a realist. Significantly, Moran is going to force his son to learn double-entry bookkeeping. In his review of Jack Yeats's *Amaranthers*, Beckett had derided allegory as "that glorious double entry, with every credit in the said column, a debit in the meant." Molloy at least is aware that he is imposing staffage on others, and he apologizes for it, promising relief in the future. Moran shows no such consideration.

The embarrassment of "clumsy artistry" reaches a climax in *Malone Dies*, in which Malone speaks of his heart "burning, with shame, of itself, of me, of them of everything except beating apparently." "Don't fret about our methods," the narrator says; "leave all that to me...."⁹ The narrator's attempt to "empty out" from his head in a "gurgle of outflow" all the characters that have peopled the previous fiction coincides with his attempt to divest himself of a dependence on visual art as a means of representing the world. This is his "last journey, down the long familiar galleries" (page 236). (Molloy had referred to his characters as a "gallery of moribunds.")

As the inmates of St. John of God's are about to be dispatched by Lemuel, the narrator declares, "The window. I shall not see it again" (page 283). He has come to associate this window with a world of artificial perception which is being superseded and rejected. Early in the novel the pane has revealed a night like those depicted in the works of Kasper David Friedrich. The pane is frosted, and Malone wishes he could breathe on it. Later the window is compared to the *trompe l'oeil* window complete with painted stars by Giovanni Tiepolo in the Bishop's Palace in Würzburg. But finally, artistic presentation no longer is sufficient: Malone must assure himself that what he sees is real. "The black night I see is truly of mankind and not merely painted on the window-pane, for [the stars] tremble, like true stars, as they would not do if they were painted" (page 237).

Violets, roses, and cupids that formerly decorated the ceiling of Malone's chamber hang down in fragments or have disappeared, but a sense of baroque extravagance remains in the window and in the white, blue, pink, and gold figures revealed in it. In the room, as in the Bishop's Palace, where Tiepolo's frescoes of each continent cover the ceiling, all heaven and earth have, through the tricks of painting, been brought into the interior so that the human body exists in an absurd scale. Malone's feet are "leagues away" (page 234), his hands are "in other latitudes" (page 234), his stick is at "one of the poles" or "the equator" (page 255), his feces might fall in Australia. If he stood up he would fill "a considerable part of the universe."

Malone—swollen, discolored, with feet thrust forward in distorted perspective, on his deathbed on "Easter week-end spent by Jesus in hell" (page 280)—is like the realistic *Cristo Morto* already identified with disingenuous artistry in "A Casket of Pralinen." He is an incongruous figure to be found among Tiepolo's allegorical baroque frescoes. The absurdity of Mantegna's morbid Christ in Tiepolo's exuberant world is, itself, ironic commentary on the disparate union of art and experience in the fiction.

Malone would like to leave this world. "One last glimpse and I feel I could slip away as happy as if I were embarking for—I nearly said for Cythera, decidedly it is time for this to stop. After all this window is whatever I want it to be" (page 237). Even as he announces his desire to leave, another parallel from painting crowds into his expression. In leaving, he would be like one of the figures in Watteau's *Embarkation for Cythera* in the Louvre, where a party of voyagers spirals out of an eighteenth-century landscape toward an indistinct destination in the far distance. The members of the procession change from real people in the foreground to undetermined cherublike forms in the distance. The scene is reminiscent of Saposcat's attempt to "glide away" out of a world of pastoral staffage and carefully arranged visual perspectives. Malone seems unable to avoid allusions to art. He is an old tourist and, like Murphy, "one of the elect who require everything to remind them of something else" (*Murphy*, page 63). But he is impatient with this tendency and is determined to make an end of it.

Therefore photographs begin to replace paintings as the main mode of self-presentation. Although we are told of photographs of the narrator and Macmann's beloved, Moll, the transition from the images of art to those of reality is not complete. "My photograph," says the narrator (*Malone Dies*, page 251), but it is a picture of an ass in a bowler. It is only a middle stage between allegory and direct representation. Furthermore, the figure is blurred by the "operator's giggle" (page 251). "Clumsy artistry," still remains. The picture of Moll at age fourteen seems more authentic, but Macmann tears it up and scatters it to the winds.

Art and allegory remain in the novel in Moll's carved ivory earrings representing the "two thieves" and the carved tooth showing the crucifixion. And, most of all, they remain in Macmann, Malone's creation. He may be found in the heart of the city near a real hotel, but he takes his form from the Colossus of Memnon, whose "planes" and "angles" define his emblematic posture. However, the process of disentanglement from art is ostensibly complete at the end of *Malone Dies*.

The Unnamable will talk of himself directly, abandoning all the characters enlisted formerly. He is also "done with windows" and "old pictures." In his curious position as observer at the center of a circle, viewing objects that pass before him at regular intervals, he contrasts the real with the conventions of art. A face might pass by: "A face ... demonstrating all a true face can do.... Worth ten of St. Anthony's pig's arse."[10] His own identity is readily available from a true photograph. "This is you. Look at this photograph.... I assure you ... look at this photograph you'll see" (page 377).

Whatever doubts remain, the question of identity no longer is obscured by art. Unlike the paintings, which obliterate and conceal experience, the photograph reveals it, and yet the process of revelation is not so final as it seems. The Unnamable does "invent another fairy tale" (page 307); he reverts to fables of Mahood and Worm. And just as he feels he is about to be grasped, he says, "Can it be they are resolved at last to seize me by the horns? Looks like it. In that case tableau any minute" (page 379). The tableau of the novel is Mahood's world in the rue Brancion, where across from the slaughterhouse for horses, he is fixed in a pot under the gaze of M. Ducroix, "the apostle of horse's meat" (page 327). The rue Brancion, the bust, and the slaughterhouse exist, but this is another stylized presentation resembling a work of art.

Even the Unnamable, who is so eager to express himself directly, has not stopped thinking of himself in terms of art. "I am Matthew and I am the angel," he says (page 301), envisioning himself as part of a scene from an unidentified painting, which is described in *Murphy* as "Luke's portrait with the angel perched like a parrot on his shoulder" (*Murphy*, page 215). This is his image of interior self-perception. He is both the poet and the Paraclete-like being that speaks to him.

And while the Unnamable may prefer a real face to one of St. Anthony's visions, the mention of St. Anthony in connection with his world is enough to recall Hieronymus Bosch's nightmarish paintings of these visions. The Unnamable's world seems analogous to Bosch's *Garden of Earthly Delights* in the Prado. The details of the Unnamable's great desert on the shores of a lake filled with talking spheres, "impotent crystalline," great perforated egg-shaped beings, disembodied ears, and bodies writhing in torment bear striking resemblance to the details of Bosch's painting. The vestiges of art persist as part of the mental landscape of the trilogy.

Direct presentation of ingenuous suffering is partly achieved in *How It Is*, in those portions that purport to be memories of the narrator's "life above." "This is my life," he insists. "No stories but mine. No more figures." Experience is depicted without the use of art forms, not even photographs. When a scene of the narrator as a young child praying at his mother's knee is presented, we are not told that it is based on an actual photograph of Beckett and his mother (pages 14-15).Instead of needing to apologize for the presence of art, the narrator seems briefly to feel himself too exposed without it. Thinking of how he will be revealed as the parts of his story unfold, he says, "Thalia, for pity's sake a leaf of thine ivy" (page 42). The old theatrical masks are gone, and he feels their absence.

The portions of *How It Is* which deal with the journey through the mud are still dominated by the influence of the visual arts. The seemingly gratuitous turnings face down, face up half-side left, half-side right; the carefully described patterns of chevrons and deasils; the dancelike movement "dextrogyre and sinestro"; and the detailed configurations of arms are not arbitrary or unprecedented. Like the movements of the angels in Blake's frontispiece to the Book of Job, the turns and spirals of Beckett's figures into and out of the world of experience are significant movements. (In this connection it should be noted that Beckett makes specific allusions to Blake's etchings for the Book of Job in *Murphy*.) The configurations of the arms recall Botticelli's illustrations to *Paradiso* from the same edition in which his Belacqua appears. There the changing angles of the arms of Beatrice and Dante indicate the degree of their progress.

In *How It Is* Beckett found the means to present experience directly and still to retain the emblematic mode that had been so important for him since the creation of Belacqua. In the fiction since *How It Is*, Beckett continues to employ this kind of emblematic statement that associates his work with the visual arts. The suitability of these works for illustration reflects the role the visual arts played in their origin: The posture of the crouched figures in *Imagination Dead Imagine* is itself a statement of their predicament. The similar figure from *The Lost Ones* is a visual condensation so graphic that the section could be extracted without being destroyed, and it was printed separately as *The North*, accompanied by Avigdor Arikha's sensitive etching of the figure. We might say of Arikha's etching, which echoes the lines of Botticelli's Belacqua, that it is out of Botticelli by Beckett.

In "Still" we can see how durable the images of art are for Beckett. The seated figures of Belacqua, Murphy, and Macmann are defunct, but still their essence remains in the description of a man seated in his room. The title suggests both the quietude of the man and the persistence of the figure. "Legs side by side broken right angles at the knees as in that old statue some old god twanged at sunrise and again at sunset."[11] Here we can recognize not only the form of Macmann but also the statue of Memnon at Thebes moved to life at sunrise and sunset. This is not lifeless art—art unmoved by experience. There is "some reason some time past this hour" why the man should be moved by the sunset. But in the process of distillation over time, it is not the experience itself, but the response embodied in forms of art, which remains.

In the margin of the facsimile of the manuscript provided in the M'Arte edition are Beckett's own drawings. They reveal his preoccupation with the visual forms in which his characters are embodied. In one of them, strong black lines perpendicular to each other trace a broad W set on its side so that its lines are perfectly vertical and horizontal—the outline of a straight-backed chair. The body that fits this form is represented by a stylized sigmoid line sketched in lighter lines. The head is a series of scribbled circles in the same lighter line. Here, once again, it is the basic sense of visual form and not the details of naturalistic presentation that prevail. From the earliest stories to "Still," this strong sense of the visual derived from art pervades Beckett's works. His fiction is partly the record of his struggle to accommodate the forms and techniques of art to the necessity of "honest" expression. The willingness to display the struggle is itself a form of honesty that Beckett has admired in contemporary visual artists and that places him in their tradition.

NOTES

1. Samuel Beckett, *Murphy* (New York: Grove Press, 1957), 84. References in the text are to this edition.
2. Samuel Beckett, "Yellow," in *More Pricks than Kicks* (New York: Grove Press, 1972), 162. References are to this edition.
3. Beckett, "Draff," in *More Pricks*, 180.
4. Beckett, "What a Misfortune," in *More Pricks*, 138.
5. Beckett, "A Wet Night," in *More Pricks*, 52.
6. Beckett, "Love and Lethe," in *More Pricks*, 87.
7. Samuel Beckett, *Watt* (New York: Grove Press, 1959), 136. References are to this edition.
8. Samuel Beckett, *Molloy*, in *Three Novels by Samuel Beckett* (New York: Grove Press, 1965), 50. References are to this edition.
9. Beckett, *Malone Dies*, in *Three Novels*, 261.
10. Beckett, *The Unnamable*, in *Three Novels*, 362.
11. Beckett, "Still," in *Fizzles* (New York: Grove Press, 1976), 48.

WOLFGANG ISER

When Is the End Not the End?
The Idea of Fiction
in Beckett

"Although I am not of the opinion that in this dark age it is only negativism that is fit for literature, nevertheless the affirmative view, even though it may from time to time criticize the 'byproducts' of the age, does smack of hypocrisy."[1] This striking statement by Ernst Fischer is to be found in an article on Beckett that presents Fischer's ideas on modern Marxist esthetics. In fact, Beckett's work offers nothing affirmative, and for this reason it has often been regarded as simply the image of an existence characterized—in the words of Georg Lukács— by the "most fundamental pathological debasement of man."[2] Such judgments are by no means confined specifically to Marxist literary criticism; they also arise when attempts are made to expound Beckett against the background of metaphysics or literary history, and they are often made with the same emphasis. Though one may suppose that even Beckett's critics do not always expect from literature an affirmative statement on the modern condition, nevertheless their judgments would seem to depend on a traditional criterion of literature, namely, that it should give a representative view of life.

Beckett's texts, however, cannot simply be reduced to the representation of a given reality; their negativeness consists precisely in the fact that they resolutely refuse to comply with this traditional criterion. If one looks for affirmation in Beckett, all one will find is the deformation of man—and even this is only half the story, for his characters frequently behave as if they were no longer concerned in their own misery; like so much else, this is already behind them, and whenever they speak of it one has the impression that the situations they mention already belong to the past. One cannot even say with certainty that

Beckett's texts confirm the misery of modern society, although they appear to do so. The moment one tries to restrict them to a specific meaning, they slide away in a new direction. Their meaning cannot be pinned down (unless one takes them to be a revelation of the limitation of "meaning" in general). However, this gives rise to objections against Beckett, as put forward by Reinhard Baumgart, who compares Beckett's works to the science of fundamentals. But the "science of fundamentals can be put into practice only indirectly and with difficulty; the practical basis for life that used to emerge from literature is thus very hard to extract from the works of Beckett. The very radicalism of the questions he raises makes his writings inapplicable to everyday life."[3] What is this radicalism of Beckett's that precludes his offering any guidelines for his reader? Beckett's works are a continual (though never completed) "exit," and each stage of the exit is only a starting-point for more "exiting." The frequency of the end in Beckett seems to imply "salvation," but we could only understand "end" as "salvation," in the normal sense of the word, if we knew what goal was in view when the "end" came. In Beckett, though, there is no mention of this goal, and if there were, then the fascination of the "end" would disappear. "The end is terrific!"[4] says Clov in *Endgame*. Beckett's characters go round and round the end with such unswerving devotion that their activity simply destroys any idea that the end is only to be seen as the desire to finish off, as the great weariness, or even as the great satiety. If these were the motives, the characters would be more likely to do and say nothing. The variations on the "end theme" are simply too numerous for them all to be regarded as merely a symptom of the longing for relief.

The recurrent indifference and apathy and the lack of concern for what actually lies beyond the end give one the impression that the end, however indefinite it may be, is a goal in itself. But when something becomes a goal in itself, it is automatically released from those standards of judgment that have previously applied. Here, analogous to "art for art's sake," we have "end for end's sake," and it is in this sense that the end appears to have a function similar to that of "salvation" without actually meaning salvation.

The end has a long history, and the fact of man's preoccupation with it would seem to indicate that the "end" does not merely mean coming to a stop, but rather that it contains other elements that can never be fully grasped, so that one tries continually to define its precise nature.

A dominant feature of this history is the Apocalypse. Perhaps this is even the starting point. In any case, the Apocalypse provides a vital precondition for men's visions and descriptions of the end: We know what happens when the end comes. This forms a constant feature in the history of man's expectations in regard to the end, and such knowledge was always regarded as unassailable, even if it was contradicted by time and circumstances. If expectations were not fulfilled (for example, if the prophesied end of the world did not take place), there was no question of abandoning one's conceptions of the end—they merely had to be adapted to the new situation. In his book *The Sense of an Ending*, Frank Kermode suggested the following interpretation for this curious phenomenon: "Men . . . make considerable imaginative investments in coherent patterns which, by the provision of an end, make possible a satisfying consonance with the origins and with the middle. That is why the image of the end can never be *permanently* falsified. But they also, when awake and sane, feel the need to show a marked respect for things as they are; so that there is a recurring need for adjustments in the interest of reality as well as of control."[5] But if the image of the end can never be permanently falsified, then the connection between origin, middle, and end has to be constantly reestablished. In order for knowledge of the end to remain permanent, life must continually be given a new interpretation—and in such a way that the interpretation coincides with life itself. In Beckett's texts, this identification between life and interpretation is constantly broken up.

The adaptability that characterizes the images of the end cannot obscure, let alone cast any doubt on, their truth content. This is also true when the meaning of the end depends on unmistakable historical circumstances, which this meaning promises to transcend. But if the meaning of the end can be adjusted to suit the requirements of different historical situations, then each time the meaning is bound to be characterized by distinct historical features. One would think, then, that history itself should show all these expectations up for what in reality they are: images of human hopes and human fears. But despite the changing contents of these images, there is never ever any suggestion, even by the latter-day eschatologists, that this is all a matter of human projections. On the contrary, the urge to construct images is so marked that even the discrediting of definite prophecies has no repercussions on this activity. But if the end can only be brought into current life by means of images, then these images, in comparison with the reality of life, must be regarded as a fiction. This lack of reality, however, does not reduce their effect but, in the light of historical experience, seems rather to heighten it. "Fictions are for finding things out, and they change as the needs of sense-making change."[6] Kermode has therefore aptly described them as "concord-fictions,"[7] for they close that very gap in human affairs that is actually caused by the end. Bacon had already pointed a finger in this direction when he said of fictions that they "give some show of satisfaction to the mind, wherein the nature of things doth seem to deny it."[8]

The fiction of the end is both a necessity and a paradox, for the end is an event that one cannot avoid and yet that one cannot hope to understand in its true nature. It is an event that must inevitably exclude any insight into itself, has to be tolerated, and yet in itself is intolerable. It is this paradox that gives rise to the creation of the fiction, for fictions alone can fill in the gaps apparent in man's knowledge. This explains the high degree of certainty about the character of the end, as evinced by all these fictions, and also explains the often radical revisions in men's expectations as new situations arise. The usefulness of these fictions can be gauged merely from the fact that the question of their truthfulness is never even considered. Indeed, the power of the fiction lies in the fact that its origin remains concealed. Thus, none of the many conceptions of the end has ever contained the suggestion that its images are designed simply to satisfy a human need—even though this is their real origin. Perhaps such a claim, if it had ever been voiced, would have been regarded as cynical, for uncovering the truth behind fictions means destroying the very thing that fiction is attempting to provide—i.e., the satisfaction of a human need. Beckett's texts aim deep down at the anthropological roots of fiction, and so they take their place within the history of "the end," not so much in the sense of another manifestation of these expectations, as in an unveiling of our own need for fictions. The violent reactions and also the nagging discomfort aroused by Beckett's texts suggest that he has hit his mark.

The negativeness of these texts would seem to consist in the fact that they refuse to satisfy our elementary needs, and that whenever we think we have found something definite to satisfy our needs, we are made to realize that what we have found is only a fiction. Furthermore, we see that we are constantly fabricating fictions in order to create reliable guidelines or even realities for ourselves, though in the end they turn out to be no such thing. These texts also show clearly that in spite of the knowledge revealed to us concerning our needs, we still cannot do without our fictions, so that these needs become the basis of our own entanglement with ourselves. And from this, no fiction can release us.

II

Beckett already touched on this subject in the *Proust* essay he published in 1931 at the age of twenty-five, when qualifying for a teaching post in romance philology at Trinity College, Dublin. Although the essay was conceived as a Proust interpretation, long passages of it are more in the nature of a manifesto, for which *Remembrance of Things Past* provided the starting point. Beckett is concerned primarily with uncovering the illusions that gave rise to Proust's central intentions, above all the identity of the "ego," as rediscovered in memory.

"The aspirations of yesterday were valid for yesterday's ego, not for to-day's. We are disappointed at the nullity of what we are pleased to call attainment. But what is attainment? The identification of the subject with the object of his desire. The subject has died—and perhaps many times—on the way."[9] To believe that memory is in a position to establish a connection—denied by life itself—between the many manifestations of the ego, means for Beckett a final capitulation to habit: "The laws of memory are subject to the more general laws of habit. ...Habit is the ballast that chains the dog to his vomit."[10] If habit could connect up the different phases of our lives, then we should have to go through life looking constantly behind us; but life itself does not run backward, so that if we allow habit to orient us, we are deceiving ourselves with fictions. The function of habit is to remove the strangeness from life; this is why we constantly have recourse to our memories. What memory retains has already passed through the filter of habit and has lost those painful sharp edges associated with first observation: Thus Beckett calls memory an "agent of security."[11] If this need for security gives rise to our projecting a meaning onto the objects before us, then we automatically cut ourselves off from those experiences that can only arise if we allow the objects to work their effect on us without sheltering behind our preconceptions of their meaning. "But when the object is perceived as particular and unique and not merely the member of a family, when it appears independent of any general notion and detached from the sanity of a cause, isolated and inexplicable in the light of ignorance, then and then only may it be a source of enchantment. Unfortunately Habit has laid its veto on this form of perception."[12]

Here we see the outline of a problem that runs through Beckett's text in something like a series of variations. The haphazardness of objects activates our need for tidy arrangements, which drives us to establish connections and link the objects together. It is this process that destroys the "enchantment of reality." For observation conditioned by habit cannot permit the experience of contingency. One might conclude that this makes literature necessary, since literature can confront us directly with something strange, and if we cannot absorb the experience of this strange object, then the possibility exists that we shall discover how our own "habit" of acquiring experience functions. We can only talk of experiences if our preconceptions have been modified or transformed by them. This is the background against which we must view the works of Beckett.

Like the *Proust* essay, Beckett's first novel, *Murphy*, published in 1937, is dominated by the attempt to expose the truth behind the commonplace. There, literary conventions are unmasked as mere devices dependent on specific situations. But unlike the Proust essay, the novel is a piece of fiction, which means that Beckett's anatomy of fiction is itself conducted through a fictional medium. The attempt to reveal the basis of fiction through fiction itself means that the process of revelation can never end.

For this reason, *Murphy*, too, is nothing but the beginning of this process. The first sentence reads: "The sun shone, having no alternative, on the nothing new."[13] The indication that the sun shone, and so had no alternative, deflates the beginning of the novel to the level of triviality. But usually the beginning is important, because it denotes the direction in which the events and their significance are to move. Beckett begins by wiping out any such significance. What is left is a form of words devoid of content and of function. *Murphy* is full of such verbal "sockets," and the reader may sometimes feel tempted to put in his own interpretative "plug" in order to supply the meaning the author has removed. If this does happen, the whole thing becomes abstruse—but only so long as one insists on regarding the novel as a representative portrayal of reality.[14]

But what is supposed to be representative about the wish of the "hero" to go into a lunatic asylum and finally to go mad himself? At

best, perhaps a withdrawal from his social environment or, less convincing, the withdrawal from body into spirit and, quite inconceivably,
the withdrawal from the recognizable forms of spiritual activity into a
movement that is recognizable only so long as it destroys everything
it has produced. As Murphy tries to bring himself back to the point
that can be identified as that which "makes him tick," so he seems to
himself to be getting farther and farther away from what he really is.
In the depths of his spirit, we learn:

> Here there was nothing but commotion and the pure forms of commotion.
> Here he was not free, but a mote in the dark of absolute freedom. He did
> not move, he was a point in the ceaseless unconditioned generation and
> passing away of line.
> Matrix of surds.[15]

What happens here has been made explicit in a different context by
Maurice Merleau-Ponty in his *Phenomenology of Perception:*

> My absolute contact with myself, the identity of being and appearance
> cannot be posited, but only lived as anterior to any affirmation. In both
> cases, therefore, we have the same silence and the same void. The expe-
> rience of absurdity and that of absolute self-evidence are mutually impli-
> catory, and even indistinguishable. The world appears absurd, only if a
> demand for absolute consciousness ceaselessly dissociates from each other
> the meanings with which it swarms, and conversely this demand is moti-
> vated by the conflict between those meanings. Absolute self-evidence and
> the absurd are equivalent, not merely as philosphical affirmations, but also
> as experiences.[16]

There are experiences that we can only have, but into which we cannot
gain any insight. One of these is the absolute contact of the ego with
itself, which is why Murphy releases himself from all worldly ties, in
order to get to the point at which in his attitude toward himself he can
finally coincide with himself.

This gives rise to a reality that cannot be penetrated by human
knowledge. Such a situation can only be presented in the manner of
absurdity, which indicates that self-evidence and knowledge exclude
one another—or, in other words, that knowledge of self-evidence does
not lend itself to be questioned. It is characteristic of Beckett's texts
that from the very beginning they are concerned with those experiences
of which we can never know anything. In *Murphy*, this is the syn-
chronization of the ego with itself; in the trilogy, it is the experience
of the end. And so in Beckett's novels, from fiction itself the impression

is drawn that no statement—not even a hypothetical one—can be made about a reality that is detached from human perception. This is the reason why the novels have an absurd effect, for inherent in the process of presentation is the awareness that what is to be presented lies far beyond the capabilities of fiction. But what is it that enables such excessive demands on the capabilities of fiction to concern us anyway? The answer may be found in the following passage in Kermode's *The Sense of an Ending:*

> ... the need we continue to feel is a need of concord, and we supply it by increasingly varied concord-fictions. They change as the reality from which we, in the middest, seek a show of satisfaction, changes.... They do this, for some of us, perhaps better than history, perhaps better than theology, largely because they are consciously false.[17]

And so fiction is able to give us such comforting answers to our human problems because it is unreal. Our compensation for what cannot be perceived is the knowledge pretended by fiction, which is "consciously false." For this very reason, the truth behind the fiction must not be revealed, and fiction itself must not be "falsified."

III

This, however, is the very thing that happens in Beckett's trilogy of novels *Molloy, Malone Dies,* and *The Unnamable,* which appeared originally in French between 1951 and 1953 and were translated into English for the most part by Beckett himself. Here, the theme of *Murphy* returns again, but on a vastly different scale. The titles of the individual sections of the trilogy draw attention to the withdrawal of the first-person narrator into ultimate anonymity. While the first-person narrator of the third novel is the unnamable, the names in the first two novels act as masks that the narrator has assumed. Hindsight reveals that the masks of the unnamable refer to particular relationships, limitations, and attitudes that, in the last novel, have lost all substance. But the unnamable is not completely free from the names that he once bore and that now stop him from relaxing in his anonymity. Clearly, one cannot get rid of fictions quite so easily.

The first-person narrators in the trilogy have an unsurpassable awareness of what is happening while they are narrating or of what happens when they try to pin down what they want to write about. It is this awareness that determines the order of sentences in the first novel. This consists of a continual alternation of statement and qualification

53

of what has been stated. The tendency, however, is not toward a consolidation of meaning, as one might normally expect from the development of a text, so much as toward a more or less complete contradiction of whatever has been stated. The first-person narrator avoids any kind of arrangement of the things he has observed. He does not want to confine them within the limits of his perception and impose an arbitrary uniformity on them; he wants, rather, to expose the deformities that occur to them through the very act of perception. But even this insight becomes an object of reflection for Molloy: "I could therefore puzzle over it endlessly without the least risk. For to know nothing is nothing, not to want to know anything likewise, but to be beyond knowing anything, to know you are beyond knowing anything, that is when peace enters in, to the soul of the incurious seeker."[18] But the words he uses also give him away.

Molloy wants peace—that is what he is searching for. This peace, however, cannot be obtained through what one knows, but only through the knowledge that whatever is knowable is nothing. This knowledge in turn is directly relevant to those experiences which we know exist, but about which we also know that insight into their very nature is denied us. One of these is, of course, the end. The question arises as to whether it can be enough for us to say about a certain situation that we know nothing. Is it not here, in fact, that we need our fictions, which, however "consciously false" they may be, at least pretend to a knowledge of the unknowable? In spite of his awareness and cool reasoning, Molloy is not completely free from the desire to imagine the end, and he falls into the very temptation to which his insight should prevent him from succumbing. "For what possible end to these wastes where true light never was, nor any upright thing, nor any true foundation, but only these leaning things, forever lapsing and crumbling away, beneath a sky without memory of morning or hope of night. These things, what things, come from where, made of what? And it says that here nothing stirs, has never stirred, will never stir, except myself, who do not stir either, when I am there, but see and am seen. Yes, a world at an end, in spite of appearances, its end brought it forth, ending it began, is it clear enough?"[19] Here the end is still visualized in detailed images, and obviously an end without such images is not conceivable. But at the same time, Molloy asks if the images are apt—and this at the very moment when the end is beginning to assume

54

the almost familiar eschatological features of a revelation. Is the peace Molloy is searching for perhaps impossible without images? If so, then the images would be the obstacles to peace, for one only creates images in terms of one's own human reality, and it is exactly this reality of which one seeks to be free. The end is therefore inconceivable without images and irrelevant with images. These are the problems developed in the remaining novels of the trilogy.

In *Malone Dies*, the first-person narrator no longer reports on different phases of his life, as Molloy had done, but simply reports on what happens when one reports. Molloy had already been aware that all representation is but an "arrangement"—tersely summed up as "Saying is inventing"[20]—and this is also assumed by Malone as he waits for his end. Right up till his death he passes time by writing, but his writing concerns writing itself. He would like to get to the point where he is only writing about the fact that he is writing. It is impossible to make the actual act of writing the object of the writing, because you cannot write unless you have something to write about, but the act of writing automatically prevents you from capturing the complete reality of the object with which you seem to be concerned. Malone is aware of this. And so he describes what results from writing as being lies. With this as a basic premise, it follows that the moment you are conscious of what happens in writing, writing itself can only be understood as a continual moving away from the false images that arise from writing. Thus the never-ending discovery of fictions created by writing remains the only possibility of writing one's way toward the truth about writing.

The truth about writing consists in the discovery of its fictional character. But why does this discovery have to be made over and over again, without end? The answer lies in the alternative course that has enmeshed Malone: "Live and invent. I have tried. I must have tried. Invent. It is not the word. Neither is live."[21] Malone's alternative is a basic dilemma of life itself. Though we are alive, we do not know what it means to be alive. If we try to find out what it means to be alive, we are forced to seek the meaning of something we cannot possibly know. And so the continual invention of images and, at the same time, the rejection of their claims to truth, provide the only means of coping with this dilemma. In this way, we do not fall victim to our own inventions, but to a certain extent we do satisfy the urge to know something about that which cannot be known. Thus we cannot abandon our fictions, but nevertheless ought to realize that they are fictions, as this is the only certain knowledge we can hope to obtain.

If we feel inclined to regard this fact as absurd, this inclination is only another expression of the fact that we are still searching for certainty where we know there can be none and that in spite of this knowledge we still take the image for the truth. In *Malone Dies*, our need for fiction is constantly frustrated. What happens here should not occur, if fiction is not to be robbed of its effect. Malone reveals the nature of this fiction, which is that fictions are "consciously false." But falsifying fictions is more than just adapting them to changing needs.

An anatomy of the fiction contained in Beckett's trilogy discloses the "complementarities" that are constantly supplied by the fictions and serve to complement and give form to that which remains inconclusive or open in each particular situation in life. The scale on which such gaps are closed can vary considerably. Every historical period will have different gaps for which "complementarities" have to be supplied. There are gaps in human affairs, too, that require to be filled in. This applies not only to the uncertainty of the end but also to the nonstop fabrication of fictions that is necessary in everyday empirical life. This is where fictions are most likely to be confused with realities, simply because they are so useful. Beckett bursts open the character of fiction as "concord-fiction" not for the sake of being destructive, but because the very composition of his texts aims at running contrary to the continual closing of gaps inherent in "concord-fiction." By betraying the fictions, he reestablishes the openness of the situations he deals with. This is the dominant trend in the third novel of the trilogy, *The Unnamable*.

This anonymous being has cast off all the fictional figures through whom he had named himself. Names had always cropped up when he had attempted to get a grip on himself in given situations. But it is difficult for him to get rid of these "vice-exister(s)."[22] Not only do they pursue him, but they also keep usurping him by telling him who he is.[23] And because this is what he wants to know, he feels that the old fictions are continually seeking to reinvent him in order to fulfill his wish. At the same time, however, he is also aware that every suggestion he writes down from these figures can only be a fiction. This knowledge enables him to avoid being continually reinvented. With something like happiness, he states: "Dear incomprehension, it's thanks to you I'll be myself, in the end. Nothing will remain of all the lies they have glutted me with."[24] This utterance is highly ambivalent. First, it means that only by accepting incomprehensibility is it possible to see through the fictions that pretend to know the unknowable; that is the situation of the unnamable at the moment in which he makes this statement. But in addition to this, it is the incomprehensibility of reality, and indeed of the ego itself, that gives rise to the creation of fiction. To pursue both lines of thought at virtually the same time seems highly problematical, but it is this very problem that the unnamable is trying to settle. With his insight, he destroys what is promised by the fictions. And this rejection of fiction, its unmasking as a lie, then becomes the condition for establishing an open situation as regards life in general. Without the production and subsequent negation of fictions, this open situation could not possibly be established. But this, in turn, means that even in cases such as the unnamable is concerned with, the usefulness of fiction cannot be dispensed with. That is to say, even the unmasked fiction cannot destroy itself. A great comfort for literature and a great nuisance for ideology!

From this state of affairs there arise two consequences. These can be described as two basic structures that are common to Beckett's prose and drama. Each individual work itself creates a certain starting point. The mere fact that something is written means that a start has been made or, alternatively, that writing has given rise to a start. If one writes, it must always be about something. This leads to the first structural feature of these texts: They consume their own starting points. But as this starting point is itself the subject of the writing, however drastically it may be reduced it can never completely disappear. Hence the second structural feature of Beckett's texts: If the content of the writing is the consumption of its own starting point, then, in accordance with its structure, it can never come to an end. Fictions, according to Kermode, are for finding things out. The fiction Beckett is constantly questioning shows that, in fact, we are alive because we cannot settle anything final, and this absence of finality is what drives us continually to go on being active.

IV

This line of thought is also apparent in the curious piece of prose written in 1965 and entitled "Imagination Dead Imagine." By imagining that the power of imagination itself is dead, we are invited to loosen our grip on the world to that extent that we should curb or annihilate our urge to interpret our surroundings.

The text begins with the sentence: "No trace anywhere of life, you say, pah, no difficulty there, imagination not dead yet, yes, dead, good, imagination dead imagine."[25] Do all traces of life disappear if we imagine that the power of imagination is extinguished? On the contrary, the text shows how, once the power of imagination has been separated from the world, its very unfixedness gives rise to a dynamism that produces continuous configurations and then swallows them up again. It is only the imagined death of imagination that brings out its inextinguishability. But whenever the power of imagination is fixed to a worldly context in which it is used to fill in the gaps there arises fiction. Beckett's novels are therefore fictional texts that do not deal with fictions, but continually strive to nullify fiction. The act of "decomposition" forms the creative impetus of these texts.

The problem that Beckett attempts to solve is: How can you picture something in words and forms that is the source from which words and forms emanate but whose inherent nature prohibits its expression in words and forms? So he tries in "Imagination Dead Imagine" to eliminate the expectation (expectation being the impetus toward meaning) in words. Beckett allows the words of "Imagination Dead Imagine" to be experienced but not to be known (in terms of meaning). The impetus toward meaning destroys the experience of the word, and for this reason Beckett cancels out all contextual references. The following passage from the middle of the text provides a good starting point for a specific, if brief, textual study: "Rediscovered miraculously after what absence in perfect voids it is no longer quite the same, from this point of view, but there is no other. Externally all is as before and the sighting of the little fabric quite as much a matter of chance, its whiteness merging in the surrounding whiteness."[26] This passage clearly illustrates Beckett's process of creation.[27] Pure chance makes this expression possible, and whether or not a specific content is generated out of the void is never firmly stated, since the whiteness of the content merges with the whiteness around it. There is no context for this specific event, and when it is placed within a context it disappears. All potential points of reference within the texts are blatantly arbitrary and contribute no unique context or meaning to the text. Yet the text is full of commands: "Go back out, move back...ascend...descend, go back in"[28] that invite the reader to a participation in the experience of the text itself. The author, at one point, exclaims that this "may seem strange."[29] By saying this he is trying to demonstrate his sympathy as a guide who recognizes the difficulty of experiencing a void of meaning. This text is not a sterile monologue; it is an invitation to participation. The words themselves seem almost to beg to be embraced on their own terms. The phrase logically negates itself, destroying its own meaning, and it is this destruction of meaning that lends the phrase its potential to be experienced by the reader.

What is "gained" by this can perhaps be summed up by a quotation from John Cage, who states in his book *Silence*: "Our intention is to affirm this life, not to bring order out of chaos nor to suggest improvements in creation, but simply to wake up to the very life we're living, which is so excellent once one gets one's mind and one's desires out of its way and lets it act of its own accord."[30]

V

Opposed to such an awakening, however, are certain difficulties caused by human behavior. Beckett's plays draw attention to these difficulties and show perhaps even more clearly than his novels the conditions that give rise to them. In a letter to his New York director Alan Schneider, Beckett speaks of his drama as the "power of the text to claw."[31] There is no doubt that his plays do claw at one, but we feel this effect above all because they lead us to an increased amount of activity. This is certainly true of Beckett's first great dramatic success, *Waiting for Godot*, which was published in 1952 and had its premiere the following year. When asked who Godot was and what he stood for, Beckett replied, "If I knew, I would have said so in the play."[32] What, then, can the audience know, and what experience will they gain from a play that refuses to divulge its meaning? In *Waiting for Godot*, as in many other of Beckett's plays, nothing is decided. Even the apparently decisive waiting of Vladimir and Estragon for Godot gradually becomes more and more aimless as the "action" proceeds. This increasing indeterminacy acts as a provocation to the audience. Waiting that loses sight of its purpose begins like a mystery but develops into mere mystification. If the waiting is an end in itself, then there arises the situation that the actions, words, and gestures of the characters become increasingly indefinite. Then not only does the waiting become aimless, but also the language of the characters no longer corresponds to what the intention of language ought to be. This expanding indeterminacy stimulates the audience into the act of "determining." The more we try to project meaning onto the aimless "action," the further we get from the characters and the nearer to our own ideas, to which we then begin to cling to an ever-increasing degree, as shown by the great *Godot* debate in the *London Times*. As the largely indeterminate situations in the text refuse to divulge who Godot is and what is the meaning of the waiting, it seems as if this play is seeking to shut out its audience. But this is something quite intolerable for us, and so the spectator who has been locked out struggles with increasing intensity to break into the play again, bringing with him all the meanings and decisions that have been withheld from him. If the play won't tell him what it means, then he will decide for himself what it ought to mean. The result is, that the spectator is, so to speak, dragged along in the wake of the play, trying increasingly hard to catch up by means of interpretation. And the harder he tries, the further behind he falls, and the play which he had tried to break into with his specific interpretations, simply goes ahead regardless of him. This gives rise to a strange experience: As the meaning projections of the spectator are incapable of removing the indeterminacy of the situations, so the two main characters seem more and more free and unconcerned. They seem to be quite indifferent to the earnestness assumed by the spectator.

Vladimir and Estragon do not possess this freedom right from the outset; it is brought to life, if not exactly created, by the resolution of the spectator to impose a definite meaning on the indeterminate situations in the play. The more the spectator feels compelled to do this, the greater the freedom of Vladimir and Estragon. The spectator's interest in Godot is disproportionately larger than that of the two protagonists. And if the spectator moves toward Godot, the protagonists move away from the spectator. If the spectator wants to know whether Godot is really God, the two men waiting seem like clowns because they do not appear to grasp the earnestness of the situation. But these situations are created, in the first place, by the spectator himself, for the determination of his attitude always brings forth a contrary reaction from the drama itself. Indeed, the text is so designed that it constantly calls forth a desire for determinacy that the spectator cannot escape but that inevitably drives him further and further into the trap of his own limitations.

Here, the problem of fiction arises again in a different, and existentially intensified manner. The spectator at a Beckett play feels for himself the need for and the consequence of "concord-fiction," which forms a basis for his act of meaning projection. The highly indeterminate actions of the characters, precisely because of the lack of consequence in these (simulated) actions, draw the spectator into the play because he wants to impose consistency, purpose, and meaning on it. But in doing so, the spectator becomes the only real person in the play. The fictional text, by its extreme indeterminacy, has led him to make the decisions he thought necessary and meaningful, but then, the moment he had made them, the characters stand round the baffled spectator and—metaphorically speaking—"experience him" in his frustration. For he is worried about something they have left behind: the closing of open situations by means of fictions. At this point we get the special and inimitable effect unique to Beckett's theater, tersely summed up by Hugh Kenner: "... for art has suddenly refused to be art and brought forward living pain."[33] A precondition for such reactions is an intensive participation in the action on the part of the spectator. And the more intensive this participation, the more fluid become the boundaries between literature and reality—and this in a play whose supposedly absurd character would seem to indicate that it had nothing to do with reality anyway. Finally, we are forced to revise, and indeed to transform, our ideas as to what is reality.

This is the tendency underlying one of Beckett's most provocative plays, *Endgame*. The title is a pointer to what is to come: The end is not to be shown, it is to be played: "Me—(*he yawns*)—to play,"[34] are Hamm's first words in this play, as he replies to Clov's statement: "Finished, it's finished, nearly finished, it must be nearly finished."[35] The degree to which Clov and Hamm are dominated by the idea of playing can be seen not only from the fact that they frequently refer to their activities as a game but also from the fact that all their activities are without consequence. When Clov smashes the toy dog on Hamm's head, the reaction is the contrary of what we expect: Hamm wants

Clov to hit him with an ax. It is little wonder, then, that in all such actions both of them are careful to remove all meaning from their game:

HAMM: We're not beginning to . . . to . . . mean something?
CLOV: Mean something! You and I, mean something! [*Brief laugh*] Ah that's a good one!
HAMM: I wonder. [*Pause*] Imagine if a rational being came back to earth, wouldn't he be liable to get ideas into his head if he observed us long enough.[36]

These are the very ideas that go whirling through the spectator's mind; he may tend to regard all the weird goings-on as part of a game, but he finds that the rules of this game are not divulged. He cannot help searching for them, and in so doing he discovers that the game could be said to run according to various codes, but these originate not in the form of the game itself so much as in the meaning projections of the spectator. If the rules of the *Endgame* have to be projected onto it by the spectator, then clearly the text itself cannot establish that any one of the possibilities is the correct one. And if one does draw up a consistent code to apply to the whole game, it can only be at the expense of all other levels of the text; and when the spectator turns his attention to those levels excluded by the "code" he seems to be fixed on, he has no alternative but to reject his own meaning projections. Thus *Endgame* compels its spectator to reject the "meanings" it stimulates, and in this way conveys something of the "unendingness" of the end and the nature of the fictions which we are continually fabricating in order to finish off the end or to close the gaps in our own experiences. By compelling the spectator to reject the meaning he himself has suggested, *Endgame* offers a new experience, unique to the world of literature, in which one is enabled to penetrate below the surface of one's own meaning projections and to gain insight into those factors that guide the individual in his personal mode of interpretation. In this way, too, there lies a chance that the individual is able to free himself from the restrictions of his own outlook. The negativeness of Beckett's texts, then, consists in the technique he uses in order to involve us in the complex process of manufacturing fictions and to open our eyes to the nature of fiction itself. If this awareness is inapplicable to everyday life, one might as well question the standards of everyday life when they cannot tolerate this awareness, or—even worse—when they attempt to suppress it.

Preliminaries

NOTES

1. Ernst Fischer, *Kunst und Koexistenz. Beitrag zu einer modernen marxistischen Ästhetik* (Hamburg-Rowohlt, 1966), 21.
2. Georg Lukács, *Wider den missverstandenen Realismus* (Hamburg: Claassen, 1958), 31.
3. Reinhard Baumgart, *Literatur für Zeitgenossen* (Editions Suhrkamp) (Frankfurt: Suhrkamp, 1966), 166.
4. Samuel Beckett, *Endgame* (New York: Grove Press, 1958), 48.
5. Frank Kermode, *The Sense of an Ending* (New York: Oxford University Press, 1967), 17.
6. Ibid., 39.
7. Ibid., 62.
8. Quoted in ibid., 63.
9. Samuel Beckett, *Proust* (New York: Grove Press, 1958), 3.
10. Ibid., 7, 8.
11. Ibid., 10.
12. Ibid., 11.
13. Samuel Beckett, *Murphy* (New York: Grove Press, 1957), 1.
14. Cf. Manfred Smuda, *Becketts Prosa als Metasprache* (Munich: W. Fink, 1970), 31 ff.
15. Beckett, *Murphy*. 112.
16. Maurice Merleau-Ponty, *Phenomenology of Perception*, transl. Colin Smith (New York: Humanities Press, 1962), 295 ff.
17. Kermode, *Sense of an Ending*, 63 ff.
18. Samuel Beckett, *Molloy*, in *Three Novels by Samuel Beckett* (New York: Grove Press, 1965), 64.
19. Ibid., 40.
20. Ibid., 32.
21. Samuel Beckett, *Malone Dies*, in ibid., 194.
22. Samuel Beckett, *The Unnamable*, in ibid., 315.
23. Cf. ibid.
24. Ibid., 325.
25. Samuel Beckett, "Imagination Dead Imagine," in *First Love and Other Stories* (New York: Grove Press, 1974), 63.
26. Ibid., 65.
27. For these remarks on "Imagination Dead Imagine" I am indebted to a paper by Jan R. Reber which he submitted in my Beckett-Seminar at Wesleyan University in the fall term 1970-71.
28. Beckett, "Imagination", 63.
29. Ibid.
30. John Cage, *Silence* (Cambridge, Mass.: Harvard University Press, 1961), 95.
31. Quoted by Hugh Kenner, *Samuel Beckett: A Critical Study* (New York: Grove Press, 1961), 165.
32. Quoted by Martin Esslin, *The Theatre of the Absurd* (New York: Anchor, 1969), 12.

33. Kenner, *Samuel Beckett*, 174.
34. Beckett, *Endgame*, 2.
35. Ibid., 1.
36. Ibid., 32-33.

THE PAGE

RUBIN RABINOVITZ

"Murphy" and the Uses of Repetition

> *What is right may properly*
> *be uttered even twice.*
> *—Empedocles*

Murphy is a novel of great beauty and complexity. These qualities are interrelated: As the work's diverse elements coalesce into a unified pattern, its beauty is revealed. Like *More Pricks than Kicks, Murphy* contains many recurring elements that are used to illuminate an underlying level of meaning. One's understanding of the work changes after successive readings: Trivial details gain significance, unambiguous statements become mysterious, latent themes emerge. Little of this is immediately apparent, however. In the time since 1938, when *Murphy* first appeared, it has been considered an undemanding work. Beckett himself once said to an interviewer, "It's my easiest book, I guess."[1] But the qualifying phrase is important: if *Murphy* is easier than other works, it is still not an easy book. Nor does Beckett truly believe that it is. In a letter to a friend he called it "slightly obscure" and said that the narrative was "hard to follow."[2]

The apparent simplicity of the novel can be a stumbling block for the unwary reader, or—to use Beckett's term—"gentle skimmer."[3] Unless one is very attentive, the novel's repetitive devices will probably be overlooked. *Murphy* contains many of these devices: reiterated passages, recurring episodes, dual sets of objects, characters with similar traits, and various types of symmetrical configurations. It is tempting, initially, to dismiss the redundancy as a stylistic flaw. But if this temptation is resisted, it becomes evident that there are far too many recurring elements for them to have been included inadvertently.

Recurring Passages

Murphy contains many phrases and sentences that are repeated, some of them more than once. There are more than 400 sets of recurring passages; about 150 of these sets contain more than two items; in all, more than a thousand individual passages are involved in the pattern of verbal repetition.[4]

Many of the recurring passages are short, easy to detect, and relatively unimportant in terms of revealing underlying meanings. This deceptively suggests that the repetition generally is unimportant. But even the more obvious recurring passages have a use: They call attention to others that are subtler. An example occurs in the following excerpt, in which Mr. Kelly advises Celia to break off with Murphy:

> Celia made to rise, Mr. Kelly pinioned her wrists.
> "Sever your connexion with this Murphy," he said, "before it is too late."
> "Let me go," said Celia.
> "Terminate an intercourse that must prove fatal," he said, "while there is yet time."
> "Let me go," said Celia.
> He let go and she stood up. (pages 24-25)

Mr. Kelly repeats an idea in parallel sentences, and Celia twice says, "Let me go": This hardly seems very significant. But in the next chapter Celia again says "Let me go" twice, this time to Murphy:

> She made to rise, he pinioned her wrists.
> "Let me go," said Celia.
> "Is it?" said Murphy.
> "Let me go," said Celia.
> He let her go. She rose and went to the window. (pages 40-41)

A comparison of the two excerpts reveals that they contain other recurring elements. The two first sentences each introduce the same archaic terms ("made to rise," "pinioned") and the concluding sentences also are similar ("He let her go..."). The repetition occurs in similar episodes: Each time Celia is seated near a man who is lying down; when she tries to get up, he takes hold of her wrists; then he releases her and she gets up. In the first of these episodes Mr. Kelly urges Celia to leave Murphy; in the second she tries to follow this advice. Murphy eventually persuades Celia to change her mind and stay with him, but her reiterated "Let me go" suggests that her remark has a figurative meaning: She is asking Murphy to make it easier for her to end their relationship.

Many of the recurring phrases call attention to subtle details that might otherwise be overlooked. In the following excerpt, about Murphy's "recreation" of tying himself into his rocking chair, it seems at first that he is honest and open in his dealings with Celia:

> She knew nothing of this recreation, in which Murphy had not felt the need to indulge while she was with him. He now gave her a full and frank account of its unique features....
>
> Nor did she know anything of his heart attacks, which had not troubled him while she was with him. He now told her all about them.... (page 30)

The recurring segments in the passage ("while she was with him. He now...") indicate that Murphy has been evasive: It is only after she finds out about his activities that Celia is given the "full and frank" accounts. Moreover, Celia is under the impression that Murphy tells her everything—this idea is similarly emphasized by repetition (pages 13, 20).

Murphy is evasive, but Celia has few secrets, even from Mr. Kelly. This becomes apparent when two passages with a recurring phrase ("might give ... pain") are compared:

> She kept nothing from Mr. Kelly except what she thought might give him pain, i.e. next to nothing. (page 11)

> "I have not spoken to you of Murphy," said Celia, "because I thought it might give you pain." (page 12)

The word *nothing*, which is repeated in the first of these excerpts, links it to a sentence that appears in the passage about Murphy's "full and frank" accounts:

> She knew nothing of this recreation....
>
> Nor did she know anything of his heart attacks.... He now told her all about them, keeping back nothing that might alarm her. (page 30)

The last sentence is tricky; it emphasizes not the similarities but the differences between Celia and Murphy. She conceals anything that might be painful; he discloses anything that might be alarming.

The repetitive devices are often used to provide clues about the characters' hidden traits and feelings. Their loneliness is emphasized in a series of related passages, each of which involves a statement about being alone, together with a modification of the original statement. The series begins when Celia says to Mr. Kelly, "You are all I have in the world," and then qualifies her remark: "You ... and possibly Murphy" (page 11). Later, when she again tells him, "You are all I have in the world," he tartly responds, "I ... and possibly Murphy" (page 18). Echoes of this conversation recur in five other passages:

> Celia, after leaving Mr. Kelly's flat, says to herself: "Now I have no one ... except possibly Murphy" (page 25).
>
> When Celia leaves Murphy, the narrator says: "Now she had nobody, except possibly Mr. Kelly" (page 35).
>
> When Murphy makes a disparaging remark about Rosie Dew's dog, the narrator refers to it as "almost all she had in this dreary *en-deçà* ..." (page 102).
>
> When Celia leaves Mr. Kelly, he says: "Now I have no one ... not even Celia" (page 115).
>
> When Neary dismisses Cooper, the narrator says: "Neary also had no one, not even Cooper" (page 115).

The tone of the qualifying phrases ("except possibly," "not even") seems cynical, but the repetition conveys a sense of despair: Most of these characters dread loneliness, and most of them become its victims. Like a leitmotiv, the reiterated formula adds significance and intensity to this theme.

Sometimes the repetition is used to reveal idiosyncracies in the narrative method. An example occurs at the end of the first chapter, in a description of Murphy in his rocking chair. Here the redundancy is doubled: A number of phrases recur within the passage, and toward the end of the novel the entire passage is repeated: "The rock got faster and faster, shorter and shorter ... soon his body would be quiet. Most things under the moon got slower and slower and then stopped, a rock got faster and faster and then stopped. Soon his body would be quiet, soon he would be free" (pages 9, 252-53). It may seem that the only point of the repetition is to stress that Murphy is rocking more quickly. But one of the reiterated phrases ("and then stopped") calls attention to an apparent paradox: Unlike most things in the world, Murphy's rocking chair does not slow down before stopping. The repeated phrase refers to an event that occurs after the chapter ends: Murphy gets the chair moving so quickly that it flips over. He is later found unconscious; how this occurred is hinted at but never explained. The omitted description is alluded to by still another recurring phrase in the passage, "soon his body would be quiet." Ostensibly it suggests that Murphy will shortly go into a trance; actually it anticipates his imminent state of unconsciousness. When the entire passage about the rocking chair is later repeated, other relevant points emerge. Again an important event—Murphy's death—occurs just after the chapter ends, and again the event is not described. The phrase "soon his body would be quiet" ironically refers to the omitted description, just as it did in the earlier episode. The recurring passages finally make it clear that the narrator is intentionally withholding details of the story.

In some instances, even apparently trivial repetitions turn out to be significant. Murphy's fiancée, Miss Counihan, habitually says "—er—" in the middle of a sentence; this she does eleven times in the course of the novel.[5] Her mannerism seems so unimportant that one barely pays attention to it. But if one compares the contexts in which the interjection occurs, a pattern becomes evident: Miss Counihan says "—er—" whenever she is about to utter a euphemism. This is never explained, however; Beckett permits readers to discover it for themselves. Two other characters, Neary and Wylie, appear in an episode in which the mannerism is important. Neary, rejected by Miss Counihan, asks Wylie for advice about winning her back. Wylie suggests that Neary tell Miss Counihan that he is "Hers to wipe her—er—feet on" (page 60). Wylie's joke goes over Neary's head, but readers who have noticed that an "—er—" signals a euphemism will apprehend its deeper meaning.

Another character whose habitual repetition is a sign of hypocrisy is Murphy's landlady, Miss Carridge. Wylie again indicates that he is aware of the meaning of her mannerism by mimicking it.[6] As his name suggests, Wylie is very shrewd; he is sensitive to nuances of speech and uses this skill to his advantage. He understands that if people dissemble, they sometimes also reveal their deeper feelings inadvertently. This idea is related to one of Beckett's techniques: Readers are encouraged to learn, as Wylie has, that minor details are often clues to hidden truths.

Cross-references

Another device used to hint at the novel's hidden meanings consists of different types of cross-references that call attention to reiterated passages. When the narrator borrows an aphorism from Neary ("Love requited ... is a short circuit"), he reminds readers where it originated and in this way also indicates that it has been repeated (pages 5, 29). Similarly, when the narrator quotes from Murphy's horoscope, he attributes the quotations to Suk, the swami who cast it; this occurs eight times.[7] In some instances quotation marks are used to indicate that passages are being repeated (see, for example, the quotations on pages 183 and 252). Sometimes the cross-references are themselves repeated and in this way become part of the pattern of verbal repetition. In the first chapter, when the narrator refers three times to a subsequent chapter, each of his cross-references is the same: "as described in section six" (pages 2, 7, 9).

Some of the cross-references are more intricate. When Cooper recalls a comment of Wylie's and repeats it verbatim, the narrator says: "It is curious how Wylie's words remained fixed in the minds of those to whom they had once been addressed. It must have been the tone of voice. Cooper, whose memory for such things was really very poor, had recovered, word for word, the merest of mere phrases. And now Neary lay on his bed repeating: 'The syndrome known as life is too diffuse to admit of palliation.'"[8] The comment Neary repeats is, like Cooper's, one originally uttered by Wylie. Neary's feat of memory is perhaps again an effect of Wylie's tone of voice; at any rate, no other explanation is given. Then—in case anyone missed it the first time around—Neary repeats the same trick: A few lines down he quotes still another of Wylie's remarks verbatim (pages 200-201, 57). At this point overtaxed credulity gives way to skepticism, and one begins to understand that the narrator is being playful. But the joke has an additional purpose as a cross-reference; it emphasizes a number of recurring passages that might otherwise have gone unnoticed.

Repeated Action

Most of the cross-references call attention to verbal repetitions, but some are used in connection with another type of redundancy involving repeated action. It may seem pointless for the narrator to mention that a gesture of Celia's resembles one of Neary's ("She despatched her hands on the gesture that Neary had made such a botch of...").⁹ But comments like this one call attention to a pattern of reiterated actions. Some actions are repeated many times and are used in conjunction with verbal repetition. When Miss Counihan sits on the edge of Neary's bed, the narrator includes the following cross-reference: "In a somewhat similar way Celia had sat on Mr. Kelly's bed, and on Murphy's..." (page 208). This comment links four episodes: one involving Neary and Miss Counihan, one involving Mr. Kelly and Celia, and two involving Murphy and Celia (pages 207-8, 24-25, 29, 39). In still other episodes a similar type of action recurs:

> Ticklepenny lies on Murphy's bed; Murphy is seated nearby in his rocking chair (page 191).
>
> Celia is on her bed; Neary moves his chair to the head of her bed (pages 232-33).
>
> Murphy lies down on Mr. Endon's bed; Mr. Endon squats on the bed (page 242).
>
> Murphy, after helping Mr. Endon into bed, kneels beside the bed (page 248).

Many of the related episodes are linked by other recurring details. Usually the person in bed is at home; the other person arrives and sits on or near the bed. In most cases the setting (appropriately enough) is a bed-sitting room. In each of the episodes an exchange between the characters redefines some aspect of their relationship, and what emerges is that—as in a royal levee—the person lying down is the more powerful. When Miss Counihan visits Neary and sits on his bed, their positions indicate that their relationship has changed. Previously he had been pursuing her; now he has lost interest and she is pursuing him. Similarly, when Neary moves his chair closer to Celia's bed, the suggestion is that he has fallen under her spell; the narrator later affirms this.

The same pattern holds in the last two episodes on the list. In the first of these Murphy is lying down and Mr. Endon is squatting on the bed. This characterizes the initial stage of their relationship: Murphy, an attendant in the asylum where Mr. Endon is confined, seems to be the dominant person. But in the next scene the situation has changed: Murphy, who wanted to become friends with Mr. Endon, realizes that he has been rejected. At this point he kneels beside the reclining Mr. Endon; as his position indicates, he now is in the inferior role.[10]

A related idea emerges in another set of parallel scenes. Celia, trying to understand why Murphy has left her, pauses as she considers various reasons. The narrator marks these intervals by saying, "A rest," as each one occurs (page 234). Later Murphy pauses in similar fashion when he thinks about why Mr. Endon would not become his friend, and again the narrator keeps repeating, "A rest" (page 250). The reiterated passages and actions point out the similarities in the two situations: Celia and Murphy are unprepared for the rejections and both are hurt by them.

Celia's unhappiness is hinted at in an episode in which she emulates the actions of a retired butler known as "the old boy." Once again, both verbal reiteration and repeated action are used to emphasize the parallels. In the first of the two scenes Miss Carridge tells Celia about the old boy's habit of pacing the floor of his room:

> "Hark," she said, pointing upward.
> A soft padding to and fro was audible.
> "The old boy," said Miss Carridge. "Never still." (page 69)

Soon afterward the old boy cuts his throat. It was presumably because he was thinking about taking his life that he paced the floor. Later Celia moves into the room he had occupied, and when it becomes clear that Murphy has abandoned her, she begins to pace the floor. Wylie calls attention to this in a passage very much like the earlier one:

> "Hark!" said Wylie, pointing upward.
> A soft swaggering to and fro was audible.
> "Mrs. M.," said Wylie, "never still. . . ." (page 228)

The similarities hint that Celia may be considering following in the old boy's footsteps, figuratively as well as literally.[11] The narrator never says whether Celia is considering suicide, and she herself remains stoically silent. But in Beckett's fiction—as in life—explanations for stoical silence are not always given.

Another series of recurring episodes involves Neary and his cycle of love affairs: As soon as a woman falls in love with him, he goes off in pursuit of someone else. Neary, whose name is an anagram of "yearn," is constantly beset by desire. This emerges in a series of recurring incidents which indicates that his relationships with Miss Dwyer and Miss Counihan are remarkably similar:

Mrs. West loves Neary; he rejects her because he loves Miss Dwyer; she rejects him because she is in love with another man (page 5).

Miss Dwyer submits to Neary; he rejects her and falls in love with Miss Counihan; she rejects him because she is in love with another man (pages 48-49).

Neary complains to Murphy, one of his students, about the pain of unrequited love (pages 4ff.).

Neary complains to Wylie, formerly one of his students, about the pain of unrequited love (pages 46ff.).

During this conversation Murphy, responding to a question from Neary, admits he finds Miss Counihan physically attractive (page 6).

During this conversation Wylie, responding to a question from Neary, admits he finds Miss Counihan physically attractive (page 60).

The story of Dives and Lazarus is used to stress how intensely Neary longs for Miss Dwyer.[12]

The story of Dives and Lazarus is used to stress how intensely Neary longs for Miss Counihan.[13]

Neary's falling in love with Miss Dwyer is explained in terms of the figure-ground concept, a central idea in gestalt psychology (page 4).

Neary's falling out of love with Miss Dwyer is explained in terms of the figure-ground concept, a central idea in gestalt psychology (page 48).

This comparison is followed by an allusion to Wolfgang Köhler, an important member of the gestalt movement.[14]

This comparison is followed by an allusion to Kurt Koffka, an important member of the gestalt movement (page 48).

Realizing that she has no future with Elliman, Miss Dwyer sleeps with Neary; he thereupon loses interest in her (page 48).

Realizing that she has no future with Murphy, Miss Counihan submits to Neary's "wishes, or rather whims"; he thereupon loses interest in her (page 199).

When Neary spurns Miss Dwyer, a new sequence involving Miss Counihan begins. The conclusion of each cycle initiates another one. Neary loses interest in Miss Counihan when he decides to become friends with Murphy; later, attracted to Celia, he forgets about Murphy.

The cyclical movement of Neary's actions also is emphasized by a circular configuration of one-sided love relationships. Neary loves Miss Dwyer at the time she is in love with Flight-Lieutenant Elliman; he loves "a Miss Farren of Ringsakiddy"; she loves "Father Fit of Ballinclashet"; he loves "Mrs. West of Passage"; she loves Neary (page 5). Even the place names in the series suggest circles or movement.

The repetition here and in other episodes introduces the idea that human activity is often mindlessly redundant. This theme is emphasized in a series of scenes where action, settings, and other details recur:

> Two scenes in the novel take place in a rooming house in West Brompton. At the beginning of each scene Murphy is alone, tied to his rocking chair. Toward the end of each scene he converses with Celia about his horoscope (pages 1-9, 28-31).

> Two scenes take place in Mr. Kelly's flat. In each one Mr. Kelly lies in bed, finds it hard to think because of a feeling that parts of his body are dispersed, and repairs his kite. At the end of the first of these episodes Celia says to herself, "Now I have no one"; at the end of the second scene Mr. Kelly tells himself the same thing. (pages 11-25, 114-15).

> Kite flying is depicted in two scenes. In each one Celia watches a boy with two kites yoked in tandem. In the first scene Celia greets the boy, who does not respond—he is singing. In the second scene the boy "did not sing as he departed, nor did she hail him." Both scenes, which take place near the Round Pond in Hyde Park, end when the rangers, crying, "All out," close the park (pages 151-53, 276-82).

> Rosie Dew appears in two scenes; both take place in Hyde Park; the Long Water (a lake in Hyde Park) is mentioned in each of them. Near the end of the first scene Rosie Dew sets out for home after recalling that "A boot was waiting for her from Lord Gall . . ."; near the end of the second scene she decides to go home after recalling that "A pair of socks was waiting from Lord Gall."[15]

> Neary sends Cooper on two missions: to discover where Murphy lives and to dispose of his remains. Each time, Cooper passes a supremely attractive pub just as it is about to open; forgetting about his mission, he remains there drinking until closing time (pages 120-21, 274-75).

The narrator seldom calls attention to these recurring episodes, and the characters who figure in them seem unaware that they are repeating their actions. It is as if they are unwilling to confront the monotony in their lives and have insulated themselves from it.

Another form of repeated action is introduced when situations described early in the novel recur toward the end. When she moves in with Murphy, Celia hopes that they will have a "new life" together.[16] She gives up streetwalking, stops visiting Mr. Kelly, and devotes herself to Murphy. The new life, however, does not last very long. This is hinted at when the words *new life* are repeated and then used ironically in a description of dead leaves falling to the ground (pages 64, 150). Later, when Murphy dies, Celia returns to her old life. Similarly, in the first scene where Celia and Murphy are seen together, she notices that he has a birthmark. In their last scene together she sees the birthmark again: She uses it to identify Murphy's corpse. Such episodes suggest that it is pointless to hope for a new life; only death brings significant changes.

Beckett has said that people usually find change unendurable and use habit, "the guarantee of a dull inviolability," to block it out of their lives.[17] This theme is introduced in the opening sentence of *Murphy* when the narrator, echoing Ecclesiastes, describes the sun shining on the "nothing new." Wylie—in a passage that Neary later repeats verbatim—points out that things "will always be the same as they always were" (pages 58, 201). Always, always: Nothing ever changes, yet everyone seems to think that things are getting better. Beckett challenges his readers with this idea. If the redundancy in *Murphy* goes unnoticed, it may be that they also have insulated themselves from the monotony and repetitiousness of life.

Duality

Another device used to hint at this repetitiousness involves pairs of characters, objects, and locales; there are, altogether, about 200 of them in the novel.[18] The device is often hard to detect because one of the items in a dual set is more conspicuous than the other. This often occurs with dual sets of characters. Two prostitutes and two landladies are mentioned in *Murphy*, but in each instance one of the two plays an important role and the other one is only mentioned in passing.[19] The novel contains many dual sets of this sort. Among the characters are two coroners, two homosexuals, two waitresses, two fortunetellers, two alcoholics, two Hindus, two alumni of Neary's academy, two scholars who write monographs (both titles are given), two unnamed doctors, two doctors with names, a set of identical twins, two men with tiny heads, and two men with heads that are disproportionately large.[20] The characters with large heads, Mr. Kelly and Mr. Endon, also have eyes that are similar. Mr. Kelly's eyes "could not very well protrude, so deeply were they imbedded"; Mr. Endon's eyes are "both deep-set and protuberant, one of Nature's jokes...."[21] Nature may be joking here, but Beckett has the last laugh.

The doctors with names, Dr. Killiecrankie and Dr. Fist, have other traits in common. They both are involved in Ticklepenny's cure for alcoholism, they speak with accents (Scottish and German, respectively), and their names contain puns based on German words. Killiecrankie's name suggests that he kills the sick—*krank*, in German, means sick—and *Faust* is the German word for fist. Dr. Fist, "more philosophical than medical, German on his father's side," may well be a distant relative of Goethe's famous doctor (page 88).

Some sets of characters are used to suggest double-dealing in amorous transactions. Wylie is attracted to Celia as well as to Miss Counihan, they are both in love with Murphy, and Murphy abandons both of them. Neary, who also yearns for Miss Counihan and for Celia, has been involved with two other women in Ireland and has deserted two wives in other countries. Celia's parents died "clinging warmly to their respective partners in the ill-fated *Morro Castle*" (page 12). Ticklepenny, Bim's minion, flirts with Murphy. Cooper's only experience with women came when he loved two of them, "simultaneously as ill-luck would have it" (page 206). Even minor characters like Flight-Lieutenant Elliman, Miss Dwyer, and Ariadne Cox participate in two relationships.[22]

Some of the characters involved in these dual sets again have traits in common. Both Miss Counihan and Celia are remarkably beautiful, eager to marry Murphy, and determined to transform him into a wage earner. Both of them later complain—using similar expressions—when his hunt for a job delays the marriage.[23] But the parallels finally serve to emphasize an essential difference. Celia, ostensibly a whore, is innately faithful; Miss Counihan is the very opposite.

Some of the characters in the novel are associated with dual sets of objects or undergo similar experiences. Celia interprets two events as omens suggesting that she should leave Murphy. Miss Counihan is vulnerable in two areas, "her erogenous zones and her need for Murphy." The old boy had two seizures before he died, "one on Shrove Tuesday, the other on Derby Day," and he ate two meals daily.[24]

Some of the dual sets, like the following examples, have common elements that link them together into pairs of doubles:

Rosie Drew offers the sheep in Hyde Park two heads of lettuce; these are twice mistaken for cabbage (pages 101-2, 106).

Murphy divides jokes into two categories; he has two favorite jokes, both about stout (pages 65, 139).

Murphy sends Celia two letters; she calls him on the telephone twice (pages 22–23).

Neary receives two similarly phrased telegrams from Cooper; he sends two similarly phrased letters to Wylie and Miss Counihan (pages 57, 199).

At times the narrator introduces the idea of duality by using the word *second* in a context in which one would logically expect to find the word *first*. After consoling Neary, Wylie feels purer "than at any time since his second communion" (page 51). Dr. Killiecrankie and the coroner have a polite quarrel at the door of the mortuary about which of them would "pass second" (page 259).

There are many dual sets involving places: Every important locale in the novel figures in some set. As the following list indicates, many of the dual sets are linked by still other common elements:

The action of the novel takes place in two countries, Ireland and England. There are two main settings in Ireland, Cork and Dublin: Two scenes are set in Dublin, two flashbacks take place in Cork. The rest of the action takes place in England, in London and at the Magdalen Mental Mercyseat.

Two rivers figure in the novel. One is Irish (the Lee, into which Neary throws two keys). The other is English (the Thames, where Celia sees a coupled tug and barge).

Two London parks are used as settings, Hyde Park and Battersea Park. Rosie Dew, Celia, Murphy, Cooper, and the boy with tandem kites all appear in parallel scenes that take place in Hyde Park. Battersea Park is mentioned twice in the novel (pages 16, 106).

During the course of the novel two characters, Miss Counihan and Neary, move from Cork to Dublin; both are in pursuit of Murphy. In Dublin each one stays first at Wynn's Hotel and then moves to another, unnamed hotel.

In London, Murphy lives in two rooming houses. Both of his landladies agree to "cook" the bill and overcharge Mr. Quigley, his uncle. Mr. Quigley lives in two cities, Amsterdam and Scheveningen.

Among the furnishings in Murphy's second rooming house are "Two massive upright unupholstered armchairs, similar to those killed under him by Balzac"; there are two references to these armchairs (pages 63, 228).

When Celia moves into a new room at Miss Carridge's rooming house, she takes two suitcases with her. The second room is "half as big . . . half as high, twice as bright" as the first one she occupied (page 148).

Murphy has lived in two cities in continental Europe, Paris and Hanover. A route he travels daily in London is compared to one he used to take in Paris, and his garret at the Magdalen Mental Mercyseat is compared to one he occupied in Hanover. The narrator says that the second garret is "not half, but twice as good as the one in Hanover, because half as large" (page 162).

The Magdalen Mental Mercyseat (or M.M.M.) is copiously endowed with dual entities. The asylum has a counterpart in Ireland that, like the M.M.M., is named for a religious figure: John o' God's. The M.M.M. is outside but not far from London; the Irish asylum is outside but not far from Dublin. Two chapters are set at the M.M.M.; John o' God's is mentioned twice in the novel.[25]

The M.M.M. is "situated in its own grounds on the boundary of two countries" (page 156). It has two staff houses and two convalescent houses. The mortuary at the M.M.M. has double-decker refrigerators, and its walls are covered with two types of climbing plants; these are described twice (pages 165, 258). Murphy's supervisors at the M.M.M. are the identical twins, Thomas "Bim" Clinch and Timothy "Bom" Clinch. It is two o'clock when Murphy begins his first shift as an attendant; his last shift ends during his second week at the M.M.M., after his second round of visits to the patients. Murphy works in Skinner's House, a building shaped like "a double obelisk"; it has two stories, and two sections (for men and for women), and its wards "consisted of two long corridors" (pages 165, 166).

The dual sets are used to emphasize two parallel themes: body versus mind, and sanity versus insanity. Murphy, a dualist in the Cartesian tradition, believes that reality has a physical component ("the big world") and a mental component ("the little world"). After arriving at the M.M.M., Murphy persuades himself that insanity is nothing more than full-time residence in the little world. If the inmates at the M.M.M. seem bizarre, it is because they are being judged by the rules of a world they have abandoned. The psychiatrists are the only ones whose behavior is irrational: They condemn the pleasures of the little world without having sampled them. The patients rightly refuse to be rehabilitated; they are happy enough as "microcosmopolitans," citizens of the little world (page 240).

The dual images suggest that the M.M.M. represents a no-man's-land between the big world and the little. Convinced that the asylum will provide him with a crossing point into the realm of mental activity,

Murphy tries to become friends with the patients. He is particularly fond of the catatonic Mr. Endon, whose condition, he feels, is closer to a philosophical breakthrough than a psychological breakdown. A solipsist manqué, Murphy hopes to study the fine points of introversion under Mr. Endon's tutelage. It never occurs to him that a veteran solipsist might have reservations about giving instructions to a figment of his own imagination.

Murphy wants to communicate with Mr. Endon in order to learn how to emulate him, but solitude is a condition for withdrawal into the self. Murphy is unwilling to give up other enjoyable activities in the big world; this "deplorable susceptibility," says the narrator, forestalls his transition into the little world (page 179). Suk also notes Murphy's tendency to equivocate: "There has been persons of this description," he says, "known to have expressed a wish to be in two places at a time" (page 32).

As Murphy grows fonder of Mr. Endon, his ability to endure isolation diminishes and his capacity for withdrawal is weakened by "vicarious autology" (page 189). Murphy remains on the border between two worlds, hoping to experience the best of both. But this is impossible; as the narrator says, "He could not have it both ways, not even the illusion of it" (page 189).

Reiterated Allusions

Another type of redundancy, similar to that of the dual sets, is based on repeated allusions. Two figures who epitomize Murphy's self-involvement and indolence are Narcissus and Belacqua; both also were important in Beckett's earlier fiction. There are two references to Narcissus in *Murphy*, and two passages about Belacqua. In each of the passages Belacqua is portrayed lazily watching the sky, just as he does in *The Divine Comedy*, and his name occurs twice in each passage.[26] References to two of Homer's heroines, Helen and Penelope, call attention to Celia's outstanding attributes, beauty and fidelity (pages 176, 149). Miss Counihan, on the other hand, is compared to Dido and Jezebel (pages 195, 199).

Another form of duality is suggested when Beckett introduces pairs of figures who are traditionally linked, like Jacob and Esau, Dives and Lazarus, or Ixion and Tantalus.[27] In one paragraph the narrator mentions two classical sculptors, Phidias and Scopas; two sculptors from more recent times, Puget and Barlach; and a matched set of caryatids, the work of Puget (pages 238-39). Beckett sometimes varies this technique by using pairs of allusions that have similar sources. Murphy, making parallel points, cites two quotations from the New Testament.[28] The narrator uses descriptions of sleep taken from two Shakespeare plays in two successive sentences.[29] Celia remembers two couplets she heard as a child; both are from Elizabethan songs.[30] When Neary complains about the pain of unrequited love, he alludes to two passages from the third chapter of Job.[31]

Some of the recurring allusions are concealed. A phrase that is twice attributed to Neary, "the big blooming buzzing confusion," actually is from an essay by William James.[32] According to James, the physical world would seem incoherent if not for the mental patterns that organize one's experience of it. A person responding directly to sense impressions would apprehend only the world's "big blooming buzzing confusion." Beckett uses this concept in stressing the differences between the big world and the little.

Murphy contains many philosophical allusions, and a number of them are involved in the pattern of duality. Often, when Beckett refers twice to the same philosopher, one of the references is much easier to detect than the other, usually because the source is given. This creates the type of dual set in which one item is more prominent than the other. The following is a list of some of the more easily identified allusions:

Pythagoreanism: Murphy is eager to learn about "what Neary, at that time a Pythagorean, called the Apmonia" (Apmonia, or *Harmonia*, is a state of attunement which the Pythagoreans considered a prerequisite for good health).[33]

Democritus: Murphy experiences "the Nothing, than which in the guffaw of the Abderite naught is more real" (Democritus of Abdera is known as the laughing philosopher—hence the guffaw).[34]

Descartes: The floor of Murphy's room is covered with "dream of Descartes linoleum" (that is, its wild pattern is associated with Descartes's famous dream of November 10, 1619).[35]

Geulincx: Murphy's conclusion that he is not of the big world is justified by a quotation: "In the beautiful Belgo-Latin of Arnold Geulincx: *Ubi, nihil vales, ibi nihil velis*" ("Want nothing where you are worth nothing").[36]

Berkeley: Neary says, "I don't wonder at Berkeley.... He had no alternative. A defence mechanism. Immaterialize or bust" (Neary is suggesting that Berkeley's immaterialism is a response to the harshness of existence).[37]

For the most part, these allusions deal with well-known concepts that illuminate the philosophical issues introduced in the novel. But one can compile another list of allusions in which, if the sources are the same, they are less easily identified. Here Beckett introduces ideas that are more obscure—and sometimes more bizarre:

> Pythagoreanism: Neary tells Wylie, "Betray me ... and you go the way of Hippasos." According to Neary, Hippasos was "drowned in a puddle" because he divulged secrets such as "the incommensurability of side and diagonal" (page 47).
>
> Democritus: Mr. Endon stares at "some object immeasurably remote, perhaps the famous ant on the sky of an airless world" (page 248).
>
> Descartes: Neary says to Murphy, "Your conarium has shrunk to nothing" (page 6).
>
> Geulincx: Wylie says that he heeds "the voices, or rather voice, of Reason and Philautia" (page 216).
>
> Berkeley: After explaining that Murphy's mind "excluded nothing that it did not itself contain," the narrator adds, "This did not involve Murphy in the idealist tar" (pages 107-8).

The first item on the list refers to a story about Hippasos, a member of the Pythagorean order. Pythagorras held that number was the underlying principle of nature. This doctrine could not be reconciled with the discovery that the ratio between the side and the diagonal of an isosceles right triangle is not expressible as a rational number. The Pythagoreans tried to keep the discovery secret; they were willing, in other words, to suppress the truth when it conflicted with the teachings of their founder.[38]

The "famous ant" in the next excerpt is one mentioned by Democritus. According to Aristotle, Democritus maintained that small objects were in theory visible at any distance. If not for the intervening air, "one could distinctly see an ant on the vault of the sky."[39] Not only is this a faulty theory of vision—Democritus also seems to have believed that the sky was solid and that insects crawled on it.

Neary's remark about the conarium (the organ that translates mental impulses into physical responses) refers to a problem in Cartesian philosophy. Descartes claimed that the function of the pineal gland was to permit the interaction of mind and body. But despite numerous challenges, he was unable to prove his theory, or even to explain how the process of interaction worked.[40]

In the next excerpt Wylie equates "Reason" and "Philautia." "Philautia" means self-love. It is a transliterated Greek word (Beckett, using the same license that permitted it to be Latinized, Anglicizes it).[41] The unscrupulous Wylie admits that reason and self-love speak to him with the same voice. Geulincx, however, arrives at a very different conclusion. Four cardinal virtues are described in his study of moral philosophy, the *Ethica*, and all are aspects of Reason. Among these virtues are Diligence, the voice of Reason, and Humility, a disdain for oneself ("contemptio sui"). These virtues can be contrasted with Philautia ("amor sui"), which Geulincx says repudiates the voice of Reason and encourages sinful behavior.[42] Wylie's assertion, then, is actually a cynical reversal of Geulincx's concept.

The idealist tar in the last excerpt alludes to one of Berkeley's hobbyhorses: He wrote a book on tar-water, which in his time was considered a cure-all. Given this doctrine of immaterialism, Berkeley's willingness to endorse a nostrum for physical ailments seems somewhat extravagant.[43]

As these summaries indicate, when the allusions are easily identified, Beckett seems to be taking the ideas he cites seriously. When they are not, he introduces a sardonic note. Beckett enjoys a bit of fun at the expense of the philosophers, but this satire is mainly directed against his own characters, Murphy in particular. If the concepts of thinkers like Berkeley or Descartes sometimes seem far-fetched, what can be said for Murphy, whose ideas are a pastiche of theirs?

Dozens of novelists have explored the depths of philosophy; Beckett's side trip to the shallows is no less instructive. The irony in the obscure allusions is his tool for avoiding the didactic solemnity that often creeps into philosophical fiction. Beckett is interested in philosophy, but for him art takes precedence over ideas. He is less concerned with either side of an intellectual argument than with the way both sides can contribute to a symmetrical aesthetic structure.[44]

Symmetry

This symmetry involves disparate types of behavior—Murphy's talk versus Mr. Endon's action—as well as opposed ideas. There are many examples of this technique: Elegant manners accompany shabby behavior; unbalanced people utter beautifully balanced sentences. A common feature in this kind of antithesis is an opposition of form and content. Again and again, descriptions of chaotic events are embodied in a style that emphasizes balance and symmetry.[45]

Many of the antitheses in *Murphy* are part of an elaborate pattern linking three sets of opposed themes: symmetry versus asymmetry, mental reality versus physical reality, and form versus content. The novel's symmetry is emphasized by formal devices; its asymmetry, by the content. The symmetry reflects the mind's tendency to impose orderly patterns on whatever it perceives; the asymmetry is a reflection of the world's blooming, buzzing confusion. The human imagination continually conjures up visions of order and integrity, but these are countered by experiences in a world where (according to the laws of thermodynamics) disorder rules. Murphy seeks respite from the world's chaos in his mind; the narrator, in his style. But there can be no respite: Disorder, no less than order, is a part of existence. This is what is finally suggested by the duality in *Murphy*. The style whispers about the perfection of what might be; the content grumbles about the chaos of what was; and together, irreconcilable, they reveal what is.

NOTES

1. "Talk of the Town," *New Yorker*, 40 (8 August 1964):23.
2. Deirdre Bair, *Samuel Beckett: A Biography* (New York: Harcourt Brace Jovanovich, 1978), 243. Beckett's comments are from a letter written to George Reavey on 13 November, 1936, before the novel was published.
3. Samuel Beckett, *Murphy* (1938; reprinted, New York: Grove Press, 1957), 84. Subsequent page references in the text are to this edition.
4. The recurring elements include repeated segments of various lengths (from a short fragment to a series of sentences); some are repeated verbatim and some have similar phrasing; see appendix 1 of Rubin Rabinovitz, *The Development of Samuel Beckett's Fiction* (Champaign: University of Illinois Press, 1984), 185-99.
5. Miss Counihan says "—er—" on pp. 52 (twice), 54 (twice), 55, 126, 129,

219, 227, and 272 (twice). The passage about "the bogs" and "the—er—fens" (p. 272) contains an allusion to Milton's *Paradise Lost* (II, 621). Beckett is suggesting that Ireland resembles Milton's Hell.

6. On p. 136 the narrator says, "Not a penny out of pocket, not one penny," in a description of Miss Carridge's reaction to the old boy's death. Miss Carridge repeats "the principle of the thing" on p. 147 and says, "I haven't a doubt, not a doubt," on p. 227. Wylie mimics her mannerism when he repeats, "You are quite sure," on p. 227.

7. The horoscope appears on pp. 32-33. Excerpts from the horoscope are attributed to Suk in pp. 63, 82, 87, 93, 138, 164, 182, and 183.

8. Wylie originally made the remark on pp. 123-24; Cooper remembers it verbatim on p. 198; the narrator's comment comes on pp. 199-200.

9. P. 35; Neary's gesture is described on pp. 4-5.

10. This idea is also suggested in a description of Clarke, who "would repeat for hours the phrase: 'Mr. Endon is *very* superior'" (p. 193). When Murphy kneels next to the bed he is "stigmatised" in Mr. Endon's eyes (p. 249). Murphy's position suggests that Beckett has in mind the Greek word from which "stigmatized" is derived: στιγμᾶτίας (one who has been branded a runaway slave). Mr. Endon's name, as a number of critics have pointed out, is derived from ενδον (within), which suggests that he has withdrawn into an inner world.

11. A few other details hint that Celia may be contemplating suicide: a rambling speech (pp. 229-30) in which she keeps mentioning words that rhyme with *death* and Neary's assumption that Cooper is referring to Celia when he says, "She is dead" (pp. 272-73).

12. Neary speaks of the love that "craves for the tip of her little finger, dipped in lacquer, to cool its tongue" (p. 5). This passage is based on Luke 16:24, where after his death Dives asks Father Abraham to "send Lazarus, that he may dip the tip of his finger in water, and cool my tongue. . . ." This allusion has been noted by Hugh Kenner; see *A Reader's Guide to Samuel Beckett* (New York: Farrar, Straus and Giroux, 1973), 60.

13. Neary's "relation toward" Miss Counihan is "that post-mortem of Dives to Lazarus, except that there was no Father Abraham to put in a good word for him" (pp. 48-49). This again (see note 12) is an allusion to Luke 16:24.

14. After Neary explains his love in terms of gestalt psychology concepts, Murphy asks, "And then. . . . Back to Teneriffe and the apes?" (p. 5). This is an allusion to the work of Wolfgang Köhler. Köhler, interned on Tenerife during World War I, spent a number of years studying apes at the Anthropoid Research Station established there by the Prussian Academy of Sciences. One result of this work was his landmark study *The Mentality of Apes* (first published in 1917; translated into English in 1925). It is likely that Beckett knows this book: The plot of *Acts without Words I* is based on experiments Köhler describes there.

15. Rosie Dew is a medium and Lord Gall is her patron: She plans to use these objects to establish contact with Lord Gall's father (pp. 103, 278). Lord Gall is the same as the character in *Echo's Bones*.

16. When Celia and Murphy first meet, they gaze at each other and then fall in love (p. 14). This suggests that the references to "the new life" (repeated

three times on p. 64) are allusions to Dante's *La Vita Nuova* (and perhaps to the beach scene at the end of the fourth section of Joyce's *A Portrait of the Artist as a Young Man*, also based on Dante's work). References to a new life occur again on pp. 130 and 150, but the hope for a new life is refuted in the opening sentence of the novel, when the sun shines "on the nothing new" (p. 1; and cf. Ecclesiastes 1:9).

17. The idea that things never change is central in *Waiting for Godot*. Beckett's comments on habit are from *Proust* (1931; reprinted, New York: Grove Press, 1957), p. 8, and see also pp. 7-12.

18. This total includes repeated incidents, pairs of objects, recurring character traits, and dual sets involving locales; see appendix 2 of Rabinovitz, pp. 200-221.

19. Prostitutes, Celia and the former occupant of Murphy's room (p. 7); land-ladies, Miss Carridge and Murphy's first landlady (p. 7). The unnamed prostitute rented a room from the unnamed landlady; Celia rents a room from Miss Carridge (p. 146).

20. Coroners, pp. 145 and 259ff.; homosexuals, Ticklepenny and Bim (p. 156); waitresses, Cathleen (p. 46) and Vera (p. 81); fortunetellers, Suk and Rosie Dew; alcoholics, Cooper and Ticklepenny; Hindus, Suk (called a swami on p. 23) and the "Hindu polyhistor" (p. 196); alumni of Neary's academy, Murphy and Wylie; scholars, the polyhistor, author of *The Pathetic Fallacy from Avercamp to Kampendonck* (p. 196), and Neary, author of *The Doctrine of the Limit* (p. 50); doctors without names, an obstetrician (p. 71) and the doctor who attends the old boy (p. 135); doctors with names, Dr. Killie-crankie and Dr. Fist (p. 88); twins, p. 165; Cooper and Wylie have "tiny heads" (p. 131); Mr. Endon and Mr. Kelly have unusually large heads (pp. 186, 276).

21. Mr. Kelly's eyes, p. 11; Mr. Endon's, p. 248.

22. Flight-Lieutenant Elliman loves Miss Farren (p. 5) and Miss Dwyer (p. 48); Miss Dwyer is involved with Neary and Elliman (p. 48); Ariadne Cox, after being deserted by Neary, falls in love with Sacha Few, who also abandons her (p. 272).

23. Celia says, "Now it was September . . . and their relationship had not yet been regularised" (p. 17). Miss Counihan says, "It was August and still she had no news of Murphy" (p. 53). A recurring episode also links these characters: Celia, at an upstairs window, watches Murphy's departure in a scene that resembles one in which Miss Counihan (also at an upstairs window) watches Wylie (pp. 142-43, 131).

24. Omens, the coin (p. 28) and the broken mirror (p. 30); Miss Counihan's vulnerability, pp. 126-27; the old boy's seizures, p. 145; the old boy, who "never left his room," is given food by Miss Carridge "twice daily" (p. 69).

25. John o'God's is mentioned twice on p. 43; chapters nine and eleven are set at the M.M.M. It seems odd that the Magdalen Mental Mercyseat should have a three-word name; this may be why Beckett expanded it in the French translation, where it became La Maison Madeleine de Miséricorde Mentale, or M.M.M.M.

26. Narcissus, pp. 186 and 228; Belacqua, pp. 78 and 112. Beckett's Belacqua watches "the dayspring run through its zodiac" (p. 78), and "the dawn break

crooked" (p. 112). Dante's Belacqua comments on the sun's position in *Purgatorio* 4:119-20.

27. Jacob and Esau, p. 23; Dives and Lazarus, p. 48; Ixion and Tantalus, p. 21. At times Beckett, emphasizing another form of duality, mentions members of these sets a second time. The word *tantalus* is used to describe a pub that tempts Cooper (p. 121), and the name *Lazarus* also occurs a second time (p. 180). It should be noted that although there are two references to the Lazarus mentioned in Luke 16 (as explained in an earlier note), the allusion on p. 180 is to a different Lazarus, the one who was raised from the dead, mentioned in John 11 and 12.

28. These are (p. 22) "The hireling fleeth because he is an hireling" (John 10:13), and "What shall a man give in exchange for Celia?" which is based on "What shall a man give in exchange for his soul?" (Matthew 16:26, Mark 8:37).

29. The quotations are on p. 239; "nature's soft nurse" is from *2 Henry IV*, III, i, 5; "knit up the sleave..." is from *Macbeth*, II, ii, 36: "Sleep that knits up the ravell'd sleave of care."

30. P. 235; the songs are "Sephestia's Song to her Child," by Robert Greene, and "What Thing Is Love?" by George Peele.

31. The allusions to Job (p. 46) are "cursed ... the day in which he was born ..." (based on Job 3:3), and "why ... is light given..." (Job 3:24).

32. The phrase occurs on pp. 4, 29, and 245; it is attributed to Neary on pp. 29 and 245. Its source is "The World We Live In," in *The Philosophy of William James* (New York: Modern Library, 1953), p. 76. The phrase did not really originate with James; he says it was first used by another, unnamed person. I am grateful to Professor Lawrence Graver for help in identifying the source of this quotation. In an interview Beckett referred to the world as "this buzzing confusion"; see Tom Driver, "Beckett by the Madeleine," *Columbia University Forum*, 4 (Summer 1961):21.

33. "Apmonia" is repeated three times (pp. 3-4). There is a joke here: αρμονία (*harmonia*) is Greek but looks like an English word when it is written in capital letters. "APMONIA" appears as a page heading in a book Beckett used for background material on the Pythagoreans: John Burnet's *Greek Philosophy*, pt. 1 (London: Macmillan, 1924), p. 45. This source was noted by Sighle Kennedy in *Murphy's Bed* (Lewisburg, Pa.: Bucknell University Press, 1971), p. 302n. The words Neary uses as synonyms for "Apmonia," "Isonomy" and "Attunement" (p. 4) are also mentioned by Burnet (p. 50). Neary's master's "figure of the three lives" (p. 90) refers to Pythagoras's division of humanity into levels represented by those who buy and sell at the Olympic games, those who compete, and those who observe (the highest level); see Burnet, p. 42. Other allusions to Pythagorean philosophy in *Murphy* are probably also based on material from Burnet's book, including the Hippasos story (p. 47; Burnet, pp. 55-56), the reference to the tetrakyt (p. 5; Burnet, p. 52), and the doctrine of the limit (p. 50; Burnet, p. 44).

34. P. 246. This idea is attributed to Leucippus and Democritus by Aristotle; see *Metaphysics* 985b. It is clear that Beckett has Democritus and not Leucippus in mind because he refers to "the guffaw of the Abderite," and Democritus is known as the laughing philospher. In *More Pricks than Kicks*

(1934; reprinted, New York: Grove Press, 1970) Democritus is identifed as the laughing philosopher (p. 162), and laughter is again associated with "the Abderite" in *Murphy* (p. 246) and *The Unnamable*, in *Three Novels by Samuel Beckett* (New York: Grove Press, 1965, p. 408). *"Nothing is more real than nothing"* (the italics are Beckett's) appears in *Malone Dies* (1956; reprinted, in *Three Novels by Samuel Beckett*, New York: Grove Press, 1965), 192.

35. P. 140. Descartes's description of his dream is lost, but its paraphrased version is given in Adrien Baillet's *Vie de Monsieur Des-Cartes*, I (Paris, 1691):81-85. Beckett is familiar with this work: see Lawrence Harvey, *Samuel Beckett, Poet and Critic* (Princeton, N.J.: Princeton University Press, 1970), 8n, 20, *et passim*; John Fletcher, *Samuel Beckett's Art* (London: Chatto and Windus, 1967), 126-27. For a discussion of Descartes's dream and its importance in the development of his philosophy, see Jacques Maritain, *The Dream of Descartes*, Mabelle Andison, trans. (Port Washington, N.Y.: Kennikat Press, 1969).

36. P. 178. My translation is based on Beckett's, which is given on p. 179. According to Geulincx, because man enjoys true freedom only in the mental world, he would do best to abstain from desiring the things of the physical world; see Arnold Geulincx, *Metaphysica, Opera Philosophica*, 2 (1891-93; facsim. reprint, Stuttgart: Friedrich Frommann Verlag, 1965), 155. Beckett drops a word, *etiam*, when he quotes the passage; the original reads, *"Ubi nihil vales, ibi etiam nihil velis."* The passage is italicized both in the original and in *Murphy*. For more material on the influence of Geulincx, see Samuel Mintz, "Beckett's *Murphy*: A 'Cartesian' Novel," *Perspective*, 11 (Autumn 1959): 156-65.

37. P. 58. Berkeley's doctine of immaterialism is expounded in his *Principles of Human Knowledge* and *Three Dialogues*.

38. It is likely that Beckett used Burnet's *Greek Philosophy* here. Neary's comments about Hippasos (pp. 47-48) are very much like those in Burnet's book (pp. 56-57). However, Burnet (like other commentators) says that Hippasos was drowned at sea, not in a puddle. That the Pythagoreans cared more for their doctrine than for the truth is again illustrated in another allusion, Neary's "unction of an *Ipse dixit*" (p. 102). According to Cicero, when they were assured that Pythagoras himself had said something ("Ipse dixit"), the Pythagoreans would accept a statement with no other proof; Cicero, *De Natura Deorum*, I, 10.

39. Aristotle, *De Anima*, 419a. The passage I have quoted is from the translation by J. A. Smith in *Introduction to Aristotle*, Richard McKeun, ed. (New York: Modern Library, 1947), pp. 190-91. Beckett uses the word *famous* in connection with the ant (p. 248) to indicate that the passage is based on an allusion, and (introducing another dual set) he does the same thing with a second allusion. The narrator's comment that Cooper "experienced none of the famous difficulty in serving two employers" (p. 197) is based on Matthew 6:24 and Luke 16:13.

40. Descartes describes the pineal gland as the locus of the mind-body interaction in *Les Passions de l'Ame*, première partie, article 31. He refers to the pineal gland as the *conarium* in letters to Mersenne dated 1 April, 30 July, and 24

December 1640 and 21 April 1641; see also Kenner, pp. 60-61. The idea of the conarium shrinking to nothing may also refer to the shrinking skin in Balzac's *La Peau de Chagrin*.

41. *Philautia*, which occurs only rarely in Latin (it is listed in few Latin dictionaries), is derived from the Greek word φιλαυτος (self-loving, selfish). The Latin form does appear in Robert Estienne's *Thesaurus Linguae Latinae* (Basil: Thurnisiorum Fratr., 1741), where it is defined as *"Amor sui ipsius."*

42. At the very beginning of the *Ethica*, Geulincx defines ethics as a study of virtue, and says a number of times that virtue is the love of reason; *Opera Philosophica*, 3:9, 12, 14, 15, et passim. According to Geulincx, *"Philautia* is love of oneself; such love is distant from virtue based on reason; indeed, it leads to sin" (3:13). Philautia is *"amor sui,"* love of oneself; humility is *"contemptio sui,"* disdain for oneself (3:28).

43. Tar-water is an infusion of tar and water. Berkeley's *A Chain of Reflexions and Inquiries Concerning the Virtues of Tar-Water* appeared in 1744.

44. Beckett once told Harold Hobson, "I am interested in the shape of ideas even if I do not believe in them. . . . It is the shape that matters"; see Harold Hobson, "Samuel Beckett, Dramatist of the Year," *International Theatre Annual* (1, London: John Calder, 1956), 153.

45. Space limitation made it necessary to omit some examples of symmetry; the deleted material can be found on pp. 89-96 of Rabinovitz.

LAWRENCE E. HARVEY

"Watt"

Beckett took part in the June 1940 exodus from Paris before the advance of the invading German army, and arrived in Vichy later that summer. It was there that he saw Joyce for the last time. The hotel in which he and the Joyce family were staying was, like most of the hotels, being evacuated, and he had to "get on, clear out." Joyce and his family went to a little town near Vichy where Madame Jolas (of *Transition* fame) had a school. Joyce stayed there until December, when he obtained a permit to go to Switzerland. Beckett started south on foot from Vichy. On the way he managed to board a train that went as far as Toulouse. There he avoided the refugee center, slept out on benches, and finally got a bus west as far as Cahors, where it was "all out" in the pouring rain. Famished, exhausted, he finally managed to find a spot on the floor of a shop dealing in religious articles, where he spent the night. Hiding in a truck the next day he succeeded in getting out of Cahors and traveling as far as Arcachon, where he was able to locate Mary Reynolds, an American he had known in Paris. She helped him find a place to stay, and he managed to obtain a little money sent under difficult conditions by his family in Ireland.

In October he returned to occupied Paris, his apartment, his books, and bread lines. In Paris he reestablished contact with Alfred Péron, a good friend whom he had first known in Dublin when Péron was an exchange student from the Ecole Normale to Trinity College. (This same reciprocal arrangement later sent Beckett from Trinity to the Ecole Normale as a *lecteur*.) It was through Alfred Péron that Beckett joined a Resistance network engaged in collecting information from various parts of France on German troop movements. Beckett classified the information, translated it into English, typed it, and in general prepared it for microphotography, after which it was sent into the free zone of France and then flown to London. In August 1942 a leader of the network was captured by the Gestapo and under torture revealed the names of its members. Péron was arrested in Anjou, sent to Drancy, and then deported to Germany. Péron's wife sent an open telegram to Beckett: *"Alfred arrêté par Gestapo. Prière faire nécessaire pour corriger l'erreur."* The telegram reached Beckett at 11:00 A.M. on 15 August 1942, and he was gone by 3:00 P.M. He was one of about thirty from a total membership of eighty that managed to escape. For some two months he moved in and around Paris from one apartment to another until he was able to get false papers and make contact with a *passeur*. In October the *passeur* led a group of ten refugees cross-country during the night into the unoccupied zone. Once again Beckett found himself in Vichy, then in Avignon, and finally in the tiny village of Roussillon near Apt in the Vaucluse, where through friends of friends he was able to find a place to stay. It was there that he worked for Bonelli (mentioned in *En attendant Godot*) and received wine in exchange for his labors. One triumph of this period was obtaining permission to glean in a field after the potato harvest. Under conditions prevailing in those days, finding a potato in the sea of mud was like finding a gold nugget. A man named Aude was kind to Beckett and others during this time, and once a week Beckett had a meal at his home. In return Beckett cut wood for Aude, helped him with the harvest, and did other odd jobs. It was in Roussillon, in the evenings, that Beckett wrote the novel *Watt*.

Something of the experience of the refugee tramping wearily along the roads of France, doing manual labor in the service of others in order to survive, living with a heightened sense of exile in the uncertainty and relative solitude that prevailed under such conditions in wartime France finds its way into *Watt*. Equally important, however, seems to have been the fact that these conditions obtained at a particular moment in the life of the author. Beckett wrote *Murphy* between 1933 and 1935 in London.[1] He wrote *Watt* approximately ten years later, between late 1942 and late 1944, when he was between thirty-six and thirty-eight years old; that is to say, more or less at the traditional midpoint of life. No doubt the break in normal existence occasioned by the war served to accentuate this passage from youth to middle age.

A Novel of the Middle Years of Man

Belacqua is a young man. His experience of the "womb-tomb" where both the world and the self die is extremely limited. All in all he is a man of the macrocosm caught between Phoebus and Narcissus. Slightly older, Murphy makes a serious attempt to enter the "little world" which is unencumbered by self or others: "But it was not enough... it had never been enough and showed no signs of being enough. These dispositions and others ancillary, pressing every available means (e.g., the rocking-chair) into their service, could sway the issue in the desired direction, but not cinch it. It continued to divide him, as witness his deplorable susceptibility to Celia, ginger, and so on" (*Murphy*, p. 179). As with Belacqua, Murphy's youth and the girls with whom he becomes involved, half in spite of himself, are largely responsible for his failure. In *Watt*, age is a powerful ally. Youth is a tension, a coming and a going. Middle age brings the hope of a staying. Near the beginning of Watt we find a prose version of the little poem "Dieppe" situated in this context:

> All the old ways led to this, all the old windings, the stairs with never a landing that you screw yourself up, clutching the rail, counting the steps, the fever of shortest ways under the long lids of sky, the wild country roads where your dead walk beside you, on the dark shingle the turning for the last time again to the lights of the little town, the appointments kept and the appointments broken, all the delights of urban and rural change of place, all the exitus and redditus, closed and ended. All led to this, to this gloaming where a middleaged man sits masturbating his snout, waiting for the first dawn to break." (page 40)

Again, there are the words of Arsene, about to leave Knott's house for good, to the newly arrived Watt: "Not that I have told you all I know, for I have not, being now a good-natured man, and of good will what is more, and indulgent towards the dreams of middle age, which were my dreams, just as Vincent did not tell me all, nor Walter Erskine, nor the others the others, for here we all seem to end by being good-natured men, and of good will, and indulgent towards the dreams of middle age, which were our dreams..." (page 62). It is in this context that Arsene uses an image strongly recalling Dante. He speaks of the servants in the house "eternally turning about Mr. Knott in tireless love" (page 62). Different as it is, *Watt* recalls the *Commedia* in more ways than one, and to begin with both are concerned with the stock-taking that may well occur *"nel mezzo del cammin di nostra vita"*:

> To think, when one is no longer young, when one is not yet old, that one is no longer young, that one is not yet old, that is perhaps something. To pause, towards the close of one's three hour day, and consider: the darkening ease, the brightening trouble; the pleasure pleasure because it was, the pain pain because it shall be; the glad acts grown proud, the proud acts growing stubborn; the panting the trembling towards a being gone, a being to come; and the true true no longer, and the false true not yet. And to decide not to smile after all, sitting in the shade, hearing the cicadas, wishing it were night, wishing it were morning, saying, No, it is not the heart, no, it is not the liver, no, it is not the prostate, no it is not the ovaries, no, it is muscular, it is nervous. Then the gnashing ends, or it goes on, and one is in the pit, in the hollow, the longing for longing gone, the horror of horror, and one is in the hollow, at the foot of all the hills at last, the ways down, the ways up, and free, free at last, for an instant free at last, nothing at last. (pages 201–2)

Watt takes Arsene's place, and when he in turn is on the point of leaving Knott's house, a successor arrives, as Watt had arrived, and the successor also is at the beginning of the middle years: "Nor was Micks a little girl, or an innocent little choirboy, no, but a big plaid man, who had seen something of the world, both at home, and abroad" (page 220). When Watt leaves Knott's house, he enters old age. His bags are "three quarters empty" (page 217). He is "an old rose now" (page 253). Finally, on page 13 of *Watt*, we find an analogy between the author, approaching forty, and Larry Nixon, who "will be forty years old next March." This is not the first time that in line 13 or on page 13 of a work of Beckett's we come upon an allusion to birth. Like Larry Nixon, Beckett was born in the spring (on 13 April), and we recall that in *Murphy* (page 180) Larry is short for Lazarus, "whose raising seemed to Murphy perhaps the one occasion on which the Messiah had overstepped the mark." The contexts of the two "Larry passages" are thematically very closely related. In both we discover again the notion, familiar to readers of the Good Friday poet, that man abandoned to postnatal suffering and solitude would be better off unborn.

The Renunciations of Watt

Very early in the novel, when we first encounter Watt, he is on his way to the railroad station to undertake a mysterious journey. After a brief conversation with Mr. Nixon, he continues on his way, and Mr. Nixon crosses the street to return to his wife and a hunchback named Mr. Hackett. Their ensuing conversation establishes the atmosphere of mystery that serves as setting for the principal theme of the novel: the need to know and the difficulty and indeed impossibility of knowing. "You cannot be in ignorance of all this," says Mr. Hackett. "Utter ignorance," replies Mr. Nixon. "I tell you nothing is known. . . . Nothing" (page 21). As it turns out, a few meager morsels of information, mostly of a speculative or downright negative character, are available: "He has no fixed address that I know of," admits Mr. Nixon (page 20).

If we put together this lack of information, lack of address, and the fact that Watt is leaving town, they lead us to the first moment in the inner development of the novel, the moment of renunciation. On the literal level it seems that Watt, "half hoping he may miss his train" and "too fearful to assume himself the onus of a decision," "refers it to the frigid machinery of a time-space relation" (page 21). Metaphorically, the quest for meaning undertaken by Watt (the quasi-homophone of "what") is at least as much an involuntary drive as a conscious decision. It comes to most men at some point in their existence but to the greater part at the start of the middle years, when the needs of youth have subsided and "the true [is] true no longer" (page 201). The quest implies an antecedent withdrawal, by things or from things. Certain realities have retreated or been pushed back. The passage that makes the first step explicit occurs about three-fifths of the way through the book. Translated from one of Watt's several variant forms of backward speech, it reads: "Abandoned my little to find him. My little to learn him forgot. My little rejected to have him. To love him my little reviled this body homeless. This mind ignoring. These emptied hands. This emptied heart. To him I brought. To the temple. To the teacher. To the source. Of nought" (page 166). Watt has given up the little he had: home, knowledge, possessions, attachments.[2] He brings with him (in Beckett's typically dualistic conception) a physical being (body, hands) and a spiritual being (mind, heart). His purpose is to find, to understand, to possess, and to love. He comes, as on a religious pilgrimage, to the temple, the teacher, the source— of nought. Before jumping to the conclusion that the journey ends in failure, it is well to recall the quotation from Democritus (*Murphy*, page 246), for whom the void was filled with atomic particles: "Not the numb peace of their own suspension, but the positive peace that comes when the somethings give way, or perhaps simply add up, to the Nothing, than which in the guffaw of the Abderite naught is more real." "Naught" suggests "Knott" (homophonous in the Anglo-Irish pronunciation), whose house is Watt's destination and his abode for a considerable period of time (the middle years). The name Knott, be- sides evoking the microcosmic state of peace so desired by *Murphy*, also calls up the idea of a riddle (knot), and indeed Knott remains ultimately enigmatic.

To return to Watt's renunciations, a large part of the novel is taken up with their nature and variety. Many of the comic, satirical, and ironic aspects of the story are dedicated to the dismissal of these less real facets of human existence. Newspapers that relate indefatigably the meaningless trivia of life end up, after an exaggerated number of rereadings, in the "ladies' house of office" (page 237). Official insti- tutions that tend to lose their vitality and fade into the shadows of routine come under fire, from the church, marriage, and the university through the shabby Irish aristocracy and railroad officialdom—and in general the unthinking and insensitive optimism that routine fosters. "All the same, said Mr. Gorman, life isn't such a bad old bugger" (page 245). Superficial and exterior also and hence less real for the author, clothes and the bodies that wear them are viewed in comic terms. Physicality find its most perfect example in the oversize buttocks that, once again, are the object of a vigorous satirical drubbing (page 157). From Watt's contorted walk to Mr. Nackybal's learned scratching to sex in Ireland (among numerous examples is Sam, of the Lynch clan, who "committed adultery locally on a large scale, moving from place to place in his self-propelling invalid's chair" [page 106]), the portrait of man's involvement with physical and intellectual surfaces is drawn with a mixture of amusement and revulsion. Watt has to a large extent been freed from the erotic possibilities that both attracted and repelled Belacqua and Murphy, but more through his greater age and lesser strength than by any act of his own will. In his liaison with the fishwoman, "Watt had not the strength and Mrs. Gorman had not the time..." (page 141). Intercourse between human beings, whether on the physical or the spiritual plane, is very partial and defective in *Watt*. The hero's departure from the community (of which apparently he had long since ceased to be an integrated member) into relative solitude finds its counterpart on the level of satire in the prolonged and hilarious pages on the nature of committees (pages 174-97).

Watt's journey is preceded and made possible by an abandonment of all that has come to seem emptied of substance. But it is also a flight from anxiety and pain and a search for peace. As in earlier works, the presence of suffering in the world is the enigma of enigmas, and Beckett unleashes his most bitter irony and succumbs to his deepest sorrow in its presence. Thus marriage and unimpeded procreation appear as the worst of follies and cruelties, as they guarantee the unending propagation of pain. Near Knott's house in the Irish countryside, "immense impoverished families abounded for miles around in every conceivable direction." Of these the author describes the Lynch family at length, and his description is a catalog of man's ills and a castigation of his optimistic blindness and acceptance. To take two of many examples, Kate Lynch is "covered all over with running sores of an unidentified nature but otherwise fit and well," while Sam Lynch (the adulterer) is "paralysed by a merciful providence from no higher than the knees down and from no lower than the waist up." In contrast to sex and religion, which are held responsible at least as immediate causes for enormous and unspeakable miseries, man's compassion is most often wholly ineffectual. Mrs. Nixon, "quivering with solicitude" ("Mr. Hackett thought she was going to pat him on the head, or at least stroke his hunch"), hardly compensates for the neglect of Hackett's mother, who left him alone to fall off the ladder and break his back while she went off to "the pub, or the chapel, or both" (pages 10, 16). Watt escapes marriage and procreation. He avoids official religion, abstains from alcohol, and is not given to futile movements of compassion. And in Watt's house he is less vulnerable to time, to the painful spectacle of natural beauty that in Beckett invariably evokes its own and man's decay and death.

We learn of Watt's separation from the world of surfaces not only through the author's irony, but also, more directly, through Watt's experience in Knott's house, where the ascesis continues and takes on a significance that goes far beyond social satire. Watt, we discover, has long since given up the search for any kind of profound inner meaning.

97

Watt "had not seen a symbol, nor executed an interpretation, since the age of fourteen, or fifteen ... [he] had lived, miserably it is true, among face values all his adult life. .... And he had experienced literally nothing, since the age of fourteen or fifteen, of which in retrospect he was not content to say, That is what happened then." In Knott's house, however, each incident of note, as it repeats itself inside Watt's head, tends gradually to lose, "in the nice processes of its light, its sound, its impacts and its rhythm, all meaning, even the most literal" (page 73). Pure form, in other words, takes over, and meaning evaporates. Again we recall Murphy's "accidentless One-and-Only, conveniently called Nothing," which results when the "somethings give way," and his flux of "forms becoming and crumbling into the fragments of a new becoming" (*Murphy*, pages 246, 112). This "fragility of the outer meaning" has a bad effect on Watt, however. It leads him to seek "for some meaning of what had passed," not for the real meaning, "for to explain had always been to exorcize for Watt" (pages 73, 78). The trouble with Watt, we learn, is that he has great difficulty, until "towards the end of his stay in Mr. Knott's house," in accepting the fact that "with all the clarity and solidity of something ... nothing had happened ... a nothing had happened ..." (pages 76, 80).

Not only events but their components, things, lose their familiar identity in the little world of Knott's house, and Watt experiences something like the anguish of Proust's young protagonist trying to go to sleep in a strange bedroom among unfamiliar and therefore terrifying objects. Man's need to domesticate the world about him, to dispel mystery by assigning phenomena to tried and true categories, is great, so great that the categories vey often substitute themselves permanently for the ever-new, ever-mysterious things about him. The experience of the microcosm, which is preceded by loss of faith in the familiar groupings or, more organically, by loss of the capacity to see things in terms of categories, was for Murphy, all in all, "so pleasant that pleasant was not the word" (*Murphy*, page 113). But Watt, especially at the beginning of his stay in Knott's house, only rarely "envisaged this dereliction with something like satisfaction" (page 84). For Proust's young protagonist the breeching of the protective fortress of habits is temporary and terror soon gives way to the relief of boredom. But eventually the workings of involuntary memory come to the rescue and restore the individual integrity of things not in the terror of unfamiliarity but in the paradisiac joy of the past resuscitated and made timeless. For Proust, then, the relationship between subject and object is never really lost completely. It is maintained, either in dullness at the level of the species or else in anxiety or ecstasy at the level of the mysterious individual. In Beckett the relationship itself is in question. Can the subject survive in unknowingness, out of contact with the objective world—including his own physical being? Such is the question at the core of *Watt*.

In the beginning the protagonist of the novel is perfectly content with categories, in fact very much in need of them. "Not that Watt desired information, for he did not. But he desired words to be applied to his situation. ... [He] would have been glad to hear Erskine's voice, wrapping up safe in words the kitchen space, the extraordinary newell-lamp, [etc.] ... And Watt's need of semantic succour was at times so great that he would set to trying names on things, and on himself, almost as a woman hats" (pages 81-83). Unfortunately for Watt's peace of mind, things have become recalcitrant. "Watt now found himself in the midst of things which, if they consented to be named, did so as it were with reluctance. And the state in which Watt found himself resisted formulation in a way no state had ever done. ... Looking at a pot, for example ... it was in vain that Watt said, Pot, pot. ... For it was not a pot, the more he looked, the more he reflected, the more he felt sure of that, that it was not a pot at all. It resembled a pot, it was almost a pot, but it was not a pot of which one could say, Pot, pot, and be comforted. ... And it was just this hairbreadth departure from the nature of a true pot that so excruciated Watt." And yet "The pot remained a pot, Watt felt sure of that, for everyone but Watt. For Watt alone it was not a pot, any more." Watt turns for reassurance to himself, "who was not Mr. Knott's, in the sense that the pot was, who had come from without and whom the without would take again." It is no use, for he makes "the distressing discovery that of himself too he could no longer affirm anything that did not seem as false as if he had affirmed it of a stone. ... He could no longer call it a man, as he had used to do, with the intuition that he was perhaps not talking utter nonsense" (pages 81-83). While Watt suffers from this situation and for a time hopes that it results simply from the difficulty with which his body adjusts to "an unfamiliar milieu" and that eventually things will "consent to be named, with the time-honoured names, and forgotten," there are times when he rather enjoys the prospect of "being so abandoned, by the last rats. ... [even though] it would be lonely, to be sure, at first, and silent, after the gnawing, the scurrying, the little cries. Things and himself, they had gone with him now for so long in the foul weather, and in the less foul" (page 84). And eventually, we learn, after Watt's world has become "unspeakable," he does indeed grow "used to his loss of species" (page 85).

The Utopia of Mr. Knott's House

Arsene's parting words tell us a good deal about the situation in which a man like Watt, at a certain age, may find himself. It is a situation defined in essentially negative terms. Watt's arrival means first of all an end to blind wandering: "The dark ways all behind. . . ." Movement does not cease altogether, but it is no longer a flight or a search or a social commitment. Instead it has become "a stirring beyond coming and going." Activity does not come to a halt, but there are no more questions, orders, explanations, for the sounds that come "demand nothing, ordain nothing, explain nothing" (page 39). Even though the new arrival in Knott's house does not find, as he hoped he would, "a situation where to do nothing exclusively would be an act of the highest value, and significance," quite different from the "superficial loitering" and "disinterested endeavour" that tormented and horrified him, respectively, in the past, he is soon reconciled to a service of "unquestionable utility . . . [and] exceptional fruitfulness" (page 41) that benefits him even more than his master. It is significant that the work done for Mr. Knott ("he peels the potato and empties the nightstool") is of a routine, manual nature, requiring no decisions and exempt from anxiety. Knott's servant goes about his tasks "calm and glad" (page 42). Knott's home is a "refuge" (page 39) and, as the etymology of the term implies, a retreat or flight back to the source. We are therefore hardly surprised to find figures of a return to the womb along with related images incorporating softness, warmth, darkness, or enclosure. Approaching Knott's house, Watt feels weak and rests by the side of the road, assuming the fetal position (page 33). Earlier, a clearly positive value is attached to the "warm nest of books and periodicals" (page 25) of the news agent who witnesses Watt's run-in with the porter in the railway station. At the end, in the insane asylum, Watt enjoys the "separate soundless unlit warmth" of his padded cell. On the level of irony, the conditions obtaining in the mind of Mr. Thomas Nackybal, the Visicelt brought back by Mr. Ernest Louit from western

Ireland in support of his dissertation, *The Mathematical Intuitions of the Visicelts*, compose a metaphorical correlative of the ideal state to be found in the womb. Apart from an almost instinctive "knowledge of how to extract, from the ancestral half-acre of moraine, the maximum of nourishment, for himself and his pig, with the minimum of labour," his mind is "an ecstasy of darkness, and of silence" (page 175).

In the amusing hoax perpetrated by Mr. Louit, Beckett takes advantage of a variant form of the myth of the good savage to satirize academia and, indirectly, man's obsessive need to know. At the same time he suggests a link between what Murphy called the microcosm of the mind and the prenatal state. Under the proper conditions perhaps the former can approximate the latter, can become, that is, a place in which one can live. The utopia of Mr. Knott's house has much in common with the "little world" of Murphy's mind. Indeed, the author employs the identical term to describe it when he writes of "the little world of Mr. Knott's establishment" (page 85). Often enough, however, the focus narrows still further to the microcosm inside Watt's skull. There, when thought stops and the body is placated and quiet, Watt experiences, in auditory terms, something closely akin to Murphy's "pure forms of commotion" (*Murphy*, page 112): "He lay on the seat, without thought or sensation, except for a slight feeling of chill in one foot. In his skull the voices whispering their canon were like a patter of mice, a flurry of little grey paws in the dust" (page 232). Such an experience, the enjoyment of pure form, is conditional upon an absence of thought or meaning. It can arise spontaneously in the mind if circumstances are favorable, or it can come from the song or speech of Mr. Knott: "The words of [Mr. Knott's] songs were either without meaning or derived from an idiom with which Watt, a very fair linguist, had no acquaintance.... Mr. Knott talked often to himself too, with great variety and vehemence of intonation and gesticulation, but this so softly that it came, a wild dim chatter, meaningless to Watt's ailing ears. This was a noise of which Watt grew exceedingly fond.... While it sounded he was gladdened, as by the rain on the bamboos..." (page 209). The phrase "rain on the bamboos" recalls the poem "Alba" and by thematic association "Dortmunder" as well, and the state of contemplative ataraxy produced in both poems through the influence of music, that is, nonreferential sound, pure form. The ghost of Schopenhauer, invoked in "Dortmunder," is with us still in *Watt*.

A number of other images are used to describe the utopia of *Watt*, all of them in one way or another suggesting a negation. On several occasions life is rendered inanimate or scaled down from the human or animal to the vegetable level. Arsene imagines himself "longing to be turned into a stone pillar or a cromlech" (page 49), and the fate of Daphne, metamorphosed into a laurel tree, is envisioned not with sadness but rather as an altogether happy way out of a disagreeable situation (page 44). Images of freedom *from* and separation *from* are further indications of a continuing process of stripping away, not un-related to Arsene's description of the three kinds of laughter as "suc-cessive excoriations of the understanding" (page 48). Existence in the macrocosm is like existence on a ladder, a constant mounting and descending, an organized relation between one thing and another, be-tween one step and another, a logical, practical, tiring business. Life in Knott's house, at least at times, is equivalent to "existence off the ladder" (page 44). In this context the joke "Do not come down the ladder, Ifor, I haf taken it away" (page 44) suggests a utopian situation. Treadmill existence has been replaced by isolation, nonrelation, re-duced mobility, and possibly a greater sense of enclosure—recalling the womb, Knott's house, and life in the mental microcosm. Much later in the novel we find a related passage with images that suggest Belacqua's cup or funnel: "One is in the pit, in the hollow... at the foot of all the hills at last, the ways down, the ways up, and free, free at last..." (page 202). Arsene's sentiments were identical when he spoke of the "sites of a stirring beyond coming and going," of a being "light and free," of "the secret places where nobody ever comes" (page 39).

The logical culmination of the tendency to reduce, negate, eliminate is *le néant*, and we do indeed find that images of nothingness, beginning with the house of Mr. Knott, are very frequent. When Beckett finishes describing Watt's aversions, little is left: "For if there were two things that Watt disliked, one was the moon, and the other was the sun" (page 33). And very shortly thereafter, "And if there were two things that Watt loathed, one was the earth, and the other was the sky" (page 36). Arsene speaks of a being that is "as the being of nothing" (page 39). Much later we learn that "In empty, in airless gloom, Mr. Knott abode.... And from it this ambience followed him forth, and when he moved, in the house, in the garden, with him moved, dimming all, dulling all, stilling all, numbing all, where he passed" (page 200). The middle years, between the contrary yearnings of youth and the decay of old age, are like Mr. Knott's house, a kind of respite between torments where "the gnashing ends" and "one is...nothing at last" (page 202). Belacqua had his "womb-tomb," his "limbo," as Murphy had his "little world," but they were occasional escapes; Mr. Knott's house, for a time at least, is Watt's world, and everything else is peripheral. When Arsene speaks of the transition from the outside world of youth to the inner world of middle age, his words describe a Belacqua, the "border man," becoming a Watt: "He will be in his midst at last, after so many tedious years spent clinging to the perimeter" (page 41). A similar figure involving the circle occurs later on in the same context of alienation from and integration into one's proper context. The painting in Erskine's room, of a circle and a point, causes Watt to wonder "how long it would be before the point and circle entered together upon the same plane... if they had sighted each other ...[whether] the artist had intended to represent...a circle and its centre in search of each other, or...a circle and a centre not its centre in search of a centre and its circle respectively, in boundless space, in endless time...and at the thought that it was perhaps this...Watt's eyes filled with tears that he could not stem..." (page 129).

All the externals that are stripped away are "other." Together they make up the illusory, insubstantial outside world. They distract. They clutter the context called Nothing, in which a man can be at home, perhaps discover the true nature of his own being. As Arsene explains, in Knott's abode the wanderer reaches his destination. Finally, for the first time, the alien, the misfit, is "the right man, at last," and "in the right place, at last" (page 40). The theme of untimeliness found in the poetry recurs in *Watt*. It is a temporal form of the spatial out-of-placeness that Lucky evokes in *Godot* when he refers to "*l'air la terre, faits pour les pierres*" (and not, he implies, for man). Outside are "the languor and the fever of the going of the coming too late, the languor and the fever of the coming of the going too soon. But to Mr. Knott, and with Mr. Knott, and from Mr. Knott, were a coming and a being and a going exempt from languor, exempt from fever, for Mr. Knott was harbour..." (page 135). Beckett's dualistic vision, in which the two halves exist in uneasy, inappropriate alliance, for once, even if briefly, gives way to a kind of mystical harmony between man and nature. Arsene describes the moment when one arrives at Mr. Knott's house and feels the "premonitions of harmony...of imminent harmony, when all outside him will be he, the flowers . . . the sky . . . the earth . . . and all sound his echo . . ." (pages 40-41). Arsene would seem to accept his creator's adaptation of the insight of Democritus that nothing is more real than nothing (*Murphy*, page 246), for in his opinion "it was not an allusion, as long as it lasted, that presence of what did not exist, that presence without, that presence within, that presence between . . ." (page 45).

If Nothing is a state more real than the one in which man finds himself in the world beyond Mr. Knott's house and garden, it is nevertheless defined primarily in negative terms. And the principal precondition for the "presence of what did not exist," to which we now come, is the absence of desire, need, will. Once Arsene "was in the sun, and . . . was the sun . . . and the wall and the step, and the yard, and the time of year, and the time of day." His "personal system was so distended . . . that the distinction between what was inside it and what was outside it was not at all easy to draw." Then "something slipped," and he finds himself back in the old dualistic fix, in an alien land as before, with the old needs, the old yearnings. The metamorphosis has been reversed: "The Laurel into Daphne" (paged 42-44). Especially as it relates *Watt* to the central predicament of Belacqua, the invocation of the myth is of the utmost importance. Belacqua was torn between two desires, figured by Apollo and Narcissus or the need to go out to the other and the need to retreat into the self, pursuit of the girl (for youth, the emblem par excellence of desire) and the flight from her. Limbo was the abolition of both needs. The laurel occupies the same place in *Watt*. Devoid of need, conscious need in any case, the tree is a part of nature and in harmony with it. There is no longer any distinction between subject and object. Turned back into Daphne, this being reenters a world of attractions and repulsions, loves and hates, comings and goings determined by needs positive and needs negative, desires for association and yearnings for solitude.

How much better would life be without *atra cura*, the "black want" of the poems. "And yet it is useless not to seek, not to want, for when you cease to seek you start to find. . . ." Satisfaction of needs merely gives rise to other needs. And fulfillment itself is considerably less desirable than the state of wanting: "When you cease to want, then life begins to ram her fish and chips down your gullet until you puke, and then the puke down your gullet until you puke the puke, and then the puked puke until you begin to like it." For Arsene, at least, the depressing fact is that the closest one can get to happiness is the state of unfulfilled desire, "to hunger, thirst, lust, every day afresh and every day in vain, after the old prog, the old booze, the old whores..." (page 44). And yet Beckett, with Schopenhauer, makes it clear enough that the root of our misery is desire, that its ablation would be felicity. Influenced no doubt by the torments of Swann needing Odette, of the narrator wanting Gilberte, Beckett ends his introduction to *Proust* with a quote from Leopardi that gives away his own view of the dilemma: *"Non che la speme, il desiderio è spento."*

Although Arsene rejects fulfillment as a way out, it seems to play some part in the ideal hypothetical solution that the author sets up. For Mr. Knott is perhaps above all the one who does *not* need. He provides the standard against which all other attempts to establish a utopian mode of existence must be measured. "For except, one, not to need, and, two, a witness to his not needing, Knott needed nothing, as far as Watt could see." Mr. Knott seems to maintain his happy state of indifference by doing things—even though he has no need to do them—that, were they left undone, might have the power to create needs in him. He wears many varieties of clothes, for example, clothes for all seasons and occasions, but indiscriminately, without regard to the season or occasion. So it is with his other activities. They are invariably explainable by his nature: that of a nonneeding being. "If he ate and he ate well; if he drank, and he drank heartily; if he slept, and he slept sound; if he did other things, and he did other things regularly, it was not from need of food, or drink, or sleep, or other things, no, but from the need never to need, never never to need, food, and drink, and sleep, and other things" (page 202).

Knott's mode of being has an effect on the surroundings. "This ataraxy covered the entire house-room, the pleasure-garden, the vegetable-garden and of course Arthur [Watt's successor on the ground floor]" (page 208). In referring to the root condition of the utopia he calls Nothing, Watt speaks of "the longing for longing gone, the horror of horror" (page 202). Not only have attraction and repulsion, or positive and negative desire, vanished. The need for desire has also been abolished, and that is the crux of the matter. Man not only desires, he desires to desire—which is disastrous. He seems incapable under ordinary conditions of living in limbo. He seeks to want. His comings and goings are purposeful, and he is forever coming and going. Only Knott "seems to abide" (page 58). And yet human progress is no progress at all, as Watt's vision after leaving Knott's house indicates. Since the flame of desire is eternally rekindled from its own ashes, all our comings and goings, which in *Watt* are figures of the needs that propel us, are futile. All motion is equivalent to stasis, since it brings us right back to the starting point: need. With Estragon and Vladimir, we move in place.

In the metaphoric structure of the novel, the sojourn in Knott's house is a time of staying and a time of nonwilling. It represents in general an end to the comings and goings that are outward manifestations of desire. The comings and goings in Knott's house are of a different nature. They are not determined by Watt. He is a servant who follows the rules of the establishment. He is not expected to make decisions.[3] His status as an obedient servant is a principal prerequisite to the tranquility of indifference (page 39), to the "will-lessness" that is the *summum bonum*. Watt enjoys Knott's "wild, dim chatter," but he is not sorry when it ceases or glad when it begins again (page 209). When he leaves Knott's house, he does so "with the utmost serenity." Only after he has left the premises does "he burst into tears" (page 208). While in Mr. Knott's house he suffers "neither from the presence . . . nor from [the] absence" of his master (page 207). And yet Watt is by no means always exempt from the common condition of need, even in Knott's house. The novel, then, appears to pose the following question: "Is there a place, like the house of Mr. Knott, in which the normal condition of need can be transcended?"

The Religious Dimension

Concern with the themes of freedom and will is traditional and of central importance in Christianity from "not my will, but thine, be done" (Luke 22:42) to the present. In the *Commedia*, a *livre de chevet* of Beckett, Dante's words *"liberi soggiacete"* (*Purg.* XVI, 80) and *"E'n la sua voluntate e nostra pace"* (*Par.* III, 85) express religious views that are very close to notions developed in *Watt*. Service, obedience, renunciation of personal will are liberating. They provide a way to "a being so light and free that it is as the being of nothing" (page 39). The renunciations of Watt are couched in religious language that suggests the ascetic preliminaries to mystic experience. Mr. Knott and his premises are often described in terms that evoke the deity. All is mobility save Knott, who "abides . . . like an oak . . . and we nest a little while in his branches" (page 57). His house is mystery and fixity. It is no easier to remain long in his presence than to be long out of it. "For there was no other place...whose mysteries, whose fixity...so thrust forth [yet] called back so soon, with such a call" (page 199). Watt rejects certain speculations about the nature of Knott as "anthropomorphic insolence" (page 202). The term *witness*, so current in religious usage, occurs on a number of occasions. A minor rebellion by Watt goes, to his surprise, unavenged: "No punishment fell on Watt, no thunderbolt..." (page 115). He reasons that perhaps his "transgression," surrounded as it was "with such precautions, such delicacies," appeared no transgression at all, that his manner was "counted to him for grace" (page 116). In language that recalls Dante's inscription over the gate of hell, the narrator speculates that Watt, while still on the ground floor, "little by little abandoned all hope, all fear, of ever seeing Mr. Knott face to face" (page 146). Arsene admits that the "dreams of middle age" were his dreams, in spite of occasional "blasphemous words and expressions." And what he knows toward the end of his stay with Mr. Knott "partakes," he asserts of "the unutterable or ineffable" (page 62).

Biblical allusions help to give a Christian tone to the vaguely religious atmosphere that permeates the novel. St. Paul comes to mind when Watt does catch glimpses of Mr. Knott, for they "are not clearly caught, but as it were in a glass, not a looking glass, a plain glass, an eastern window at morning, a western window at evening." Mr. Knott likes a small number of rather down-at-the-heels servants, "for to seediness and shabbiness and fewness in number he is greatly attached." Although the expression "give glory" is not used, we hear a faintly ironic echo of its meaning when Arsene states that the purpose of these servants is "to make much of [Knott]" (page 59). Through a footnote, we learn that both Arsene and Watt have an "eleventh hour vision, of what might have been" (page 82). Mr. Knott rests on the seventh day (page 86). Arsene must leave Mr. Knott's establishment "before the cock crows" and leaving he will perhaps long "to be turned into a stone pillar" (page 49). Later the narrator, like Veronica,[4] has compassion on Watt and wipes his face with a cloth. And like Mary Magdalene he anoints his face and hands. The examinations committee leaves the university in reverse order "so that the first was last, and the last first" (page 196), which is perhaps not without relation to the backward speech of Watt's post-Knott days. Occasionally a clear allusion to a well-known prayer reinforces the religious atmosphere. Thus "as it was in the beginning, is now, and ever shall be" turns up in the form: "As it was now, so it had been in the beginning, and so it would remain to the end" (page 131).

In one especially crucial area, the analogy between Knott and the deity seems to hold. The satire of religion that we have already noted goes beyond an attack on institutions. Beckett suffers from the knowledge of the suffering of his fellows, and his pain emerges in the form of bitter irony that links the mystery of evil and the mystery of divinity. The news agent, "a man of more than usual acerbity" who seems "to suffer from unremitting mental, moral and perhaps even physical pain," is short and limps dreadfully. Once he gets started he moves rapidly, "in a series of aborted genuflexions" (pages 25-26). The same implicit question, to serve or not to serve under such conditions, arises in connection with the "faithful emaciated dog" (page 97), endowed with free will, which is supposed to eat Mr. Knott's leftovers—whenever there are any. The principal garbage men attached to the service of Mr. Knott, who "exploit" (page 98) the dogs, are members of the malady-ridden Lynch clan, whose ailments seem to be an expansion of the case of Job, utilized by Beckett in the poem "Text." The metaphysical protest reaches paroxysmal proportions in the description of the later activities of Sam and Watt in the mental institution. They take delight in stoning birds, especially the confiding robins, which they destroy in great numbers. They grind the eggs of larks into fragments under their feet "with peculiar satisfaction." But their favorite friends are the rats, to which they feed frogs and baby thrushes, "or seizing suddenly a plump young rat, resting in [their] bosom after its repast, [they] would feed it to its mother, or its father, or its brother, or its sister, or to some less fortunate relative." It is on such occasions, they agree, that they come "nearest to God" (pages 155-156). Close upon this ferocious, if theologically dubious, passage comes a double juxtaposition that associates "Knott, Christ, Gomorrha, Cork" (page 156).

To identify Knott and the Divinity is as risky as equating Godot and God. For one thing, the asylum where Watt tells his story to Sam is also described in terms borrowed from the Bible (page 151) and used there to describe heaven ("In my Father's house are many mansions" [John 14:2]). For another, many of Knott's actions have surely never been associated with the god of any known religion: his habits of dress and his gastronomic preferences, for example. Certain aspects of his nature also give pause. In the addenda we learn that "Mr. Knott too was serial..." (page 253). There was a time, then, when Mr. Knott, unlike God, did not yet exist.[5] However, one prime characteristic, valued highly by Watt, is shared by Knott and the Divinity: an absence of need. Belacqua did spend more than two months at one stretch in his "umbra" ("Dream," pp. 38-40), but he was never able to duplicate the feat again, let alone approach the all-time record of his namesake in purgatory. The consuming curiosity of Watt violates the indifference requisite to the limbo that he too would inhabit. Everything in Mr. Knott's little establishment, on the other hand, is organized with a view to eliminating all need—save the need "not to need" and "a witness to his not needing" (page 202). Only this minimal link to the macrocosm intrudes on the self-sufficiency of his private world.

If we turn now to Lucky's speech in *En attendant Godot*, we find a pertinent description (like the portrait of Mr. Knott, half-satirical and half-serious) of the deity who exists "*hors du temps de l'étendu*" in a state of "divine apathie... divine athambie... divine aphasie" (pages 71-72). Characterized, like Murphy's microcosm and Belacqua's cup, by negative attributes, this timeless, spaceless condition is all but sealed off from the world of men. The triple qualification suggests the trinitarian God, but the absence of feeling or suffering, of brilliance ($\Theta\alpha\mu\beta o\varsigma$) and of speech would require stretching and a different sequence to work specifically against the power, wisdom, and love traditionally associated with the Father, Son, and Holy Spirit. The three terms describe accurately enough, however, the indifferent, darkly mysterious, and uncommunicative Almighty of Beckett's vision, and, curiously, they apply equally well to the desirable state sought in the sanctuary of mind by all Beckett's early protagonists, including the "I" of a number of poems—and to Mr. Knott. "Apathie" for Belacqua is "a beatitude of indolence... in a Limbo purged of desire" ("Dream," page 38). "States of peace" describe the corresponding experience in *Murphy* (page 112). "Dispassionate" Anteros is summoned to "choke ...regret" in "Return to the Vestry" (pages 35-39). The untroubled calm of "ataraxy" pervades the house and grounds of Mr. Knott, and only when he passes beyond the gate does Watt's total "serenity" give way to "tears" (page 208). Similarly, "athambie" turns up as grayness, dimness, absence of sun and glare, gloom, half-light; while "aphasie" translates as hush, country of quiet, silence, softness of sound, dim meaningless chatter.

In the privileged and relatively rare experience of inner being Beckett finds his utopia, the beatific condition so prized by a succession of fictional surrogates. Its excellence can only be adequately described (as Proust's narrator describes the workings of involuntary memory) by recourse to religious imagery. In the negative Mr. Knott we have the postulate of a human mastery of this godlike mode of being, described as a very real Nothing in *Murphy*. Knott's characteristics and actions stem from the imaginative postulate. His achievement accounts for the supernatural aura that surrounds him. By comparison with Knott, Watt is indeed an apprentice—in some ways a singularly inept one. Because he is older, however, and relatively free of the erotic distractions that plagued his younger forerunners, he has some degree of success. Because his effort is serious and moving even while remaining comic, he emerges as a strangely impressive and haunting figure in the Beckett canon.

If Watt is middle-aged, Knott is an old man, as we learn from Arthur's encounter with Knott's contemporary in the garden (page 252). Certain passages indicate that age is an important ally in the conquest of inwardness. Watt's reaction when Arthur relates his encounter is especially noteworthy: "There had been a time when [knowing] ... that Mr. Knott too was serial ... would have pleased him...." (The knowledge of a reduced distance between apprentice and master might have raised Watt's expectations.) "But not now. For Watt was an old rose now, and indifferent to the gardener" (page 253). The indifference of old age, antidote to the poison of curiosity that inhibits the imitation of Knott, resembles the deific "apathie" in *Godot*. It may be the open sesame to the asylum where he passes his declining years and where he comes to resemble Knott in more ways than one. His abode brings to mind the Magdalen Mental Mercyseat, where Murphy cultivates the "sanctuary" (page 177) that he calls his "dungeon in Spain" in admiring imitation of patients successfully "immured in mind" (page 180). No less compellingly, the situation of Sam and Watt recalls Belacqua's experience of limbo: "the mind at last its own asylum, disinterested, indifferent..." ("Dream," page 39).

In *Watt* Beckett probes the microcosm more searchingly and more seriously—but seldom without the skeptical queries of irony and laughter. In "Dream" the Alba suspects Belacqua of being "inextricably Limbese" and promises to leave him to "rot away in his darling gloom" if she turns out to be right (page 173). Even at the asylum, as he acquires dimensions lacking in Belacqua and Murphy, Watt does not cease to be a comical figure. The parallel between a microcosmic deity and microcosmic man (made in His image?), each cruel in his self-enclosed indifference, implies a radical criticism of inwardness. As certain passages in part 3 appear to suggest, Watt's solitude at the end may be less beatitude and fulfillment than the anxiety of a continuing, if changed, need. Ultimately, religious metaphor takes on more than metaphoric value, and the vaunted inner existence seems more the calvary of an exile than a heaven of untroubled bliss.

The Fly in the Ointment of Microcosmos

In the motif of the serial and the nonserial we can see more clearly why Watt, better equipped in some ways than his precursors, is far from wholly successful in his undertaking. In a lamentation over the return of the days, the months, and the seasons (which includes biographical references to Beckett's early years at Cooldrinagh in Foxrock: "the larch turning green every year a week before the others," "the consumptive postman whistling *The Roses Are Blooming in Picardy*"), Arsene ends the year in April (when Beckett was born) with the words "and then the whole bloody business starting all over again." Later in the book Watt follows in his footsteps, attaching "great importance" to the question "Was the picture a fixed and stable member of the edifice...[or] a term in a series, like the series of Mr. Knott's dogs, or the series of Mr. Knott's men, or like the centuries that fall, from the pod of eternity?" (page 131).

Little by little Watt comes to the opinion that no "presence" ever changes in Mr. Knott's house; only appearances, surfaces change, but they are in a process of unending change. Although he has a will to know, he can learn little from the phantom forms of a world in eternal flux. Reluctantly, then, Watt, who has not attempted to get at underlying meaning since the age of fourteen or fifteen, who has lived "among face values all his adult life," feels impelled to seek some other meaning, to find reasons and causes, to penetrate—beneath the accidents—the mystery of being (page 117). Watt's curiosity, however, does not lead him to pursue truth for its own sake. He works at the "ancient labour" of trying to find out only in order to exorcise the demons of desire. The conceptions that Watt has no *need* for at the moment he puts aside like an umbrella in readiness for a rainy day. He tries to distinguish truth, "whatever that is," from falsehood, "whatever that means," but he feels that it is "greatly to be deplored" that he cares to do so (pages 135-36, 226). Watt seeks, then, not knowledge itself but freedom from the epistemological craving that "disquiets" him.

Paradoxically, a very large part of the novel is given over to Watt's extraordinarily persistent attempts to know. With the oil of information he again and again momentarily dims the flames of curiosity, only to see them burn again with a new intensity. Through his principal character Beckett explores a whole gamut of types of knowledge, ways of learning, and obstacles to understanding. The identity-card types of data that are wholly exterior reveal nothing of the essential being (page 21). With Mr. Spiro (whose name suggests air, in this case of the hot variety) erudition is down the drain (page 29). Intuition fares only slightly better, and any hope that primitive man, blessed with an underdeveloped cerebrum, might have access to nonrational sources of discernment is laughed out of court in the episode of Mr. Nackybal, the Visicelt (page 198).

In the same fell swoop academic research and group attempts to reach truth are ridiculed in Arthur's comical story of the examinations committee with its deaf recording secretary. Eyewitness evidence is invalidated by Watt's hallucination. Experience itself is like the "sterile pus" used in Watt's "course of injections" (page 253). We can learn neither from the outer world nor from dreams (page 232). The tools of logic and mathematics (and sometimes music) are of no avail. Religious faith is not enough (page 192). The motives for human actions escape us (pages 240, 245). Ultimately, man's intellect is ill-adapted to the task, his memory imperfect, his senses untrustworthy. Fatigue, desire, imagination, convention, time, and circumstances of life are distorting lenses. But the receiving subject is no less flawed than the transmitter. And the mode of communication and the conditions under which the message is transmitted must share the blame. "Watt spoke also with scant regard for grammar, for syntax, for pronunciation, for enunciation . . . [in] a voice *at once* so rapid and so low . . . [that] much fell in vain on my [Sam's] imperfect hearing and understanding, and much by the rushing wind was carried away, and lost for ever" (page 156).

Arsene warns beforehand of the futility of the quest in his anecdote about one Mr. Ash, who had buttonholed him in a snowstorm on Westminster Bridge and who, unsolicited and at great inconvenience to himself, had dug out his grossly inaccurate watch to give him the time of day just a moment before Big Ben struck the hour. This bit of knowledge—painful to come by, undesired, wrong, and superfluous—is according to Arsene "the type of all information whatsoever" (page 46). Watt, for whom knowledge is no more than a means by which he hopes to vanquish the "dis-ease" of the intellect and find asylum, might have spared himself the effort. The hunger to know is insatiable at a certain time of life, and as Beckett writes in *Proust*, "Wisdom . . . consists not in the satisfaction but in the ablation of desire" (page 7).

Watt opens with a symbolic departure from the city. Its structure resembles a three-stage *rite de passage* (in this case a passing from maturity to old age): The hero goes out, spends a period of initiation in a privileged locus, and returns equipped with new power or wisdom. Like Arsene before him, Watt will acquire a certain wisdom in Knott's house, an inexpressible and "quite useless" (page 62) wisdom. Arsene compares his sagacity to that of "Theseus kissing Ariadne, or Ariadne Theseus, towards the end, on the seashore . . ." (page 63). Sagacity is the awareness of coming separation, living in the knowledge that we are given over to sorrow and loss. When Watt leaves the ground floor of Mr. Knott's house he is already well along the road to such sagacity:

> What had he learnt? Nothing.
> What did he know of Mr. Knott? Nothing.
> Of his anxiety to improve, of his anxiety to understand, of his anxiety to get well, what remained? Nothing.
> But was not that something?
> He saw himself then, so little, so poor. And now, littler, poorer. Was not that something?
> So sick, so alone.
> And now.
> Sicker, aloner.
> Was not that something? (page 148)

The one thing we can know is our own want, our own lack and need. Since Mr. Knott needs nothing, he knows nothing of himself (page 203). Were Watt himself to reach his goal, the nirvana of nonneed, he too would cease to be conscious of his own being, since that being is unknowable except as need, and Beckett's paraphrase of Descartes would seem to be "I need; therefore, I am." *Film* (1965) expresses anew this cornerstone concept in the edifice of Beckett's works through yet another attempt to escape the pain of awareness, inflicted either by the gaze of the other or the reflexive contemplation of the self, in a limbo of unself-conscious being.

The need to know destroys utopia. *Watt* is perhaps more than anything else a long development of the story of Eden. The fruit of the tree of knowledge is forbidden fruit, and the penalty for disobedience is banishment from the garden. From one point of view, Watt's departure from Mr. Knott's house and garden is indeed symbolic. For the most part he has never really lived there, and his leaving simply expressed his inability to be an unthinking, unneeding part of the innocent, peaceful "nothingness" of nature. Like Arsene he could not remain a laurel tree, one with the sun and the garden and the time of day and year. Leaving Eden, Adam and Eve saw their nakedness and were ashamed. Watt understands better than ever his own increasing indigence. Such wisdom is dearly paid for (page 50). In his description of the varieties of laughter as "successive . . . excoriations of the understanding," Arsene comes finally to the deepest level of wisdom, to the mirthless laugh, "the *risus purus*" or "laugh laughing at the laugh" (page 48). This is the moment of self-consciousness, when man discovers that his need to know has led ultimately only to the sure knowledge that he is a creature with a need to know—a need that has lost him Eden.

Arsene admits ruefully that "wiser [he] could hardly become without grave personal inconvenience" (page 50). Perhaps the aging Watt too began to weigh inquisitiveness in the balance. By the time he moves from the ground floor to his new duties upstairs, he is too tired to revise a faulty hypothesis or seek a finished formulation. Even his need is no longer certain: translated, "Deen did tub? Ton sparp." (page 166) comes out "But did need? Praps not." His experience in Mr. Knott's house is termed a "long dwindling supposition" (page 131), and in his final indifference as he leaves the establishment we may see a reflection of Leopardi's lines, quoted by Beckett in *Proust* (page 7): *"In noi di cari inganni/non che la speme, il desiderio è spento."* Watt in the asylum with Sam is certainly a changed person. His speech progresses from one form of inversion to another in a parodic mirror image of the logic of permutations and combinations he was wont to utilize.

He even walks backward. Like Dante's wrongheaded soothsayers, Watt pays for his attempts to "see." At the end he cannot even see where he is going. He has a peculiar and obscure way of talking; he progresses blindly; he has, in short, become an artist.

The protagonist abandons reason at the end and gives up the attempt to know for the attempt to make. He becomes a storyteller, but one who by this time is so convinced of the inadequacy of ordinary language that he feels compelled to invent verbal structures that are more closely related to his experience. Beckett's metaphor of Watt's backward language is related to his own view of the creative process. In conversations in 1961 he spoke of writing as a "groping in the dark," an enterprise that required the writer to "see with his fingers." We find, then, at the heart of Beckett's artistic credo, a correspondence between the intellectual darkness in which man is doomed to live and the irrational organization of words imposed upon the serious artist who wants to say something valid about the conditions of human existence. We find the symbolic darkness inside the egg in *Whoroscope* and its relation to the "starless inscrutable hour" denied to the fictional Descartes. More than thirty years later, the characters in *Comment c'est* live out their lives plunged in a similar obscurity.

NOTES

1. A curiously autobiographical note occurs in *Watt* on page 212, where Beckett writes that sometimes in the early hours of the morning his protagonist "went to the window, to look at the stars, which he had once known familiarly by name, when dying in London. . . ." Since for Beckett man is always in the process of dying, the phrase "dying in London" may be taken as roughly equivalent to "living in London." It was Samuel Beckett, of course, who was "living-dying" there during the years of misery following the death of his father. In the *Watt* passage the author speaks briefly not as narrator but as author. He testifies to the ambiguous relationship between creator and character, the same and yet distinct. Two notions are implicit in his statement. First, the Proustian idea of the multiple self: Beckett-Murphy must die in order to make way for his successor, Beckett-Watt. Second, a view more characteristic of Beckett: On the one hand each self is fictional in the deepest sense of the word. Man knows his own being, if it exists, imperfectly at best. His literary creations are phantoms of his imagination, without grounding in reality. Neither Murphy nor Watt is Beckett. On the other hand they resemble each other in too many ways to be thought of as wholly arbitrary. If one, as the *Watt* passage suggests, can be thought of as the prolongation of the other,

it is because each bears some relationship to a mystery-shrouded but permanent core of being. The trilogy, and in particular *L'Innommable*, bears witness to the tension between such a despair and such a faith.

2. The parallel to Beckett's own renunciations when he left home, country, religion, profession is strikingly apparent.

3. Cf. Belacqua in "Ding-Dong." Incapable of deciding which direction to take, he must wait for a sign.

4. Cf. Samuel Beckett, "Enueg II," in *Poems in English*, the collected works of Samuel Beckett (New York: Grove Press, 1970), 26.

5. In any consideration of the religious dimension of Watt it is essential to keep in mind Beckett's consistent separation of Christ, seen as man, the suffering servant, himself a victim, and the Divinity, enigmatic source of the mystery of evil. Arsene, describing himself as much as Watt, suggests the stigmata when he refers, in another context, to head, side, hands, and feet (p. 39). Later Sam likens Watt, and himself, to this same Christ (p. 159).

ERIC P. LEVY

"Mercier and Camier": Narration, Dante, and the Couple

Beckett kept his third novel, *Mercier and Camier*, on the shelf for twenty-five years before reluctantly allowing its French publication in 1970. The book was apparently more valuable to him as an exploration of expressive forms than as a work of art in its own right. Indeed, the novel is clearly a kind of pivotal exercise, for here we can see Beckett on the one hand stressing the type of futile dialogue he was to perfect a few years later in *Waiting for Godot* (the French edition was published in 1952), while on the other hand further developing the system of narrative mirrors so useful in *Murphy* and *Watt* for expressing the experience of Nothing.

We do not have to read very far into *Mercier and Camier* to discover that the story as much concerns the narrator as the two eponymous heroes. With the first sentence the narrator thrice intrudes the first person pronoun, founding his own subjectivity on the adventures of the two characters: "The journey of Mercier and Camier is one I can tell, if I will, for I was with them all the time."[1] In recounting the futile existence of his characters, the narrator is somehow trying to grasp his own, but the attempt remains unsuccessful, for their vain wandering only mirrors his confusion. They cannot understand their journey because it has been imposed upon them, and the narrator is improvising as he goes along: "So let him wake, Mercier, Camier, no matter, Camier, Camier wakes.... Why? No knowing. No knowing such things anymore" (page 103).

Under these severe circumstances, how can the characters preserve the narrator who so exploits them? Part of the answer appears in Beckett's brief article on the painter Henri Hayden. There, in phrases that illumine his own work as much as his immediate topic, Beckett looks beneath the rubble of collapsed conventions for the last safeguard and testament of subjectivity and finds it "quite simply in the saving of a relation, a separation, *a couple*, however impoverished the components: the I with its possibilities of acting and receiving, the rest in its docility as the given" (my translation and italics).[2] The couple, of course, has become a renowned institution in Beckett's fiction, and Mercier and Camier are its first representatives (the novel was written around 1945). The couple's function is to protect subjectivity by assuring its relation to a world by which it is bounded, any world, even that of its own torment or solitude. Such, for example, is the relation between Hamm and Clov in *Endgame*. Hamm is the center whose world of experience Clov confirms and defines. But Mercier and Camier have their roles less well differentiated, and for this reason the Unnamable later calls them a "pseudo-couple" (*Unnamable*, page 297).[3] Both are subjects; each props up the other so that together they may inhabit a world in which subjectivity—their own and the narrator's—persists. Sometimes the task is more than they can manage: "And there were times they would look long at each other, unable to utter a word, their minds two blanks" (page 17).

The world they inhabit is their journey, and that journey boils down to a question about purpose: "What were they looking for?" (page 23). Subjectivity, then, knows itself only as a striving to know what it is doing and who it is. Here Beckett reduces the polarity between self and world to its simplest form: the endless bumping of self against the walls of its own ignorance. The walls at least confirm its independent existence. The only truth ever revealed to Mercier and Camier involves the same paradox that runs through all Beckett's works—the need to have a need is all that keeps the subject going: "Finally a great light bathed their understandings, flooding in particular the following concepts. There are two needs: the need you have and the need to have *it*" (page 72). Needs, by pointing to a deficiency in the subject, always imply a world outside where they can be gratified. In Beckett's reflexive universe where the subject turns more and more tightly in upon himself, the external world has been completely lost, and need now refers to the worst deficiency of all—the need for continuous proof of personal existence in a world of others.

This proof comes fitfully and negatively to Mercier and Camier and only when witnessing or causing the death of some other, as the fat lady or the constable. Death is the unique event in this redundant universe, the sole thing that, happening but once to a given individual, can confirm his individuality. All other acts and occasions are cyclic, recurring endlessly, varying only according to local circumstance. Consequently, the reaction of Mercier and Camier to each of the two deaths they behold is significant. The first restores Camier's will:

> Let this be a lesson to us, said Camier.
> Meaning? said Mercier.
> Never to despair, said Camier, or lose faith in life. (page 33)

The second convinces Mercier that he and Camier live as two different subjects, each of whom needs the other to remain a subject: "We would never have hit on it alone, said Mercier" (page 94). Each makes the other's relation to the world a little more secure. These restitutions are fleeting, however. Eventually, the two separate and recede into darkness.

The narrator emphasizes that the journey is in search of subjectivity by modeling it upon the greatest itinerary of the soul in western literature: Dante's *Divine Comedy*. It is not so much a case here of *Mercier and Camier* paralleling or mimicking the *Divine Comedy* as of the later work being superimposed upon the earlier spiritual voyage. Hence, at every moment we can see, underneath the wanderings of this Beckettian couple, the Dantean convictions that they cannot even glimpse. The gap between the two works makes *Mercier and Camier* at once pathetic and pointless, for the couple retain Dante's earnestness ("Men less tenacious might not have withstood the temptation to leave it at that," page 71) but have lost all notion of goal or end. Imagine Dante and Virgil traversing Hell, Purgatory, and Heaven a thousand times, with no memory of their entrance, no hope of an exit, no means of judging those they meet, and no way of evaluating their own experience. Eventually, the stage would be reached where there is nothing in Dante to distinguish him from Virgil and vice versa. That is the starting place for Mercier and Camier. Unlike Dante's, their journey is morally neutral. At various points, as we shall see, they slip directly from Hell to Paradise with no increase or remission of their suffering. Most of the novel, however, relives the *Purgatorio*, because it is here that we can best gauge the utter futility of their striving. As our discussion will show, Mercier and Camier can make no progress; they pass no fewer than four times through the same purgation for the same sin. Yet they are not the only ones thus ensnared. With them we shall find the narrator in various disguises, for he is vainly attempting the greatest purgation of all—release from the need to go on searching for his own subjectivity. After charting the connections with the *Divine Comedy*, we shall be in a position to consider how the novel is superimposed upon another world as well: Beckett's narrative one stretching all the way back to *Murphy*. Against this double background, the narrator of *Mercier and Camier* will yield even more of his secrets.

The first chapter opens, as we might expect, with a strong echo of the first canto of the *Inferno*. Where Dante, overcome by fear of three predatory beasts, does not at first recognize Virgil, whom Beatrice has sent to guide him, Mercier sees "in the morning mist a shape suggestive of Camier's" (page 8), but it takes forty-five minutes for them to remain long enough in the same place finally to meet. Instead of moving Mercier and Camier steadily forward from this point in Hell, the rest of the first chapter projects the couple against the background of the *Purgatorio*, placing them sometimes in the earthly Paradise at the summit of the Mountain of Purgatory, sometimes at its base, near the entrance to Hell. The implication is clear: wherever the couple wander they always remain in the same unresolved situation. The "small public garden" (page 9) where they greet each other is dominated by a single enormous tree that recalls not the entrance to Hell, but the earthly Paradise just above Purgatory. There (canto 33), the forbidden tree is an immediate symbol of divine goodness: "Whoso robs that tree or rends it offends with blasphemy an act against God...."[4] With Beckett it becomes just another item progressively desecrated in the endless round of corruption and generation: "The stifled giant's days were numbered, it would not cease henceforward to pine and rot till finally removed, bit by bit" (page 10). Another little detail derives from this part of the *Purgatorio*. From time to time in the novel, Mercier makes rather cryptic utterances that cannot be explained by the immediate context but which come directly from the *Divine Comedy*. The first of these occurs in chapter 1: "A drunken woman passed by, singing a ribald song, and hitching up her skirts" (page 13). This apparition duplicates that of the "ungirt harlot" Dante spies in the earthly Paradise (canto 32). Mercier and Camier are far worse off than the lowest of Dante's damned, for their universe admits of no redemptive or structuring principle. Indeed, the little garden is invaded by two copulating dogs, echoes of the beasts that menace Dante. Even here, Mercier and Camier feel the presence of the damned of the First Circle whose sighs are the first Dante hears: "I sense vague shadowy shapes, said Camier, they come and go with muffled cries" (page 19). The ranger who disturbs the couple and surveys their eventual departure, "his bunch of keys in his hand" (page 20), recalls the warder at the gate of Purgatory who holds the keys given him by St. Peter. Since we cannot tell whether Mercier and Camier are leaving or entering Purgatory when they quit the garden, the first chapter has succeeded in suspending all notions of direction or end, retaining only that of indifferent movement.

Chapter 2, gathering and blending elements from each of the three cantos, grinds away the last hope of a definite conclusion to a journey that can by now mean nothing. The strangely silent crowd that buoys Mercier and Camier along the town streets recalls the "shadowy shapes" intuited by Camier in the previous chapter. Yet, before we can trace their descent deeper into Hell, the couple reach a crossroads that abruptly returns them to Purgatory. Camier's question "Which way do we drag ourselves now?" (page 42) echoes the First Terrace (canto 10), where Virgil and Dante lose their bearings. Camier's follow-up remark, "Then let us turn back," explicitly contradicts the warder's warning in the previous canto of the *Purgatorio*: "Enter, but I bid you know that he who looks back returns outside." The confusion over the "mixed choir" (page 25) that Camier hears and Mercier dismisses as a "delusion" duplicates the debate Dante holds with himself on the First Terrace (canto 10), trying to decide whether he hears singing: "In front people appeared and the whole company, divided into seven choirs, made two of my senses say, the one: 'No,' the other: 'Yes, they sing.'..."

After this, the Dantean references shift even more swiftly. Mercier, in a fit of rage, smashes the malfunctioning umbrella and curses God: "And to crown all, lifting to the sky his convulsed and streaming face, he said, As for thee, fuck thee" (page 26). Here two cantos are compressed. The beating rain belongs to the Third Circle of the *Inferno* (canto 6), but the great malediction is hurled much later in canto 25 by the thief Vanni Fucci, who shakes his fists: "Take that, God, for at Thee I square them!" A few lines later, with no transition, Mercier and Camier stand inside Helen's apartment. This is Paradise and she is Beatrice. The connection with Beatrice will grow clearer later on, but we can note now the ease with which Mercier and Camier enter and leave her domain. She can offer them only diversion, not permanent repose, and certainly not vision. The ailing cockatoo languishing in the room, its feathers "blazing in ironic splendour" (page 27), is a sorry version of the Eagle of Divine Justice, "preening its feathers" in canto 19 of the *Paradiso*.

The next morning the couple resume their wanderings, and their journey, far from unfolding confidently, is whirled cruelly against three of the most significant moments in the *Purgatorio*, shattering any vestiges of purpose or meaning. The fatal accident involving the fat woman recalls the collision of the ecclesiastical chariot and the eagle in canto 32. Mercier's delighted reaction—quite the opposite from Dante's response to this vision of lingering weakness in the earthly church—borrows from the last lines of the *Purgatorio*, where Dante, cleansed in the River Eunoe, emerges "remade": "Ah, said Mercier, that's what I needed, I feel a new man already" (page 33). The remark is a hollow one; a few lines later the chapter ends with Mercier passing one hand over his rain-soaked face: "He had not had a wash for some time" (page 34). Here we are transported back to the opening of the *Purgatorio*, where Virgil, wetting his hands with dew, washes the grit of Hell from Dante's cheeks. Life itself is Purgatory for Mercier and Camier, who do again and again what they have already done, what they can never do for good.

Chapter 3 begins deceptively. The first-person voice recounting its childhood seems, through almost two pages, to belong to the narrator, for he is the only narrating "I" encountered so far. However, the speaker this time turns out to be a garrulous old man, Mr. Madden, who is sitting opposite the couple in a slow train. This stage of the journey is clearly back in Hell; when Mr. Madden disembarks, he calls to them: "Not alighting? said the old man. You're quite right, only the damned alight here" (page 40). A little digging will disclose what area of the *Inferno* this interlude entails. Mr. Madden's long monologue about "springing from the loins of a parish priest" (page 39) and verbally knocking into people ("Then up I'd get, covered with blood and my rags in ribbons, and at 'em again," page 39) recalls the Fourth Circle of the *Inferno*, where damned souls, including a disproportionate number of tonsured clerics, wheel in a great circle and collide repeatedly with each other. In a passage whose end we quoted earlier, the Unnamable associated Mercier and Camier with the same circle: "Two shapes then, oblong like man, entered into collision before me. They fell and I saw them no more. I naturally thought of the pseudo-couple Mercier-Camier" (*Unnamable*, page 297). The Fourth Circle is connected with Mercier and Camier, not from their point of view, but from that of the narrator who invents their pratfalls. We see now the reason both for Mr. Madden's confusing entry into the chapter and his invocation of the Fourth Circle: he is taking a journey, but unlike theirs, his is purely verbal. No other character in the book, aside from Mr. Conaire, whom we shall meet in a moment, delivers long monologues, for such utterances are the dubious privilege of the narrator alone. The particular Hell to which he belongs is different from but just as insufferable as that which his creatures inhabit. Hence, Mercier responds with amazement to his suggestion that all three of them alight together: "This puts a fresh complexion on it, said Mercier" (page 39). A change of Hell might be interesting.

They finally get off one stop after Mr. Madden and proceed to the inn of Mr. Gall, alias Mr. Gast. Their difficult reception there recalls the defiant refusal of the devils to let Dante and Virgil past the gate of Dis. Once admitted, Mercier and Camier go upstairs, and during their absence another wayfarer, Mr. Conaire, enters. If we attend to clues, it becomes obvious that he is a double of Mr. Madden and hence another reflection of the narrator. Both Madden and Conaire are extremely talkative, carry walking sticks, and take a profound interest in the couple. The episodes involving each are termed "interlude" in the chapter summary, the only ones so designated in the entire novel. Finally, Mr. Conaire refers to the "other hell calling me back" (page 53); we can determine which part by considering his bald head, for the tonsured clerics of Mr. Madden's Fourth Circle are also bald.

The clinching proof that Mr. Conaire, like Mr. Madden, is an image of the narrator appears in a series of hints near the close of the chapter culminating, if we untangle the Dantean references, with Mr. Conaire and the couple exchanging roles. First, Mr. Conaire shrieks at the horrors of childbirth and the pudenda of adult women. This recalls Dante's balking at the passage through fire on the Seventh Terrace of Purgatory (canto 27), where lust is purged. At the end of his outburst, Mr. Conaire sees his auditors "smiling at him as at a child" (page 54), exactly how Virgil regards the reluctant Dante, shying at the flames: "[He] smiled as one does at a child that is won with an apple." Immediately after his painful purgation, Dante falls asleep. This is imitated in the novel where, directly following his little agony, Mr. Conaire is informed that Mercier and Camier have fallen asleep. That the couple exchange roles with Mr. Conaire should come as no surprise when we consider him as an image of the narrator, for, as we have already seen, the narrator admits at the outset that their story is simply a means of preserving his subjectivity.[5]

The opening of chapter 4 mingles this canto with the next. The barren field in which Mercier and Camier find themselves is yet another version of the earthly Paradise, the setting of that next canto (28). The goat prancing along the hedgerow recalls the one to which Dante compares himself after passing through the flames. The narrator draws out the parallel, for it soon becomes obvious that he is comparing the goat to both himself and the couple; all of them move in circles: "Would it continue thus all round the field? Or weary first?" (page 56). Dante's sudden sensation of lightness after casting off the burden of sin is recalled in Camier's remark, following his disposal of an envelope of miscellaneous junk: "So, he said, I feel lighter now" (page 57). Camier is trying, as he says a little later, to disencumber himself of "life in short" (page 66), but this is something that the Beckettian Purgatory never quite manages.

The futility of their intentions is underscored near the end of the chapter when Camier decides to abandon their precious raincoat. Such a gesture, instead of completing the purgation, only lands them right back in Hell. Mercier says, "I should have liked to launch it" (page 65), and worries that, if they simply leave the garment on the ground, "some verminous brute" (page 66) will seize it. The words introduce a detailed interpolation from cantos 16 and 17 of the *Inferno*. The launching recalls Dante's throwing his belt into the infernal pit to signal the winged monster, Geyron, on whose back he and Virgil fly to the Eighth Circle or Malebolge. Camier's advice, "lente, lente, and circumspection, with deviations to right and left and sudden reversals of course" (page 67), follows Dante's description of the flight to the point of actually quoting two words from the Italian text (17:115). Mercier's remark "...if I look up I'll fall down" (page 67) simulates Dante's dizziness. The chapter ends, as does Dante's flight, with the reaching of a different part of hell: "Cheer up, said Camier, we are coming to the station of the damned, I can see the steeple" (page 67).

As soon as the couple enter the town (chapter 5), they go to Helen's, where the "two-fold light of lamp and leaden day" (page 71) that illumines their troilistic amusements points back to Dante's amazement in canto I at the brilliance of Paradise: "... and of a sudden it seemed there was added day to day, as if He that is able and had decked the sky with a second sun." When they leave at noon the next day, Camier remarks on "the pretty rainbow," a feeble copy of the beatific vision that fills the last canto of the *Paradiso*, in which Dante beholds the three circles of colored light, the first two "reflected by the other as rainbow by rainbow...." The chapter ends with the couple again trudging off, and this time their journey will take them right through Purgatory with no digressions. Soon after leaving Helen's, they see an old man reminding us of Cato at the base of the mountain of Purgatory. Then follows a series of significant details: the fog (page 78) that wraps Mercier derives from the spiritual fog that Cato directs Virgil to wash from Dante's face before commencing the ascent. The narrator plays then with the word *shadows*, echoing the third canto, in which Dante, not realizing that only his body, still alive, casts a shadow in Purgatory, marvels at Virgil's lack of one. Finally, the strange image of Mercier looking at his feet "as through shifting seaweed" makes sense when related to the swaying ocean reeds with which Virgil is instructed to clothe Dante in canto I. Here, in each case, the chapter neutralizes the tremendous energy these three details contain in the *Purgatorio*.

Chapter 6 continues the movement through Purgatory by shifting to Camier waiting alone in a pub for Mercier, whose sudden entrance alarms everyone. The narrator can only note the reaction; he cannot explain it. Yet his extended comparison of the clientele to a flock of sheep "startled by some dark threat" recalls Dante's description in canto 3 of the troop of souls' frightened response to his shadow: "As the sheep come forth from the fold by one and two and three and the rest stand timid...." The narrator is stressing the link between Mercier and Dante by making the otherwise "not easily affected" (page 81) pub clientele partake of the souls' unease. The couple then leave the pub, and their aimless steps take them faster and faster through Purgatory. Their dialogue leaves a trail of hints. First Mercier: "By the ingle, said Mercier, snug and warm, they drowse away. Books fall from hands, heads on chests, flames die down, embers expire, dream steals from its lair and towards its prey. But the watcher is on the watch, they wake and go to bed..." (page 86). Here we rush through a number of cantos. The cozy "ingle" points to the shoulder of rock in canto 4 upon which Belacqua, the man of sloth, sits. The creeping dream and alert watcher derive from canto 8, where at night, snakes, symbolizing the sinful dreams before which the sleeping soul is still vulnerable, weave down to the Valley of the Princes in Antepurgatory, and are driven away by two guardian angels.

The brutal encounter with the constable at the end of the chapter brings the couple for a second time to the Seventh Terrace, for their Purgatory is cyclic and futile. Mercier's question about the location of the whorehouse and his defense of "venery" (page 92) identify the theme of lust proper to the Seventh Terrace while Camier's "scream of pain" recalls Dante's torment in the flames. Finally, Mercier's cryptic remark that puzzles Camier, "The flowers are in the vase and the flock back in the fold" (page 94), compresses two passages from the *Purgatorio* that immediately follow the fire. The flowers come from Dante's dream of Leah (canto 27) "going through a meadow gathering flowers and singing...." The flock, coming from the same canto, we have already met in chapter 4. It revives Dante's comparison of himself to a goat in a flock and Virgil and Statius to his shepherds: "... as the herdsman who lodges in the open passes the night beside his quiet flock...." Mercier and Camier may triumph over the policeman, but the circular Purgatory in which they revolve will bring them back to the same flames by the end of the next chapter, and yet again in the final chapter.

Chapter 7 takes Mercier and Camier on another run through Purgatory. The chapter begins with a "descriptive passage" (page 98) whose mention of altitude, sea, mountain road, and a small valley for sleeping echoes the plan of Antepurgatory and the ascent beyond. Sure enough, at the close of the passage Mercier points to a wooden cross near the road, recalling the figured pavement of the First Terrace (canto 12) that commemorates the painful deaths of the proud. The narrator's identification of the grave as that of a nationalist is one of Beckett's little jabs agains his native Ireland. Mercier's admission, "I don't think I can go much further" (page 101), repeats the similar one Dante utters several times in the *Purgatorio*. The sudden approach of darkness, making everything "blurred and fuzzy, as if you were going blind before your very eyes" (page 101), duplicates the dense smoke that renders Dante temporarily "blind" on the Third Terrace, where anger is purged (canto 16). Mercier's offer to take Camier's hand repeats Virgil's order to Dante: "See that thou art not cut off from me."

The night the couple pass in some ruins derives from the Fourth Terrace, in which sloth is atoned for (canto 18) and which Virgil and

Dante enter near midnight. The Dantean purgation of sloth by its contrary, continuous movement, appears in the narrator's desire to close his story at this point ("Here would be the place to make an end," page 103), but he is unable to do so: "But there is still day, day after day, afterlife all life long, the dust of all that is dead and buried rising, eddying, settling, burying again" (page 103). The cycle that drives him on makes him propel the couple out of their shelter before dawn to resume the journey and so continue through Purgatory. Camier's wave to Mercier ("But even to the dead a man may wave," page 106) duplicates Virgil's salute to Statius on the Fifth Terrace (canto 21) while the giant tree at the crossroads derives from the one similarly placed in the next canto. Camier's hesitation and flight down one of the forks "as into a burning house" (page 107) repeats once again the wall of fire in Canto 27.

In chapter 8, the couple's encounter with Watt, hero of Beckett's preceding novel, shunts them back several cantos. Camier's failure to recognize him recalls Dante's inability to recognize Forese Donati on the Sixth Terrace (canto 22). Their talk of Camier's saintly mother revives the praise Forese heaps upon his widow, Nella. The couple and Watt walk toward the sunset into a pub, just as Dante, Virgil, and Statius in canto 25 walk toward the setting sun to enter the Seventh Terrace. Watt's mention of "the utilities I was stuck with at birth" (page 113) echoes Statius's account of conception and the creation of the soul in the same canto. Watt's agonized outburst, "Bugger life!" (page 114) and his subsequent torpor ("Watt seemed asleep," page 117) reenact a fourth and last time Dante's passage through fire. Despair of life is the sin from which neither Watt nor the couple can even be cleansed. Mercier's jest "Blessed be the dead that die" (page 115), mocks the admiring benediction Guido Guinicelli confers upon Dante just before the latter enters the fire: "Blessed art thou ... who, to die better, takest freight of experience from our bounds!" In Mercier's world there is no experience but the same experience of vacancy repeated. Finally, Camier's cryptic utterance, "the goat" (page 117), points back again to canto 27 and Dante's simile after passing through the flames.

The book ends with Mercier and Camier sitting on a bench at dusk by a river, trying to spot flowers in the distance. The rather disappointing results contrast sharply with Dante's vision of the river of light and the multifoliate rose (*Paradiso*, 30). Camier's parting gesture of "pouring over" (page 122) the river recalls Dante letting his "eyelids drink" of the celestial river in this canto. Mercier's concluding vision of darkness ("Alone he watched the sky go out, dark deepen to its full," page 122) brings us to a brutal inversion of the beatific vision at the end of the *Paradiso* and Dante's hymn to "Light Eternal." Such is the "apparent consummation"[6] Beckett's Purgatory allows.

The advent of Watt together with Mercier's recollection of Murphy ("I knew a poor man named Murphy," page 111) make it clear that Dante's world is not the only one against which the journey of Mercier and Camier is projected. There is also Beckett's, and of this the book contains much evidence. The pub owner, Mr. Gall, whose name is quietly changed to Mr. Gast, seems a suspiciously close relation to Mr. Gall, the piano tuner, in *Watt*. Mr. Graves also makes an appearance in both novels. The old man that Mercier spies "carrying under his arm what looked like a board folded in two" (page 76) recalls not only Cato, as we suggested, but the narrator of "The End," a story written about the same time as *Mercier and Camier*: "I had perfected my board. It now consisted of two boards hinged together, which enabled me, when my work was done, to fold it and carry it under my arm" (page 157).[7] The narrator who accompanies Mercier and Camier is the same one who propels Murphy, Watt, and all the rest on their way. Just before meeting Watt, Mercier voices his intimation of the narrator's presence: "Like the presence of a third party, said Mercier. Enveloping us. I have felt it from the start" (page 100). This journey and all the other ones are so many attempts to forge the narrator's subjectivity through a plurality of personae.

At this point the worlds of Dante and Beckett intersect, and the narrator resembles Belacqua.[8] Before entering Purgatory proper, Belacqua must spend a second lifetime in Antepurgatory dreaming over his first lifetime wasted slothfully on earth. The Beckettian narrator, on the other hand, with no hope of eventual bliss, must pass an interminable present dreaming of a past that was never his, reliving through the couple and other characters a subjectivity that he never had. As we have already seen from his first sentence, the narrator has no self beyond the characters he invents. He attempts through Mercier and Camier not only to gain his subjectivity, but at the same time to express the futility of his search for it. Otherwise the self he gains would not be his. In different words, the narrator does not want any old self; he wants just enough to let him utter his need for one, since that need defines who he is. He is caught in the endless cycle of trying to express his own lack of self, and his efforts can have no genuine conclusion. This repetition is the very essence of sloth, the deadly sin of Belacqua—reviewing the same tedium again and again, without the energy to seek something new and fresh, something with a purpose.

By sending the couple on their meaningless journey, the narrator gives them just enough subjectivity to know what they are missing: "Looking back on it, said Camier, we heard ourselves speaking of everything but ourselves" (page 119). The murmurs noted in the last sentence of the novel, while Mercier sits alone in the dark, are the clearest expression of what the narrator has been approaching all along. They enter most of Beckett's works and intrude, for example, when Molloy is stranded between remaining himself and becoming one of his characters, A or C: "Then the murmurs began again" (*Molloy*, page 13). Heard by a subject who never realizes that he is their author, the murmurs are a Beckettian convention signifying the inability of that subject to be himself. They are the sound of his own endless dissolution, and for that there is no purgation. The elaborate and repetitious journey of Mercier and Camier is simply an alternative expression of this experience of interminable dissolution in which the notions of beginning and end or definite self and world no longer apply.

NOTES

1. *Mercier and Camier*, trans. Samuel Beckett, 7. All quotations are from the 1974 Grove Press edition.
2. Samuel Beckett, "Henri Hayden, homme-peintre," *Documents* (22, 1955), reprinted in *Disjecta* (New York: Grove Press, Inc., 1984), p. 151.
3. References to *Molloy* and *The Unnamable* are to the1965 Grove Press edition of *Three Novels by Samuel Beckett*.
4. Dante, *The Divine Comedy*, 2: *Purgatorio*, trans. John D. Sinclair (New York: Galaxy, 1961). All other quotations from Dante are taken from Sinclair's translation of this work, the *Inferno*, and the *Paradiso*. Since Sinclair's prose translation cannot always be perfectly matched with the corresponding lines of the Italian text, I have restricted myself to citing directly the specific cantos under discussion. The reader will have no difficulty determining which book of the Divine Comedy is under discussion, if he remembers that the numbering of the circles belongs to Hell and that of terraces to Purgatory.

5. From this point of view, it is hard to agree with Raymond Federman's contention that Camier's rejection of Mr. Conaire symbolizes the rejection of fictional realism. See his *Journey to Chaos* (Berkeley: University of California Press, 1965), 164.

6. "Dante...Bruno. Vico...Joyce," in Samuel Beckett and Others, *Our Exagmination Round his Factification for Incamination of Work in Progress* (London: Faber, 1972), 22.

7. "The End," trans. Samuel Beckett, in *Stories and Texts for Nothing* (New York: Grove Press, 1967), 67. Ruby Cohn has also noted this connection. See her *Back to Beckett*, 66.

8. The connection with Belacqua is by no means an innovation in Beckett criticism. Much of the groundwork was done in Walter A. Strauss' "Dante's Belacqua and Beckett's Tramps," *Comparative Literature*, 2 (Summer 1959); 250-61. We can note here that Belacqua's bowed posture recurs throughout Beckett's fiction whenever the narrator incarnates himself. We meet it once in *Mercier and Camier* with Mr. Madden: "Mercier, whose back was to the engine, saw him as he stood there, dead to the passengers hastening towards the exit, bow down his head till it lay on his hands at rest on the knob of his stick" (page 40).

GEORGES BATAILLE

Molloy's Silence

What the author of *Molloy* is telling us is demonstrably the most out-rageous of all truths: that there is nothing but inordinate fantasy, that everything is fantastical, extravagant, unquestionably repellent, but also that what is repellent is splendid. To put it more precisely, *Molloy* is repellent splendor incarnate. At the same time there is no narrative more necessary nor more convincing; *Molloy* shows us not merely reality, but reality in a pure state: reality at its most indigent and inevitable, the fundamental reality, which is always in front of us but which fear always separates us from, which we refuse to see and which we always strive to avoid being engulfed by, which is consequently known to us only under the elusive form of anguish.

I myself would be Molloy if I took no notice of cold, or hunger, or the numberless discomforts that oppress a man given over to nature, to the earth and the rain, to the vast quicksand of the world. Yet even so I can testify that he is a figure both you and I have met; in the grip of a timorous craving, we have met him at street corners, an anonymous figure consisting of the ineluctable beauty of rags, apathy, and an indifferent gaze, the age-old swarm of ordure; at a loss, to be sure, as regards being, and, like us, a derelict as regards doing.

In that reality which is the true depth or residue of being, in those utter vagrants that we have often encountered but immediately given up for lost, there is something so universal, something so intrinsically blurred, that we can imagine nothing more anonymous. So much so that the very word *vagrant* that I have just used dishonors them, though *wretch*, in spite of possessing the ostensible advantage of being less precise, would dishonor them equally. What we see is so very much the basis of being (though the mere phrase *basis of being* scarcely begins to circumscribe it) that we identify it immediately: We cannot give it a name, it is elusive, crucial, slippery, it is *silence*. . . . What we in our impotence call *vagrant* or *wretch*, which in truth is *unnamable* (though even unnamable is a word calculated to enmesh us), is no less dumb than death. We know in advance the futility of even trying to speak of this ghost who haunts the streets in broad daylight. Even if we were to know the precise circumstances and conditions of his life (?) and wretchedness it would be of little help: This man—or rather, this being to whom, in employing such a word, we attribute being (a word he at once epitomizes and, as it were, exhausts)—and hence language itself, suffers from an irremediable deficiency. No speech we could have with him could be other than ghostly, a specter of speech. Speech would estrange us, restoring us to some semblance of humanity, or to something other than what holds us spellbound,[1] this wreckage in the street: the *absence* of a human dimension.

But there is no reason to suppose it was Samuel Beckett's intention to describe this "basis of being" or this "absence of a human dimension," as I have called them. It seems to me unlikely that he would see Molloy as the epitome of a vagrant (or whatever we elect to call this aspect of the unnamable), as Molière, for example, might have seen Harpagon the miser or the misanthrope Alceste.

I know almost nothing, I must say, of the intentions of the author of *Molloy*, and the little I know of the author does not add up to very much either. Born in Ireland in 1906, he was a friend of James Joyce and has to some extent remained his disciple. His friendships—or his contacts—would seem to have been with those who knew Joyce in France. Before the war he wrote a novel in English (*Murphy*), which he translated into French before the outbreak of war. Bilingual, he seems to have chosen to write in French since then. One should add, however, that the manifest influence of Joyce on Beckett will not serve to account for Beckett, even though both authors interest themselves in language as possibility, as ruleless game, creatures of impulse as they seem to be, in spite of their stubbornness, their concentration. And certainly this wide-eyed confidence, like that of a blind man, when it is applied to the creative convulsions of language precisely indicates the great gulf between Beckett and Molière.

But is there not also some point in regarding this separation, this absence of human feature, as what links the *formless* figure of Molloy to those of the miser and the misanthrope? Only an incontinent flux of language could accomplish the feat of expressing such an absence (an incontinence and a flux that are themselves equivalent to negation and also equivalent to the absolute absence of that "discourse" without which the figures of the miser and the misanthrope would lack their finished *form*, without which we could not conceive them). And reciprocally, it would seem as if the surrender of the writer, no longer content to reduce writing to the mere business of expressing his intentions, ready to respond to its intrinsic possibilities, albeit confusedly, in the deep currents that flash across the wavelike agitation of words, under the weight of a destiny to which he cannot help but succumb, leads of its own accord to the *formless* configuration of *absence*. Molloy (or the author) says,

> All I know is what the words know, and the dead things, and that makes a handsome little sum, with a beginning, a middle and an end as in the well-built phrase and the long sonata of the dead. And truly it little matters what I say, this, this or that or any other thing. Saying is inventing. Wrong, very rightly wrong. You invent nothing, you think you are inventing, you think you are escaping, and all you do is stammer out your lesson, the remnants of a pensum one day got by heart and long forgotten, life without tears, as it is wept.[2]

This is not the manifesto of a movement, but rather the expression, among other things, of someone determined to expose a façade, signing the death warrant of a literature made of language, preferring a speech disheveled by the wind and pitted with holes, but with the kind of authority that a ruin cannot help but have and that no mere movement can ever possess.

In this way, without his having willed it or, it may be, in order that he may will it or, better still, so that he may not have to will it, literature, no less fatally than death—under the aegis of an imperative necessity, each taking his own route to the summit, even when one is left no choice—leads inexorably to the unsoundable depths of *Molloy*. This remorseless advance may seem like the most arbitrary of caprices, but its gravity gives it the character of a fated outcome. Language calcifies that calculated world which our culture, our activities, our very edifices make manifest in the domain to which we attach significance, but it does so at the cost of reducing our culture, activities, and habitations to one and the same level. Free of these shackles it need no longer be a matter of empty mansions left to the gentle mercy of the wind and rain; the word is no longer the signifying factor, but rather the crippled form that death, in its indirect way, must inevitably take.

Only indirectly, however. Death itself must be the last silence, irreducible to imitations; and a literature congruent with silence can only be an atoll of incongruous words. Wherever it arrogates to itself the same meaning or the same direction as death, this silence cannot be more than parody. But this is by definition not true language; literature may indeed already have possessed the same properties as silence but recoiled from taking that last step which would be silence indeed. And by the same token Molloy, who is its incarnation, is not death pure and simple. For a dead thing evinces a profound apathy, or an indifference to all possibility, whereas Molloy's apathy recognizes its limitations only in death itself. Molloy's interminable wanderings in the forest (which, if only because he is on crutches, are equivalent to a kind of death) differ from death in one particular: habit or perseverance *in* death. They possess that tenacious negative quality which at once shapes life *and* renders it shapeless—much as literature finally *is* silence in its disavowal of rational language but nevertheless remains what it is, literature. The death of Molloy is in the life that obsesses him, the life one is unable to take one's leave of. "But did it make such a difference after all, as far as the pain was concerned," says Molloy (agitated though not as yet anguished by the aggravation of his infirmities):

whether my leg was free to rest or whether it had to work? I think not. For the suffering of the leg at rest was constant and monotonous. Whereas the leg condemned to the increase of pain inflicted by work knew the decrease of pain dispensed by work suspended, the space of an instant. But I am human, I fancy, and my progress suffered, from this state of affairs, and from the slow and painful progress it had always been, whatever may have been said to the contrary, was changed, saving your presence, to a veritable calvary, with no limit to its stations and no hope of crucifixion, though I say it myself, and no Simon, and reduced me to frequent halts. Yes, my progress reduced me to stopping more and more often, it was the only way to progress, to stop. And though it is no part of my tottering intentions to treat here in full, as they deserve, these brief moments of the immemorial expiation, I shall nevertheless deal with them briefly, out of the goodness of my heart, so that·my story, so clear till now, may not end in darkness, the darkness of these towering forests, these giant fronds, where I hobble, listen, fall, rise, listen and hobble on, wondering sometimes, need I say, if I shall ever see again the hated light, at least unloved, stretched palely between the last boles, and my mother, to settle with her, and if I would not do better, at least just as well, to hang myself from a bough, with a liane. For frankly light meant nothing to me now, and my mother could scarcely be waiting for me still, after so long. And my leg, my legs. But the thought of suicide had little hold on me, I don't know why, I thought I did, but now I see I don't.... (pages 78-79)

It goes without saying that so faithful an attachment to life cannot possibly strike one as reasonable. In fact, it is not even a matter of saying that death itself is the rationale for this probity. This would only make sense if death—or existence *in* death (or, for that matter, death in existence)—could have a meaning, whereas the only meaning death can have reposes in the fact that, in its way, its lack of meaning is itself a meaning, a parody of meaning perhaps but, ultimately, a quite finite meaning, which the world of significance obscures. The same blind goal also informs *Molloy*, which is sustained throughout by so much inexhaustible verve that one reads it no less impatiently than one would the typical novel of disturbing vicissitudes.

Lasciate ogni speranza voi ch'entrate....

Dante's line would make an apt epigraph for this quite remarkable book, whose uninterrupted (indeed unparagraphed) exclamation explores with persistent irony the extremities of indifference and wretchedness. Isolated passages offer only a faint and empty notion of this outrageous journey, a journey that, paradoxically, the narration organizes as if it were a huge epic, wrecked and at the same time sustained by its irresistible, inhuman impetus (it is hard indeed to take Molloy at his word when he says, "by human chance," since, at the low point of his unhappiness, he monstrously indulges an incongruity, obscenity, and moral indifference that all mankind, in anguish, and ill by very virtue of its scruples, rejects). Abandon all hope ... but only in a sense, for rather than actually quoting these mournful words, the violence of Beckett's irony imposes them upon us. Consider the moment when, having been molested and brutalized by the police, Molloy records precisely the point at which they cease to be applicable:

While still putting my best foot foremost [he says in his naïveté] I gave myself up to that golden moment, as if I had been someone else. It was the hour of rest, the forenoon's toil ended, the afternoon's to come. The wisest perhaps, lying in the squares or sitting on their doorsteps, were savouring its languid ending, forgetful of recent cares, indifferent to those at hand ... Was there one among them to put himself in my place, to feel how removed I was then from him I seemed to be, and in that remove what strain, as of hawsers about to snap? It's possible. Yes, I was straining towards those spurious deeps, their lying promise of gravity and peace, from all my old poisons I struggled towards them, safely bound. Under the blue sky, under the watchful gaze. Forgetful of my mother, set free from the act, merged in this alien hour, saying, Respite, respite. (page 21)

This might advantageously have been left implicit. I don't say the book would have been the better for it, but one or two passionate phrases strike one as out of place. The reader might have been satisfied with less; its very subtlety seems designed to bolster up the intrinsic debility of literature, which can only conquer those forces that threaten to defeat it by actions of brutal simplicity, and then only with difficulty. The passage is in some respects a failure, though it is the key passage in the book, a creative tension of this magnitude never failing to dissipate gloom. All hope, certainly, all rational designs, are here mired in indifference. But it almost goes without saying that, at this moment, within the confines of the present, there was nothing that would have served, nothing that could have served. Nothing, not even a feeling of tolerable inferiority, not even a limb linking Molloy to the expiation of his crimes—nothing, in short, that would not have demeaned him and humiliated him to some degree. The book proceeds calmly, obtusely, on the point of silence:

> But perhaps I was mistaken, perhaps I would have been better advised to stay in the forest, perhaps I could have stayed there, without remorse, without the painful impression of committing a fault, almost a sin. For I have greatly sinned, at all times, greatly sinned against my prompters. And if I cannot decently be proud of this I see no reason either to be sorry. But imperatives are a little different, and I have always been inclined to submit to them, I don't know why. For they never led me anywhere, but tore me from places where, if all was not well, all was no worse than anywhere else, and then went silent, leaving me stranded. So I knew my imperatives well, and yet I submitted to them. It had become a habit. It is true they nearly all bore on the same question, that of my relations with my mother, and on the importance of bringing as soon as possible some light to bear on these and even on the kind of light that should be brought to bear and the most effective means of doing so. Yes, these imperatives were quite explicit and even detailed until, having set me in motion at last, they began to falter, then went silent, leaving me there like a fool who neither knows where he is going nor why he is going there. (pages 86-87)

In the end such an expiation, to which Molloy is condemned, enjoins him to leave the forest at once. And though Molloy only ever dreams of losing the thread, the thread imposes itself upon him with such overwhelming force that nothing in his customary hebetude can make him disobedient to it. Unable any longer to walk, he proceeds to crawl like a slug:

> Flat on my belly, using my crutches like grapnels, I plunged them ahead of me into the undergrowth, and when I felt they had a hold, I pulled myself forward, with an effort of the wrists. For my wrists were still quite strong, fortunately, in spite of my decrepitude, though all swollen and racked by a kind of chronic arthritis probably. That then briefly is how I went about it. The advantage of this mode of locomotion compared to others, I mean those I have tried, is this, that when you want to rest you stop and rest, without further ado. For standing there is no rest, nor sitting either. And there are men who move about sitting, and even kneeling, hauling themselves to right and left, forward and backward, with the help of hooks. But he who moves in this way, crawling on his belly, like a reptile, no sooner comes to rest than he begins to rest, and even the very movement is a kind of rest, compared to other movements, I mean those that have worn me out. And in this way I moved onward in the forest, slowly, but with a certain regularity, and I covered my fifteen paces, day in, day out, without killing myself. And I even crawled on my back, plunging my crutches blindly behind me into the thickets, and with the black boughs for sky to my closing eyes. I was on my way to mother. And from time to time I said, Mother, to encourage me I suppose. I kept losing my hat, the lace had broken long ago, until in a fit of temper I banged it down on my skull with such violence that I couldn't get it off again. And if I had met any lady friends I would have been powerless to salute them correctly. (pages 89-90)

But suppose that this extravagant grotesquerie is of no account, these massive phantasmagorias wearying, and leave us utterly indifferent.

It's quite possible to react like that at first. But one's objections to the absolute absence of what ordinarily constitutes interest are overruled by the passion and power with which the author convinces us to the contrary. The frantic momentum of collapse that animates this book, the very antagonism the reader feels for the author, is such that not for a moment is the reader left free to withdraw into indifference. Could this momentum have been achieved without a powerful motive, and an equally overwhelming conviction, informing its inception?

As I suggested, we have no right to suppose that the writer began with an articulated plan. The kind of nativity I have cast for Molloy is not a matter of careful composition but rather the only one that would be appropriate to the elusive reality I have been attempting to sketch: a reality of mythical dimensions—monstrous, a product of the sleep of reason. Two analogical truths (death and the absence of humanity) can take shape in us only under the aspect of myth, which is the living specter of death. So much absence of reality cannot be conveyed in the clear distinctions of normal discourse, but there can be no doubt that death and inhumanity, both equally lacking in being, are not a matter of indifference in the life we lead, since they are its limit cases, its backcloth and its ultimate reality. Death is not merely a hidden door at which anguish awaits us; the void in which even wretchedness must come to grief, while it absorbs us totally and discomposes us, is nothing other than that death which, as the object of our anxiety, bears the positive index of the whole of humanity. In the same way this grotesque figure balanced miserably on his crutches represents the truth of our malady, a malady that follows us no less faithfully than our shadow; it is our very dread of such a figure that conditions our human gestures, our well-groomed attitudes, and our crystal-clear phrases. By the same token this figure is in some sense the horizon into which the human show must ultimately fade, if only to shroud itself: oblivion, powerlessness.... It is not so much a matter of misfortune yielding feebly to wretchedness; Beckett is concerned with that indifference in which man forgets his own name, forgets he is man even, being perfectly indifferent to his most repugnant misery. "Yes, there were times when I forgot not only who I was, but that I was, forgot to be" (page 49): This is how the mind, or absence of mind, in Molloy is laid bare. And there is unquestionably some sleight-of-hand here. Molloy, or rather the author, *writes*: and what he writes about is his intention of writing in such a way as to shrug off any responsibility for what he has written. Never mind that he should tell us, "I have always behaved like a pig." There is not a single human taboo that has not here been engulfed by an indifference that would like to be definitive but cannot be; and how *could* one be other than indifferent when doomed to so imperfect an indifference? If the author reneges upon his decision to behave "like a pig" and foregrounds his mendacity by ending his book

> Then I went back into the house and wrote, It is midnight. The rain is beating on the windows. It was not midnight. It was not raining. (page 176)

it is because this is not Molloy—Molloy in all truth commits himself to nothing because he writes nothing.

The Page

An author who writes like this, gnawed by indifference to what he is writing, might easily pass for a buffoon were it not for the fact that the reader is himself embroiled in comparable buffooneries, every bit as casuistical, even when they originate in the innocence of ingenuousness. The naked truth of our human comedy is not so readily accomplished. Indeed, before it can occur, we must not only renounce all our affectations but completely obliterate them and, as a direct consequence, know nothing, like the impotent cretin Molloy: "not knowing what I was going to do, until it was done." We can only undertake for ourselves the quest for Molloy, like Moran in the second part of the book. Moran (clearly in some respects a patent fiction), a man of regular habits but with the whims of a self-indulgent widower, is something of a desperate character; he is the protagonist of a second part in which, Molloy having disappeared, he is sent out to look for him. As if the prostrated figure of the first part had not sufficiently epitomized the silence of this world, the futile quest for him on the part of Moran reads like a conditioned response to the necessity of giving up that measureless universe of absence in which Molloy is perfectly irrecoverable as a presence. But by going in quest of an inaccessible Molloy, Moran—gradually stripped bare, and more and more infirm—is little by little and in his turn reduced to the same grotesque mode of locomotion as Molloy in the forest.

This is the way in which literature cannot help but corrode existence and the world, reducing to nothing (though this nothing is awful) the strategies whereby we proceed confidently from one outcome to another and from one achievement to another. It does not exhaust the possibilities of literature. And certainly Beckett's employment of a language more expressive than utilitarian opens up, on the contrary, a domain of delight, bravado, and irrational audacity. But the two domains—of terror and pleasure—are more contiguous with one another than we might have supposed. Would the consolations of poetry be comprehensible to one who shunned terror, and could authentic despair be in any way different from that "golden moment" which Molloy experiences in the arms of the law?

Translated by John Pilling

NOTES

1. I remember having had a long talk with a tramp when I was very young. It occupied most of a night I spent waiting for a train in a small railway junction. He, of course, was not waiting for a train; he had simply sought the shelter of the waiting room, and towards morning he left me to prepare his coffee over his campfire. He was not exactly the figure I am speaking of, being quite a chatterer, more so than even me. He seemed satisfied with his lot and, as an old man, took pleasure in expressing his satisfaction to the boy of fifteen or twenty I then was. I listened in astonishment. Yet the memory I have of him, together with the incredible dread it still provokes, never fails to inspire in me the silence of a brute beast. (Meeting him so distressed me that a little later I began to write a novel in which a man who met him in the country killed him, perhaps primarily in the hope of acquiring the same animality as his victim.)

   On another occasion, driving through a forest with friends, we came upon a man by the side of the road, stretched out on the grass in broad daylight, drenched by a downpour. He was not asleep; he may have been ill; he did not reply to our questions. We indicated our willingness to take him to a hospital, but so far as I recall he made no reply whatsoever or, if he did take the trouble to respond, it was by way of a massive snarl of repudiation.

2. Samuel Beckett, *Molloy*, in *Three Novels by Samuel Beckett* (New York: Grove Press, 1965), 31–32. References in the text are to this edition.

MAURICE BLANCHOT

Where Now?
Who Now?

Who is doing the talking in Samuel Beckett's novels, who is this tireless "I" constantly repeating what seems to be always the same thing? What is he trying to say? What is the author looking for—who must be somewhere in the books? What are we looking for—who read them? Or is he merely going around in circles, obscurely revolving, carried along by the momentum of a wandering voice, lacking not so much sense as center, producing an utterance without proper beginning or end, yet greedy, exacting, a language that will never stop, that finds it intolerable to stop, for then would come the moment of the terrible discovery: When the talking stops, there is still talking; when the language pauses, it perseveres; there is no silence, for within that voice the silence eternally speaks.

An experiment without results, yet continuing with increasing purity from book to book by rejecting the very resources, meager as they are, that might permit it to continue.

It is this treadmill movement that strikes us first. This is not someone writing for beauty's sake (honorable though that pleasure may be), not someone driven by the noble compulsion many feel entitled to call inspiration (expressing what is new and important out of duty or desire to steal a march on the unknown). Well, why *is* he writing then? Because he is trying to escape the treadmill by convincing himself that he is still its master, that, at the moment he raises his voice, he might stop talking. But is he talking? What is this void that becomes the voice of the man disappearing into it? Where has he fallen? "Where now? Who now? When now?"[1]

He is struggling—that is apparent; sometimes he struggles secretly, as if he were concealing something from us, and from himself too, cunningly at first, then with that deeper cunning which reveals its own hand. The first stratagem is to interpose between himself and language certain masks, certain faces; *Molloy* is a book in which characters still appear, where what is said attempts to assume the reassuring form of a story, and of course, it is not a successful story, not only because of what it has to tell, which is infinitely wretched, but because it does not succeed in telling it, because it will not and cannot tell it. We are convinced that this wanderer who already lacks the means to wander (but at least he still has legs, though they function badly—he even has a bicycle), who eternally circles around a goal that is obscure, concealed, avowed, concealed again, a goal that has something to do with his dead mother who is still dying, something that cannot be grasped, something that, precisely because he has achieved it the moment the book begins ("I am in my mother's room. It's I who live there now."),² obliges him to wander ceaselessly around it, in the empty strangeness of what is hidden and disinclined to be revealed—we are convinced that this vagabond is subject to a still deeper error and that his halting, jerky movements occur in a space that is the space of impersonal obsession, the obsession that eternally leads him on; but no matter how ragged our sense of him, Molloy nevertheless does not relinquish himself, remains a name, a site within bounds that guard against a more disturbing danger. There is certainly a troublesome principle of disintegration in the story of *Molloy*, a principle not confined to the instability of the wanderer, but further requiring that Molloy be mirrored, doubled, that he become *another*, the detective Moran, who pursues Molloy without ever catching him and who in that pursuit sets out (he too) on the path of endless error, a path such that anyone who takes it cannot remain himself, but slowly falls to pieces. Molloy, without knowing it, becomes Moran, that is, becomes an entirely different character, a metamorphosis that undermines the security of the narrative element and simultaneously introduces an allegorical sense, perhaps a disappointing one, for we do not feel it is adequate to the depths concealed here.

Malone Dies evidently goes further still: here the *vagabond* is nothing more than a *moribund*, and the space accessible to him no longer offers the resources of a city with its thousand streets, nor the open air with its horizon of forests and sea that *Molloy* still conceded us; it is nothing more than the room, the bed, the stick with which the dying man pulls things toward him and pushes them away, thereby enlarging the circle of his immobility, and above all the pencil that further enlarges it into the infinite space of words and stories. Malone, like Molloy, is a name and a face, and also a series of narratives, but these narratives are not self-sufficient, are not told to win the reader's belief; on the contrary, their artifice is immediately exposed—the stories are *invented*. Malone tells himself: "This time I know where I am going. . . . It is a game, I am going to play. . . . I think I shall be able to tell myself four stories, each one on a different theme."[3] With what purpose? To fill the void into which Malone feels he is falling; to silence that empty time (which will become the infinite time of death), and the only way to silence it is to say something at any cost, to tell a story. Hence the narrative element is nothing more than a means of public fraud and constitutes a grating compromise that overbalances the book, a conflict of artifices that spoils the experiment, for the stories remain stories to an excessive degree: Their brilliance, their skillful irony, everything that gives them form and interest also detaches them from Malone, the dying man, detaches them from the time of his death in order to reinstate the customary narrative time in which we do not believe and which, here, means nothing to us, for we are expecting something much more important.

It is true that in *The Unnamable* the stories are still trying to survive: The moribund Malone had a bed, a room—Mahood is only a human scrap kept in a jar festooned with Chinese lanterns; and there is also Worm, the unborn, whose existence is nothing but the oppression of his impotence to exist. Several other familiar faces pass, phantoms without substance, empty images mechanically revolving around an empty center occupied by a nameless "I." But now everything has changed, and the experiment, resumed from book to book, achieves its real profundity. There is no longer any question of characters under the reassuring protection of a personal name, no longer any question of a narrative, even in the formless present of an interior monologue; what was narrative has become conflict, what assumed a face, even a face in fragments, is now discountenanced. Who is doing the talking here? Who is this "I" condemned to speak without respite, the being who says: "I am obliged to speak. I shall never be silent. Never"? By a reassuring convention, we answer: It is Samuel Beckett. Thereby we seem to draw closer to what is of concern in a situation that is not fictional, that refers to the real torment of a real existence. The word *experiment* is another name for what has actually been experienced—

and here too we try to recover the security of a name, to situate the book's "content" at the stable level of a person, at a personal level, where everything that happens happens with the guarantee of a consciousness, in a world that spares us the worst degradation, that of losing the power to say, "I." But *The Unnamable* is precisely an experiment conducted, an experience lived under the threat of the impersonal, the approach of a neutral voice that is raised of its own accord, that penetrates the man who hears it, that is without intimacy, that excludes all intimacy, that cannot be made to stop, that is the incessant, *the interminable*.

Who is doing the talking here then? We might try to say it was the "author" if this name did not evoke capacity and control, but in any case the man who writes is already no longer Samuel Beckett but the necessity that has displaced him, dispossessed and dis-seized him, which has surrendered him to whatever is outside himself, which has made him a nameless being. The Unnamable, a being without being, who can neither live nor die, neither begin nor leave off, the empty site in which an empty voice is raised without effect, masked for better or worse by a porous and agonizing "I."

It is this metamorphosis that betrays its symptoms here, and it is deep within its process that a verbal survival, an obscure, tenacious relic persists in its immobile vagabondage, continues to struggle with a perseverance that does not even signify a form of power, merely the curse of not being able to stop talking.

Perhaps there is something admirable about a book that deliberately deprives itself of all resources, that accepts starting at the very point from which there can be no continuation, yet obstinately proceeds without sophistry and without subterfuge for 179 pages, exhibiting the same jerky movement, the same tireless, stationary tread. But this is still the point of view of the *external* reader, contemplating what he regards as only a tour de force. There is nothing admirable in inescapable torment when you are its victim, nothing admirable in being condemned to a treadmill that not even death can free you from, for in order to get on that treadmill in the first place, you must already have abandoned life. Esthetic sentiments are not called for here. Perhaps we are not dealing with a book at all, but with something more than a book: Perhaps we are approaching that movement from which all books derive, that point of origin where, doubtless, the work is lost, the point that always ruins the work, the point of perpetual unworkableness with which the work must maintain an increasingly *initial* relation or risk becoming nothing at all. One might say that the Unnamable is condemned to exhausting the infinite.

> I have nothing to do, that is to say, nothing in particular. I have to speak, whatever that means. Having nothing to say, no words but the words of others, I have to speak. No one compels me to, there is no one, it's an accident, a fact. Nothing can ever exempt me from it, there is nothing, nothing to discover, nothing to recover, nothing that can lessen what remains to say, I have the ocean to drink, so there is the ocean then.[4]

How has this come about? In his essay on Genet, Sartre shows how literature, in expressing the profound *mal* whose constraint Genet first endured and then transformed into an exaction of his own, gradually afforded him the power to raise himself from passivity to action, from the formless to a face, and even from a blurred poetry to a sumptuous and determined prose.

> *Notre-Dame des Fleurs*, without the author's suspecting it, is the journal of a cure, a conversion: in it Genet disintoxicates himself of himself, and turns toward others; this book makes the process real: born of a nightmare, an organic product, a condensation of dreams, the epic poem of masturbation, it opens line by line a stumbling passage from death to life, from dream to waking, from madness to health.

This is a form of experience we might call classical, its traditional formulation given in Goethe's phrase *poetry is deliverance. Les Chants de Maldoror* serves as an illustration: By the power of metamorphoses, by the passion of images, by the recurrence of ever more obsessive themes, rising gradually from the night's darkness and by means of the night itself, a new being seeks the reality of his own face in the light of day; thus Lautréamont is born. But it would be a mistake to think that literature, when it seems to lead us to daylight, leads us to the tranquil enjoyment of rationality, to a life of proportions observed, regulated, and viable. The passion of the common day, which in Lautréamont already ascends to the dangerous exaltation of banality, the passion of common speech, which destroys itself by becoming the ironic affirmation of the cliché and the pastiche, also impels him to self-destruction in the limitless daylight in which an exemplary destiny puts his death beyond our grasp.

Similarly, in Genet's case, Sartre has shown that if literature seems to provide a way out for the man, to facilitate the success of his mastery, it also—just when everything is going nicely—suddenly reveals the absence of a way out suitable for *him,* or even exposes the absolute failure of his success and dissolves into the insignificance of an academic career.

At the time of *Notre-Dame*, the poem was the way-out. But today: conscious, rational, without immediate apprehension for the future, in short, without horror, why should Genet write? To become a man of letters? Just what he does not want to be. We realize that an author whose work results from so deep a need, whose style is a weapon forged with so precise an intention, whose every image, every argument so manifestly resumes his entire life, cannot suddenly begin talking about something else. Loser takes all: by winning the writer's status, Genet loses at once the need, the desire, the opportunity, and the means of writing.

The fact remains that there is a classical manner of describing the literary experience: We see the writer happily delivering himself of his darker self, which becomes, almost miraculously, the very felicity and clarity of the work in which it is expressed and in which the writer finds a refuge and still better a fulfillment of his solitude in a free communication with other men. This is what the last incarnation of Socrates, who was Freud, tried to persuade us of by insisting on the virtues of sublimation and by his continuing confidence—so moving, so innocent, so naïve—in the powers of consciousness and of expression. But matters are not so simple, and we must recognize another level of experience, one where we see Michelangelo in torment, Goya possessed, the gay and lucid Nerval hanging from a streetlamp, Hölderlin dead to the rational possession of himself because he yielded to the excessive movement of the poetic transformation. How does this happen?

We can here suggest only two fields for consideration: the first, that for the man producing it the work is not a site where he resides, peaceful and protected, sheltered from life's difficulties; perhaps he thinks himself, as a matter of fact, protected from the world, but this is only in order to be exposed to a much greater, much more ominous danger, since it finds him without arms against it: the very danger that comes to him from outside, from the fact that he stays outside himself. And against this danger he must not defend himself; on the contrary he must surrender to it, give himself up to it. The work demands that the man producing it sacrifice himself for the work, become other, not *an*other, not merely "the writer" with his duties, his satisfactions, and his interests, but *no one*, the empty, actuated site where the summons of the work reverberates. It is here that the experience of the work is also, for the man who writes it, an ordeal in which his integrity is at stake, in which he enters a world of metamorphoses that has never yet been directly approached.

Clemens Brentano, in his novel *Godwi*, speaks feelingly of the "self-annihilation" effected by the work. And perhaps we are concerned here with a more radical change that does not consist of a new disposition of soul and spirit, that does not content itself with dividing me from my ego, that is not even related to the particular contents of this or that book, but to the fundamental exaction of the work.

But why does the work require this transformation? We might answer: because it cannot find its point of departure in the familiar, the habitual, the commodity of an available reality, because it requires the unaccustomed, what has never been thought, seen, or heard of before; but this answer, although true, seems to be somewhat beside the point, to miss what is essential. We might answer again: because it deprives the writer living in a world where he has appropriated expedients, relied on the continuity of past and future achievements, participated willy-nilly in the truth of a common intention, of that world, offering him instead the space of the imagination as the locus of his action; and in fact *The Unnamable* evokes something of this malaise of a man fallen out of the world, eternally hovering between being and nothingness, henceforth as incapable of dying as of being born, haunted by his creatures, meaningless ghosts he no longer believes in.

Nevertheless, this is still not the right answer. We will find it rather in the movement which, as the work tries to reach its conclusion, bears it toward that point where it is at grips with impossibility, where the flux and reflux of the eternal recommencement draws it on: excess of impotence, sterile prolixity, a spring, a source that somehow must be dried up in order to become a *resource*. Here the voice does not speak, it *is*; in itself nothing begins, nothing is said, but it is always new and always beginning again. The writer is the man who has heard this voice, who desires to make himself its mediator, to impose silence upon it by pronouncing it. He is the man who has surrendered himself to the incessant, who has heard it as a voice, who has entered into an understanding with it, has fulfilled its requirements, has lost himself

147

in it and, nevertheless, for having properly sustained it, has brought it within his grasp, has uttered it by firmly referring it to this limit, has mastered it by measuring it.

It is this approach to *origin* that makes the experience of the work still more dangerous, dangerous for the man who bears it, dangerous for the work itself. But it is also this approach that assures the experiment its authenticity, that alone makes of art an essential research, and it is by having rendered this approach evident in the nakedest, most abrupt manner that *The Unnamable* has more importance for literature than most "successful" works in its canon. Try listening to "this voice that speaks, knowing that it lies, indifferent to what it says, too old perhaps and too humiliated ever to be able to say at last the words that might make it stop." And try descending into that neutral region where the self surrenders in order to speak, henceforth subject to words, fallen into the absence of time where it must die an endless death:

> ... the words are everywhere, inside me, outside me, well well, a minute ago I had no thickness, I hear them, no need to hear them, no need of a head, impossible to stop them, impossible to stop, I'm in words, made of words, others' words, what others, the place too, the air, the walls, the floor, the ceiling, all words, the whole world is here with me, I'm the air, the walls, the walled-in one, everything yields, opens, ebbs, flows, like flakes, I'm all these flakes, meeting, mingling, falling asunder, wherever I go I find me, leave me, go toward me, come from me, nothing ever but me, a particle of me, retrieved, lost, gone astray, I'm all these words, all these strangers, this dust of words, with no ground for their settling, no sky for their dispersing, coming together to say, fleeing one another to say, that I am they, all of them, those that merge, those that part, those that never meet, and nothing else, yes something else, that I'm quite different, a quite different thing, a wordless thing in an empty place, a hard shut dry cold black place where nothing stirs, nothing speaks, and that I listen, and that I seek, like a caged beast born of caged beasts born of caged beasts...

Translated by Richard Howard

NOTES

1. Samuel Beckett, *The Unnamable*, in *Three Novels by Samuel Beckett* (New York: Grove Press, 1965), 291.
2. Beckett, *Molloy*, in ibid., 7.
3. Beckett, *Malone Dies*, in ibid., 180-81.
4. Beckett, *The Unnamable*, 314.

J. E. DEARLOVE

The Voice and Its Words:
"How It Is"

In discussing Beckett's works it is frequently useful to divide his career into three segments: the early period of exploration in English extending from pieces like "Assumption" and "A Case in a Thousand" to *Watt* (up to 1944), the middle period of French prose and the narrator-narrated beginning with *Mercier and Camier* and including *How It Is* (1946-60), and the later period of the enigmatic short pieces from "Imagination Dead Imagine" through the present (1965-   ). Useful as it otherwise may be, however, a tripartite division of the Beckettian canon obscures an important shift in the conceptual framework of Beckett's pieces. *How It Is* does not present simply a continuation of the techniques and themes developed in the trilogy. Instead the book marks a turning point in Samuel Beckett's career from an exploration of the limitations of the human mind and an emphasis upon definitions of the self, to an identification of the self with the voice and an acceptance, if not a celebration, of the life of the imagination. Indeed, *How It Is* enables Beckett to surmount the attitude of disintegration *L'Innommable* once caused in him[1] by directing attention not to the divorce of the mind from the external world, but rather to the internal worlds the mind creates. Chaos is accommodated not by the creation of structures appropriate for an uncertain and fluid universe, but rather by the celebration of the artificiality of structure itself. *How It Is* reduces everything to a voice speaking in the eternal present creating its own universe. This interior focus in turn makes possible the highly self-conscious and arbitrary constructions of Beckett's recent fictions.

I

The works written prior to *How It Is* are concerned with the problems of a mind-body dualism. From Belacqua scoffing "at the idea of

150

a sequitur from his body to his mind,"[2] to the Unnamable trying to say who he is even though there are no names or pronouns for him (page 404), we see Beckett's characters trying to bridge the gap between the mind, which Murphy describes as a "large hollow sphere, hermetically closed to the universe without" (page 107) and what Neary refers to as "the big blooming buzzing confusion" (page 4) of the world. The problem for Beckett's characters, as for the post-Cartesian philosophers to whom Beckett frequently alludes, is that action, speech, identity, and thought become problematic once the mind is isolated from the material world. Ultimately, Murphy's quest to become immersed in the dark flux of the mind's third zone, "where he could love himself" (page 7), is a self-destructive quest that can be accomplished only by annihilating that physical part of himself "which he hated" (page 8).

Watt's efforts to superimpose the rational constructions of his mind upon the irrational world he encounters meet with no greater success. No matter how many hypotheses he formulates, nor how many generations of "needy local men" he traces to guarantee the feeding of "two famished dogs" (pages 91-117), Watt can never "penetrate the forces at play ... or even perceive the forms they upheaved, or obtain the least useful information concerning himself, or Mr. Knott" (page 117). Knott cannot be known: the rational mind, incapable of knowing the irrational, can only combine and permute its own limited elements. Those limitations are explored further in the triology as the first person narrator proffers a consciousness experiencing itself. From Molloy's inability to recall his name (page 22) and Moran's contradiction of his own report (page 176), to Malone's inventory of stories and possessions (pages 181ff.), to the Unnamable's continuing effort to say the words that will put an end to words (page 369), we see Beckett's successive narrators struggling to define themselves in relation to the external world and to the words they speak. Even after the Unnamable renounces foreign objects and "vice-existers" as terms in his self-definition, he is still forced to rely on a language learned from others (page 314). The result is an infinitely repeating pattern in which some larger category is always necessary to encompass the speaker and his definition, to contain the perceiving mind and its self-perceptions.[3] While Beckett's early pieces portray a mind-body dichotomy, his works of the narrator-narrated investigate the restrictions that dichotomy imposes upon the mind.

The pieces written after *How It Is*, on the other hand, turn from an emphasis upon the mind's limitations to considerations of its imaginative constructions. References to, and comparisons with, an unreachable external reality are replaced by detailed descriptions of objects that exist only in the inner world of the mind's creations. Portrayals of a mind creating stories are omitted in favor of the deliquescent creations themselves. Moreover, these creations often pay tribute to the imagination. "Imagination Dead Imagine" is based on a paradox: Imagination is necessary to envision a state in which imagination is dead. Without imagination there is no motion, no emotion, no voice, no thought, "no trace anywhere of life" (page 63). The identification of color, sound, and even life with imagination is continued in "Ping," which catalogs what is finally over. Significantly, the last elements in this catalog to be over are not the "heart breath" nor even the blue eyes, but the murmurs that are too indistinct to be quoted directly, too fleeting to be recorded. They belong to the world of the imagined, the "never seen," "invisible," "no trace."

Yet it is precisely in these nonmaterial murmurs and their postulations of what is not that vitality persists. Like existence, the piece itself is over only after the final murmur has ended and the last *ping* has faded away. Just as the imaginative murmurs provide variety and vitality in "Ping," so too those sentences associated with imaginary constructions provide mystery and meaning in "Lessness."[4] Four of the six groups of sentences Beckett wrote in composing *Lessness* are relatively simple: They describe setting and body—the known or observable aspects of the present situation. The last groups of sentences, however, deal, not with given data, but with the imaginative and mental, postulating things that are not except in the mind, in dreams and figments and illusions. The mere mention of these illusions enriches the entire work by relieving the gray endlessness. By presenting figments and impossible futures, Beckett forces us to see what does not and cannot exist in the "true refuge" except through the imagination.

Even if they do not describe the self-contained and fanciful constructions of "Imagination Dead Imagine," "Ping," and "Lessness," Beckett's other later works embrace the imagination without lamenting its dissociation from material reality. For example, unlike the trilogy, *Fizzles* is not obsessed either with defining the narrator or with labeling, controlling, and hence divorcing him from his stories. Indeed, the narrator's identity and location are often difficult to determine. Sharp divisions between mind and world are blurred. The Unnamable's urgency to say his pensum and to find the correct words is gone. Instead, the words as stated are accepted as adequate, even if incomplete, depictions of the way it is. Everything "needed to be known" is known, imagined, and said; there is nothing beyond the world of the fiction: "Closed place. All needed to be known for say is known. There is nothing but what is said. Beyond what is said there is nothing. What goes on in the arena is not said. Did it need to be known it would be. No interest. Not for imagining" (page 37). The sense of self-sufficiency suggested in *Fizzles* is central to "Enough." As the title implies, the work is concerned with the moderate and the balanced. Even in a minimal world there can be too much—too much of silence, too much of speech, too much remembered, too much forgotten: "All that goes before forget. Too much at a time is too much. . . . Too much silence is too much" (page 53). The piece deals with calm acceptance and the "eternally mild" (page 59). Instead of the commitment to an unending pursuit of futile quests saying, "You must go on, I can't go on, I'll go on" (*The Unnamable*, page 414); instead of the rebellious claim that "to be an artist is to fail, as no other dare fail";[5] instead of these, "Enough" hesitantly and tentatively proffers the reconciliation, calm acceptance, and perhaps even the affirmation of a narrator who feels it is enough to have spoken at all, of a narrator who can accept the inevitable failure of his quest saying, "Stony ground but not entirely. Given three or four lives I might have accomplished something" (page 54). The piece, though a reduced and even minimal literature, is itself enough. When chaos cannot be captured, it is enough to have created an image that fleetingly gestures toward the void. When imagination is divorced from material reality, it is enough to have written words that wipe out everything but a sense of unity with the passing image (page 60).

2

The transition from rebellious questing to tentative acceptance, from examination of the mind's limitations to exploration of its creations, from external definitions of the self to internal identifications with the imagination, is first expressed in *How It Is*.[6] By directing the narrator's attention to the self-creating powers of the voice and by eliminating external referents and efforts to locate oneself in opposition to an exterior order, Beckett frees both the voice and his fiction to consider earlier themes and subjects within a new framework. The more the voice must rely on its own words for both its existence and the wherewithal to endure, the more ambiguous its postulations become. Where everything is produced by and contained within a speaking voice, nothing need be ultimately affirmed or denied. *How It Is* is bound only by self-imposed limitations. Unencumbered by the problem of sequiturs between body and mind, the voice creates its own space, time, identity, and even style.

The shift in Beckett's framework begins with the reduction of everything to a voice speaking in an eternal present. Whereas *Molloy, Malone Dies*, and even *The Unnamable* contains vestigial characters with bits and scraps of a plot still clinging to them, *How It Is* reduces even those fragmentary characters and plots until there remain only the archetypal elements of the panting, the murmur, the dark, and the mud. Of these elements, only the murmur in the mud has the capacity to differentiate, to individuate, to create. This imaginative murmur, then, is the source and substance of the universe—of the Pims and Boms, the sacks and tins, the memories and images. Only through our reading of the voice's whey of words does the narrator assume an identity or existence. Indeed, as the initial and final "stanzas" reveal, the book itself is literally a quotation of the voice's narration. Instead of a three-part division of eternity, we have the perpetual present formulation of a voice creating itself in the here and now. When the voice ceases, so does *How It Is*, and our journey through its bizarre world ends.

The structure of *How It Is* intimates the overriding importance of our voice for that work. The presence or absence of the voice distinguishes the journey of part one from the abandon of part three (page 21). Likewise, the couple of part two is subdivided by the momentous discovery that Pim "can speak then that's the main thing" (page 56). Repeatedly the narrator anticipates the return of his voice (for example, page 60). If it is not with relief, at least it is without objection that he finds this voice "back at last in my mouth" (page 106). Like Watt seeking to make a pillow of words, the narrator seeks solace in saying something, anything, to himself (page 43). Just as the typography of *How It Is* consists of print and spaces, so too the universe consists of words and silences (page 13). The narrator no longer searches for a "language meet for here" (page 17); yet only through that language can he live (page 129).

Although the importance of the voice is emphasized by the structure, its nature remains ambivalent: "This voice is truly changeable" (page 15). Indeed, the voice freely contradicts and revises itself. The narrator asks a question, then denies his capability of asking such a question (pages 92-93); he describes motions he makes to hear Pim's watch, then concludes "all that beyond my strength" (page 58); he posits a word, then retracts it as "too strong" (page 55, 115). Uncertainty increases as the voice points out its own faulty transmission. Not only do we depend on some less than assuring witness, but this witness himself depends on a less than definitive narration. Like Sam in *Watt*, the witness is trying to transcribe a story of which he hears only "bits and scraps" (page 15) and "little blurts midget grammar" (page 81) that come too fast and end too soon (page 81). In spite of its ambiguity and uncertainty, however, the voice is consistent in its modes of operation. It remains loyal to the self-imposed limitations of the way the story is told. Reality is not really an issue. Phrases such as "It's one or the other" (page 11), "I remember . . . or I forget" (page 8), and "It's not said or I don't hear" (page 18) become refrains. Nothing, not even an ending, need be established irrevocably. The narrator may be engulfed in the mud, may be part of an unending cyclical progression, may be shat into the light. He may be the only figure who exists, or may be diffused into the great collapse of a million Pims and Boms. Unlike the trilogy characters, he may even die: "I am not dead to inexistence not irretrievably" (page 69). The narrator's only self-imposed rule of order for dealing with permutations is that "justice" be maintained. This justice is itself nothing more than the preservation of symmetry. Every Bom must be a Pim for equivalent periods of time (page 125). Every four yards to the north must be balanced by four yards to the south (page 47). As in *The Lost Ones* and "Imagination Dead Imagine," the narrator uses his mathematics to create verbal diagrams (page 47). Ironically, in an uncertain world of undifferentiated mud, we know precisely how the narrator crawls—if he really does crawl. Likewise, the narrator's "dear figures" yield the percentage of words lost (if they are lost) (page 95), and enable a contrast between Pim's "iso" buttocks (if Pim exists) and the narrator's own "ratio [of] four to one" (page 37). The voice is thus consistently operating according to the abstract postulations of systems such as "mathematics astronomy and even physics" (page 41), in an inconsistent world lacking the "history and geography" that gave time and place to mimetic novels.

The ambivalence of the voice is due not only to its uncertainty about the universe it postulates, but also to its ambiguous source. Although the narrator purports to be murmuring in the mud, at the same time he attributes the voice to some external person or thing that he is at best only quoting: "I say it as I hear it" (page 7). As in *The Unnamable* there is a sense that the words are part of some pensum taught by and belonging to a "them" or "it" (page 108). But there is no longer any urgency to define "who is speaking that's not said any more it must have ceased to be of interest" (page 21). Nor are we concerned whether the narrator speaks from obligation, necessity, or desire; whether he uses his speech "freely" or not (page 18). The narrator accepts without desperation the realization that his words can pass through him and beyond his control. Moreover, he uses the externality of the voice as the first premise in the proof of its divinity. If the voice is other and is the source of words, it may be the source of the murmurings of all Pims and Boms (page 76). The voice is prime matter and prime mover. Like the Christian God it is creator and trinity, "the voice quaqua from which I get my life ... of three things one" (page 113). It is to this "voice quaqua the voice of us all" (page 138) that the narrator assigns the "minimum of intelligence" required to validate his universe by hearing and noting our murmurings and by filling the "need of one not one of us an intelligence somewhere a love who all along the track at the right places according as we need them deposits our sacks" (pages 137-38). The tasks are not too difficult, since "to hear and note one of our murmurs is to hear and note them all" (page 138). The external divinity not only creates us by giving us words, but it also confirms us by listening to us repeat them (page 137).

But just as rationalists' proofs of God's existence led to agnosticism, so too the narrator's deduction leads to doubt. Given his world, it is unlikely that a voice as powerful and intelligent as his divinity would endure a system whereby it would hear its own story endlessly repeated. Since it is impossible to stop the cycle without causing injustice (page 139), the voice would be forced rather to formulate a system eliminating himself as divinity and "admitting him to peace at least while rendering me in the same breath sole responsible for this unqualified murmur" (page 144). The narrator has thus gone full circle. Beginning with a voice that he locates externally, he goes on to construct a universe over which such a voice would be the divine intelligence, only to end by acknowledging the errors of his system and his own responsibility for the voice.

Perhaps it is only in a Beckettian universe that a narrator can without contradiction assume responsibility for an external voice. The consistency, or at least compatibility, of such claims is due to the paradoxical nature of the voice. It is both external and internal, universal and individual (page 7). Internality is emphasized by the soundless voice of the journey (page 18). No qualitative difference accrues between silent and audible murmurings, between "two cries one mute" (page 48). The voice and its significance lie beyond mere vocalization. The essential and internal nature of the voice is also supported physiologically. Murmuring and panting are similar processes. An end will not come until both have stopped (pages 104-5, 106). The voice, the pant, and even the fart are all defined by the same elementary description. Foreign matter is brought into the body, it is processed, waste products are expelled: inspiration, respiration, exhalation; ingestion, digestion, excretion. The application of voice to this pattern undercuts western veneration of the mind. In the archetypal world of mud, dark, pant, and murmur, it is the murmur with its ability to invent that must bear the burdens normally associated with the mind, imagination, and thought. With embarrassing ease principles concerning human understanding can be plugged in to the description—perception becomes foreign input, thought becomes processing, and ideas become mere waste products equivalent to the less inspiring and more earthy pant or fart. The voice, the pant, and the fart are the basic life process, are the hiss of air that bestows existence on the little that's left of the narrator:

> escape hiss it's air of the little that's left of the little whereby man continues standing laughing weeping and speaking his mind nothing physical the health is not in jeopardy a word from me and I am again I strain with open mouth so as not to lose a second a fart fraught with meaning issuing through the mouth no sound in the mud

> it comes the word we're talking of words I have some still it would seem at my disposal at this period one is enough aha signifying mamma impossible with open mouth it comes I let it at once or in extremis or between the two there is room to spare aha signifying mamma or some other thing some

other sound barely audible signifying some other thing no matter the first to come and restore me to my dignity. (page 26)

On another level the words restore the narrator to his dignity because they are that dignity. The voice creates the narrator, who in turn embodies that voice or, as the narrator says, "I personify it it personifies itself" (page 112). He can have no desires beyond those the voice grants him (page 12). He can make no judgments independent of the voice's evaluations (page 37). He ceases to exist when the voice leaves him and returns to himself only when the voice returns to him (page 95). Life is presented at its minimal point—"my life last state last version ill-said ill-heard ill-recaptured ill-murmured in the mud" (page 7).

When the ill-said creates its fictitious worlds and material universe out of undifferentiated, soundless, and scentless mud (page 25), attention no longer need be directed to the height of Cuchulain's statue[7] or to the location of the Unnamable's jar. Geographic division becomes less important than the perception that the primeval mud (page 11) is the protoplasm from which all else is derived and to which all things return. The mud is both "humanity restoring" drink and food (pages 27, 28) and the excrement of billions (page 52). Although the narrator imposes directions upon the vast plains of mud (page 47), his compass references are only arbitrary divisions of a purposeless tack. The eastward movement is metaphorically meaningless. It cannot be a movement toward the sunrise with its conventional association of rebirth because birth, sunrise, and even the earth's rotation belong not to the mud, but to "life above in the light" (page 123). Nor can it be a journey toward death, for "death [is] in the west as a rule" (page 123). At best the journey from west to east, from left to right, is analogous to the motion of words across the printed page. The voice's geography belongs to its medium of words.

Likewise, objects depend on the voice's narration. The objects presented are purposely simple, few in number, grudgingly given, and rigidly controlled. Unlike the trilogy where characters, plots, and objects proliferate until they escape control, until for example, Malone does not know why his own character Sapo "was not expelled when he so richly deserved to be" (*Malone Dies*, page 190), the objects here are contained and carefully labeled (pages 8, 9, 11, 25). They never attain independent existence but rather always remain subject to the voice's postulations. By revising his description of Pim's watch (page 58), the narrator calls the materiality of that watch into question. The sack steadily depreciates from one of the early certainties (page 8), to an incidental object, to one of the "not true" (page 145). Indeed, the narrator is able to envision himself without sacks or other anomalous objects, "quite tiny," sustained only by the air and the mud (page 17). Unlike the conventional flashback, however, the narration denies the validity of a past and the possibility of a future. As in *Happy Days*, once a state is ended, it is as though it never existed. One "knows one's tormentor only as long as it takes to suffer him and one's victim only as long as it takes to enjoy him if as long" (page 121). If there is "no more Pim [there] never [was] any Pim" (page 74). The narrator is displaced in time, cut off from a causal world, denied a heroic past and a golden age (pages 10, 54). The lack of a future denies him any hope or goal (page 143). He cannot deal with questions such as what would happen if he were to lose the opener or if the sack were finally empty (page 9). Nor can he predict that no one will ever come again to shine a light on him (page 15). The narrator is forced to return to the "vast stretch of time" (page 7) of the present with its only certainties of the mud, the dark, the pant, and the murmur.

In this timeless world, the narrator speaks to fill in the void, discussing things and desires he no longer has in preference to not speaking at all (pages 12–13,16, 18). The whole work becomes his effort to find the "there wherewith to beguile a moment of this vast season" (page 91). Raising a hand, fluttering it, covering a face with it (page 14), fluffing hair (page 24), and drinking the mud (pages 27–28) constitute the busy work and stage business that pass the time.

In this intensely insistent *now*, death and its counterfeit—sleep— assume importance as possible sources of relief. Death, never entirely ruled out (pages 23, 69), is one of the things in which the narrator can perhaps believe (page 21). Indeed, death pervades the work. The tins are described as being "hermetically under vacuum on their dead for ever sealed" (page 92); the sack helps the narrator keep dying in a dying age (page 17); the narrator is either born into death or dying at birth (page 70). Although suicide is a recurrent thought (pages 40, 87), it does not seem to be a viable outlet, perhaps because the narrator is concerned about the family honor (pages 83, 84), perhaps because he is unable to find a satisfactory method of ending his present condition (page 63), or perhaps because he will not be freed, even in death, from the eternal present and the need to pass the time. Death is not the lowest level in an infinite, downward spiral (pages 20–21). One slips lower and lower but nevertheless one continues to persist (page 22), to endure "the same kingdom as before . . . the same it always was I have never left it it is boundless" (page 43).

Just as death is portrayed as a desired but unattainable relief, so too sleep is made increasingly important and improbable. The narrator invents his breath bag to keep conscious track of the precious unconscious moments. He cannot simply sleep until rested, but must measure that sleep in half-hour intervals (page 19). Life is the interval "from one sleep to the next" (page 23), with value placed not on the intervals but on the sleeps. Sleep offers escape from "all the doing suffering failing bungling achieving" (page 23) that compose the waking moments. But as sleep's significance mounts, so does the narrator's insomnia. Diminishing references to his naps terminate in the narrator's acknowledgment that he no longer does sleep (page 40). The desire for the solace of sleep is raised to a religious appeal and then denied. Sleep is what one seeks for in vain, has no right to, does not deserve, and yet must pray for, "for prayer's sake when all fails" (page 36).

Denied escape from the "vast season" of the present, the narrator explores the implications of his existence. Like a tree falling in an uninhabited forest, does a voice speaking in the eternal present need some "other" to hear its words and confirm its existence? As in *Film*, the narrator can examine the structural and dramatic convenience of Berkeley's dictum *Esse est percipi* (to be is to be perceived), without attaching any "truth value" to the idea. The actual reality of a witness is less an issue than are the images and theories resulting from the narrator's felt need for one.

Like the presence or absence of a voice, the presence or absence of another is a major structural device. It is the fact of the couple rather than the role of tormentor or victim that is important: Part four is unnecessary to our narration because it is essentially a repetition of part two (page 131). The journey and the abandon are themselves defined in terms of the "other." The journey is a quest without hope and without the "all-important most important other inhabitant" (page 13). Yet even in that solitude there remains the dream "of a little woman within my reach and dreaming too it's in the dream too of a little man within hers" (page 13). Or, if that dream is too hopeful, there is an emergency dream of an alpaca llama in whose fleece one may huddle (page 14). Part three presents not simply man alone, but man abandoned, rejected, and aware of his lack of the other. The need of another simply for its otherness manifests itself in the narrator's relationship with his sack. During the journey the sack is the only available other. By being an external object against which individuation may occur, the sack becomes the first sign of life (page 8). More than a thing to be manipulated or an object to be possessed, the sack assumes almost sexual relationships with the narrator, who cradles and caresses it (page 44), makes a pillow of it to lie "soft in my arms" (page 46), murmurs endearments to it (page 17). The narrator clings to the sack not from fear of losing it (page 10) or from expectation of any profit from it (page 66), but because it admits of his own existence.

Like the sack, the narrator's people evolve out of his felt need for a witness. Long before they are named, Krim and Kram appear as listener and scribe. The narration technically cannot exist without their recording of the narrator's stream of words (page 7). Their transcript is the book we hold and read. Yet Krim and Kram are unreliable witnesses. Not only do they "lose the nine-tenths" (page 81) of what is being said, but their whole capacity for comprehension is made questionable by their inability to determine whether the narrator and Pim are alive (page 93). Moreover, the narrator denies them an independent existence, even abandoning his own viewpoint in one scene to speak their thoughts (page 81). At one point he tells us there is no witness, no scribe (page 84). At another, like Watt dealing with the Lynch family, he postulates generations of Krims and Krams to ensure continual observation (page 80). Pim is similarly undermined. Pim is the necessary other. Only by feeling that Pim is there, can the narrator feel he himself is there still (page 92). However, Pim's reality is questionable. Like Krim and Kram, Pim may be only a figment of the narration (page 27). Not only does the narrator, as he says, "efface myself behind my creatures when the fit takes me" (page 52), but he also quite blatantly assumes their names (page 60) and lives (page 72) and "plays" at being them (page 57). The hope for another who will penetrate the voice's hermeticism is destroyed.

By making the narrator's existence and identity dependent upon a voice whose nature is ambivalent, whose postulations are uncertain, and whose auditor is problematic, Beckett has diffused his work into an intangible, paradoxical vastness. He has gone beyond Proust and Joyce and the problems of temporal identity. As in *Ulysses*, identity is continuous and successive. The narrator is the same ancient voice throughout and he is three figures who cannot recall earlier stages. But

Beckett destroys the perimeters of the self in space as well as in time. The narrator is not only the ancient external-internal voice, but he is also the spoken and the heard voice. His existence is contingent upon the other; no sharp divisions separate him from that other. In such a schema there is no real difference between being Pim or Bom, between section two and four. Joy and sorrow, tormentor and victim, "I" and "he" all merge as identity is denied definitive borders and as existence is diffused into spoken and heard, Pim and Bom, I and Other.

Because everything in *How It Is* depends upon the diffuse, narrating voice, the form in which the voice creates its universe is as important as the content of that universe. In a world without past or future, cause or effect, there can be no subordination. The omnipresent now is experienced without punctuation and without the interlocking memories that made the well-made sentence possible. In such a universe the major concern is to pass the time while waiting for an end that will not come. The lack of hope removes urgency from the verbal games the voice plays with itself to fill in the void. But even in these games, the self-imposed limitations of the voice's universe must still be obeyed. In a world that has rejected traditional time, place, and identity, the voice can no longer ask how it got here, whence come its possessions, or even whether it exists: ". . . how I got here no questions not known not said and the sack whence the sack and me if it's me no question impossible too weak no importance" (page 7). Where everything, including identity, is ambiguous, pronouns become indefinite and names generic. Pim is victim: Bem is the tormentor already endured: Bom is the tormentor to come. Where nothing is certain, language itself begins to dissolve. Not only does the voice begin to contradict itself, but it also rejects its words as too strong (pages 115, 127).

Where there is no external order, all becomes a free-flowing mental construction. The lack of permanent and concrete connections is reflected in everything from the failure of the couple to communicate to the splitting apart of normal syntax groups. In a prose that intimates an entropic universe breaking down in the mud, there can be little imagery. The colors, gestures, near-metaphors, and almost-symbols that survive are few in number and sparingly used. Whereas earlier works are greatly concerned with the degenerating bodies of their characters, *How It Is* is almost amorphous. It is the voice that captures our interest. Its references to eyes, ears, hands, and heads are neither insisted upon nor pursued as physical realities. The body fades into surreality (page 28). Even the eyes become strangely unseeing eyes. The important vision is mental rather than material. Hence the voice's need for two kinds of eyes: the blue to deal with the physical and "the others" at the back (page 8) for the psychical.

Unlike the self-consciously artificial images of the later works, the images in *How It Is* are of "earth sky a few creatures in the light some still standing" (page 8). The narrator may begin with himself alone, but his narration is irresistibly drawn toward real or imaginary others: "The first is always me then the others" (page 88). We see a woman worrying over a child (pages 10-11), a boy praying at his mother's knees (page 15), a boy and a girl walking hand in hand (pages 29-31), a youth meeting Jesus in a vision (page 45). The events Pim recalls are traumatic sunderings of relationships, when some bizarre and fatal accident breaks another's back. His wife, Pam Prim, falls or jumps from a window (pages 76-78), his father falls when a scaffolding collapses (page 78), and his dog Skom Skum is run over by a dray (page 85).

Yet as familiar as the images initially appear, they are as different from the images of Beckett's earlier works as they are unlike the rotundas, boxes, and cylinders of the later pieces. Whereas the Unnamable's "delegates" tell him "about man," provide him with "the lowdown on God," give him "courses on love, on intelligence," and teach him "to count, and even to reason" (*The Unnamable*, pages 297-98), the voice's images do not create intellectual or emotional bonds between him and their "few creatures in the light" (page 8). Although the narrator begins by saying he has only old dreams, things, and memories (page 7), he quickly revises this statement. In a world without a definable past or sleep, there can be no memories nor any dreams. Therefore the narrator chooses to call the things he sometimes sees in the mud "images" (page 11). Unlike memories, the images are impersonal and independent of an external reality. There is neither recall by the narrator of the life the images portray (page 8) nor any question of, or even desire for, returning to such a life (page 8). Moreover, the images cannot be controlled (page 32). They come without warning or choice at irregular intervals (pages 10, 15). In a rather strident passage the narrator compares the sudden emanation of images to an infant befouling his crib. "I pissed and shat another image in my crib never so clean since" (page 9). He is unable to manipulate the figures in order to see them better. He cannot tell if the figure on the bed with his head in his hands is young or old (page 18). Nor can he stop the couple when their images pass through him (page 32). If he awaits their return, he waits in vain (page 32). His viewpoint as an outsider is often limited and distorted: "...I watched him after my fashion from afar through my spy-glass sidelong in mirrors through windows at night..." (page 9). The distance between the narrator and his images, and the comparative happiness of the images, makes the narrator's own position more desolate. Although he may once have been a boy in the company of a little girl friend under the sky of April or May, he is so no longer. Although he responds to his impression that the couple is looking at him by trying to appear friendly and respectable (page 29), the gesture is futile. When the scene ends he is still alone, unseen, in the mud: "I realize I'm still smiling there's no sense in that now been none for a long time now" (page 31). His consciousness of the figure's improvement—"better than he was better than yesterday less ugly less stupid less cruel less dirty less old less wretched" (page 9)—forces the narrator's recognition of his steady decline from bad to worse (page 9). The very relief offered by the images of "earth sky a few creatures in the light" (page 8) makes the return to the mud that much more devastating, makes the losses of "the humanities I had" (page 30) that much more noticeable.

Like the images from life above in the light, the reduced and restricted imagery of *How It Is* offers both relief from, and a heightened awareness of, the barrenness and desolation of the narrator's world. This dual effect is particularly true of colors because they are used only in reference to the life above in the light. Blue belongs to the blue sky of a world where there is a possibility of beauty, happiness, and other people; a world where, rather than crawling face down in the mud, a boy can lift his eyes to the sky (page 15) and a couple can walk with "heads high ... eyes open" (page 29) through "glorious weather egg-blue sky and scamper of little clouds" (page 29). These blue and white skies bring with them a sense of exhilaration, liberation, and expansion. They come to represent all that is lacking in a decaying world. They are linked with the fertility Pam Prim denies (page 77), with a graceful, flowing movement antithetical to the halting crawl (page 27), with the vision that is past of meeting Christ in a dream (page 45). The colors are vibrant, startling, and solid. We see red tiled roofs (page 15) and "emerald grass" bedecked with a colorful "dream of flowers" (page 29). We are confronted by "blue of a sudden gold and green of the earth of a sudden in the mud" (page 21). Hence, when the images dissolve, when there is "no more blue" (page 106), when "the sky goes out the ashes darken" and we are returned to the mud (page 32), then the absence of color is that much more noticeable, that much more decimating.

The movement from vibrancy to pallor to "impenetrable dark" (page 11) suggests the ultimate incommensurability of colors to the world of the mud, the dark, the pant, the murmur. A similar evocation and subsequent diminution occurs in Beckett's presentation of religious language without any religious underpinnings. God, Jesus, and heaven are neither believed nor denied: They are simply irrelevant. Just as in *Murphy*, in which the mental hospital, shaped like a church without an altar, presents a Christian icon without its hope of salvation, so here too the religious imagery proffers symbols lacking completion and confirmation. The narrator is a distorted and parodic Christ figure who understands everything but forgives, disapproves, and loves nothing (page 41). Divine forgiving is replaced by an attitude that "divine forgetting [is] enough" (page 79).

In the mud it is the images and not the Kingdom of Heaven that lie beyond "the approaching veils" (page 87). In fact, it is in the image of the boy sleeping in the sun (page 45) that the closest approximation to a religious vision and affirmative experience occurs. The youth meets Jesus in "an image not for the eyes made of words not for the ears" (page 45). The importance of that vision for the narrator is supported by its reappearance in two other passages. In the first the narrator tells Pim of his religious experience and "the feeling since then vast stretch of time that I'd find it again the blue cloak the pigeon the miracle he understood" (page 70). But Pim's understanding is quickly negated by the narrator himself, "the childhood the belief the blue the miracles all lost never was" (page 70). It is to this sense of loss that the final mention of the vision refers. The setting of the scene is repeated, "ten twelve years old sleeping in the sun at the foot of the wall" (page 85), but this time the veils fall before the vision can come. That brief moment when a boy of ten or twelve dreamt of meeting Jesus contains all of the peace the world of the mud will ever know. Christ is not denied, but the possibility of reaching him is irrevocably past: "...

what have I said no matter I've said something that's what was needed
... said it was me ten twelve years old sleeping in the sun in the dust
to have a moment's peace I have it I had it..." (page 86).

In an ambivalent world where everything, even the hopes of religion,
can be reduced finally to a voice creating and correcting itself, a refrain
of "something wrong there" is inevitable and natural. Inevitable because where nothing is certain, any statement must be only relatively
true. Natural because where everything is self-consciously fictive, correction and revision can be flatly announced. Yet at the same time the
refrain is disconcerting as it abruptly destroys any suspension of disbelief we may have willed. The prose demands that we, like the narrator,
agonize over and experience the present formulation without the me-
diation of even the most minimal fictions. Moreover, we are required
to draw upon our own resources to discern what is wrong and where.
The errors themselves are significant in a work in which "my mistakes
are my life" (page 34).

There are three or four basic categories our refrain labels as erro-
neous. It is used to negate any statements implying a continuity with
the past, a predictable future, or a possibility of change. The narrator
can say neither that he has steadily gone from bad to worse (page 9)
nor that he crawls toward a ditch that will never come (page 16) nor
that one day he and Pim will travel together (page 57). The refrain is
also appended to any statements granting credence to other bodies or
objects. It is wrong to speak of Pim's timepiece (page 40), of Krim's
knowledge of the couple (page 93), or of the couple itself as "two little
old men" (page 54). We are uncertain one body exists, let alone others.
A voice may be posited, but a choir of such voices must be undercut
(page 107). The narrator knows only himself, not "[him] who is coming
towards me and [him] who is going from me" (page 116). References
to the narrator's own body are themselves problematic. Although the
hand controls a large amount of the book's imagery, its activities are
repeatedly crippled by the refrain. Unsure whether the hand is really
disintegrating, whether the thumb has dropped off (page 28), we have
no assurance that the fingers and thumb do hold a sack (page 34), that
the hand does flesh Pim's buttocks (page 37) or feel his cheek (page
56), that a hand ever descends on an arse for the first time (page 121),
or even that the hands exist and can be seen lying "tense in the mud"
(page 43).

Finally, the refrain contradicts statements the narrator makes about his own cyclic theory. Unable to determine ultimately whether there is eternal recurrence or eternal presence, he finds fault with both systems. In a cyclic world it is incorrect to call anything a first or last member, to say that a clinking tin is the "first respite very first from the silence of this black sap" (pages 24-25). Likewise, in a cyclic world one is not simultaneously Pim and Bom and the roles should not be equated in the conjugation of their names (page 115). The "inevitable number 777777" (page 140) cannot be, at the same time, Bom to 777778 and Pim for 777776. But if the world is an eternally present now, one cannot alternate roles and be "now Bom now Pim" (page 115). Everything must stem from the essential present of the abandoned where the narrator has a voice with which to create the other parts. It is difficult to imagine any other formulation (page 129): it is impossible to depict any other order (pages 116-17). *How It Is* is only a voice speaking in the present and creating a universe of Pims and Boms, sacks and tins, voiced and voiceless. Any statement that tries to ignore or circumvent this essential fact will naturally have "something wrong there" and will inevitably be undermined by the refrain. The prose style of the narration insists upon our facing "how it is present formulation" (page 129).

Every element in *How It Is* from typography to time, from "objects" to "others," derives from a voice narrating itself. The imaginary worlds the voice creates assume the ambivalence and uncertainty surrounding that voice. Although everything depends upon a stream of words, the source of those words is ambiguously external and internal just as identity is indistinctly I and Other. Existence and continuation are the present act of speaking. Time is only the now against which words are spoken. The already-mentioned and not-yet-said fade into irrelevance. Murphy's concerns for mimetic details, like the Unnamable's desires for self-definition, are replaced by a voice speaking in the eternal present. Instead of examining the limitations of the mind/body dichotomy, the work explores the fluid universe of the mind and its imagination. The murmurs in the mud mark a shift from exterior orders to internal fabrications. Just as the speaker and his narration intimate the way it is for us, so too the voice and its words suggest how it is in Beckett's canon.

NOTES

1. In the Shenker interview (pp. 1, 3), after describing *L'Innommable* as a work of "complete disintegration," Beckett confides: "The very last thing I wrote— *Textes pour rien*—was an attempt to get out of the attitude of disintegration, but it failed."

2. Beckett, *More Pricks Than Kicks* (New York: Grove Press, 1972), 29. Other Beckett works referred to in this chapter and cited parenthetically will be to the following Grove Press editions: *Watt* (1959), *Murphy* (1957), *Three Novels by Samuel Beckett: Molloy, Malone Dies, The Unnamable* (1965), *Fizzles* (1976), and "Imagination Dead Imagine," "Ping," and "Enough" in *First Love and Other Shorts* (1974).

3. Beckett's infinitely repeating pattern is often observed; for example, see also Hugh Kenner, *Samuel Beckett: A Critical Study* (Berkeley: University of California Press, 1968), David H. Hesla, *The Shape of Chaos: An Interpretation of the Art of Samuel Beckett* (Minneapolis: The University of Minnesota Press, 1971), and the articles, especially those of David H. Hesla and Edouard Morot-Sir, in *Samuel Beckett and the Art of Rhetoric* (Chapel Hill: North Carolina Studies in the Romance Languages and Literatures, 1976).

4. Samuel Beckett, "Lessness," *New Statesman* 79 (1 May 1970):635.

5. Beckett, "Three Dialogues," 21.

6. Samuel Beckett, *How It Is* (New York: Grove Press, 1964).

7. In his article "The Thirties," in *Beckett at 60* (London: Calder and Boyars, 1967), A. J. Leventhal recalls receiving an urgent postcard from Beckett requesting that he "measure the height from the ground of Cuchulain's arse"— referring to the statue in the Dublin General Post Office. As Leventhal points out, Beckett needed this information to be certain Neary actually could "dash his head against [Cuchulain's] buttocks, such as they are" (*Murphy*, 42).

JOHN PILLING

Shards of Ends and Odds in Prose: From "Fizzles" to "The Lost Ones"

In a letter to me, Beckett said that the *Fizzles* dated from after *How It Is*, and there seems a certain logic in his following the "fundamental sound" of *How It Is* with six short texts that "break wind noiselessly" and fizzle out shortly after they have begun. The fact that Beckett saw fit to publish them together with *Still* and *For to End Yet Again* also suggests that they are the first attempts at a minimalism that, in the last twenty years or so, has been Beckett's standard practice, in prose and drama. But this dating has been questioned, notably by J. D. O'Hara, who sees the *Fizzles* as throwbacks to the *Texts for Nothing*, and on first French publication (in the Les Editions de Minuit house magazine) there were indeed hints that they were written at the end of the 1950s rather than at the beginning of the 1960s. The confusion is worse confounded by the fact that, in the three separate editions (English, French, and American), Beckett juggles the order of the texts, as if in some doubt about exactly how they relate one to another and to the much more important *Still* and *For to End Yet Again*. It seems safest, in the absence of hard and fast evidence, to attempt first a broad overview of the texts in question, and then to see what each individual "fizzle" contributes to the problems of language and being that have always been at the heart of Beckett's enterprise.

Any experienced reader of Beckett will be struck, on reading the *Fizzles*, by the plethora of motifs that have been encountered before. "Afar a bird," for instance, alludes to the end of *From an Abandoned Work*[1] and refers obliquely to *How It Is*: "someone divines me, divines us, that's what he's come to, come to in the end," (page 26). "I gave up before birth" alludes to the end of *Malone Dies* (page 32), the basic situation of which seems also to lie behind "Horn came always." Horn, in that "fizzle," is reminiscent of Gaber in *Molloy*, and the obsession in "He is barehead" with moving in a straight line calls to mind Molloy's problems in part one of the same novel. The "sounds...of fall" in "He is barehead" (page 11) remind one of Molloy's "world collapsing endlessly"; the "childhood sea" of "Old earth" (page 44) recalls the first *Text for Nothing*; the "I-he" confusions of "Afar a bird" and "I gave up before birth" are similar to the fourth *Text for Nothing*.

But there are also a number of motifs that point forward, rather than backward, in time: the "ruinstrewn land" of "Afar a bird" (page 25) makes one think of *Lessness*, *For to End Yet Again*, and *La Falaise*; the tree of "Old Earth" points forward to *Sounds* and *As the Story Was Told*; "still, standing before a window" (at the end of "Old Earth," page 44) is analogous to *Still*, which is also prefigured at the beginning of "He is barehead" (pages 7-8). "He is barehead" contains the "fancy" (page 14) of *All Strange Away*, the labyrinthine structures of *The Lost Ones*, and the faint, remote sounds that are referred to again in *Sounds* and *As the Story Was Told*. "He is barehead" contains references to Murphy (who also "never wore a hat"[2]) and to the Brunonian maxima and minima of Beckett's 1929 essay on Joyce. There are also several literary references: to Milton's *Samson Agonistes* ("a little further on" in "He is barehead," page 10), to Shakespeare's *Hamlet* (the "journey ...from which it were better I had never returned" in "Horn came always," pages 21-22) and to the end of Dante's *Inferno* ("I see the sky" in "Old Earth," page 44), which Beckett also refers to in *Text 9* and *The Lost Ones*, section 4.

The *Fizzles* are clearly, therefore, transitional works, full of what "He is barehead" calls "fresh elements and motifs" (page 15) but far from being liberated from elements and motifs that are, in Beckettian terms, comparatively ancient. But despite these transitional features, the *Fizzles* are surprisingly homogeneous and form, no doubt with a judicious sprinkling of hindsight, a genuine collection, with a number of points of contact between the separate texts. "He is barehead," for instance, ends with "these bones of which more very shortly, and at length" (page 15); and "Afar a bird" and "I gave up before birth" attempt to reduce the "he" of the "I-he" dichotomy to bones, in order that the "I" may achieve independent, authentic being.[3] The "body seen before" of "Closed Space" (page 38) reminds us that the Murphy-like figure of "He is barehead" is precisely a body we have seen before.

There is a new sense of purpose about the self-addressed admonitions of the respective speakers: "I won't go on about worms, about bones and dust" ("I gave up before birth," page 32); "I'll let myself be seen before I'm done" ("Horn came always," page 20). Almost all the texts, as befits Beckett's attempt to "break wind noiselessly," are concerned, to a greater or lesser degree, with sound and silence. There is, too, a pervasive concern throughout with the problems of beginning and ending, announced in the first sentence of *For to End Yet Again*, surfacing again in "Afar a bird" ("I'll feed it all it needs, all it needs to end," page 27), and reaching a kind of high-water mark in "He is barehead" where "with one thing and another little by little his history takes shape" (page 14).

Of the individual "fizzles," only two ("He is barehead" and "Old Earth") are really noteworthy, since "Closed Place" returns to *The Lost Ones* material, and two of them ("Afar a bird" and "I gave up before birth") are almost identical. "Horn came always," with its mention of a "session" (page 21), is mainly interesting in its anticipations of *As the Story Was Told*, which is a much more satisfying piece of work. It is surely symptomatic that the texts in which Beckett seeks to immure the "I" inside a "he" figure ("Afar a bird" and "I gave up before birth") and the text in which the "I" is obscurely dependent on an external agent (the Horn of "Horn came always") are markedly inferior to the text in which a narrative is entrusted to a mostly disinterested "he" ("He is barehead"), and also to the text that seeks to remove dichotomies altogether ("Old Earth"). For immediately after the *Fizzles*, Beckett wrote the "last person" narrative *All Strange Away*, and afterward only once (in *Enough*) reverted to the first person.

"He is barehead" has an allegorical feel about it, as if Beckett is consciously employing the metaphor of a road to comment on the nature of the narrative that is being told. But it is an extraordinarily physical text as well and reads at times as if the "he" is striving to get born. Beckett is clearly here (as the remark about worms in "I gave up before birth" confirms) more concerned with life than with death, and the open air obviously offers more "life-giving" properties than the subterranean passages the figure is stumbling through. This figure is at least striving to get born, whereas the "I" of the later "fizzle" freely admits to having given up before birth. But it seems almost as if the allegorical form of the story is precisely what prevents the achievement of real being, and by the time of "Old Earth," with its positive

171

approach ("It will be you, it will be me, it will be us"), it is apparently "too late" (page 43). The "long gaze" at the end of the text seems promising, but it is followed by "gasps and spasms" that indicate "another body" is being born (page 44). These are certainly the two most complex "fizzles," no doubt because they are decisively oriented toward what "Old Earth" calls "moments of life" (page 44), which inevitably involve Beckett in the problem of "being seen" (page 20). It cannot be irrelevant, in this connection, that "Closed Place," in the original French, bears the title "Se voir." Beckett seems to be striving in the *Fizzles* for the "ejaculation" that he told Lawrence Harvey would be the "most perfect form of being," if it could ever be achieved.[4]

It is obvious that none of the *Fizzles* breaks wind quite as noiselessly as Beckett would wish, which is why no doubt he has applied this unflattering sobriquet to them. But there are signs, in both the two best pieces, that Beckett is on the way toward mastering the "syntax of weakness"[5] that reaches its most impressive form in *Still*. The dislocated syntax of "Old Earth" may seem at the furthest remove from the careful, almost pedantic, only momentarily ruffled syntax of "He is barehead"; but the overall effect is strangely similar, and they are both much mellower in tone than, for instance, "Afar a bird," with its "little panic steps" (page 27). The extraordinary statement in "Horn came always" to the effect that "What ruined me at bottom was athletics" (page 22), which seems at first reading a rather tasteless *jeu*, is no doubt intended to indicate to us that Beckett's "late" period will be more a matter of stillness than of movement. Nothing could be better adapted to portraying this than the minimalist forms Beckett has chosen to adopt, and it cannot be accidental that he speaks, in "He is barehead," of "the minima, these two unforgettable" (page 14), when the volume does indeed contain two unforgettable "minima," *Still* and *For to End Yet Again*. It is, in short, clear that the *Fizzles* are more than just prose "ends and odds," and "in view of their importance, contribute to enrich" (page 15) our understanding of Beckett's post–*How It Is* achievement.

It would be difficult to overestimate the importance of *All Strange Away* (1963-64 written "on the way to *Imagination Dead Imagine*"); it contains in embryo almost all the elements from which Beckett was to construct the strange and yet compelling world of his recent prose. However, it must be said that it offers less immediate rewards than

Enough or *Imagination Dead Imagine* and is more hybrid in manner than *Ping* or *The Lost Ones* or *Lessness*. In its own way, though, it is quite as uncompromising and remarkable as any of the later texts and offers us a wider emotional range than most of them. This is partly explained by the fact that Beckett is here experimenting with a manner and with material that offer new possibilities at a time when he had been feeling, in the *Fizzles*, the regressive pull of the old. In the subsequent works he restrains his wildness and operates over more manageable areas; the equanimity of *Enough* and the thudding monosyllables of *Ping* are the result of paying prolonged attention to the individual component parts of *All Strange Away* and investigating its "residual" possibilities. But *All Strange Away* offers us what Beckett calls in *The Lost Ones* our "first aperçu" of the way his imagination will be working in the 1960s and 1970s and has a freshness and immediacy about it that makes even its elusiveness attractive.

Imagination Dead Imagine is the residual precipitate of *All Strange Away* and is a much more controlled piece of work, more coherent, more accessible, and (despite its apparent dryness) more moving. Instead of concerning himself, as in *All Strange Away*, with the volatile willfulness of the creative faculty of imagination, Beckett contents himself, in *Imagination Dead Imagine*, with one imaginative projection only: the rotunda of the last part of *All Strange Away*, now populated by two figures lying back to back. This concentration on a single object enables Beckett to avoid the diffuseness of the earlier text and allows him to present a more considered view of the workings of the imagination than was ever possible in the turbulent flurry of *All Strange Away*. *All Strange Away* is a fascinating torso but shapeless and prolix; *Imagination Dead Imagine* is a finished piece of work, as Beckett obviously realized when he published the latter and suppressed the former.

The residual text consists of a skeletal prologue, two distinct "sightings" of the rotunda and a melancholy epilogue, and possesses a formal perfection quite alien to its successors, *The Lost Ones* and *Ping*. The prologue, for all its brevity, is a distinct advance on the opening of *All Strange Away*, which reverts to the weariness and self-disgust of the *Texts for Nothing*. *Imagination Dead Imagine* begins with a refusal to accede to resignation, which is rewarded by a sudden and magical intuition:

No trace anywhere of life, you say, pah, no difficulty there, imagination not dead yet, yes, dead, good, imagination dead imagine. Islands, waters, azure, verdure, one glimpse and vanished, endlessly, omit. Till all white in the whiteness the rotunda.[6]

Beckett is now intent, it is clear, on expunging all external realities ("islands, waters, azure, verdure") and exploring the inner world of his own skull. The impulse to subject this interiorized world to accurate measurement, first manifested in *All Strange Away*, seems somehow more natural and less obsessive here, as if it had been engaged in as a matter of course rather than a matter of pressing necessity: "No way in, go in, measure... Two diameters at right angles AB CD divide the white ground into two semicircles ACB BDA. Lying on the ground two white bodies, each in its semicircle. White too the vault and the round wall eighteen inches high from which it springs" (page 63). Beckett confirms the new clarity of his vision by demonstrating that the world he has conceived is a much more substantial one than anything in *All Strange Away*: "Go back out, a plain rotunda, all white in the whiteness, go back in, rap, solid throughout, a ring as in the imagination the ring of bone" (page 63). This movement out and back has now lost all the thematic resonances it once had and is used now simply to establish, as in a control experiment, whether the existence of the rotunda is spatially determined. Beckett repeats the movement a moment or so later: "Go back out, move back, the little fabric vanishes, ascend, it vanishes, all white in the whiteness, descend, go back in" (page 63).

The imperative mood that dominates the beginning of this text contrives to make these movements seem more like physical activities than mental strategies. But this is only a way of imaging cerebral adjustments in a manner that will guarantee their being apprehensible. There is, in any case, no danger of our interpreting a text as oblique as this in a severely literal way, when it is clear that Beckett is trying to identify the optimum conditions in which imaginative enterprise can flourish. The imagination is free to roam through space as it will but runs the risk of losing, by diversifying its maneuvers, the substantial object it has been fortunate enough to come upon.

Beckett stresses that the workings of the imagination are at once mysterious and determined, arbitrarily granted and yet controlled by specific determinants. The object can be "rediscovered miraculously" (page 65) only if the imaginative mind adopts the privileged "point of view" that has already proved beneficial ("there is no other," Beckett tells us). This bi-focal attitude allows Beckett to stress the imagination's consuming need for some talismanic object that it may work upon, but at the same time to stress the haphazardness that is an unavoidable concomitant of exercising the imaginative faculty at all. Beckett is also at pains to point out that the imagination can never operate in exactly the same way twice and that it is always, in a sense, "at the end of an era," as Wallace Stevens said.[7] Imagining has become, for Beckett, less and less a matter of exercising the will and more and more a matter of waiting for the mercies vouchsafed by inspiration. It is only natural, therefore, for Beckett to feel at the end of this text that more has been lost than has been gained, since the miraculous perception of the rotunda cannot be retrieved by any conscious striving on his part and can only be altered out of all recognition in the unlikely event of a third "sighting" being permitted to occur. The more involved Beckett is in an active way, the more likely it is that he will unbalance the delicate equilibrium of forces that has created this bizarre and compelling vision.

In his first aperçu of the rotunda Beckett stresses the strangeness of the mechanisms that it contains but is clearly impressed by the extreme systematization that obtains within it:

> . . . wait, the light goes down, all grows dark together, ground, wall, vault, bodies, say twenty seconds, all the greys, the light goes out, all vanishes. At the same time the temperature goes down, to reach its minimum, say freezing-point, at the same instant that the black is reached, which may seem strange. Wait, more or less long, light and heat come back, all grows white and hot together, ground, wall, vault, bodies, say twenty seconds, all the greys, till the initial level is reached whence the fall began. (page 63)

There is clearly an element of reciprocation here; the systematization of the mechanism is matched by the systematization of the prose. Beckett is not interested as yet in deciding which systematization is primary or which conditions the other. He simply presents the mechanism and the description of the mechanism as indissolubly bound together, in a state of relative equilibrium.

The second aperçu of the rotunda, after its "absence in perfect voids," is much less tranquil and harmonious, although "externally all is as before": "But go in and now briefer lulls and never twice the same storm . . . In this agitated light, its great white calm now so rare and brief, inspection is not easy" (page 65). The prose is much less musclebound than previously, as if Beckett were intent on achieving a reciprocation similar to that achieved in the first aperçu. We begin to feel the pressure of great emotion behind the studiedly dispassionate description of the bodies: "Sweat and mirror notwithstanding they might well pass for inanimate but for the left eyes which at incalculable intervals suddenly open wide and gaze in unblinking exposure long beyond what is humanly possible" (page 65). This is the germ of the style that dominates *The Last Ones*, the long, unpunctuated sentence that openly courts awkwardness and wins through to a kind of resolution despite its angularities. Beckett is avoiding in *Imagination Dead Imagine* the formulaic strain that he has always found it difficult to resist, and adopting here a more supple syntax that will enable him to exploit the self-canceling effects he has found even more irresistible since his adoption of French in 1945:

> Piercing pale blue the effect is striking, in the beginning. Never the two gazes together except once, when the beginning of one overlapped the end of the other, for about ten seconds. Neither fat nor thin, big nor small, the bodies seem whole and in fairly good condition, to judge by the surfaces exposed to view. The faces too, assuming the two sides of a piece, seem to want nothing essential. (pages 65-66)

The tonal and syntactical fluctuations here suggest that the imagination is finding it difficult to sustain its scientific dispassionateness and is becoming involuntarily embroiled in the lives of the figures it has summoned up. There is a gnawing sense on Beckett's part of the inadequacy of remaining content with the measurable superficies, and a growing willingness to draw inferences and attempt conclusions that have nothing to do with scientific evidence at all:

> Between their absolute stillness and the convulsive light the contrast is striking, in the beginning, for one who still remembers being struck by the contrary. It is clear, however, from a thousand little signs too long to imagine, that they are not sleeping. (page 66)

Suddenly the epilogue, as poignant and elusive as the prologue, destroys all trace of serenity and tranquillity. The merest touch of emotional warmth and nostalgic regret breaks all the tenuous barriers between the creative mind and the bodies it has created: "Only murmur ah, no more, in this silence, and at the same instant for the eye of prey the infinitesimal shudder instantaneously suppressed" (page 66). If we are again reminded here of *The Lost Ones*, as the prose shrugs off its potential lugubriousness and pulses with life, we should not forget that *The Lost Ones* takes such moments in its stride and has no difficulty in "whispering the turmoil down"[8] again, whereas at the end of this text there is nothing but wreck and turmoil:

> Leave them there, sweating and icy, there is better elsewhere. No, life ends and no, there is nothing elsewhere, and no question now of ever finding again that white speck lost in whiteness, to see if they still lie still in the stress of that storm, or of a worse storm, or in the black dark for good, or the great whiteness unchanging, or if not what they are doing. (page 66)

The imagination, robbed of its talismanic object after its predatory and illegitimate appropriation of the object's otherness, is left at the end without anything meaningful that will make sense of its continuing hypotheses. Beckett has been stimulated into activity by the fact that there is "no trace anywhere of life," has been granted two miraculous visions of a private world, has tried to infiltrate this world and then recoiled from its severity, and been forced to remember at the end that "life ends" and "there is nothing elsewhere." It is as dispiriting a conclusion as Beckett has ever allowed himself, with a cluster of negatives that makes even the "screaming silence of no's knife in yes's wound" seem endurable.

In the absence here of any "yes" that might be set against the "no's" as at the end of *How It Is*, we may be tempted to think that Beckett's search for "a new no, to cancel all the others" (as the eleventh *Text for Nothing* puts it) is over. But *Text 2* offers an ironic gloss on this idea and stresses the impossibility of "a new no" ever being found: "a new no, that none says twice, whose drop will fall and let me down, shadow and babble, to an absence less vain than inexistence. Oh I know it won't happen like that, I know that nothing will happen..."[9] The twice-repeated "no" at the end of *Imagination Dead Imagine* leaves us with a kind of "absence," but not one that could be described as "less vain than inexistence." It is too close to inexistence for that. The elliptical syntax of the last few phrases suggests finally that there is once more "no trace anywhere of life," as at the beginning. The sharp point of "no's knife" is at its most exquisitely painful at the end of *Imagination Dead Imagine*.

Enough is preeminently a narrative of separation—what *How It Is* would call "abandon"—containing at the same time (and conflating)

the other two elements of *How It Is*, the "journey" and the "couple."
It is also a narrative from beyond the grave, like "The Calmative" or
Play or *Not I*. The separation takes place at a time when the "he"
figure is close to death, and it is associated, in the narrator's mind,
with a loss of meaning that is a kind of death. This helps to account
for one's feeling that this is a strangely "romantic" kind of text for
Beckett to be writing at this stage of his career and means that we
should not summarily dismiss (as perhaps we should like to do) "romantic" readings of it. But the more one considers the narrator's first
description of the separation, the more one's suspicion grows that the
"romantic" reading is reductive and misguided.

In *Imagination Dead Imagine* the "islands, waters, azure, verdure"
are peremptorily omitted; in *Enough* we see the narrator presenting a
transfigured and semifictional world that can be traversed with comparative ease. In his subsequent writings Beckett has abandoned the
"old earth" along with the idea of the quest and the idea of the couple.
Enough remains fascinating because it offers us the last tantalizing
glimpses of the real world, before we are engulfed by the imaginary
constructs of the texts that follow it. Beckett is well on the way here
to constructing a paradise that need not necessarily be lost, the paradise
of the imagination.

The Lost Ones is an exploratory text written in 1966 in French (first
titled *Chacun son dépeupleur*, the last words of the first sentence, but
finally published under the title *Le Dépeupleur*). The final French title
is (like the English title of *Sans*) a coinage of Beckett's that he found
impossible to translate into English. One reason for the disparity between the French and English titles is doubtless the fact that Beckett
could not rely on his English readers' catching the allusion to the line
of Lamartine's (*"Un seul être vous manque, et tout est dépeuplé"*), which
is embedded in the coinage. But it is possible that Beckett also felt,
after changing the title of *Sans* to *Lessness* (and thereby advertising the
idiosyncratic linguistic surface of that text), that a simpler and more
generally descriptive title was more suited to the material he was trans-
lating. For *The Lost Ones* is in many ways the simplest of Beckett's
post–*How It Is* prose, the most easily approachable, the least fraught
with potholes for the unwary.

This is not to say that *The Lost Ones* lacks subtlety, however, for—
as critics have not been slow in realizing—it requires as concentrated
an attention as any of Beckett's other recent work if its felicities are

to be appreciated. *The Lost Ones* reads like an intriguing exercise in openly fleshing out the skeleton of a fiction, in full view of an audience with suspended disbelief, like the Shakespeare of *Cymbeline* or the Yeats of *The Death of Cuchulain*. The very artlessness with which the job is done inspires in a sympathetic reader a kind of tremulous wonder, as if the writer can hardly hope to succeed in seeing his precarious enterprise through to a conclusion. Beckett did indeed abandon *Le Dépeupleur* because he could not see how to bring to an end a world that was going about its business almost without reference to him and that grew more elaborate and complicated with each attempt he made to describe it, but he partially remedied this situation in 1970 by the addition of a final paragraph divorced in time from the events that occupy the main body of the text. And yet it is difficult to feel—despite the intrinsic interest of the final section—that this was an entirely satisfactory strategy, however important it may have been to Beckett (usually, it should be noted, content to abandon works that are slipping out of control). Perhaps the prime reason for the addition was Beckett's realization that his forte (even in his new, more abstract manner) was not the plight of a multitude—however many multitudes of readers might identify with it—but rather the plight of an isolated individual, a figure entirely alone in a universe puzzling in the extreme, without the benefit of resources and companions that might explain it, a "lost one" indeed.

Between his first French drafts and the final published version Beckett dropped the topic headings preceding each section and outlining—in severely abbreviated form—the primary contents of each. He had obviously realized that these titles ("Ladder Law," "Place," "Zenith," etc.) were unhelpful and irritating and interfered with the continuity of the text. The text reads more smoothly without them, if one can speak of smoothness in such an angular piece of prose. *The Lost Ones*, as it stands, for all its unfinishedness, preserves an evenness of tone and coherence of purpose that would only be disturbed by reminders of how atomized its components are. Indeed, the more familiar with the text one becomes, the less it seems to be a rehearsal of already established material and the more it resembles a deeply considered, and admirably restrained, exploration of *terra incognita*.

Reading *The Lost Ones* in its proper chronological place among the last works, one is struck immediately by the dispassionate tone, no doubt a reaction to the restrained passion of *Enough*, the work that immediately preceded it. But *The Lost Ones* is actually much closer in subject matter to *Imagination Dead Imagine*, and ought perhaps to be seen as written in reaction to that work, as *Ping* (according to Beckett) was later composed in reaction to *The Lost Ones*, and *Lessness* in reaction to *Ping*. Beckett has retained, in slightly modified form, the light and heating systems of *Imagination Dead Imagine* but increased the population of the enclosed space (a cylinder, rather than a rotunda) one hundredfold. The desire to populate a space, resisted since his early days, was obviously something he could resist no longer, not least because he was now dealing with material from which "all strange" elements could be purged "away," a world "all known" as *Ping* would put it. It is this mania for completeness and accuracy that drives Beckett to adopt the pedantically dry and remote voice of *The Lost Ones*, and it is a new confidence in his ability to describe things more fully and more plainly that accounts for the increasingly frequent admissions of emotional involvement that give the text its haunting quality and engage the reader's almost anesthetized sensibility.

The first section of *The Lost Ones* ("Séjour" in the original French drafts) outlines with exemplary plainness the primary facts of life in the cylinder:

> Abode where lost bodies roam each searching for its lost one. Vast enough for search to be in vain. Narrow enough for flight to be in vain.... The light. Its dimness. Its yellowness. Its omnipresence as though every separate square were agleam of the same twelve million of total surface. Its restlessness at long intervals suddenly stilled like panting at the last. Then all go dead still. It is perhaps the end of their abode.[10]

It is immediately noticeable, even this early in the text, that whenever a sentence exceeds a very short breath pause, an awkwardness and potential ambiguity (quite foreign to the lapidary clarity striven for) begin to affect the surface of the prose. But at this stage the desire to convey information in as unvarnished a manner as possible proves strong enough to throttle the skepticism, puzzlement, and confusion that later bulk much larger. Beckett even becomes quite chatty, or as chatty as his declarative manner will allow him to be:

> Consequences of this climate for the skin. It shrivels.... A kiss makes an indescribable sound. Those with stomach still to copulate strive in vain. But they will not give in. Floor and wall are of solid rubber or suchlike. Dash against them foot or fist or head and the sound is scarcely heard. Imagine then the silence of the steps. (pages 8-9)

"Imagine then" is quite without the admonitory tone of Beckett's self-addressed injunctions to "imagine" the elements of *All Strange Away*; it is as if there is still someone left to address one's remarks to. There is a relaxed informality about most of *The Lost Ones* that co-exists oddly with its moments of *hauteur* or bluntness, but which reflects a new equanimity on Beckett's part, as for instance, in the last sentence of the first section—"So much for a first aperçu of the abode" (page 13)—which is signally different from Beckett's irritation at the end of the first paragraph of *Enough*—"So much for the art and craft." (In *First Love*, page 53.) So equable is the prose that there is even a certain blandness about it. But at the point where this threatens to turn into self-satisfaction Beckett promptly punctuates it: "Such harmony only he can relish whose long experience and detailed knowledge of the niches are such as to permit a perfect mental image of the entire system. But it is doubtful that such a one exists" (pages 11-12). The studied remoteness of the narratorial voice, less tremulous than that of *Enough* but in its own way quite as personal, allows Beckett the rare opportunity of being both clinically cold and implicitly involved:

> ... the need to climb is too widespread. To feel it no longer is a rare deliverance.... Their solitary attempts to brain themselves culminate at the best in brief losses of consciousness.... Woe the body that rashly enters [the tunnel] to be compelled finally after long efforts to crawl back backwards as best it can the way it came. (pages 10, 12)

As the work proceeds the oscillation between dispassionate description and passionate involvement increases to the point where one is no longer certain quite which is which, and one begins to ask oneself whether the former is not in fact a more genuine commitment to the "lost ones" situation than the latter. But the personal note is kept to an absolute minimum in order that the times where it does intrude may strike with maximum force.

In the second section Beckett introduces for the first time a system of categorizing the inhabitants of the cylinder. The first and second categories prove no problem; there are those "perpetually in motion" and "those who sometimes pause" (page 13). The third category, labeled the "sedentaries," involves Beckett in finer and more problematic discriminations and reveal to him not only the folly of his obsession with accuracy but also the first paradox he has encountered in what has seemed to be such an ordered world: "Paradoxically the sedentary are those whose acts of violence most disrupt the cylinder's quiet" (page 14). When he moves to the fourth category, the "vanquished" (as they are later called), they detain him even longer. Beckett is clearly impressed by the way the vanquished are afflicted from time to time by the desire to rejoin one of the categories they have previously been part of, their eyes "possessed of the strange power suddenly to kindle again" (page 15) with hope. But he cannot forbear from commenting on how essentially hopeless they (and the members of the other categories) are and reminding us, in one of the shortest and most decisive sentences in the work, how irremediable and desiccated their existence is:

> And far from being able to imagine their last state when every body will be still and every eye vacant they will come to it unwitting and be so unawares. Then light and climate will be changed in a way impossible to foretell. . . . In cold darkness motionless flesh. (pages 15-16)

The third section increases the tension of the work by striving to provide a summary of all the information about life in the cylinder that has been offered so far. One begins to become aware of a strange pressure in Beckett's language that is more than simply a longing for scientific accuracy: "Omnipresence of a dim yellow light shaken by a vertiginous tremolo between continuous extremes. . . . Corresponding abeyance of all motion among the bodies in motion and heightened fixity of the motionless" (page 16). There is a desperate quality about these weighty sentences that suggests Beckett is feeling the strain of keeping up the Olympian calm that has marked his enterprise from the beginning. At the same time he contrives to complete an acceptable summary of what has gone before (much fuller than the summaries of material that occupy every third chapter of *Mercier and Camier*) and thereby to extend his investigations of life in the cylinder into areas one would scarcely have believed possible from a reading of the first three sections.

The fourth section (originally titled "L'Issue" in the drafts, and published separately prior to the publication of a full French text of *Le Dépeupleur*) deals with a topic reminiscent of the ninth of the *Texts for Nothing*: the possibility of a way out. Beckett introduces the idea with a cunning cluster of clichés that cast an ironic shadow over the whole of the subsequent discussion: "From time immemorial rumor has it or better still the notion is abroad that there exists a way out" (pages 17-18). The ironic note is maintained by a wry reference to the Romantic poets that Beckett has long had a love-hate relationship with (one recalls here that Lamartine had provided him with a title) and a subtle allusion to the last words of Dante's *Inferno*, reminding us once more of the ninth *Text*, which also ends by referring to them:

> One school swears by a secret passage branching from one of the tunnels and leading in the words of the poet to nature's sanctuaries. The other dreams of a trapdoor hidden in the hub of the ceiling giving access to a flue at the end of which the sun and other stars would still be shining. (page 18)

By associating these hopes with the fabrications of literature Beckett hints (as later in *Lessness* when talking of the "blue celeste of poesy") that they are really only a snare and a delusion, and proceeds to demonstrate that such fictions prevent the population of the cylinder from realizing that their predicament is "issueless." In the conclusion to this section Beckett increases his irony to the point of outright condemnation, although he cloaks his severity with a tactful withdrawal at the end: "So much for a first aperçu of this credence so singular in itself and by reason of the loyalty it inspires in the hearts of so many possessed. Its fatuous little light will be assuredly the last to leave them always assuming they are darkness bound" (pages 19-20).

The fifth section ("Zénith" originally) is the briefest and really only a footnote to the fourth, reminding us of the way a restless idealism has consumed the lost ones and turned them into "amateurs of myth" (page 21). The sixth section reverts to more dispassionate appraisal of the complicated "ladder law" that obtains in the cylinder, and the sentences here are almost without exception longer and more awkward than those we have previously encountered, as if to mirror the complexity of the laws being enunciated. At the same time it becomes clear that a considerable amount of discipline and even violence is needed to prevent the "abode" from transforming itself into "pandemonium" (page 26). This is perhaps the last work of Beckett's in which we find the violence that is so evident in *How It Is* or in Molloy's relations with his mother. But one can almost hear the people of the cylinder murmuring resignedly to themselves, "It's our justice," in the manner of *How It Is*, and the absolute obedience of those who are reprimanded is both chilling and strangely charming: "This docility in the abuser shows clearly that the abuse is not deliberate but due to a temporary derangement of his inner timepiece easy to understand and therefore to forgive" (page 26). The "*tout comprendre, c'est tout pardonner*" allusion (developed from *How It Is* [New York: Grove Press, 1964], page 41, "understood everything and forgave nothing") is faintly disturbing, as if man has unjustifiably arrogated to himself the eternal and ubiquitous tolerance of God. But we find the same "docility" and tolerance operating in the injunction "not to do unto others what coming from them might give offence" (page 58.) This smacks faintly of the homely ethic of Kingsley's *The Water Babies* but seems to derive from a section of Burton's *Anatomy of Melancholy*[11] (a work Beckett silently quotes from in the poem "Enueg 1"). Beckett has always been prepared to allude to what Yeats called "the accumulated wisdom of the world," but perhaps nowhere else has he embedded his allusions so deeply and subtly as in *The Lost Ones*. The glazed surface of the prose effectively prevents our penetrating what lies behind the impassive detachment of the speaker. The rehabilitation of cliché and dead metaphor that Beckett has been engaged in since the days of the Trilogy has here been superseded by a prose that seems able to include the tritest elements alongside the most arcane and reduce them all to one enveloping common denominator.

The next three sections are all short and come to life only in the description (section 8) of the "semi-sages" who "inspire in those still fitfully fevering if not a cult a certain deference" (page 28). Beckett has long been fascinated, since his first attraction to Dante's Belacqua, by figures who have abandoned appetite and accepted their condition as "issueless," and the sentence that ends the eighth section is full of a kind of stunned admiration that the "semi-sages" have conquered the desire to retaliate that periodically afflicts even the best-intentioned of the other inhabitants of the cylinder. Beckett maintains tension by introducing conclusive and decisive sentences like this—the tenth and fourteenth sections end with utterances of a similar kind—into a work that is sometimes threatened with the "docility" it is intent on examining. Alternatively Beckett ends a section on a hesitant note, with a sudden alteration of the angle of vision, as for instance in the ninth section: "Which suitably lit from above would give the impression at times of two narrow rings turning in opposite directions about the teeming precinct" (page 29).

The tenth section offers more variety than almost any other, oscillating between the "picturesque detail" (page 30) of a youngish woman with a baby at her breast and the incipient permutation of the description of how the four categories of inhabitants will in some unthinkable future be reduced to one only: the "vanquished" (as happens in the fifteenth and final section). However, most of Beckett's time in this section is taken up with the "devouring" eyes that he had first alluded to in *Imagination Dead Imagine*. The fact that Beckett amplifies his account with the one really memorable metaphor in the text is an indication of how important the question of vision has become for him. Embedded in the desiccation that surrounds it, this elaborate metaphor operates with the force of an epic or Miltonic simile and cannot but remind us of the sand heap referred to in *Endgame* and dramatically in front of us in *Happy Days*:

> Then the eyes suddenly start to search afresh as famished as the unthinkable first day until for no clear reason they as suddenly close again or the head falls. Even so a great heap of sand sheltered from the wind lessened by three grains every second year and every following increased by two if this notion is maintained. (page 32)

The increased frequency hereabouts of the stock phrase "if this notion is maintained" (clearly a distant relative of *All Strange Away*'s "if this maintained") is a measure of how the text has changed in character since the beginning. Beckett is now in the position of asking himself questions—there is another self-addressed question in the eleventh section—and is more and more reliant on retiring from the immediate purlieu of his gaze if he wants to understand the life of the cylinder. The sentence beginning "An intelligence would be tempted to see..." (page 33) reminds one of the figure in the first section whose "detailed knowledge" of this world would allow him to possess "a perfect mental image of the entire system," and despite Beckett's disclaimer about the likelihood of this being possible, it is clear that we are in the grip of a very knowledgeable intelligence for much of the time. Beckett actually prefigures the end of *The Lost Ones*—unknown to himself, since it was only completed four years later—by introducing into this tenth section a sense of history that has been signally lacking heretofore: "But never again will they ceaselessly come and go who now at long intervals come to rest without ceasing to search with their eyes. In the beginning then unthinkable as the end all roamed without respite..." (page 34). It is clear that Beckett has begun his most epic recent effort *in medias res*, perhaps in the hope that (in the words of "He is barehead") its history may "take shape," and only in the final section do we feel that we are, as we have for a long time come to expect of Beckett, at an end.

The eleventh (and second-longest) section continues the tenth's interest in eyes and elaborates on the light that permits the eyes to operate at all: "The ear finally distinguishes a faint stridulence as of insects which is that of the light itself and the one invariable. . . . The sensation of yellow is faintly tinged with one of red. Light in a word that not only dims but blurs into the bargain" (page 38). Although the synesthesia that connects sound and vision here is reminiscent of *All Strange Away* (which also makes use of the color red), it is obvious that the eyes are now in a much more parlous condition:

> . . . the slow deterioration of vision ruined by this fiery flickering murk and by the incessant straining for ever vain with concomitant moral distress and its repercussion on the organ. And were it possible to follow over a long enough period of time eyes blue for preference as being the most perishable they would be seen to redden more and more in an ever widening glare and their pupils little by little to dilate till the whole orb was devoured. (pages 38-39)

Beckett returns to these "burnt eyes" in the fifteenth and final section in a mood of dispassionate inquiry. But at this point he cannot leave the topic without commenting on his own proclivities and subjecting them to a subtle critique: ". . . the thinking being coldly intent on all these data and evidences could scarcely escape at the close of his analysis the mistaken conclusion that instead of speaking of the vanquished with the slight taint of pathos attaching to the term it would be more correct to speak of the blind and leave it at that" (page 39). A similar moment of revelation occurs toward the end of this eleventh section when, after dealing with the relationship between light and temperature (less systematized than in *Imagination Dead Imagine*) and postulating "a single commutator" with a switch that turns them on and off, Beckett makes explicit for the first time what we have long suspected: "For in the cylinder alone are certitudes to be found and without nothing but mystery" (page 42). But our wholehearted acceptance of this statement as the premise on which all the conclusions of *The Lost Ones* depend is affected by the absurd self-confidence of a statement made six sentences previously: "This is a disturbance analysis makes short work of." Analysis has always been a mixed blessing in Beckett's work (especially perhaps in *Watt* and *How It Is*) and has usually been more a cause of disturbance than a cure for it. As Beckett states quite categorically in the twelfth section, "All has not been told and never shall be" (page 51). Indeed the analysis that forms the basis for *The Lost Ones* seems to suffer a kind of elephantiasis that must have been one of the "intractable difficulties" that prevented Beckett's completing the work to his satisfaction.[12]

The twelfth (and longest) section of *The Lost Ones* is in many ways the dullest because the exploration of a new subject (the question of queueing for the ladders) does not involve Beckett in any of the tensions and ambiguities that inevitably arise from returning to a subject already dealt with. Only at the end of the section, where an unprecedented cluster of rhetorical questions occurs, do we feel the pressure characteristic of the best parts of *The Lost Ones*. And even here there is a kind of bathos in the evasive and timid withdrawal from the subject of future anarchy: "Is not the cylinder doomed in a more or less distant future to a state of anarchy given over to fury and violence? To these questions and many more the answers are clear and easy to give. It only remains to dare" (page 52). The answer to this question and the two questions that precede it is presumably yes. But such an answer brings into being a dread that is at the furthest remove from the self-satisfied confidence and optimism that dominates *The Lost Ones*. As a prophecy it is actually a good deal less accurate than those of the previous section, since as the final paragraph makes clear, violence and anarchy actually diminish as life in the cylinder becomes subject to greater and greater entropy and gradually rigidifies.

The last three sections are, by contrast, among the most interesting and complex. The thirteenth begins with Beckett apparently on the point of abandoning his empirical approach in order to investigate the effect of the climate on the souls of the inhabitants. But the soul has never been so interesting to Beckett as the body (even the "soul landscape" of *Watt* is relegated to the addenda), and it is scarcely surprising that the body should remain of primary importance here: "This desiccation of the envelope robs nudity of much of its charm as pink turns grey and transforms into a rustling of nettles the natural succulence of flesh against flesh" (page 53). The wryness of tone that characterizes so much of *The Last Ones* reaches a kind of climax at this point as Beckett concentrates on the rare instances of sexuality in the cylinder: "The spectacle then is one to be remembered of frenzies prolonged in pain and hopelessness long beyond what even the most gifted lovers can achieve in camera" (page 54). A similar wryness informs the conclusion to the section, which returns to the question of the periodic lulls that bring all life in the cylinder to a stop. One suspects that the "vivacity of reaction as to the end of a world" (pages

54-55) is as much Beckett's as the inhabitants', whose emotional attitude to their situation is rarely so clear-cut or so lively. But there is still a real sadness in Beckett's voice at the thought that they have been denied the relief of ending and must recommence their several quests "neither glad nor even sorry" (page 55).

The fourteenth section maintains the thirteenth's emphasis on the physical but dwells (like the final section) on an individual figure rather than a group. Not even the striking image of the "mere jumble of mingled flesh," (page 59)—which is what those queueing for the ladders have become—can compete with the female figure who provides a point of fixity from which others can take their bearings. As in *All Strange Away* the female figure is huddled up in a corner, head bowed, her hands gripping hold of her legs. Her passivity is of the extreme kind that has always fascinated Beckett and is at quite the opposite end of the spectrum from the violence that follows an infringement of the ladder laws. Like her predecessor she is quite unable to resist the close inspection that is basic to the searchers' quests for their lost ones, and in the final section she suffers the most intense and dramatic inspection of all from the last searcher to thread his way towards her.

It remains unclear why Beckett returned to *The Lost Ones* some four years after he had abandoned it. But it has long been obvious that Beckett is obsessively interested in the face-to-face confrontation of two figures, and in concluding *The Lost Ones* he reverts to the situation so memorably dramatized at the end of *Murphy*. Beckett stresses that the most important figure for the last searcher is the first vanquished and finishes this somewhat dehumanized work with a moment of strange tenderness:

> There he opens then his eyes this last of all if a man and some time later threads his way to that first among the vanquished so often taken for a guide. On his knees he parts the heavy hair and raises the unresisting head. Once devoured the face thus laid bare the eyes at a touch of the thumb open without demur. In those calm wastes he lets his wander till they are the first to close and the head relinquished falls back into its place. (page 62)

The doll-like movements of Mr. Kelly (in *Murphy*), which seem so mechanical and opportunist, here give way to a withdrawal so absolute that one cannot but be moved by it. Indeed, when life in the cylinder is finally brought to a halt, one cannot help feeling an immense relief: "Hushed in the same breath the faint stridulence mentioned above whence suddenly such silence as to drown all the faint breathings put together" (page 62). The last words, however, referring us back to that "unthinkable past" when the first searcher "bowed his head" and became one of the "vanquished," offer no relief at all. There is a lingering suggestion that "if this notion is maintained" (page 63) the world of the cylinder will be "possessed of the strange power suddenly to kindle again" and thus once again become a place of systematic polity teetering on the edge of anarchy.

This is perhaps Beckett's last (and admittedly very tenuous) attempt at the circularity of form that once used to obsess him. Almost all the other late pieces end *in medias res* or in an attempt to erase the reality the text has brought into being. Even in *Lessness*, in which the permutations could be continued indefinitely, the last paragraph has a decisiveness that prevents us harking back to the beginning, and the "unthinkable" futures alluded to at the end of *Imagination Dead Imagine* and *For to End Yet Again* are too unpredictable for us to feel that things will necessarily go on endlessly repeating themselves. It is as if Beckett had realized that circularity of form was as vulgarly plausible as any other concatenation and determined (since *How It Is*) to write in a resolutely linear way, without regard for the overall neatness of shape that was once important to him. When we recall that *Malone Dies* ends in a clutter of strangulated phrases, *The Unnamable* in utter turbulence, and even *Watt* (despite its formal ending) in a heap of fragments—and how many of the shorter texts have had to be abandoned—it is clear that the circularity of *Molloy* is the exception rather than the rule. Beckett has not changed so radically as to suggest that the future will be different from the past, but he has become less convinced that this will inevitably be the case, perhaps out of fear that we will begin to derive some solace from his pessimism. With a mind like Malone's, "always on the alert against itself," he has retained the ability to disquiet us more consistently than any other modern writer of comparable stature.

NOTES

1. Samuel Beckett, *Fizzles* (New York: Grove Press, 1976), 25. References in the text are to this edition.
2. Samuel Beckett, *Murphy* (New York: Grove Press, 1957), 73; Samuel Beck-

ett, *Molloy* in *Three Novels by Samuel Beckett* (New York: Grove Press, 1965), 14.

3. Beckett's first collection of poems was called *Echo's Bones and Other Precipitates*, Paris, Europa Press, 1935. The story of Echo and Narcissus in Ovid's *Metamorphoses* has remained central to Beckett's writing.

4. L. Harvey, *Samuel Beckett, Poet and Critic* (Princeton: Princeton University Press, 1970), 441.

5. Harvey, *Samuel Beckett*, 249.

6. Samuel Beckett, *Imagination Dead Imagine*, in *First Love and Other Shorts* (New York: Grove Press, 1974), 63. References in the text are to this edition.

7. W. Stevens, *The Necessary Angel* (New York: Knopf, 1951), 22.

8. Quoted from "Assumption," *transition*, 16-17 (June 1929), 268.

9. Samuel Beckett, *Stories and Texts for Nothing* (New York: Grove Press, 1970), 131.

10. Samuel Beckett, *The Lost Ones* (New York: Grove Press, 1972), 7. References in the text are to this edition.

11. R. Burton, *Anatomy of Melancholy* (London: Everyman Edition), 166. I owe this discovery of source to Peter Murphy.

12. Beckett's own description, at the head of *The Lost Ones* material he gave to the Reading University Beckett Archive, MS 1396/4/45.

MARJORIE PERLOFF

Between Verse and Prose:
Beckett and the
New Poetry

The opening paragraph of Samuel Beckett's *Ill Seen Ill Said* begins as follows:

> From where she lies she sees Venus rise. On. From where she lies when the skies are clear she sees Venus rise followed by the sun. Then she rails at the source of all life. On. At evening when the skies are clear she savors its star's revenge.[1]

How shall we characterize this strange discourse, a discourse that is surely no closer to *prose*, which I shall define here, following Northrop Frye, as "the arrangement of words ... dominated by the syntactical relations of subject and predicate"—in other words, the sentence— than it is to *verse*, which is the arrangement of words dominated by "some form of regular recurrence, whether meter, accent, vowel quality, rhyme, alliteration, parallelism, or any combination of these."[2] Indeed, if we had to choose one term or the other to designate this passage we might well want to call it verse:

> From whére she líes
> she sêes Vénus ríse.
>
>   Ón.
>
> From whére she líes
>   when the skíes are cléar
> she sêes Vénus ríse
>
>   fóllowed by the sún.
> Then she ráils at the sóurce of âll life.
>
>   On.
>
> At évening when the skíes are cléar
> she sávors its stár's revénge.

Six dimeter lines, five of them rhyming, followed by three trimeters made up primarily of anapests, the whole bound together by the alliteration of voiced and voiceless spirants: "she lies," "she sees Venus rise" (twice), "skies" (twice), "sun," "she rails," "source," "she savors," "stars." The paragraph—or is it a strophe?—is punctuated twice by the refrain word *on* (which rhymes with *sun*).

But of course the text is not, strictly speaking, verse either. For one thing, Beckett chose not to lineate it, and for many readers this very choice determines the status of the text as prose. For another, *Ill Seen Ill Said* is written in what are, despite the indeterminacy of reference, primarily normal grammatical sentences: "From where she lies she sees Venus rise"—adverbial modifier, subject-verb-object.[3] What makes us want to lineate this particular sentence are two things: its binary rhythm, reinforced by rhyme (x / x / x x / x /), and the appearance of the word *on* immediately following, where *on*, pointing to nothing perceivable, breaks up the linear flow of successive sentences. Throughout *Ill Seen Ill Said*, we shall run into this odd prose-verse ambiguity; either a single unit can be construed both ways or a "poetic" unit is directly followed by a prose one, as in this example at the end of the second strophe:

> Rigid with face and hands
> against the pane she stands
> and marvels long.

A little imagist poem, one might say, followed by the matter-of-fact sentence, "The two zones form a roughly circular whole."

Whatever we choose to call Beckett's series of disjunctive and repetitive paragraphs (sixty-one in all), *Ill Seen Ill Said* surely has little in common with the short story or the novella. Yet this is how the editors of the *New Yorker*, where Beckett's piece first appeared in English in 1981, evidently thought of it, for like all *New Yorker* short stories, it is punctuated by cartoons and, what is even more ironic, by a "real" poem, Harold Brodkey's "Sea Noise." Notice that the reader immediately knows—or is supposed to know—that Brodkey is a poet and Beckett a fiction writer, not only because "Sea Noise" is designated a poem in the issue's table of contents, but also because its placement on the page, framed by white space, distinguishes it from *Ill Seen Ill Said*, which is printed in standard *New Yorker* columns. Yet if we examine the sound structure of Brodkey's poem, we find that the rhythm of recurrence is, if anything, less prominent here than in the Beckett "prose." The four stanzas are of irregular line length (9, 6, 9, 7); the stress count ranges from one ("and cúrsive") to five ("ínterló-cutóries [báritóne]"); rhyme occurs only once, at the end of the poem ("lie"/"reply"); and alliteration and assonance are not marked. Unless we assume that poetry is defined by the sheer decision of its maker to lineate the text, or unless we want to call "Sea Noise" a poem because it is built around a single extended metaphor (the witty analogy of sea:shore = professor:class), there is no rationale for the classification the *New Yorker* has implicitly adopted.[4]

The meaning of this classification is worth pondering, for it represents, in microcosm, the orthodoxy of every major literature textbook and literary history as well as of most classrooms in the United States and Britain, which is that Beckett is a writer who, like the young Joyce or the young Faulkner, wrote in his dim youth some negligible, clotted lyric poems but whose real work belongs to drama and fiction. As such, we don't teach Beckett in our poetry courses or include him in discussions of contemporary poetry and poetics. The index of any major book on the subject—say, Robert Pinsky's *The Situation of Poetry*—will bear this out. And yet the irony is that contemporary poets are increasingly using forms that cannot be properly understood without the example of Beckett's astonishing "lyrics of fiction"—to use Ruby Cohn's apt terms—or, as I shall call them, his "associative monologues." Perhaps, then, it is time to rethink our current procedures of canon making. In what follows, I shall use *Ill Seen Ill Said* as an example.

The landscape of *Ill Seen Ill Said* has familiar Beckett contours—a dying old woman, an empty room in an isolated cabin, a pasture with a "zone of stones" that may or may not be a cemetery, and a cluster of obsessive objects: a kitchen chair, a skylight, a buttonhook hanging from a nail on the cabin wall, an antique coffer, a trapdoor. The colors of Beckett's composition are stark black and white—black night, black figure of the woman, black room at night, black greatcoat of the unknown man silhouetted against the setting sun, "Black as jade the jasper" that flecks the white of the granite (tomb) stone (42); white moonlight, white stones "more plentiful every year" (22), white walls, long white hair that "stares in a fan" (25), white disc of the dial on the clock face, and, above all, the white face above the black dress.

In the course of Beckett's narrative, the woman is seen as in a series curvature. To the point at certain moments of its seeming unfit for service. Child's play with a pliers to restore it. Was there once a time she did? Careful. Once once in a way. Till she could no more. No more bring the jaws together. Oh not for weakness. Since when it hangs useless from the nail. Trembling imperceptibly without cease. Silver shimmers some evenings when the skies are clear. Close-up then. In which in defiance of reason the nail prevails. Long this image till suddenly it blurs.

She is there. Again. Let the eye from its vigil be distracted a moment. At break or close of day. Distracted by the sky. By something in the sky. So that when it resumes the curtain may be no longer closed. Opened by her to let her see the sky. But even without that she is there. Without the curtain's being opened. Suddenly open. A flash. The suddenness of all! She still without stopping. On her way without starting. Gone without going. Back without returning. Suddenly it is evening. Or dawn. The eye rivets the bare window. Nothing in the sky will distract it from it more. While she from within looks her fill. Pfft occulted. Nothing having stirred.

Already all confusion. Things and imaginings. As of always. Confusion amounting to nothing. Despite precautions. If only she could be pure figment. Unalloyed. This old so dying woman. So dead. In the madhouse of the skull and nowhere else. Where no more precautions to be taken. No precautions possible. Cooped up there with the rest. Hovel and stones. The lot. And the eye. How simple all then. If only all could be pure figment. Neither be nor been nor by any shift to be. Gently gently. On. Careful.

Here to the rescue two lights. Two small skylights. Set in the high-pitched roof on either side. Each shedding dim light. No ceiling therefore. Necessarily. Otherwise with the curtains closed she would be in the dark. Day and night in the dark. And what of it? She is done with raising her eyes. Nearly done. But when she lies with them open she can just make out the rafters. In the dim light the skylights shed. An ever dimmer light. As the panes slowly dimmen. All in black she comes and goes. The hem of her long black skirt brushes the floor. But most

SEA NOISE

The professorial sea
scribbles mile after mile
of waves. Rustling
and cursive,
the script is crawling,
lullingly sunlit,
illegible,
a green thesis
            (of the sea).

Near the shore, it rises,
ranks of old men emeritus,
snuffling, green-gowned;
it propounds upon shoals
interlocutories (baritone):
"Tomb? Tomb?" Also, "Box? Box?"

Across the lower sand,
a bubbling push,
flat-disembodied beard,
vaporous spirit of tumbling
polar bears,
exploded brides,
gravel-scattering asks,
"Which human hunger
            is least respectable . . . tibble, tibble?"

To which the sand,
with a student hiss,
aglaze in a rushing film,
utters, in a withdrawn whisper,
the delicate lie,
the bubbling polysyllables
of its mostly uninteresting reply.
                        —HAROLD BRODKEY

*   *

often she is still. Standing or sitting. Lying or on her knees. In the dim light the skylights shed. Otherwise with the curtains closed for preference she would be in the dark. In the dark day and night.

Next to emerge from the shadows an inner wall. Only slowly to dissolve in favor of a single space. East the bed. West the chair. A place divided by her use of it alone. How more desirable in every way an interior of a piece. The eye breathes again but not for long. For slowly it emerges again. Rises

anne Burgess

from the floor and slowly up to itself in the gloom. The semi-glo[It is evening. The buttonhook g[mers in the last rays. The pallet s[to be seen.

Weary of the inanimate the ey[her absence falls back on the twe[Out of her sight as she of th[Alone turn where she may she k[her eyes fixed on the ground. On[way at her feet where it has come[stop. Winter evening. Not to be[cise. All so bygone. To the tw[then for want of better the wido[eye. No matter which. In the dist[stiff he stands facing front and[setting sun. Dark greatcoat reac[to the ground. Antiquated block[Finally the face caught full in the[rays. Quick enlarge and devour be[night falls.

Having no need of light to see[eye makes haste. Before night falls of film shots, sitting in her chair and watching the moon rise outside her window, or eating a bowl of slop, or opening the antique coffer and finding a "scrap of paper" on whose "yellowed face" appear "in barely legible ink two letters followed by a number. Tu. 17, Or Th." (35). These indoor scenes are punctuated by outdoor shots of the woman, occasionally followed by a lamb but mostly alone, making her way through the pasture toward the zone of stones, where she is confronted by the enigmatic "twelve," alternately advancing and receding, as she is drawn again and again to one particular stone (apparently her husband's tombstone although Beckett never specifies): "Blindfold she could find her way" (5).[6] In this Stonehenge-like setting, she often sits in the moonlight, rigid against the stone. But in the course of the seasons, some things change: There is, for example, the moment when the third finger of the left hand is lost: "A swelling no doubt... preventing one panic day withdrawal of the ring" (29). At a later moment, she tears up the piece of paper found in the coffer:

> The sheet. Between tips of trembling fingers. In two. Four. Eight. Old frantic fingers. Not paper any more. Each eighth apart. In two. Four. Finish with the knife. Hack into shreds. Down the plughole. On the next. White. Quick blacken. (54)

After this moment, "only the face remains," and the time is envisioned when there will be no more trace even of it, when "the coats will have gone from their rods and the buttonhook from its nail" (56). "Farewell to farewell" (61).

Unlike such earlier monologues as "Enough" (1967), in which the speaking voice is that of the old woman herself, *Ill Seen Ill Said* is the product of "the voice of us all" as Beckett calls it in *How It Is*,[7] the strange ventriloquist voice, outside and detached from the woman's own consciousness, that obsessively recounts her every movement and guesses at her feeling as she moves from cabin to pasture and back again in the course of successive winters. We can surmise that the "relentless eye" (26) that "return[s] to the scene of its betrayals" (23) is Beckett's own, that the writer is trying to exorcise the painful image of what he imagines his mother's last days to have been, especially with respect to her response to his dead father. But, as always in Beckett, the autobiographical mode is turned inside out; the old woman's Book of Hours is recited by a debased or parody bard who can barely articulate the words to define her movements. Her "story," that is to say, comes to us only in broken fragments as it presents itself to the impersonal voice whose fate is to "ill see ill say" it.

Here the word *trace* is central, the bard's mission being to "erase" the "trace" of the "face" that forever haunts his sleep and his waking. *Ill Seen Ill Said* represents one of the rare cases in Beckett's oeuvre in which such erasure seems to be successful; here is the sixtieth strophe:

> Absence supreme good and yet. Illumination then go again and on return no more trace. On earth's face. Of what was never. And if by mishap some left then go again. For good again. . . . Till no more trace. On earth's face. Instead of always the same place. Slaving away forever in the same place. At this and that trace. And what if the eye could not? No more tear itself away from the remains of trace. Of what was never. Quick say it suddenly can and farewell say say farewell. If only to the face. Of her tenacious trace.

And so in the final section "trace" gives way to "grace": "Not another crumb of carrion left. Lick chops and basta. No. One moment more. One last. Grace to breathe that void. Know happiness" (61).

Because the old woman is forever "ill seen" by the "relentless eye," just as her story is forever "ill said" by the speaking voice, the verbal units of which Beckett's narrative is made are like bits of flotsam: words, phrases, clauses—these do not cohere; indeed, the levels of discourse are entirely inconsistent. For what sort of English is this?

> The cabin. Its situation. Careful. On. At the inexistent center of a form-less place. Rather more circular than otherwise finally. Flat to be sure. To cross it in a straight line takes her from five to ten minutes. Depending on her speed and radius taken. Here she who loves to—here she who now can only stray never strays. Stones increasingly abound. Ever scanter even the rankest weed. Meagre pastures hem it round on which it slowly gains. With none to gainsay. To have gainsaid. As if doomed to spread. How come a cabin in such a place? How came? Careful. (2)

One thinks immediately of Stephen Daedalus walking on the beach: Beckett's next strophe, for that matter, contains the phrase "Invisible nearby sea. Inaudible," confirming the allusion. The difference between *Ill Seen Ill Said* and the "Proteus" chapter of *Ulysses* is that the words of the latter monologue still have a center—Stephen's consciousness—from which they emanate, whereas the words and phrases in Beckett's passage emanate from no identifiable source. Is it, for instance, the woman who thinks "Careful. On," or is it the voice that "ill tells" her story? That voice is occasionally capable of straightforward articulation—"To cross it in a straight line takes her from five to ten minutes"—but then it lapses into riddle ("here she who now can only stray never strays"), into mock Elizabethan pentameter ("Éver scánter éven the ránkest wéed"), and into pun and archaism ("it slowly gains. With none to gainsay. To have gainsaid"). Sometimes we hear the voice of fairy tale ("Meagre pastures hem it round on which it slowly gains"), sometimes of nursery rhyme: "To have gainsaid / As if doomed to spread." But no tone lasts long: after this little jingle, we come back to modern colloquial speech—"How come a cabin in such a place?—followed by the elliptical "How came?" and the repetition of "Careful."

Wherever we look in *Ill Seen Ill Said*, we find this curious mixture of voices and discourse patterns: straightforward reportage ("The two zones form a roughly circular whole" [3]); inversion, usually coupled with ellipsis ("To the twelve then for want of better the widowed eye" [18]); archaism ("In the way of animals ovines only" [3]; "Rigidly horrent it shivers at last" [26]) parodic literary allusion, usually in tetrameter or pentameter ("The lids occult the longed-for eyes," "On centennial leave from where tears freeze" [23]; "Sweet foretaste of the joy at journey's end" [57]; "Empty-handed she shall go to the tomb" [43]); mock balladry ("Time will tell them washen blue" [21]); tongue twister ("Winter in her winter haunts she wanders" [9]; "Panic past pass on," "Will they then never quiver" [29]; "To scrute together with the inscrutable face" [55]); and series of short staccato questions ("Who is to blame? Or what? They? The eye? The missing finger? The keeper? The cry? What cry?" [29]), where rhyme ("eye"/"cry") provides further formalization. The result is often a kind of babble:

> What is it defends her? Even from her own. Averts the intent gaze. In-criminates the dearly won. Forbids divining her. What but life ending. Hers. The other's. But so otherwise. She needs nothing. Nothing utterable. Whereas the other. How need in the end? But how? How need in the end? (10)

It is impossible to tell from whom or from what the woman is to be defended or even who "her own" are. "Avérts the intént gáze" (perhaps a garbled version of Herbert's "Bids the rash gazer wipe his eye" in "Virtue") is syntactically and rhythmically parallel to "Incríminates the deárly wón," but the second phrase doesn't follow from the first, and indeed the referent of "the dearly won" is undecidable. Even if we conclude that death ("life's ending") will finally defend the woman against the vicissitudes of life, we still don't know to whom "The other's" refers. The abrupt phrase leads not to anything semantically related but to wordplay: "The other's. But so otherwise. . . . Whereas the other." And so it goes on.

How should we interpret this querulous, compulsive, sometimes maddening babble? In the course of the sixty-one strophes, repetition, both of words and of phrases, becomes increasingly insistent, culminating, as I have shown, in the variations on the word *trace* contained in the final sections. The repetition of the title is particularly telling. The first allusion to it comes in the eighth strophe, and even then, only to its first part: "And only half seen so far as a pallet and a ghostly chair. Ill half seen" (8). "Ill seen" does not recur until strophe 22— "First zone rather more extensive than at first sight ill seen"—whereas "Ill said" does not appear until strophe 25: "Which say? Ill say." Both finally appear together at roughly the midpoint of the monologue: "Such bits and scraps. Seen no matter how and said as seen" (28). This is an important aphorism: what is "seen" is "said," no matter how badly. Or, as the voice says in strophe 23, "The eye will return to the scene of its betrayals." After this moment in the monologue, the words "ill seen ill said" become more prominent: the full title appears in strophe 41—"Such the dwelling ill seen ill said"—and the phrase now becomes increasingly insistent: "Day no sooner risen fallen. Scrapped all the ill seen ill said. The eye has changed. And its drivelling scribe" (49). But although the "drivelling scribe" now seems inclined to scrap the whole story, to forget about that which is "ill seen, ill said," it takes another ten strophes to "efface" the "tenacious trace" of the "face," to cease seeing the "Full glare now on the face present throughout the recent future. As seen ill seen throughout the past neither more nor less" (58).

In charting this thematic development, the question of prosody is central. The peculiar babble of Beckett's monologue, its consistent and abrupt dislocations and deflations, reflects the speaking voice's repeated attempt—and repeated failure—to articulate what it perceives or imagines, to achieve coherence out of what is ill seen and can only be, at best, ill said.[8] To express this peculiar inexpressibility, prose is inadequate, for prose, as Frye points out, "is the expression or imitation of directed thinking or controlled description in words. . . . It is not ordinary speech, but ordinary speech on its best behavior, in its Sunday clothes, aware of an audience and with its relation to that audience prepared beforehand" (*Critic*, page 18). Rather, what we hear in *Ill Seen Ill Said*, as in Beckett's related lyrics of fiction like "Imagination

Dead Imagine" and *The Lost Ones*, is what Frye calls the *associative rhythm*:

> One can see in ordinary speech . . . a unit of rhythm peculiar to it, a short phrase that contains the central word or idea aimed at, but is largely innocent of syntax. It is much more repetitive than prose, as it is in the process of working out an idea, and the repetitions are largely rhythmical filler, like the nonsense words of popular poetry, which derive from them. In pursuit of its main theme it follows the paths of private association, which gives it a somewhat meandering course. Because of the prominence of private association in it, I shall call the rhythm of ordinary speech the associative rhythm. (*Critic*, pages 21-22)

Because the "associative rhythm represents the process of bringing ideas into articulation, in contrast to prose or verse which normally represent a finished product" (*Critic*, page 99), twentieth-century writers have been especially interested in formalizing its properties:

> The naïve assumption that any poetry not in some recognizable recurrent pattern must really be prose clearly will not do, and we have to assume the existence of a third type of conventionalized utterance. This third type has a peculiar relation to ordinary speech, or at least to soliloquy and inner speech. We may call it an oracular or associational rhythm, the unit of which is neither the prose sentence nor the metrical line, but a kind of thought-breath or phrase. Associational rhythm predominates in free verse and in certain types of literary prose. (*EPP*, page 886)

In verse, Frye notes, the associative rhythm "very seldom predominates over meter before Whitman's time; about the only clear examples are poems written in abnormal states of mind, such as Christopher Smart's *Jubilate Agno*" (*EPP*, page 890). What Frye calls "free prose" ("the associative rhythm influenced, but not quite organized, by the sentence"), on the other hand, is found much earlier: in seventeenth- and eighteenth-century diaries and letters, in Swift's *Journal to Stella*, Sterne's *Tristram Shandy*, and before these in Burton's *Anatomy of Melancholy*, that "tremendous masterpiece of free prose, where quotations, references, allusions, titles of books, Latin tags, short sharp phrases, long lists and catalogues, are all swept up in one vast exuberant associative wave" (*Critic*, pages 81, 83).

It should be clear by now that *Ill Seen Ill Said* similarly sweeps up references, allusions, short sharp phrases, neologisms, and contorted elliptical clauses into an associative monologue; indeed, Beckett's fiction *The Unnamable* (1958) is one of Frye's repeated examples of the

199

associative rhythm. Note that "associative" does not simply mean conversational: the discourse of *Ill Seen Ill Said* is, on the contrary, highly formalized: "The eye will return to the scene of its betrayals. On centennial leave from where tears freeze. Free again an instant to shed them scalding" (23). No one, surely, talks this way. But then if we want to be technical, we would have to say even more emphatically that no one writes this way either. Consider the following:

> It is now the left hand lacks its third finger . . . a swelling no doubt of the knuckle between first and second phalanges preventing one panic day withdrawal of the ring. The kind called keeper. Still as stones they defy as stones do the eye. Do they as much as feel the clad flesh? Does the clad flesh feel them? Will they then never quiver? This night assuredly not. For before they have—before the eye has time they mist. Who is to blame? Or what? They? The eye? The missing finger? The keeper? The cry? What cry? All five. All six. And the rest. All. All to blame. All. (29)

The abrupt phrases with their repetition—"a swelling no doubt," "as stones," "clad flesh," "eye," "finger," "keeper," "cry," and "all" (this last word five times)—follow the paths of private association in a radically nonlinear way. The panic experienced when the ring cannot be withdrawn has nothing to do with the kind of ring in question; yet the voice moves from "withdrawal of the ring" to "The kind called keeper" and from there to the stones in the ring: "Do they as much as feel the clad flesh?" In response to the questions "Who is to blame? Or what?" further questions burst out like pellets—"They? The eye? The missing finger? The keeper? The cry? What cry?"—and the answers are framed around repetition of the word *all*: "All five. All six. And the rest. All. All to blame. All." The pedantic talk of "phalanges" and "clad flesh" finally gives way to this stark reality.

"A kind of thought-breath or phrase," a rhythm neither that of regular recurrence as in verse nor of sentence-making as in prose—this is the mode of Beckett's associative monologue as it fumbles to articulate meaning only to lapse yet again into what is almost a dyslexic reading of the "still shadowy album" (8). Beckett has been extending the formal limits of this mode since the time of the trilogy (*Molloy, Malone Dies, The Unnamable* [1951–58]). In *How It Is* (1964), for example, the successive blocks of type are made up of abrupt phrasal groupings, each containing two or three stresses, whose truncated syntax, repetition, archaism, and foregrounding of rhyme and metrical units anticipate the poetic texture of *Ill Seen Ill Said*:

to speak of happiness one hesitates those awful syllables first asparagus burst abscess but good moments yes I assure you before Pim with Pim after Pim vast tracts of time good moments say what I may less good too they must be expected I hear it I murmur it... (*How It Is*, page 25)

Note the pervasive rhyme ("happiness"/"abscess," "first"/"burst," "say"/"may"); the intricate pattern of alliteration and assonance ("asparagus burst abscess but," the repetition of *good*, the parallelism of "before Pim with Pim after Pim" and "I hear it I murmur it"); and the interjection of "yes I assure you" cutting into the so-called narrative. The germ of *Ill Seen Ill Said* is literally found among these fragments:

my life last state last version ill-said ill-heard ill-recaptured ill-murmured in the mud brief movements of the lower face losses everywhere (*How It Is*, page 7)

We can scan this as follows:

```
//  //  //x  //  //  /x/x
//x  xx/  //x  xx/x/
//  /x/
```

Here the spondees, some with an unaccented tail, and cretics create an almost liturgical rhythm.

Free prose as Beckett develops it is, in other words, very close to free verse. Once this point is understood, we can come to terms more readily with such anomalous texts of the seventies as John Ashbery's *Three Poems*, a book dismissed by certain critics as not being poetry at all because it is written in prose.[9] The book-cover blurb is not entirely helpful; it states that *Three Poems* "partakes of what amounts to a new literary form: not at all 'prose poetry' in the traditional sense, it is one in which the resources of prose are used toward an end which is nevertheless poetic."[10] The latter part of this assertion is certainly true: *Three Poems* is distinctly not a medley of prose poems in the tradition of, say, Baudelaire's *Spleen de Paris*. But neither has Ashbery quite invented a "new literary form"; readers of Beckett will recognize the mode of a typical paragraph unit:

There are some old photographs which show the event. It makes sense to stand there, passing. The people who are there—few, against this side of the air. They made a sign, were making a sign. Turning on yourself as a leaf, you miss the third and last chance. They don't suffer the way people do. True. But it is your last chance, this time, the last chance to escape the ball. (page 4)

Like Beckett's free prose, Ashbery's contains sentences that are correct grammatically but have indeterminate referents: the "event" the photographs depict is not specified, nor does the text ever explain what it means to stand "there" or how one can "stand" and be "passing" at the same time. Repetition is used here as in Beckett's associative monologues to present the process of "working out an idea," of getting at a meaning: "They made a sign, were making a sign" and "But it is your last chance, this time, the last chance" bring to mind a tried and true fairy-tale motif—the story of the three caskets, for instance. Again, fairy tale yields to abrupt interjection—"True"—and little rhyming units are foregrounded:

> The people who are there
> few against this side of the air
>
> Turning on yourself
> as a leaf
>
> They don't suffer the way people do
> True

These jingles modulate, in turn, into elliptical abstractions. Ashbery's open-ended strophe continues in the next unit:

> of contradictions, that is heavier than gravity bringing all down to the level.
> And nothing be undone. (page 4)

"Down to the level" of what? one wonders. The faintly archaic phrase "And nothing be undone" provides no answer. Grammatically, it may be either an imperative ("And let nothing be undone!") or an indicative ("And nothing can be undone"); in either case, "And" acts as false conjunction.

From paragraph to paragraph, from present to past to future tense, and from "I" to "he" to "we" and back again to "I," often within the space of a single sentence or sentence fragment—Ashbery's prose repeatedly shifts, as does Beckett's, from the mundane ("an open can of axle grease" [page 5]) to the recondite ("it sets the hydra in furious motion, pullulating beyond the limits of the imagination" [page 36]), from colloquial speech ("That's the way it goes" [page 90]) to formal locution ("There are dark vacancies the light of the hunter's moon does little to attenuate" [page 8]). The appearance in discordant contexts of characters from fairy tales and classics—Childe Roland, the Red Queen, Don Quixote. Hop-o'-My-Thumb—recalls Beckett's parodic references to Shakespeare in *Ill Seen Ill Said* (Edmund's blinding of Gloucester in *Lear*, for example, appears in garbled version in strophe 51: "Closed again to that end the vile jelly or opened again"). *Three Poems*, however, is not as fully narrative as Beckett's associative monologue. Ashbery's interpolated stories and parodic film clips are subordinated to the larger meditation in which they are embedded. That meditation, despite its radical fragmentation and shifting reference, is never as detached as Beckett's "voice of us all." But the movement of the whole, its representation of the struggle to control thought and articulate meaning without ever quite finding a point of rest—this is strikingly reminiscent of the poetic mode Beckett had made his own by the early sixties.

In *The Poetics of Indeterminacy*, I have tried to show how this mode has been assimilated and transformed by such performance poets as John Cage and David Antin. But it is in the work of the younger "language" poets of the eighties that the associative paradigm has really come into its own. In such texts as Ron Silliman's *Tjanting* and Lyn Hejinian's *My Life*, the basic unit is not the verse line or the sentence but the short phrase of irregular length and "primitive" syntax, often marked by inversion and ellipsis. Repetition, whether of phoneme, word, or phrase, becomes the main binding device, sound often carrying the burden of meaning. Again, poets like Charles Bernstein in "Dysraphism" and Lydia Davis in *Story and Other Stories* are producing texts that may be called pieces, lyrics of fiction, collage, assemblage, *bricolage*, free prose—perhaps the name is finally less important than the recognition that we are living in a world of new literary organisms.

In a recent *Georgia Review* symposium prompted by Christopher Clausen's essay "Poetry in a Discouraging Time," a number of distinguished poets and critics try to come to terms with Clausen's contention that contemporary society no longer values poetry:

> The virtual extinction of poetry as a cultural force, though long predicted, is a recent event; it happened within living memory. Whether a second "rescue" is possible remains to be seen, for while the cultural changes attendant on the rise of science undoubtedly altered the position of poetry, they did not make its decline inevitable.[11]

Clausen speculates on what course of action might make poetry once again play a central role, but clearly both he and most of his respondents are gloomy about the prospect. There is much intelligent debate about the relationship of poetry to science as well as to the mass media, but what I find curious is that no one seriously questions Clausen's tacit assumption that when we talk about poetry we are referring to the lyric poem as that paradigm has come down from the romantics. The names cited again and again in this symposium on "The Place of Poetry" today are those of Wordsworth, Shelley, Tennyson, and Eliot.

Perhaps it is time to question our continuing faith in romantic and modernist paradigms for poetry. Can the "time" really be quite as "discouraging" as Clausen takes it to be in a year that witnessed the publication of a text as intricately poetic as *Ill Seen Ill Said* in a popular magazine like the *New Yorker*? Perhaps, in other words, the "death of poetry" Clausen and his fellow symposiasts talk about is more sensibly construed as the gradual and inevitable evolution of the free-verse lyric—a form that after a hundred years of use has become as conventionalized and trivialized as the Elizabethan love sonnet was by the end of the sixteenth century—into a literary mode that can accommodate verse and prose, narrative and lyric, fiction and nonfiction, the verbal and the visual. If, as Wayne Booth rightly points out in his response to Clausen, sophisticated younger critics today may prefer to read *New Literary History* or *Critical Inquiry* rather than "'the best novel, play, or collection of poems of the last year—one praised extravagantly by reviewers in whichever journals you respect most,'" perhaps it is because some of the so-called critical journals are currently publishing pieces that might well have more "literary" interest than, say, John Updike's *Rabbit Is Rich* or Peter Shaffer's *Amadeus* or Robert Bly's newest collection of poems, to mention just three "imaginative works" that have indeed been praised by a wide variety of reviewers.[12] Guy Davenport's "Ernst Machs Max Ernst" is a case in point: a lyrical collage essay, it first appeared in *New Literary History*, as did Cage's *assemblage*, "Diary: How to Improve the World (You Will Only Make Matters Worse) Continued, 1970-71."[13] Are these works we can dismiss as nonimaginative, as belonging to the discourse of the sciences?

Perhaps the familiar distinction Aristotle made between *poema* (the poem) and *poiesis* (the process of making a poetic construct) can point the way toward an understanding of what poetry is becoming in our time. Beckett, whose very earliest lines, in *Whoroscope* (1930), already displayed a curious resistance to lineation,

> Hey! pass over those coppers.
> sweet millèd sweat of my burning liver!

The Page

> Them were the days I sat in the hot-cupboard
> throwing
> Jesuits out of the skylight.[14]

has himself nicely defined the new associative paradigm in a strophe near the end of *How It Is*:

> but all this business of voices yes quaqua yes of other worlds yes of someone in another world yes whose kind of dream I am yes said to be yes that he dreams all the time yes tells all the time yes his only dream yes his only story yes (*How It Is*, page 145)

NOTES

I gratefully acknowledge the assistance of the Guggenheim Foundation in making my research for this article possible.

1. Samuel Beckett, *Ill Seen Ill Said* (New York: Grove Press, 1981), paragraph 1. All further references to this work will be included in the text. *Ill Seen Ill Said* was translated by Beckett from his original French, *Mal vu mal dit* (Paris, 1981); the first English publication appeared in the *New Yorker*, 5 October 1981, 48-58. Since the *New Yorker* edition is important to my argument, I refer to *Ill Seen Ill Said* by paragraph, or strophe, number rather than by page number.

2. Northrop Frye, *The Well-Tempered Critic* (Bloomington: Indiana University Press, 1963), 21. All further references to this work, abbreviated *Critic*, will be included in the text. Northrop Frye, "Verse and Prose," in Alex Preminger, ed., *Princeton Encyclopedia of Poetry and Poetics* (Princeton: Princeton University Press, 1974), 885. All further references to this work, abbreviated *EPP*, will be included in the text.

3. I discuss the question of reference in Beckett's poetry in *The Poetics of Indeterminacy: Rimbaud to Cage* (Princeton: Princeton University Press, 200-247).

4. Contemporary prosodists, perhaps because they must account for the difficult case of free verse, generally do equate verse—and hence implicitly the poem—with lineation. For example, Charles O. Hartman, in his recent *Free Verse: An Essay on Prosody* (Princeton: Princeton Univesity Press, 1980), observes that, difficult as it is to define the word *poetry* "rigorously and permanently," verse can be distinguished from prose quite readily: "*Verse is language in lines*. This distinguishes it from prose. . . . This is not really a satisfying distinction, as it stands, but it is the only one that works absolutely. The fact that we can tell verse from prose on sight, with very few errors . . . indicates that the basic perceptual difference must be very simple. Only lineation fits the requirements." (page 11)
   But as I have just shown in the case of Beckett and Brodkey, what looks like verse may sound like prose and vice versa. The "basic perceptual dif-

ference" between the two is surely not as simple as Hartman suggests. I discuss the question from a somewhat different angle in "The Linear Fallacy," *Georgia Review* 35 (Winter 1981):855-69.

5. See "Lyrics of Fiction" in Ruby Cohn, *Back to Beckett* (Princeton: Princeton University Press, 1973).

6. Twelve is, of course, a number with multiple symbolic connotations—especially in the New Testament and the book of Revelations. But I think Beckett has in mind especially the twelve signs of the zodiac, whose conjunction symbolizes cosmic wholeness; in this sense, "the twelve" relate to the astrological symbolism of the "zone of stones" (Stonehenge). Nevertheless, "the twelve" are purposely unspecified; their identity is finally as elusive as that of the man in the greatcoat or the stone itself.

7. Samuel Beckett, *How It Is* (New York: Grove Press, 1964), 138. All further references to this work will be included in the text.

8. For a related discussion of voice in *How It Is*, see Hugh Kenner, "Shades of Syntax," in Ruby Cohn, ed., *Samuel Beckett: A Collection of Criticism*, (New York: McGraw-Hill, 1975), 30-31.

9. See, e.g., Charles Molesworth, "'This Leaving-Out Business': The Poetry of John Ashbery," *Salmagundi* 38-39 (Summer–Fall 1977):30, 39.

10. John Ashbery, *Three Poems* (New York: Viking Press, 1972). All further references to this work will be included in the text.

11. Christopher Clausen, "Poetry in a Discouraging Time," *Georgia Review* 35 (Winter 1981):705. Clausen's essay summarizes the argument of his new book, *The Place of Poetry* (Lexington, Ky.: University Press of Kentucky, 1981).

12. Wayne C. Booth, "Becoming Dangerous Again," *Georgia Review* 35 (Winter 1981):753.

13. Davenport, "Ernst Machs Max Ernst," *New Literary History* 9 (Autumn 1977):137-48. John Cage, "Diary: How to Improve the World (You Will Only Make Matters Worse) Continued, 1970-71," *New Literary History* 3 (Autumn 1971):201-14.

14. Beckett, *Whoroscope*, in *Poems in English*, The Collected Works of Samuel Beckett (New York: Grove Press, 1970), 12.

DOUGALD McMILLAN

"*Worstward Ho*"

Try again. Fail again. Fail better.

Samuel Beckett's new piece of short fiction is both familiar ground and, as its title suggests, a progression into new territory. Beginning with Belacqua Shua in *More Pricks than Kicks*, a series of overlapping Beckett protagonists have been struggling "on" toward unattainable relief from compulsion. They are either compelled from without to push "on"[1] in a physical journey in quest, flight from pursuers, or movement in some abstract pattern. Or else they are compelled from within to "say on" (page 7) until some story is completed or there are no more words to use up.

Each new Beckett character in a new situation is also another stage in an apparently endless progression. Like one of these characters, Beckett seems compelled to present all of the possible situations. Together, the succession of protagonists is his attempt to exhaust his own mind. *Worstward Ho* is thus, as the narrator informs us, the "latest state" (page 46) in the process of "all gnawing to be naught. Never to be naught" (page 46).

An unidentified speaker ruminates to himself. Slowly out of the verbiage a vision emerges of narrator represented by a skull "oozing" words out of one black hole. He is observing an old man and a child who plod hand in hand toward a final scene at a graveyard, where they observe the bowed back of an old woman. In its starkest outlines Beckett presents the essentials of a life cycle: love (presumably), birth, paternity, death, loss, and return in memory.

The multiple puns of the title point out and define the movement "on" through space, time, and the Beckettian dimension of words. (In Beckett's world characters are located not only in space and time, but on a verbal continuum, their position defined by how much they have said and still have to say.) The movement is toward "the worst"—but significantly only *toward* that point. The real worst is that the speaker is not yet able to arrive at the worst. Finality is unattainable.

207

Worstward Ho is in the most apparent sense "Westward Ho!" through space. The comparison of the plodding of the man and the boy toward the graveyard with the pioneers' arduous trek across the American plains suits well to portray the experience here. It points out first of all the ironic contrast of expectations. (Notably, Beckett's "Ho" lacks an exclamation point.) It also suggests a landscape devoid of many individual marks of the humanity that traverses it and yet not the ultimate abstraction which a desert might represent. Similarly, there are only enough details of specific depiction of the man and the boy in this landscape to convey the impression of an individual experience. This experience, although highly abstract, is not yet the ultimate universal abstraction we might imagine as possible. As usual with Beckett, we are in a quintessentially penultimate world.

The graveyard, which is the destination of the westward trek, represents the "worst" presumably because it is where the mind must confront the memory of the dead—the "shades" as the narrator calls them (pages 12, 13).

This spatial movement is also "worstward" because while it leads toward a distant point on the horizon, it does not confer any distance from the observing narrator. In visual paradox, the man and the boy plod "unreceding on" (page 24).

Throughout Beckett's work, movement toward the west retains the conventional association of passage through time. The movement here is both forward and backward in time. There is progression toward the final, most recent scene in a life cycle; but that is a moment of memory and so, as the speaker says, "back is on." Like the movement through space, the movement through time confers no distance or respite from painful events and is therefore toward the worst.

More than "Westward Ho!" through space and time, the title points to a journey through dubious linguistic terrain: Worst*word* Ho. The process is so exhaustive that it leads through "worsening words" (pages 28, 29) and it requires the ungrammatical form "worser" (page 31) to express the state beyond bad and worse but not yet the worst.

It is one of the tricks of the mind to track consciousness back across any verbal matter it may have encountered, however trivial or tawdry. Beckett, the sophisticated Irishman who left English for the distilled formality of French, is now faced with a mind that insists upon pressing forward even through clichéd American colloquialisms.

At the end of this process there is the word *nohow*. The text begins,

"Somehow on. Till nohow on," and ends "nohow on." Even for lin-guistically democratic American westerners, *nohow* is a markedly aber-rant usage, almost as much a part of the clichéd portrayal of rustic Americans as *begorra* for Irishmen or *wee* for Scots. It is usually a double negative used where *anyway* would be the accepted form. Beck-ett's mind has taken him not only in the direction of the low level of discourse of American western colloquialism, but to a superlatively bad specific example of it. *Nohow* is also the worst word because as the final destination of this linguistic trek, it is a disastrous confirmation of the impossibility of ever reaching an end: There is not any "know-how," expertise, or any other known means of progression to a final state. It also suggests the time when even the search for the impossible means will have been abandoned—the time when *nohow on* will replace *on anyhow*. Finally, and most importantly, *Nohow* presents Beckett's most recent summation of the balanced alternatives of his persistent dilemma. On the one hand, *No!*—the negative acknowledgement and shrinking away from the impossibility of it all. On the other hand, *How?*—the commitment, albeit questioning, to find a way to continue.

Worstward Ho is deceptively unprepossessing at first—traversing a landscape which Beckett himself acknowledges as "mere-most mini-mum" and undesirable. But as his most recent attempt to exhaust the possibilities of language and of his own mind, it reveals upon closer examination Beckett's characteristic linguistic control and brilliance. It is all the more impressive, moving, and enjoyable because of his willingness to go on in the face of the dubious medium imposed upon him by his own mind.

NOTES

1. Samuel Beckett, *Worstward Ho* (New York: Grove Press, 1983), 7. Subsequent references in text.

THE STAGE

MacGowran on
Beckett

You have said that your first involvement with Beckett's plays had a profound impact on you and your career.

It certainly did. Up to that point, I was an average working actor, I suppose, making a reasonable living doing movies, television shows, and plays. But as a result of playing Beckett, my whole attitude to life changed—he expanded my potentialities as an actor very, very much.

What originally brought you and Samuel Beckett together?

I think it all arises from the fact that I am a frustrated writer, as all my life I've been chasing good literature no matter who wrote it and trying to find if the person was alive, so that I could talk about it with him. And it happens that in 1957 I was doing a small part in a play for the BBC called *All That Fall*, and I was struck tremendously by the writing. It seemed to me to be profound and yet ironically funny, in a style I had never come across before. I didn't know then who Beckett was—I'd never heard of him. I thought he was a Frenchman whose work had been translated into English. I was stimulated to read all I could of his work, and then I spoke to a producer about getting me an introduction to Beckett. I was getting so involved in his work that I had to meet the man. It wasn't just idle curiosity—it was a compulsion. At that time Beckett's work was difficult to understand and I thought finding out his way of life and thinking might add a dimension to the writing. When I did meet Beckett finally I discovered he was a Dublin man, born about three miles away from where I was born.

Do you think that the affinity you have for his work has anything to do with the fact that you are both from Ireland?

I cannot deny that part of it must be connected with that. A lot of the rhythms he uses in his work are native to my ear, because we not only come from the same country, but from the same city which has its own recognizable idiosyncracies of speech. With the exception of Lucky's speech, I had no problems with any of the rhythms that other people have problems with because I recognize them straight away as being Celtic rhythms. This "kinship" and my love for his work led to a very affectionate relationship. Since then I have worked in close association with Beckett, going to him before performing in any of his plays to get a definitive interpretation of the work. I have always felt, you know, that his plays are not so complicated as people would like to think—that there is an underlying simplicity.

How does Beckett work as a director? Does he give you a fair amount of freedom in the role?

Yes, if you feel like doing something that is not against the value of the text or what he's trying to say, it's all right. But if you are lost as to what to do, he will tell you that he would like a move made in that direction and the head held a certain way—very detailed, very detailed indeed. But he allows you any amount of freedom you want, provided he feels it doesn't conflict with the text.

Does he begin by explaining to you the point of the play and the effect he's trying to get?

Yes, he does, but only when you are doing his work. For the casual person who asks him questions, he just doesn't feel he can answer them, because they're not going to be involved in his work—they're only curious—but when it concerns doing his work he will open up completely about it. He's often been questioned about *Waiting for Godot*. Because Godot begins with *g-o-d*, people have got the idea that he's referring to God. But he categorically states that that is not the point at all, that it doesn't mean God at all. The whole play's about waiting.

But waiting for something?

Waiting for something, whatever it may be, whatever personal thing a person's waiting for—if they have the patience to survive and wait for it, it may happen. He writes about human distress, not human despair. Because Estragon and Vladimir live on a kind of hope that, if it doesn't come tomorrow, it'll come the next day or the next day. There is the same idea in the novel *The Unnamable* when he says, "I can't go on, you must go on, I'll go on."

When you played Lucky, what sections of Godot *did you discuss with Beckett?*

The rhythm of Lucky's speech. That speech has always been a problem to most actors. Because I had access to Beckett—I got from him what it means and also the rhythms of the speech, which are terribly important. Every time I've seen *Godot*, Lucky's speech has been a jumble—you couldn't make anything out, it's delivered so quickly. But this needn't be the case. When Beckett was trying to explain the rhythms to me, he said, "I can't explain what a rhythm is except that it's iambic pentameter or trochaic; outside that they are just specific rhythms of my own." And I said, "Well, the only way we can do it is if I hear them." So he recorded Lucky's speech for me on a tape recorder and I listened to that many, many times. That is how I got the rhythm of the speech, and from those rhythms I could actually hear what was being said. It's really one long sentence that ends with the conclusion that man "wastes and pines wastes and pines."

In the early part of the play when Vladimir makes biblical references, how did you handle that? What is Beckett's attitude toward that?

There's a sentence from St. Augustine that reads, "Do not despair; one of the thieves was saved. Do not presume; one of the thieves was damned." Beckett said that is the key to the whole play, the shape of what he needed. Vladimir questions the fact that only one of the gospels refers to the thieves. Estragon, who says he's forgotten all he's read about the Bible—he remembers the maps and the blue sea, but nothing else—has read it all and thrown it all aside as a lot of nonsense. He says, "People are bloody ignorant apes." Whereas poor Vladimir tries to puzzle out why only one of the four refers to the thieves and the others make no reference to them at all, to Estragon it doesn't matter.

I think sometimes the roles are reversed. I think Estragon is the one who has read and known everything and thrown it away and become completely cynical. Vladimir, who appears to be the brighter of the two, is in fact the half-schooled one, madly trying to find out answers and pestering Estragon the whole time. Otherwise, Estragon couldn't quote Shelley as he does and misquote him deliberately: "Pale for weariness of climbing the heavens and gazing at the likes of us." This gives you the impression that Estragon has read everything and dismissed it.

When you were developing the role of Vladimir, did you find it necessary to talk with Beckett about the difference between the two?

Yes, and he said to me, "Treat it as a movable force meeting an immovable object" (Vladimir being the movable force and Estragon being the immovable object). But, he said, "They are interdependent; one needs the other." Estragon has so many nightmares, he must have someone to talk to. And Vladimir could not bear to be alone, because he cannot find any answers to the questions he is seeking. He hopes Estragon will provide the answers. Also, part of Vladimir is very much concerned about the plight of mankind. After Pozzo and Lucky fall down and Pozzo keeps shouting for help, suddenly Vladimir says that they are the only ones who can lend assistance: "Let us make the most of it before it is too late."

When you played Lucky, what was your approach to the scene in the second act when Pozzo and Lucky return, one dumb and one blind? Again, did you talk to Beckett about it?

No, I didn't find I had to talk to him very much about that. In the first act Lucky is an extremely damaged person mentally—hence his speech disintegrates because his mind is disintegrating. Pozzo says, "I am bringing him to the fair, where I hope to get a good price for him." They arrive back in the second act when Pozzo hasn't been able to get rid of Lucky because he's blind and he needs the halter to hold on to. But there can be no communication because Lucky has gone dumb and cannot answer; he has said all he has to say and can say no more. But they remain interdependent.

Did you envisage the play as taking place in the present time or as though it were in the future?

I just saw them as two men isolated in an area where people weren't about. I didn't play it in any futuristic sense; I played it as happening in the present time.

What about Endgame, *in which you played Clov?*

Endgame presented different problems. The world upon which Clov looked, through the window, was a world devoid of anything, any human living being. So perhaps this could be taken as a futuristic play, an example of genocidal factors, of races that have been killed off. The world upon which Clov looks is more a moon-scape than an earthly vision. That's why *Endgame* is the harshest of the plays and the most tragic. There's less laughter to be found in *Endgame* than any other play—except for little moments like when Clov discovers he's got a flea or the dummy dog with the leg and sex missing.

The reason Clov doesn't leave at the end is because Hamm puts a doubt into his mind whether he does see life outside or not. If he did see life outside, Clov would escape, and Hamm wouldn't worry because he would take in the new life to help him. I have part of the original manuscript of this scene; it's much longer than the English translation and Clov talks at great length about what he's seeing outside. But Beckett wanted to leave a doubt about the existence of human life and he cut that sequence out, so as to make Clov less sure of going. Hamm says, "I don't need you any more." Clov doesn't like the fact that he's not needed—he must be needed. That is why he never leaves.

Is that Beckett's attitude toward it—that Clov will not leave?

Yes. Clov will not go because he cannot face what's outside without anybody. He's achieved one thing: He will not answer the whistle any more. But he's still dependent upon Hamm no matter what happens.

Did you discuss Endgame *in some detail with Beckett?*

Oh yes. Actually, the best *Endgame* we ever played was directed by Beckett in Paris in 1964. I got Patrick Magee to play Hamm, and I played Clov, and we got two very good character players to play the dustbin people. Beckett came over and spent six weeks directing it. He didn't go on the program as director, because there was a young director who let Beckett take over. Beckett is a marvelous director of his own work, but he's a strict disciplinarian. The play ran for nine weeks in Paris, then for two seasons at the Aldwych Theatre in London and was still playing to packed houses when we closed it.

What was Beckett's interpretation of the play as he approached it from the point of view of a director?

Interdependency—that man must depend upon his fellowman in some way no matter how awful; a love-hate relationship between Hamm and Clov that exists right through the play.

So he put the major emphasis on their relationship, rather than the "something" that's taking its course outside?

Yes. Harold Pinter came to see it one night. He dashed around afterward—he's an honest man, Pinter, and a very good playwright influenced by Beckett's work. He said to me and Pat Magee, "You know, it's not what you were saying to each other, it's what was happening in between that gave me tickles up my spine." So you see, the relationship was working. This is what Sam made sure would happen— that the relationship he wanted between Hamm and Clov was taking place. Clov takes an insane delight in saying, "There's no more pain-killer," and when he wheels Hamm to the center, he *doesn't* wheel him to the center. Clov is constantly *not* doing what Hamm wants him to do. Hamm knows he's not in the center; he has a sixth sense for knowing. He places a terrible curse on Clov when he says, "One day you'll be blind like me . . . except that you won't have anyone with you." This hurts Clov; this worries him a lot. So they hurt each other mentally. They're mentally both very damaged people anyway.

Did Beckett ever talk about what it was that has decimated the population and left only Hamm and Clov?

218

No, never. It's some vision—there is a visionary in Beckett. The seeds of *Endgame* were in fact in Lucky's speech—"In the great deeps, the great cold on sea, on land and in the air"—referring to the return of the world to its former state of a ball of fire or the glacial age that will get rid of all the population and perhaps, by sheer luck, two people will remain. Lucky also says, "In the year of their Lord six hundred and something. . . ." Beckett can't remember the actual date, but he read it somewhere, and it was nearest to a glacial age the earth ever got in mankind's time.

Though there is the suggestion in Endgame *that the flea might be the first chain in the development of a new race of humans.*

That's right, and it's so awful that they want to kill it quickly before it starts, because the same thing will happen again.

In Hamm's story, he refers to the baby who was brought to him by the man who came crawling. . . .

I played it as if Clov was the person who was brought there by the man, so that the story is not really fiction at all. It's a retelling of those early years, which Clov may or may not remember because he has been there so long.

What was Beckett's attitude toward Hamm's parents, who were in the dustbins?

I think he feels that's the way most of us, in later life, treat our own parents—we put them into homes and we give them the minimum kind of treatment to keep them alive for as long as we can. The human race generally does that to an aging parent and this was his conception of how stark it could be—putting them into dustbins and giving them a biscuit or a biscuit and a half a day, anything to keep them going just for a while.

I gather then that Beckett would dismiss the critical approach to Endgame *that says it takes place in the mind of one man and the parents in the dustbins symbolize subconscious repression.*

He would reject that idea completely. People may think that because the play makes it possible to think that way. But I know for a fact that that's not Beckett's idea of what's happening.

In Happy Days, Play, *and* Act Without Words II *with the goad, there's an external force that seems to make the characters function. Have you ever talked to Beckett about what that is?*

No, I haven't. He told me he was going to write a play called *The Goad*, but then he called it *Acte sans Paroles II* (Act Without Words II). It's a mime I don't care for very much myself because I know more or less what he's talking about: that life won't let man alone, that it will prod him into doing things that he's got to do every day no matter what happens. Even in Sam's own life, he's got to write, as he said, "With nothing to express, no desire to express, but with the artist's need to express." So the goad is based on the fact that there is some factor every day that makes you get up and do the things you should be doing. I've played the other one—*Acte sans Paroles I*—very frequently.

Have you asked him what it is off-stage that throws you on?

Yes, it's a combination of rejection forcefully or being thrown into the world from a woman's womb, over which you have no control. You're thrown into a world where you must survive. You didn't ask to be born, so to speak; you are born, possibly against your own will, but you are born nonetheless. And that is even a form of rejection, in a way, in that you are rejected or ejected by the mother. And the character in the mime is, too, because he's flung violently backward and lands on his back, has to roll over and onto his feet, and then takes all the frustrations that life has to offer him. Everything that he finds comfort in suddenly goes, and he finds discomfort. But he goes on trying to find where the comfortable thing lies, until he becomes conditioned to failure, if you remember, and then all the good things that he was looking for come and he ignores them—they're no good to him any more.

Isn't he the only Beckett character who obviously gives up completely in the end?

Now that you mention it, he is the only one who has just been beaten and subjected and brainwashed to such a degree that he has nothing left. He seems to be the only one that I know of his characters that has nothing left at the end except to sit there and wait for death.

Before Beckett wrote Eh, Joe *for you, did he tell you he was going to do it?*

He told me he was writing a television play for me, but I didn't know what it was about until it was ready. It was the most grueling twenty-two minutes I have ever had in my life, because as you know the figure is silent, listening to this voice in his head that he is trying to strangle the memory of. It's really photographing the mind. It's the nearest perfect play for television that you could come across, because the television camera photographs the mind better than anything else. As that camera comes closer and closer, you must see the effect it's having on this man—but not to the extent that he goes into all kinds of grimaces externally. The words are having an effect on him as he attempts to strangle the voice in his head, which he finally does. It's a little victory he has at the end in dismissing the voice; he finally crushes it.

Do you know why he wrote the play for you?

No, I just accepted it. He didn't say why he wrote it for me but thought that I would do it very well. I mean, in his idea, it was the right kind of play for me, and it turned out to be one that I did very well, even though it was very exhausting. Jean-Louis Barrault did it in French, and I think somebody else did it in German, but Sam thought my version was the best.

That Beckett wrote a play for you in which you have no lines to speak suggests he has a very visual approach to what his plays are to be like.

Very. He is in touch with everything apart from the word itself.

One of the things that struck me about Beckett is a similarity between some of Chaplin's early films and Beckett's plays. Has he ever talked about that?

He has. He was one of the greatest enthusiasts of the old silent movies

221

that you could find. Chaplin, Buster Keaton, all those people, they were all part of his youth, and he was very influenced by them. You see this coming out in his work every now and then in the vaudevillian kind of touches you get here and there.

So Beckett sees himself as a comic?

When I asked him, "How much laughter do you expect from my anthology [*Beginning to End*]?" he said, "As much as you can get." But it's ironic laughter, an extension of slipping on the banana skin. I think Beckett has the ability to write one line that contains tragedy and laughter at the same time.

Is that why you find Beckett an optimistic playwright? I know you've been quoted as saying that.

Yes, but he's not entirely optimistic. There are the moments of pessimism and doubt, which I think are normal to us all. Otherwise, he's as optimistic a writer as any you'll find—but he's a realist. He talks of the human condition as it is, and sometimes it's not very pleasant in the world today. He's got no rose-colored glasses; he dispensed with them long ago. He sees life as it really is and has tremendous compassion for humankind. Man's inhumanity to man upsets him gravely.

You're implying that Beckett is really a highly realistic playwright?

Absolutely. He's the greatest realist I know of this generation. He's an extreme realist. Pinter has said openly in the press, "Beckett to me is the acme of all the great writers of this generation. Without Beckett, I would not be writing. He rubs my nose in the shit and the more he rubs it in it, the more I like him." And this, I think, is a great compliment from one very good playwright to another.

Many of Beckett's characters like Krapp and Vladimir have physical problems....

They all have some physical problem or another. For instance, Hamm is blind and unable to move, while Clov cannot sit down. This is not just imagination. There are people in the world, Beckett has discovered, who do suffer from these kinds of things, and yet they're related, they're married to each other—in a love-hate relationship, maybe.

When Beckett gave up teaching French at Trinity College, Dublin, he left suddenly, because, as he said to me, he felt he was teaching something he knew nothing about. That decision was the birth of a writer. He came to London and took a job as an attendant in a mental home for a year. That influenced him very much—I know that *Murphy*, his first novel, came out of his experiences as a mental attendant. And, then, he has seen many people who were handicapped severely in some way. When he was young, there was a war pensioners' hospital very close to where he was born. He saw them regularly every day—they were in various stages of physical disability. I am sure these experiences have influenced the fact that his characters are largely damaged people.

Beckett has said to me often, "People must think I had a very unhappy childhood, but I hadn't really. I had a very good childhood, and a very normal childhood as childhoods go. But I was more aware of unhappiness around me"—not in his own home, but just in people—"than happiness." So the sensitive chords in Beckett's nature were attuned to the unhappiness in humankind rather than the happiness.

In Endgame *and several of the other plays there are references to the fact that a play is going on. Does he do that deliberately as a kind of theatrical device?*

Yes, he does. Pozzo said, "Where are we? It isn't by any chance the place known as the Board?" The "board" is the stage, so that conveys that they know it's a play that's going on. He wants to make the audience feel that it's a play that's taking place and not what really is happening.

When you work with Beckett, does he treat the plays that he has written first in French and then translated into English as equivalent plays, that is, does he make references back to the French text as being different from the English version?

Yes, he does. There was a point in *Endgame* that worried me. When Clov realizes that he's had a little victory over Hamm, he starts humming, and Hamm, if you recall, says "Don't sing," and Clov says, "One hasn't the right to sing anymore." Hamm says, "No," and Clov says, "Then how can it end?" I said to Beckett, "I'm really not quite sure what that means." He said, "Well, that was a difficulty in translation I had. When I wrote it in French, there is a French proverb which is well known, 'Everything ends with a song,' and I could not translate that proverb, which is particularly French, into English unless I did it that way." You see, it was more readily understood in French, Clov intimating that this is the end of their relationship.

Has he ever talked to you about his artistic goals?

No, never, though he said to me once, "Writing is agony." Even winning the Nobel Prize didn't please him. He didn't want it. He didn't want any limelight thrown on him. I think he felt, since James Joyce never got the Nobel Prize, that he wasn't entitled to it at all. And he said, "I certainly won't go to Stockholm to take it. I'll send my publisher if you insist." I think in fact he's given most of the money away. He's a very generous man—if anybody approaches Beckett with a real problem, financial or otherwise, he will help them out. He lives up to what he believes about helping mankind, but he would not want to discuss it himself, because he doesn't want to take any credit.

Do you find a growing awareness of Beckett as though the world is catching up to his vision?

I still think he is slightly before his time, but I think what he is trying to say will become more and more evident as the years go by. I find the easiest audience to play to are students who just seem to know what he is talking about, whereas the middle-aged group are not so tuned in on Beckett.

But his characters tend to be older people.

He doesn't write about young people at all, because he doesn't see life from that point of view. He only writes about what he knows and what he has seen. He's never found anything in the younger people that he felt he had to write about.

Do you feel that he writes himself into his work at all?

I do, but I can't specifically say where. At certain points, I think he appears in his own novels, without even, perhaps, being aware of it. But there's no play I know of that I could equate with Beckett himself or anything about him.

Where do you think Beckett will go from here as a playwright?

That's anybody's guess. He's been reducing and reducing his writing to practically sentences and nothing more now. So I don't know what the next tangent will be, because he's reduced everything now to utter simplicity. *Lessness*, which is the last one he wrote, is only a very slim volume, but it contains very powerful poetic imagery. After this, I don't know—he's pared things down, shorter and shorter, until silence is perhaps the only answer.

Blin on Beckett

TOM BISHOP: Which of the plays of Samuel Beckett have you directed?

ROGER BLIN: All of his first plays, *Godot* in 1953 and *Fin de partie* [*Endgame*] in 1957. Then, later, I directed *La Dernière Bande* [*Krapp's Last Tape*]; Jean Vilar was the producer, when he was at the Recamier. It was with an actor called R. J. Chauffard, who was extremely good. Unfortunately, Beckett didn't like it very much—perhaps because he would have preferred me to play Krapp myself. I was probably too tired at the time to do it. . . . Then I directed *Oh les beaux jours* [*Happy Days*] with Barrault producing.

BISHOP: How did you first meet Sam? Was it to do *Waiting for Godot*?

BLIN: Well, we first met in 1948. He had recently finished writing *Godot* and had just sent off the play. His wife, Suzanne, was taking care of all this. At that time I was director at the Gaité Montparnasse. I'd just directed Strindberg's *Ghost Sonata*. Without knowing me at all, Beckett had been to see the play. In fact, he'd been twice. After that, he sent me his play *Waiting for Godot*, together with his first play, *Eleuthéria*, which I'm just about the only person to know.

BISHOP: You're certainly very lucky to have seen it. It's a manuscript that very few people have seen.

BLIN: Perhaps, to be diplomatic, I should have started with *Eleuthéria*, which presented more difficult casting problems than *Godot*. There are more characters in it. If I had put on *Eleuthéria*, it would have been interesting in itself. At least it would have revealed a new author. But it wasn't only reasons of convenience that made me choose *Godot*. I was very impressed by the quality of the play. But I had to persist

226

for four years in order to get it put on. My associates (who incidentally have since died), who had the money, didn't want to be involved, asking what sort of play it is that hasn't got a single female part and in which, at the human level, there is no story at all. So I looked elsewhere. I showed the script to everybody I knew, at least to all those who were involved with the little theaters and, therefore, might conceivably be interested. All to no avail. I encountered the same reaction of amused disbelief more or less everywhere I turned. But that made me even more determined to do it. So I got a few friends together—three friends, in fact—and we started working on the play. The friends didn't always stay the same, because some of them got discouraged. But Latour and Raimbourg stayed faithful throughout.

I didn't intend to act in it at all at first. It happened by chance. Everybody pictured me as Lucky. But they didn't know Jean Martin. I thought that there would be too much work to do to allow me to act as well as direct. The friend playing Pozzo finally pulled out. The play frightened him, and he didn't understand it very well. For him, Pozzo represented a kind of traitor, not at all genuine. But that's simply not true. So I had to look around for someone else. I pictured Pozzo as physically tall, fat, bald, and perhaps the oldest of the characters. Finally, three weeks before the play opened, I took the part on myself. I already knew the text well enough to fill in Pozzo's lines at rehearsals. So eventually, I found myself creating a role that really isn't in my nature. I don't think Pozzo should be played by a failed tragic actor.

BISHOP: Did Sam play an active part in rehearsals?

BLIN: He attended rehearsals. In fact, he followed all the painful stages I went through at the time—with a certain amount of anguish! I had only had one actual proposal from the Théâtre de Poche. But there wasn't enough room on the stage to install a tree. And, of course, you must have a tree in *Godot*! Finally, I offered the play to Jean-Marie Serreau, who, a year earlier, had opened the Théâtre de Babylone. He accepted it with the idea of putting it on later. Then, when he found himself in the position of having a knife at his throat, he said all right, if we're going to die, let's at least die in beauty.

In the meantime, I did something I hadn't thought of doing, since it wasn't my normal practice. I submitted the play to the commission that offers grants for first plays. There was no news until, one day, I met Georges Neveux, who is a good friend of mine. I said to him, "Georges, you've probably got a play called *En attendant Godot* in your drawer at the moment that I submitted to the commission."

"Yes, I remember seeing the title. It's probably lying under a pile of scripts."

So I said to him, "Would you do me the favor of reading it?"

The next day I received a letter saying, "Bravo! I'll fight for it; it's a remarkable piece of work; I'll do everything I can." Coming from a dramatist, that was praise indeed. Particularly as Neveux is a very intelligent man. So that was how I managed to get the very welcome windfall of 500,000 francs, or something like that—500,000 old francs, of course.

BISHOP: Without which I suppose the play might never have been put on?

BLIN: Exactly. I took the play to Serreau, who, after a year, had just about come to the end of the road. He'd had a fair number of failures and was in quite a lot of difficulty. But it was at that point that he said, "All right, then, let's do it."

So I started working with the actors again and it was then I found I had to take on the part of Pozzo myself. That was how eventually we came to open on 3 January 1953. Sam came to rehearsals. He couldn't tell me exactly how he saw the characters. All he knew was that they wore bowler hats. So I really had to make an effort; at the very least I needed to have an oneiric revelation concerning the relationships among the characters in order to visualize them. While working with my friends, I'd had in mind men of a rather uncertain age, with faces like clowns. Of course, it hadn't escaped me how closely the play was related to the circus, in its names, the brevity of its opening lines, and so on. So I imagined it taking place in a circus ring. That idea lasted for about a week. I realized that the second act couldn't be situated in the circus idiom. And also, if the circus was certainly there, it should remain in the background. It had to be felt within the play, as it were. But not in its actual setting. After all, Beckett was sufficiently grown-up to have written, "The play takes place in a circus ring," if that was the way he wanted it! So: A country road, in a little theater, with a tree. For the tree, I did a drawing of a rather pathetic-looking tree, and because of the smallness of the stage, it couldn't be very large. So someone made it like that. Afterward, we had the same tree built in three bits so that it could be taken around with us on tour. The grand tour. The first grand international tour of *Godot*, you might say! Each actor carrying a third of the tree. That's right, they each carried a third of a tree in their suitcase! That's how we took off. In a very small way, as you see. And there was a remarkable first night. An enormous success. It all came together.

BISHOP: An immediate success?

BLIN: Well, one couldn't say that the play was cursed, though right up to the time it was performed, it certainly seemed as if it were. Afterward, there were those who were against it and those who were in favor of it. But most people really did feel something. And of course, over a period of four years, we'd had enough time to put in some very good work with the actors. I started from a sort of idea or image that Vladimir should be smaller than Estragon and that he should be restless, always on the move. This was because more than anything else I started out from their respective illnesses, rather than from their psychology or from any kind of symbol. I started with the lowest dimension, the lowest level.

BISHOP: The feet, the kidneys, the bladder trouble...

BLIN: Yes, Vladimir wants to piss all the time, so he's restless. The one who has trouble with his feet wants to sit down as much as he can. The fat one, Pozzo, who's got heart trouble, waddles along, holds forth at length, swanks about—and then there's Lucky, who's completely decrepit and who's afflicted with a slight trembling that, at first, I wanted him to adopt only from time to time. But Jean Martin got into it so well that he managed to tremble for a whole forty minutes without stopping! At first I didn't approve of this. I'm not in favor of clinical studies, and the play is above that sort of thing. But he could do it so consistently well and with a kind of conviction that it really was quite extraordinary. So I recognized that with Jean Martin it was probably necessary. He did it so well that he brought out a whole dimension of cruelty that is clearly there in the play. The very image of cruelty. I know that some spectators left in part because of that. They left at the moment of his crisis. Martin in full flow was really incredible. He's the finest Lucky I've ever seen.

BISHOP: To what extent would you say that there was humor in this play?

BLIN: The humor is absolutely vital to it.

BISHOP: More so than in *Endgame*?

BLIN: As much. It's very much the same.

BISHOP: Yet I've always had the impression that the Anglo-Saxon productions I've seen of *Godot* and *Endgame* underlined *humor* rather more than yours did. Take Gogo's various "*C'est vrai*" replies ["Ah!" in English] throughout the play. They are sometimes given quite a mixture of tones, both comic and tragic.

BLIN: I knew from the beginning that it was a tragic play, a tragicomedy. I realized—and I was delighted—that this was a play that was going to explode most of the contemporary theater, the boulevard theater as well as the avant-garde or the pseudo-avant-garde. At times I had to fight against the actors' own tendency to stress the play's pathetic side. It's a problem I had, for instance, in Holland when I directed the play once in Haarlem. Well, I'd been to see the play....

BISHOP: Were the actors playing in Dutch?

BLIN: That's right. I'm referring to the melancholic side of Vladimir in the second act. I said, no, no, that's not it at all. The play doesn't finish with the second act; it can go on. There might well be a third day and then a fourth day. All right. We got that resolved, and in the end it all went extremely well. Then, sometime later, while they were playing in the provinces, I went along to a performance, without letting them know I was in the audience. And there was poor Vladimir crying at the end—absolutely weeping his heart out!

BISHOP: And you didn't resist!

BLIN: Yes, I did. I stopped Raimbourg as well. He had a bit of a tendency to do this as well. Since then I've been asked to direct *Godot* again. They asked me to do it at the Comédie Française.

BISHOP: Doesn't that interest you?

BLIN: Beckett doesn't want that. But while Raimbourg is still alive, I couldn't imagine doing it without him. I couldn't imagine reviving the play without him.

BISHOP: Did you see the production Beckett directed himself in Berlin in March 1975?

BLIN: No—unfortunately, I didn't. Matias saw it. It seems it was very, very funny, really excellent. I regret I missed it. I should have gotten over there. Unlike our production, Beckett chose a tall Vladimir and a short, lively Estragon. And I've also been told he added some songs and a lot of stage business. That's a freedom he probably wouldn't have allowed me.

BISHOP: Certainly not twenty years ago.

BLIN: That's perfectly legitimate, of course. And always within a general choice of color: gray or grayish. That's why he's been accused of miserabilism. Ninety-five percent of the directors who have directed *Fin de partie* and *Godot* fall into the trap of overemphasizing the circus element. You have to sense the circus there—but only under the surface. And as far as bright colors are concerned, Sam rather liked my first Pozzo, who was quite colorfully dressed, wearing a cape with quite a lot of red in it.

BISHOP: Yes, I saw photographs of your costume.

BLIN: I modeled it to some extent on nineteenth-century English engravings. Hunting parties, for instance. There was John Bull. Figures like that. The image of the gentleman farmer came into it a bit as well.

BISHOP: And wasn't Sam happy with that?

BLIN: On the contrary, he was. He wasn't against it at all. Not at all. On the other hand, perhaps he did find it a little strange that I should have dressed Lucky in a sort of red and gold French-style dress coat with black trousers and a striped sweater. He would have liked him to be dressed more prosaically—like a railway-station porter. The reason was that in the back of my mind, I had a surrealist image I couldn't get rid of. But then, I've always approached the theater in a rather baroque sort of way. At the time it's fair to say that I couldn't imagine a play without there being some baroque element involved. Now I think I've got away from all that. But at the time...

BISHOP: As Beckett's plays have become more and more abstract—*Play* and *Come and Go*, for instance—do they still interest you as much as the earlier ones did?

BLIN: Yes, indeed! I got an enormous amount of pleasure out of working on *Happy Days* with Madeleine Renaud. When Sam first offered me the play, I thought of a number of different actresses who, physically, would have looked quite comic in the part, and certainly much funnier than Madeleine—a fat woman with big breasts, for instance. Then I realized that Winnie covered such a wide gamut of feelings and language that to cast a comic actress of that kind in the part would have amused everybody for about five minutes at the most. It was when I realized this that I decided to offer it to Madeleine Renaud, thinking that she would be able to do justice to all its varying moods. To the extent that she had acted in Feydeau, so she could cope very well with all that business in the first part of the play where, pitifully, the woman carries on with her life, when it seems impossible for her to carry on; but with her bag, she's got all her everyday possessions with her and she goes on with a kind of life. Something happened, and I thought that she would do all of that superbly well. And that proved to be the case. But I also thought that, in the second part, she would be able to fade away, physically and progressively, while still carrying on with the game. Her game. A pitiful game with ever more reduced means. Going on until she has nothing left to go on with. Movement is reduced to turning her eyes and sticking out her tongue. It's a horrible and yet a marvelous play. Yes, so much pleasure!

For me *Godot* meant the discovery of an author. It was something enormously exciting, to which I could devote myself wholeheartedly.

Then there was the friendship with Sam, which began only a year after I received the play. I wrote to him. Straightaway. Then we met. We were each very intimidated by the other.

BISHOP: But since then, have you discussed his plays with him when you have directed them? Or does Sam tend to withdraw and stand in the wings?

BLIN: Sam became a lot more confident after *Godot*. Much more confident about his own plays, about the theater in general, and about the phenomenon that is theater, with which he wasn't acquainted, but which he intuited brilliantly.

BISHOP: Just as he understood instinctively the phenomena of television, radio, or cinema.

BLIN: That's right. With *Fin de partie*, he attended rehearsals much more frequently. In fact, he had ideas about the play that made it a little difficult to act. At first, he looked on his play as a kind of musical score. When a word occurred or was repeated, when Hamm called Clov, Clov should always come in the same way every time, like a musical phrase coming from the same instrument with the same volume. I thought that this idea was very much a product of the intellect and would result in an extraordinary rigor. He didn't see any drama or suspense in Clov's imminent departure. He would either leave or he wouldn't.

BISHOP: For Beckett, did he leave? Was there no suspense?

BLIN: No. Because that was of no interest to him. From the moment Clov announced that grain upon grain, there's a heap, it's understood, everything else is just words and a few other things. With maybe a little theatrical effect with the arrival of the child, or rather the pseudo-arrival of the child. And Hamm should always sound the same in his anger. And that's how we played it in London. Starting the play too much in high gear. Then I noticed after three days that we were modulating this a little. In other words, I was toning it down for the sake of the audience. And of course, a real live actor simply can't change suddenly from anger to laughter as if you're turning a switch.

233

Anger grows out of a laugh that's just ending, and so on. That is flesh and blood. It's what I might call the harmonics of the business. In fact, I know later Sam used to poke fun at all the harmonics that I used to go on about. But in the revival at the Théâtre 347, he wanted to make the play even grayer. He cut out the song.

BISHOP: Had he also cut out the arrival of the child?

BLIN: No, that stayed in. We didn't cut that. But it was merely indicated, suggested, that's all.

BISHOP: Sam immediately cut out a whole section of text about the child in the English text. He never translated that into English.

BLIN: Perhaps he was wrong. That part came from me. I felt instinctively that Hamm should reach such a low point that he might never recover, never resume sufficiently to make the effort to go on. That explains why perhaps I made the end a little too dramatic. So Hamm uttered a sort of cry, barking out his call for Clov one last time. Maybe. I know other actors have played him as if he stays in a constant state of good health, high colored, with makeup like a clown.

BISHOP: Yes, but it doesn't work at all well. I've seen them play it like that too.

BLIN: That comes partly from those who seem to think that the comic adds color and that color is in itself more comic than gray. But it's the way in which someone acts that can be comic. It's the way an effect is created, that allows you to achieve a searing kind of comedy. It won't be funny simply because you give Hamm red cheeks or dress Clov in a certain way or give him a red nose. I think if Chaplin and Buster Keaton had had to be subjected to the horrors of Technicolor, we wouldn't have what we have from them. There is a kind of arabesque of gesture that can be achieved in black-and-white with a flat print and without any photographic gimmickry that is far more striking than anything you can attain by means of effects.

BISHOP: When you put on a Beckett play, what is your relationship with the text as it's written?

BLIN: As far as I'm concerned, I don't have any specific personal theatrical style. With writers of this standing, I simply try to push them as far as they will go. By stressing what they are. But I don't try to put on what could be identified as a "Blin" play.

BISHOP: That's to say, you push Beckett's work in a different direction from Genet's, for instance?

BLIN: Yes. There are plays that I direct where the direction is invisible. Absolutely. It works completely by itself. While with others, like Genet's *Les Paravents* (*The Screens*) or Strindberg's *Le Songe* (*The Dream Play*), which I've just directed in Zürich, I live with ideas, with an aesthetics that can offer the play the best I'm capable of.

BISHOP: You mean you serve the text?

BLIN: Yes. Because I get more pleasure in doing this than in trying to find things to say that would be, "This is going to be a 'Blin' production. It's going to be tremendous. It doesn't fit the text very well. But I don't give a damn about the author." I know directors who think, "For me all playwrights are dead, at least I treat them as if they were dead. I take what they've done and I simply use it." Of course, you can always find ordinary enough texts, mediocre ones, or mere scenarios with which you can amuse yourself doing this. You can have fun with a show; I am all for the show. Really I am. With great texts, until they have passed into history what one must do is serve them. That is the case with Sam's plays today.

Translated by James Knowlson

235

ALAN SCHNEIDER

Working with
Beckett

Through twenty theatrical seasons, I have happily carried a typescript by Samuel Beckett with me to rehearsals through more than that number of productions—in Washington or Texas or San Francisco, in New York's off-Broadway, and twice even on to Broadway itself. On three occasions, those scripts had never before been performed—*Happy Days* (1961), *Film* (1964), and *Not I* (1972). On four others—*Waiting for Godot* (1956), *Endgame* (1958), *Krapp's Last Tape* (1959), *Play* (1964)— the scripts were receiving their first production in English and/or in the United States. And more than a dozen other times, I have carried these same or other scripts of his through a proscenium arch, onto the thrust stage, or out directly into the middle of an audience—something Mr. Beckett had neither expected or entirely understood. In these twenty years, there have been few times when I had not just finished directing one Beckett work or another or was not actively planning to do another one.

Did I gravitate to Sam at once, immediately recognizing his dramatic genius? Truthfully, I'm not sure. When I first read *Endgame* in manuscript, I told Barney Rossett, Beckett's American publisher, that it seemed to me like a combination of *Oedipus* and *King Lear*. This was before either Jan Kott's book or the Brook-Scofield production, so I must have had the correct sympathetic vibrations. But did I recognize it then as a major work of the twentieth century? And that first time I watched *Godot* at the Babylone in Paris back in 1954, without catching more than a portion of its French dialogue, I did at least respond emotionally enough to its stage directions to try—at that time unsuccessfully—locating the playwright to have him translate it into English for me. One year later, when I first read the English text, I remained

236

equally intrigued and baffled, trying to figure out which one of those two fellows was which. But when a producer happened to offer the play to me to direct, I at once accepted. Even though at that time, as now, I had serious reservations about both the producer and the play's viability for Broadway audiences. But the moment I started to work on the text itself, I was hooked, as I have been on every one of them ever since.

Which of the almost dozen different plays of his which I've directed, I am always being asked, do I prefer? That's like asking a parent to pick out a favorite child. Or making a mountain climber name his favorite peak. All I can really say is that they've all spoiled me for the lowlands. I tend to prefer the Beckett play I'm working on at whatever moment I'm asked. Though, perhaps, *Krapp* and *Happy Days* seem to be most human and moving. Or *Endgame*. Or *Godot*, which is no longer a play but a condition of life. Let's just say: The one I favor is the one I'm going to be working on next. On all of these working occasions, with the one exception where Beckett was told that the shooting of a very unusual filmscript absolutely required his physical presence, my favorite playwright has never wanted to venture forth from his Parisian privacy to face the periods of production à l'Americaine. So that in a real sense, this present account of my experiences with his plays might more accurately be labeled "Not Working with Beckett"; or "Working with Beckett's"; or, perhaps most exactly, "Working on Beckett."

Sam's continued reluctance to cross the Atlantic to be with me in rehearsal is no proof that he is the shadowy recluse pictured by his interviewers. Actually, he remains the most accessible of men and authors—though only to his friends. He has, after all, taken an active role in most of his French productions; and he has even managed to cross the Channel in order to be of assistance to directors George Devine and Donald McWhinnie. And he has regularly journeyed to Berlin himself to direct new productions of his plays at the Schiller Theater. Why then never to New York except for *Film*? Does he trust me or mistrust me so much? Is he not interested enough in the American theater's attempts at his plays, in contrast to his feelings about what the European stage does with them? Does it take Buster Keaton to get him over here?

Sam could answer those questions better than I can. But my own impression is that the truth, as always with Beckett, is much simpler. New York is just too far away and too noisy, the job of getting here too demanding. Nor does he especially favor either press conferences or cocktail parties, occupational hazards he has discovered to be endemic to the American production process. Nor, I am supposing, have his early publishing experiences (prior to Grove Press) with American commercialism and commercial Americans endeared him generally to our jangled rhythms and demands. He prefers to stay away if he can, gently but firmly declining all manner of invitations, whether they come from Harvard or the neighborhood of Washington Square.

Not that I've been content to have him stay away. In the theater, I agree with my friend and Sam's, the late Jackie MacGowran, that we most of the time seem to be trying to keep the author out but with Beckett we feel just the other way around: We want him in. To hold our hands through the darkness. To illuminate the dots, interpret the ellipses, and explain the unexplainable. To hover and fume (though he'd never let us see). So although he'd never actually been there, I've always rehearsed as though he were in the shadows somewhere watching and listening, ready to answer all our doubts, quell our fears, and share our surprises and small talk. Sometimes, without sounding too mystical or psychotic, I've felt that he was indeed there, and that I might easily be talking with him. Once we all did talk to him, when we nicknamed the light that flicked from urn to urn in *Play*, "Sam."

In work then, all of his texts—and that word includes both dialogue and stage directions—have always been "Sam's" to me, a marriage in absentia, in which I have loved, honored, and obeyed as though he were always with me. Every actor and actress cast by me for a Beckett production, every designer of setting and costumes and lighting—and posters—every producer and would-be producer has had to deal with me on this one fundamental premise: We're doing Sam's play more or less in the way he'd want it to be done; "at least insofar as I as the director can understand that and transmit it to you." Whatever else may be happening, we're not trying to put anything over on Sam.

Having Sam actually at rehearsals, however, would have made my problems easier. At least, deciding what he really wanted or meant at any given moment would have been immediately possible, without anyone's taking or not taking my word for that. Resolving all those inevitable differences of opinion or interpretation of each word and each moment. And clearing up his specific technical demands, all those complications that those simple little Beckett plays with one or two characters and hardly any scenery, manage to be loaded with: undersized ashcans and oversized urns, parasols that burn up on cue but not before, carafes that fly without twisting slowly, slowly in the wind, a Mouth that floats unsupported in space, and a Figure with head and arms lit up but with feet invisible.

And, best of all, with him there, it would have been more possible to adapt and change something. Because like the rest of us, whenever Sam goes to work on a given production, he understands its uniqueness and special problems. Something for some reason (whether acting or technical) doesn't seem to be working, or might be more interesting with some slight variation. A line doesn't sound exactly right coming from that particular actor, or the actor cannot deal properly with a certain prop. When, for example, I wanted to add an overhead lamp to Krapp's den, it took me some weeks to get up the nerve to ask Sam. Had he been there, he would have seen the pool of light that such a lamp at once created and agreed at once—instead of getting a description and a request from me and answering back, "Yes, of course." When I wrote to explain that "weir" was too unfamiliar a word for us, suggesting "dam" as an alternative, Sam came back with "lock." As well as, years later, Erskine for Arsene, which was too specifically French. How much more leeway we would have always had if only he had been with us day by day!

I have always held to the old-fashioned belief that a first production—certainly of a living author, especially of an author as clear and explicit in his directions to all concerned as Beckett has always been (and is increasingly becoming)—should try to bring to stage life the author's play. Should a director disagree, significantly or violently, he shouldn't be doing that play. Nor do I believe that the creative ego has necessarily to feed on the principle of contradicting the author or trying to substitute for, elaborate upon, evade, or elude the author's own point of view, or to use the text as simply the starting point for the director's virtuosity. Interpretation is one thing—like *Hamlet*, *Godot* will always be different when filtered through a director's temperament and the imponderables of casting—but interpolation is quite another, not to mention extrapolation, and the intrusion of a subtext that clearly distorts instead of illuminating its text.

Not too immodestly, I hope, I admit that my directorial mind is quite capable of conceiving *Godot* with an all-female cast—and, in fact, had one such in an acting class I once supervised long enough ago to have included several performers since elevated (?) to stardom. Nor am I any longer appalled at the idea of Vladimir and Estragon as homosexuals—but reject it as I have thousands of other ideas equally unrelated to the play. Let's say the idea of having the two playing cat's cradle with string all through the graveyard scene. I've seen (or myself used) *Godot's* tree bedecked, in the second act, with the greenest of ribbons, balloons, rubber bands, even spaghetti, even leaves (real or stylized); but the idea (which graced a recent highly praised version) of not having the tree onstage at all is not one I can immediately respond to, even in theory. Nor do I yet understand why having Hamm and Clov ad lib a hodge-podge of pop-art songs and slogans, not to mention having Clov sit and Nell and Nagg pop in and out like box puppets at various times not even suggested by the text, or opening the play with Nelson Eddy and Jeanette MacDonald singing away on a gradually running-down record, is necessarily preferable to honoring the lines and pauses by trying to discover why Beckett put them there in the first place—and doing something theatrically interesting with that knowledge. Shakespeare, of course, is being done (including sometimes by myself) in everything from bathing suits to cave-man outfits with all the concomitant details. I once did *Macbeth* with six witches (though I am now embarrassed to admit that only three appeared to the audience at any given time; the others were doubles who made the witches seem to be able to fly through space). And Beckett will one day be performed in seventeenth century armor or space suits with *Godot* as an extra-terrestrial intelligence, as well as set to music (*Godot* already has been). But in the blessed meantime, at least within the author's own span of life and awareness, I utterly reject the "colored lights" school of production and favor an author's inalienable right to the relative satisfaction of his own intentions, limited as they may be.

I got into my very first troubles with a Beckett production early in the game, on my first *Godot*, when I actively resisted Bert Lahr's open desire to be top banana, with Tom Ewell as second banana. Very simply, Bert wanted to relegate the role of Vladimir to that of straight man. In the instance of Lucky's speech, he wanted to cut it out entirely "since nobody understands it anyway"; at the very least, since I would neither cut it nor let him go offstage during the speech, he insisted on doing lots of comic business all through it so that no one would have to listen and be bored. After all, they had come to see Bert and not the actor playing Lucky, whoever he was—and to hear Bert repeat his familiar "Onnnggg-onnnggg" in response to his recurrent realization of his fate instead of Mr. Beckett's simpler and very ordinary (but how extraordinary) "Ahh." The fact that Bert was superbly eloquent in many of his own manifestations of Estragon's character didn't make my choices easier. Eventually, another director more willing to accept and deal with Bert's insecurities took the play to New York—and away from Beckett.

When the original off-Broadway producers of *Endgame* at the Cherry Lane wanted to bring a gag man in to amplify Sam's (and my) lack of humor, or when one of the actors who replaced our original Clov wanted to explore less conventionally than had the author what the character might be doing in the play's opening sequences instead of climbing up to look out those two windows, I demurred both times—on the play's own stated premise that nothing is funnier than unhappiness. And when Buster Keaton wanted to keep sharpening the end of a broken pencil until it got smaller and smaller and eventually disappeared, a "bit" he told me he had always used successfully, I explained—quietly, I trust—that we were only doing what was in the shooting script, funny or unfunny as it happened to be. All the way down to someone's repeated suggestion while we were doing *Not I* to blow up the Mouth on to a giant full-stage color TV screen so that the audiences at the Lincoln Center Forum would be able to see and understand the play better. Not I, said I.

This attitude on my part, by the way, has not prevented a few of my not-so-friendly neighborhood critics, who feel that I have somehow hypnotized Sam into giving me a stranglehold on his work, from accusing me of seriously distorting his plays. I shudder to think what such nongentlemen of the press would have said about me had I actually tampered with Beckett's texts and intentions even a fraction of the extent to which certain recent productions (some not authorized and sometimes not paying royalties) have done—in the process being praised for transmitting the author's "true" intentions. One leading critic has even blamed me for adding bananas and other extraneous business to my most recent version of *Krapp's Last Tape*. The revisions in some of Krapp's pantomime were the result of Sam's own experiences in Berlin, which of course the critic had no way of knowing about. The bananas, however, are quite apparent in the text. What such critics do not at all understand is that I didn't have to hypnotize Sam. He's just been burned too many times elsewhere by too many people in too many ways.

With all my Beckett productions, then, I have been more faithful than the pope himself often required. And since Rome (or in this case, Paris) has never except for that once come to me, I have always gone to Paris, to get the full benefit of the author's "stutherings," as he once described them. Before each production, including that first one, I've sailed or flown or trained or driven—at the production's expense, if possible; if not, on my own—to spend whatever time with Sam he could give me. Punctual as a churchbell, he always comes first to my hotel, the boulevard Raspail's modest l'Aiglon, which I found by accident of fate back in 1949 on my first pre-Beckett visit and have stayed in ever since, later to discover it was around the corner from Sam and an old favorite of his. I sit with him in his favorite cafés and restaurants, sometimes in his apartment around that corner. We eat, drink, wander through the Luxembourg Gardens or elsewhere in Montparnasse. I badger him with all the questions and problems that I've jotted down or that occur to me as we walk and talk. Sometimes, we don't even mention the play, although we do get into everything else—from the state of the damnation to my daughter's schooling. He is fond of her, remembering her as a little girl playing in front of l'Aiglon. When he speaks with the waiters, Sam always seems completely French to me—and to the waiters; when he talks with me, he's very Irish.

As much as possible, those conversations are like ones we would be having if he were in New York at rehearsals, and the atmosphere is very like that of the Village, although somewhat more pleasant because we're in Paris. Naturally, it's impossible to anticipate even a fraction of what may happen during production or actually does. But while such preliminary meetings cannot be as valuable as the real day-by-day give and take of rehearsals, they are not without benefits or concrete results.

Over the years, the benefits have increased and the results intensified, and the meetings between us have mellowed from that first formal conference he so grudgingly granted to "the American director" of *Godot*, whose name he didn't know. My questions have gotten less general and silly, more carefully thought through and phrased. The answers have come more willingly, even if they have not always been complete ones. And I have been able to interpret them more precisely because I have understood the pauses as well as the words.

That very first time, I asked Sam who or what Godot was, though luckily not what it "meant"; and he told me, after a moment of deep reflection in those seemingly bottomless blue-gray eyes, that if he had known, he would have said so in his play. The last time I came over to talk about a production, it was to encourage him to write a companion piece to Hume Cronyn's rendition of *Krapp's Last Tape*, bringing along the companion-lady in question to inspire him. It turned out that Sam liked the lady and happened to have something in his trunk, or in his desk, that if he could do a bit of work on it, it might fit her nicely. He did, it did, and we did it—after a few days of questions and thoughts and wanderings and cafés. On all the visits in between, I've always asked him everything I could think of, and Sam has always tried to answer as fully and as specifically as he could. And at the end of it all, after he's delivered me in his rusty tin buggy of a Citroën in the Invalides air terminal or the Gare du Nord, he always has sent me homeward with the same farewell:

Do it anny way you like, Alan; anny way you like.

Once, Sam came over to join me in London, where we went together to see the original English *Godot*, then playing at the Criterion. It had just transferred from a successful run at the Arts, although the theater was not full and people were walking out all during the performance, sometimes loudly venting their British spleen. Sam sat next to me in various sections of the stalls for four or five nights in a row, staring in somewhat stunned amazement at the proceedings on stage and in the audience, occasionally leaning over to whisper to me: "They're doing it ahl whrang," referring to what was taking place on the stage. One evening, while we were backstage in the absence of the director, who happened to be the youthful Peter Hall, I had to prevent Sam firmly from giving out an array of written notes to the actors. Under the mistaken assumption that I was part of the opposition to his production, I'm afraid, Peter Hall has never forgiven me. But at least I did learn what Sam considered to be "ahl whrang." So that I could eventually go back and do it "anny way" I liked. As if I actually could.

But even after I've gotten back each time, there have always been afterthoughts, new questions, new explanations. Never has there failed to be a further exchange of ideas and problems between us, a dialogue via airmail. Continued and regular cross-currents of air-letters, post-cards, or just little pieces of paper, typed or printed, or scrawled so unintelligibly as to challenge the top cryptographer for the CIA. Over the years now, seemingly hundreds of them, suddenly part of theater history though once read and reread and studied and cherished for their apt responsiveness to a particularly crucial confusion.

Since that brief initial inquiry into the cosmic nature of *Godot*, Sam has never wanted to discuss with me (or anyone else) the metaphysical backgrounds or symbolic meanings of any of his plays; nor have I pressed him in this direction. As Beckett himself once wrote about Joyce, Sam is after all basically "not writing about something, he is writing something." His plays are not about things, they are themselves things. His work is a "matter of fundamental sounds," he once explained, with the pun intentional; and the overtones should be let fall where they may without being verbalized or pinned down at every turn. Nor does he want to try to tell me something already either obvious or not there.

Not that my reluctance to pursue philosophical trails with him means that I am totally uninterested in intellectual matters or don't enjoy these pursuits—especially away from valuable rehearsal hours and with people who don't have to act them all out on stage on opening nights. Besides, Sam is enough of a theater man himself to understand more and more the futility of trying to act out abstract themes on stage. Explanations of philosophical meanings provide marvelously satisfying speeches with which the director can impress his actors but very little practical help for them. How does one, after all, play "the end of history" or "the decline of western values"? One has to sit in a certain way against the mound, or turn over a certain way over a certain shoulder at a certain time with the spectacles held in a certain hand. Theatrical truth, as Brecht said and Beckett knows, is concrete.

And when it comes to concrete matters, our transoceanic message service has never failed to function so as to further illuminate the plays. How long should one of those famous "pauses" really take—in relation, say, to a "long pause" or, when it gets there, a "maximum pause"? Sam could give me the actual counts if I would ask him—though I never did—and although he doesn't own a stopwatch. But then he

244

doesn't own a tape recorder either, and look what he figured out for Krapp to do! It's a matter of his own innate sense of rhythm. Should Winnie's glasses be on or off at this or that point in the play? Would it be better for her to be holding the toothbrush in her left hand or her right—so that she can take care of other required matters with her other hand? And so on.

When Sam was directing *Happy Days* in Berlin a season or so ago, he carried all those answers, and a few thousand others, with him in a completely detailed cross-lined notebook, practically Cartesian in its organization of information and insight. But even before that notebook existed, it was all down logically in his head—and not only for *Happy Days*—and quite willingly shared with me whenever I was able to ask the proper questions.

The literal meaning of a line that seemed unclear, the source of a quotation, a desirable pattern of behavior or movement—these were all not mysteries but knowledge to be shared. The pace of *Godot* should always be kept light and quick, he feels; in fact, that is a basic rhythm, a common denominator for most of his plays. The "tree" is, of course, not to be a representation of the tree on stage at all, with hands outstretched as it usually is for the branches, but one of the basic positions of yoga: the sole of one foot resting in the groin, with the two hands clasped together as if in prayer. That makes infinite sense—and not just comic nonsense—of Estragon's next line: "Do you think God sees me?" Sam once even drew a small diagram to show me exactly what he meant. And I have hidden away somewhere some lovely and even more detailed pen-and-ink sketches from him outlining Willie's exact optimum path around the mound when he comes visiting Winnie. If Beckett hadn't become a writer, he could have quite well found other uses for his pen.

Nor is Sam unwilling to discuss his characters as people, although he's more concerned with their external than with their internal qualities. And never with their symbolic significances or "meaning." Yes, Vladimir is more or less restless and roams around the stage; Estragon is more or less still and sits down a lot. The Mouth is "on fire" and must keep on talking in short rapid bursts (separated by those perennial dots, of course) because she has to. The Mouth is totally unaware of where she is or of a Figure watching her. The Figure is aware of and sees the Mouth but has no effect on it. No, there's nothing in the text to indicate whether the Figure is male or female. And Krapp looks at his watch at regular intervals not just because he is bored or wants to know what time it is but because he wants to see if enough minutes have gone by for him safely to have another drink. Then he goes for that other drink anyhow. And that clink of glass without the siphon is telling us that he's saying the hell with it here and taking the last shot straight up instead of with soda, as he should, to dilute the alcoholic content. (How many otherwise intelligent drama critics have talked about the "wine" Krapp is drinking!) As Jackie always called it, Sam's "underlying simplicity" is never simple—but it's there if one only looks for it.

Once, when my entire cast of the first off-Broadway *Endgame* insisted that I write to Beckett to find out why Hamm's and Clov's faces were red while Nell's and Nagg's were white, the answer came back like a slap: Why is Werther's coat green? In other words, because the author had decided that he liked that particular color. Or colors. Or when Sam thought that both Jessie and I were asking too many foolish questions about the birth, life experience, and physical circumstances surrounding that solitary floating Mouth, he finally decided that enough was enough: "I no more know where she is or why than she does," he wrote. There was only the text and the stage image, both of which he had provided for us. "The rest is Ibsen." Or, as I used to tell Jessica Tandy when I felt that she wanted to probe too hard into recesses that didn't have actual existence, this was Samuel Beckett and not Arthur Miller. If one once started to worry about where Winnie got her groceries or how she managed to discharge her bodily functions, one could get into a lot of unanswerable questions. And into another play.

Oh yes, those inquisitive *Endgame* actors, not pacified, decided among themselves that Nell and Nagg, being older, had less efficient circulatory systems so that the blood couldn't get to their faces so easily. This without informing Sam—who would have been eminently surprised at this revelation. And Hamm and Clov had high blood pressure—though luckily neither Sam nor our audiences needed to know that.

The key to my directing of Beckett, then, may be described as that of dealing simultaneously with what I have come to call "the local situation" (in contrast to that other more cosmic one) and his rhythmical and tonal structure, his specific style or "texture." In principle, that is no different than when I am directing Shakespeare or Chekhov; in practice, one is more concerned in Beckett with the juxtaposition of specific sounds and silences, movement and speech, instead of with, say, the handling of iambic pentameter and Elizabethan footwork. The needed intertwining of comedic and serious tones in Chekhov is matched by a parallel necessity in Beckett, though framed in a more formal and less naturalistic pattern. Although *Krapp* to me has always seemed almost Chekhovian in its blend of emotional colors, Krapp himself is both Trofimov and Pischchik—and perhaps, Epihodov as well.

Dealing with "the local situation" simply assumes that I try to concern myself primarily with who the characters are as human beings, and what their human situation is. What are they doing, wanting, getting, not getting in a given scene? How do they change or not change? What happens to them in the play? How do they affect their own situation, and the other characters? What is their awareness of and reaction to the various events of the play? (It is not, for instance, the "significance" of the burning of the umbrella in *Happy Days* that can be acted but Winnie's reaction to that burning.) Most importantly, what is their physical, their sensory, reality?

Of course, examining the "local situation" also means that I have to consider how the characters got there, or even perhaps why. Is Clov that same small boy whom the father, crawling on his belly, brought to Hamm years ago? What happened to the Mouth in April in that field? But not in the same manner or to the same extent that I explore those questions of background and motivation in Ibsen or in Chekhov. How, after all, did Winnie get into that pile of sand in the first place? The answer is that she's always ("the old style") been there. The sand, though "real" to her, is to Beckett a stage world only, a theatrical metaphor, a stage image. The sand, that mound into which she eternally sinks—why?—is simply the condition of her existence. Just as, in some other type of drama, a character's job or position in society is given to us. Or just the character's happening to be there in order to fulfill a function or complete a relationship. All of those seemingly accidental but necessary and unquestioned coincidences that make possible even the entrances and exits in any supposedly realistic play.

I accept Winnie's dominating presence in the mound, the literal absence of legs in the first act and of anything below her neck in the second, as I accept Picasso's lady with several faces or Dali's bent

247

watch. Though in spite of a century of nonrepresentational art, we are still more familiar and more comfortable with the most outrageous juxtaposition of circumstances masquerading as "reality" than we are with the simplest and most direct of metaphors: let us say, our inevitably vanishing existences, for example. But we don't have to go on being uncomfortable, and the plays of Sam Beckett, I am pleased to know, have moved us a few miles up the road toward understanding of that.

Metaphor or not, though, it is the sensory reality with which the director must be primarily concerned. Winnie should be hot as well as cosmically happy and unhappy. It has never mattered who Godot really is, although we keep on asking and those convicts at San Quentin have always known. Nor even who told Vladimir and Estragon that they had to wait for him. It's the two hours of their lives and of our playing time that count. It's how they wait. Clov cannot sit down, for whatever reason; and a generation of American actors have, within my experience, offered up various answers—from arthritis through gonorrhea to hemorrhoids—although their audiences were not always able to diagnose those exact causes. So long as they were interesting and theatrical, I don't mind—and I'm sure Sam wouldn't have. Nagg and Nell are elderly, cold, hungry, sleepy, somewhat deaf, not so good at seeing, without legs, and feel a certain way about their son Hamm keeping them cooped up in those ashcans. These qualities can be acted, while the concept of the "older generation discarded" or the "dead past put onto the garbage heap" or "the flower of French civilization" cannot. Even though Sam tells us very clearly that they lost their shanks at a special time and place, Sedan, which has a distinctive echo of meaning for the French nation, although the rest of us have forgotten what happened there.

At the same time, every Beckett play—from the extremely formal *Not I* to the extremely informal *Krapp's Last Tape*—possesses its own specific tonality, its special texture. That which distinguishes it from anyone else's work. Almost any page of Beckett can be immediately identified as his. Because of his particular vision of the universe and of mortal man's frail fate in it. But also because of his specific technique of organizing and orchestrating the formal elements involved. The sparseness and simplicity of his language, juxtaposed against its passages of poetic musicality. The balance and tension of its various rhythms and sounds and images. His repetition of words and phrases. The constant interplay of parallel and opposing ideas and themes: counterpoint, auditory and visual. The carefully worked-out opposition of lines and the interrelating of opposites. And other notes of dramatic music.

As the Royal Court's George Devine, one of the earliest and most loyal of Beckett's supporters and interpreters, once explained his own view of the Beckett terrain: "One has to think of the text as something like a musical score wherein the 'notes,' the sights and sounds, the pauses, have their own interrelated rhythms, and out of their composition comes the dramatic impact."

It is only through constant attention to both Beckettian "texture" and the "local situation" that his plays can be presented faithfully. For the repetition of three dots contains a specific clue to both character reality and dramatic meaning. And I have always tried to deal with both these aspects without distortion or distraction. Through whatever means. I have talked or not talked with my actors, before or during the work. I have both demanded and given way, read them portions of Beckett's letters to me or kept them to myself. I have gone up on stage to demonstrate a special move or piece of business I wanted done in a certain way, or waited for the actors to come up with their own version—as with the choreography of Vladimir's song about the dog. Helped by Beckett's own pauses, I have always worked out the "beats" in the text—with the proper intentions, adjustments, circumstances, and other standard underpinnings. Most of all, I have tried to cast only those actors whom I felt to be suitable and agreeable to Beckett's world—and not cast those who would deny or destroy that world.

After all these years, there are a number of actors (and directors) who still do not respond to Beckett, or avoid doing his plays. They feel he limits them too severely as artists, removes their creativity and individuality, constricts them too rigidly in their physical and vocal resources. They tell me that he must hate actors because he denies them the use of their own impulses, as well as more and more of their physical selves. After all, if they cannot move freely about the stage, cannot use the full range of their voices and bodies—their very means of reaching their audiences—what are they but impersonal or even disembodied puppets of his will? Now he's even down to strapping them into some sort of medieval torture chamber, closing off their faces, including their eyes—the windows of the stage souls—in order to leave only a mouth visible on stage. What's next, they ask me, the uvula alone, pinpointed on a darkened stage? And no words for them to speak?

I do not agree. Nor did Jackie, the Irish-born actor and friend of Beckett. Before his death, Jackie told an interviewer that Beckett's "feeling for precision in inflection, rhythm, and movement seems almost severe, but not for a moment does he restrict the imagination or inventive feeling of others except if it is outside the framework of what is being interpreted. He creates a freedom in working which actors do not often enjoy in the theater today, and that freedom is always the bedfellow of true discipline."

How right Jackie was and yet how difficult it is still to explain to those actors who do not want to understand that it is precisely because Sam so admires them and so respects their abilities that he trusts them to be extraordinarily effective even with certain of those abilities confined or even removed. We have known for centuries that an actor can hold us and move us when he has full range onstage. But that he can reach us as powerfully or more so with only his face or his eyelids or his mouth, or with lips and teeth and voice alone, that is fantastic. And theatrical. And worth exploring further.

After all, do we think that Beckett hates or despises the English language because he uses so many simple one- or two-syllable words instead of availing himself of its entire range of syllabification and richness? Does he deny that language its strength and virtues because he has gone in the opposite direction from Joyce or Giraudoux or Yeats toward greater and greater selection and bareness? Is he uninterested in language itself because he makes use of only a small portion of those possibilities he knows it possesses? Of course not.

Yet even this sort of analogy has not and does not satisfy his critics on the stage and in the audience. They still complain or get angry when Beckett doesn't cater to their expectations or fit in with their past habits, though they can no longer accuse him so readily of heresy or hoax. They do continue to avoid him or in praising him not bother to read his plays or attend his productions. Years ago, Ralph Richardson turned down the part of Estragon because Beckett was unable to inform him adequately of the exact extent of Pozzo's holdings (although Richardson later had the good grace in his autobiography to confess his error). Everybody turned down Hamm for me once, as well as Krapp. In fact, dozens of actors, those of the first rank and others, have in the past turned down Beckett roles; today, more and more star names have begun to think of the plays as stage or screen vehicles for themselves to be manipulated toward their own personalities or purposes. In Paris, Madeleine Renaud and Jean-Louis Barrault have been doing *Happy Days* for years; over here, I tried in vain once to interest Lynn Fontanne and Alfred Lunt. Eventually, the last time around, I did get Jessica Tandy and Hume Cronyn, though I had a hard time talking him into doing Willie. And even the gracious Miss Tandy, if I'm not giving away too sheltered a confidence, despaired nightly of the various restraints, literal and metaphorical, placed upon her by author and director in *Not I*. She could not wait to be forever free of its head clamp, blackened makeup, and stichomythic pace.

As to my own feelings of confinement, I have none. When I limit my imagination to the boundaries set for me by Sam, I feel with Jackie that I am not so much limiting as freeing myself, just as a sonnet writer who has something he wants to express may not be bound tighter but actually guided into greater complexity by the demands of its rhyme scheme—or any artist always is by the specific limitations of his materials. When I direct Shakespeare or Brecht there are also limitations involved, though in those cases they are inherent, thus perhaps seemingly more flexible, than imposed. When I direct Beckett, I know and trust him and respond to him so directly that I can allow my own impulses and imagination to flow through his pulse beats—even though some of the critics may still say that I am abdicating my directorial responsibilities, that I am betraying Beckett by being too loyal.

Once I did put a bowler hat instead of a toque on my Hamm, but I did not consider that a betrayal of Beckett, just a practical adjustment to the fact that the actor playing the role simply did not look right in any toque we could find or make. Only once have I felt that I actually did betray Sam's real intentions. When we were doing the first production of *Play*, whose text is constructed so as to be spoken twice, the preview audiences at the Cherry Lane seemed to resent the repetition, sitting there stony-faced and bored the second time around, instead of offering up greater attention and more laughs. At the same time, our actors didn't relish the idea of speaking the lines the first time as rapidly as both Beckett and I wanted them to. They felt that the audiences didn't have a clue as to what was going on and that they were losing their laughs. (The same conflict took place, by the way, during rehearsals of the original London production; it was eventually resolved—in Sam's presence—by a rearrangement of the repetition, but with the actors both times speaking so rapidly that, Rosemary Harris told me, they could hardly catch their breaths.) After continued urgent requests by our producers and against my better judgment and previously held position, I wrote to Sam explaining that perhaps New York audiences were more sophisticated (or jaded) than all others and were actively resenting this supposed slur upon their intelligence. I asked him if he would mind if during a few of the previews we experimented with playing the text through only once and spoken a bit more slowly just to see how it would go. He wrote back his approval, without making apparent his underlying tone of sadness and disappointment.

We tried it only once through in the rest of the previews, where it seemed to be getting more of a response, and eventually in performance. Not that the change saved us. In spite of reasonably favorable notices, the production ran only a few weeks, which it would probably have done anyway, even had we played it as originally intended. They just were not ready for the play. But I realized as I have so often, before and since, that I should have stuck to my instinctive guns, done the show the way the author had conceived it. By distorting his writing we diluted his play and still did not "succeed." Doing it his way, we might also have "failed" him but at least on our own terms. Nor has that play always been successful when performed elsewhere. But at least its quality and dramatic audacity have now been accepted.

It was not until many years later, and most indirectly because he would never tell me himself, that I learned how hurt Sam had been by my decision. By then I had learned my lesson.

Those theater people who are not willing to trust, not ready to go along on a production or part of a greater equilibrium than that provided by their reflexes—or ego—cannot understand my pleasure and gratitude and joy at having been associated with Samuel Beckett's work. Not because of his fame but because of his quality. Sam's feeling for precision, for order, has always been for me a most uncategorical imperative. His rhythms, his insights, his vision of the theater have rarely, if ever, restricted my own. On the contrary, he has deepened my own experience as a working director more than any other playwright—perhaps more than anyone outside of my own immediate family.

Without, I hope, waxing overly sentimental, I must confess that I have always felt both privileged and inspired to have worked so long and so often with him—if not as directly as I would have chosen had not a particular accident of geography intervened, yet no less fully or richly. To quote the words of Sam's favorite French publisher, Jérôme Lindon, "I have never met a man in whom co-exist together in such high degree, nobility and modesty, lucidity and goodness." Sam has not only changed my life, both professionally and personally, but become part of it. From that moment, almost a quarter century ago but still seeming as though yesterday, when he first wrote to me that "the Miami fiasco does not distress me in the smallest degree, or only insofar as it distresses you," there has not been a day when I did not think of him or feel him present in my work and life. There is nothing I would not do for him, onstage or off.

Last season, while substituting for Zelda Fichandler as a somewhat inadequate producing director at Washington's Arena Stage, I had one of my few satisfactions in bringing into being an extraordinary production—on the order of accomplishment, I believe, of Peter Brook's *Marat/Sade* or *Dream*—by a leading Romanian director, Liviu Ciulei, of Georg Büchner's *Leonce and Lena*. Written about 1830, the play had never been professionally presented in this country; yet it was as contemporary in feeling as though it had been written today. While we were in previews, a sizable portion of our subscription audience walked out in high dudgeon that we could inflict this particular pain on them, then proceeded to bombard both Zelda and myself with letters expressing their keen resentment of such "trash" (although by the time we opened—and the favorable notices came out—they were a little less sure). I thought once more of Samuel Beckett and of Miami Beach, about 1956, and realized once more how little had actually changed in the theater. It was Harold Hobson, writing in the London *Sunday Times* not so long ago, who best expressed my feelings: "This complacent inability to recognize the highest, this apparently natural enmity towards the exaltation of the spirit . . . checks one's heart."

My heart, I am well aware, has been checked often throughout my

253

theater life, as has everyone's, although the causes always differ. But it is Sam Beckett's exaltation of the spirit that has taught me the one basic truth: that in spite of everything or whatever, one goes on, with or without sand in those bags; that in the theater as in all of art the only thing that counts is the work itself, the need to go on with that work at the highest possible level—not to be distracted or disturbed by success or failure, by praise or blame, by surface or show, analysis or abstraction, self-criticism or the criticism of others. This is especially important when that work is of Beckett's order of magnitude, possessed of Beckett's sublimity, his degree of compassion, his eloquent understanding of the potentialities both of the stage and of human frailty. After twenty years of working with him, I can only be grateful that whatever theatrical fates that be have put me into the same universe of possibility with him.

HERBERT BLAU

Notes from the Underground: "Waiting for Godot" and "Endgame"

There is nothing so stimulating as nothing, at least now and then.
—Max Frisch, *Diary*

You could not be born at a better period than the present, when we have lost everything. —Simone Weil, *Gravity and Grace*

HORATIO: *Oh, day and night, but this is wondrous strange!*
HAMLET: *And therefore as a stranger give it welcome.*

A woman once asked Chekhov: "What is the meaning of life?" He replied, "You ask me, what is life? It is just as if you had said, what is a carrot? A carrot is a carrot; that is all there is to it."

I have a feeling he really knew there was more to it than that, but a goodly amount of art in our time has been created or talked about to put off people who are always looking for meaning. That is why so much of it has acquired the reputation of being without meaning. The artists encourage this. Eliot says he would tell us the meaning of *Sweeney Agonistes* if he knew; Beckett says he would tell us who Godot is if he knew. In a discussion after our production of *Godot*, a chemist insisted it couldn't be a good play because there was no meaning, no message. "I want to know the message," he said, pounding the table.

Well, all you can say to that is, if there is a message it's not glad tidings. And when you're really aroused you may insist in return that an empirical scientist ought to know better than that—that a carrot is a carrot is a carrot, overstating the point.

Even so: After we satisfy our aesthetic egos and get rid of the boors by saying the thing *is*, or "nothing happens, twice," we can settle down and say a good deal about the meaning of *Waiting for Godot*, as we could about the carrot if pressed to it. If, however, you work on the assumption that "a carrot is a carrot; that is all there is to it"—nobody dramatizes the idea better than Beckett.

As for the despair that is the "objective content" of Beckett's plays, he has given the best answer to that: If it were all dark, everything would be easy, but there is the light, too. You might say Beckett begins where Chekhov leaves off. I remember a drawing by Robert Edmond Jones of the last moment in *The Cherry Orchard* as produced at the Moscow Art Theater: a brooding pointillist darkness; a sliver of light, like the vertical beam of the Cross (which you complete in your mind), the slumped figure of old Firs crawling toward the couch to die. Look again: It might be the opening of *Endgame*. Adjust your eyes to the darkness. Now you see the closed shutters, the covered furniture, the spaces on the walls where the pictures had been. The decrepit motion of the servant is the last residue of pure behavior. It is the gravitational field in which Beckett works. If you stay with it, it may even become lively. I recall a speech by an official of the Peace Corps, who said that people today *do* want to act. He quoted Confucius: "Better to light a single candle than to curse the darkness." A Beckett play lights a candle *and* curses the darkness.

For a man who has *chosen* loneliness, there is something unreal about the theater, a betrayal: the public premises, the assumption of a contained space, actors, others, an audience. As though in penance, the drama contracts to a needle's eye. The action crawls through the eye out of time, "in the dark, in the dark mud, and a sack—that's all"; or there is "a voice which is no voice, trying to speak" (I am writing from his conversation), then the crawling, the mud, "the form of weakness." When you try to imagine the play before it comes off the printed page, you may think of Beckett's favorite sculptor, Giacometti, whose figures yield, in metal, as much to the air as the air needs to surround them.

The true rhythm of Beckett's plays: "I can't, I must." When the voice rises it can be apocalyptic: "Mene, mene? Naked bodies.... Your light dying! Listen to that! Well, it can die just as well here, *your* light."

One might say about Beckett in the theater what Walton said about Donne, who slept in his winding sheet but appeared to preach in Saint Paul's when he should have been on his deathbed: "And, when to the amazement of some beholders he appeared in the Pulpit, many of them thought he presented himself not to preach mortification by a living voice: but, mortality by a decayed body and a dying face." Donne, like Beckett, was a man of great erudition. His most searching devotions were born of the Plague. So in *Godot*, the tramps look over the rubble of the audience and say, "A charnel house! A charnel house!" In one little diabolic canter, we have the decay of Western civilization and Beckett's opinion of the modern theater. If, however, the cultural diagnosis seems merely misanthropic, let us go back a few years before *Godot* to another voice, renowned for grandeur and hope: "What is Europe now? It is a rubble-heap, a charnel house, a breeding-ground of pestilence and hate." It is the atmosphere out of which *Godot* was born—the despair, hunger, and disease of postwar Europe—being defined by Winston Churchill.

As Beckett didn't invent despair, neither does he rest in it. Salvation is a fifty-fifty chance ("it's a reasonable percentage"[1]); his favorite parable: the two thieves, one of whom was saved. Because Chance leads Power in the end—Pozzo tied to Lucky—the protective device, the living end, is laughter, "down the snout—How!—so. It is the laugh of laughs, the *risus purus*, the laugh laughing at the laugh, the beholding, saluting of the highest joke, in a word the laugh that laughs—silence please, at that which is unhappy." So Nell: "Nothing is funnier than unhappiness, I grant you that. But...."[2] The laughter dies like the funny story told too often. The trick, perhaps, is to find another way of telling it. Technique again, to baffle the fates, and time. But when technique fails—as it must—more rage. So Hamm: "Use your head, can't you, use your head, you're on earth, there's no cure for that! (*Pause.*) Get out of here and love one another! Lick your neighbor as yourself!" (*Endgame*, page 68.)

The message is clear—but the message is not the meaning. As we wade through the boots, the gaffes, the bicycle wheels, the ubiquitous pipes and spools, the circular dogs, the colossal trivia and permutations of loss, the spiritual mathematics of his withered heroes and amputated clowns, you may be bewildered. But then you accept them as a matter of fact: fact—each world to its own protocol. For instance: A man needs a hat to think. "How describe this hat? And why? When my head had attained I shall not say its definitive but its maximum dimensions, my father said to me, Come, son, we are going to buy your hat, as though it has pre-existed from time immemorial in a preestablished place." Where did Lucky's second hat come from? It was just *there*. In our second production of *Godot*, when Didi and Gogo were terrified by the invaders who never came, Gogo hid behind the tree and Didi jumped into a hole we had cut into the front of the stage. Then, using a technique borrowed from the cowboy movies, he tossed his hat in the air to test the enemy. No shot, all clear. One picks up his hat and proceeds. On opening night, Didi threw his hat into the air. No shot. But nothing came down. It was perfect. One picks up Lucky's old hat and proceeds.

For those willing to play the game, the acrostics are alluring, the virtuosities entrance. But at the end of the wild-goose chase we are entangled in the net of inexhaustibility. That, rather than exhaustion, is Beckett's real subject. "You're right," says Didi, "we're inexhaustible." (*Waiting for Godot*, page 40.) That, too, is terrifying. It's funny, but then it's no longer funny. Lest we think the universe too inscrutable to bear: The hat thrown up by Didi (Ray Fry) had stuck in the light pipe above. "So much the better, so much the better." It's the proceeding that counts.

One learns, in doing them, that the plays—with their whoroscopic revelations and buried performances—are always looking in on themselves, throwing up readings, telling you how to do them. If any dramatist has the right to speak of drama as an ado about nothing, it is Beckett. And he means what is *there*. The picture waits to be turned. The window asks to be looked out of. The tree is meant to be done. The empty landscape waits to be recognized. The boots wait to be worn. Beckett may say (at a café in Paris), "That cup, that table, those people—all the same." And yet which of the New Wave—hovering over images with the camera's mind—can invest man-as-object with so much humanity? Why, tree, boot, bowler, and black radish seem more human than the people in other plays.

As for uncertainty of meaning, just perform what he tells you to perform, and you will feel—as if by some equation between doing and feeling—exactly what you need to feel, and in the bones. Climb up the ladder like Clov, backing down the rungs as he must, and you will know why he walks as he does. Speak the speech of Lucky trippingly on the tongue, clutching through all the eschatological gibberish at the loose ends of western philosophy, and you will know—if you follow the rhythm—the full, definitive exhaustion of thought. Let the tramps and Pozzo pummel you at the same time, and you will know what it is to be "finished!" Try keeping Hamm's chair *exactly* in the center of the stage, and you will know what a tortuous thing it is to wait on him. Try to hang yourself upon the tree—go ahead, try it—and you will see, decidedly, the degree to which the tree is useless. Eat Gogo's carrot and try to carry on a conversation, and you will know quite materially that a carrot is a carrot.

On the physical level, the inexhaustibility of the plays is just plain exhausting. Even thinking is a physical task, not only for Lucky. Look at Didi's face agonized with the effort to use his intelligence. Our actors discovered the physical investment demanded of them in this apparently intellectual play, as they discovered a new conception of character-in-action. Indeed, Beckett has fulfilled on stage the idea of character advanced by Lawrence in his famous letter to Edward Garnett. Not character defined by "a certain moral scheme," but character as a "physiology of matter . . . the same as the binding of the molecules of steel or their action in heat. . . ." Not what the character *feels*, for "that presumes an *ego* to feel with," but what the character "is—inhumanly, physiologically, materially. . . ." Lawrence speaks of another ego with allotropic states, in which the individual goes through transformations "of the same radically unchanged element. (Like as diamond and coal are the same pure element of carbon. The ordinary novel would trace the history of diamond—but I say, 'Diamond, what! This is carbon!')"

Like Lawrence, Beckett is out to recover *wonder*, the mysterious harmony of man-in-nature, man-as-nature. But characteristically, like chipping a hairline in marble with a nib, he does this in the form that puts character—in all its flux and transformation—in *separate bodies* before you. By an act of histrionic juggling in which they perform no-action, the two tramps convince us they live one-life. Between them—urinating, eating carrots, putting on boots, scratching the head, playing charades—they compose an identity. While habit may be the great deadener, bare necessity gives energy. The rhythm is a continuum of crossed purposes and lapsed memory. How did they get that way? As Gogo says, unable to recall what happened the shortest time before: "I'm not a historian." (*Waiting for Godot*, page 42). For the actors, identity has to be rehearsed into being. As there is no biography, there is no other way.

Nevertheless, instead of demeaning men by reducing them to tramps in an inscrutable dependency, *Godot* restores the idea of heroism by making the universe their slave. They are, as Simone Weil says of being (in a book with a title that describes the play, *Gravity and Grace*), "rooted in the absence of a place." What would it be without them? "To see a landscape as it is when I am not there," she muses. Unimaginable. "When I am in any place, I disturb the silence of heaven and earth by my breathing and the breathing of my heart."

Because the waiting, for all its avowed purpose, is purely gratuitous, it is bound to look comic—especially when, as with Pozzo, the heart seems to stop. If, like Chaplin, the tramps are victims too, there is a comparable sweetness in the terror. And unconscious power: Godot is concealed in their names.

The movement is circular, like a worn-out wheel of fortune at a deserted fairground, mysteriously turning. Having come out of history like shadows, the tramps are nothing but, and something more than, the concrete fact of the time they pass. And the question of time in the theater is limned in their every gesture. Time-in-space. If the landscape needs one of them, the one needs the other. And, as we sit superior to their impotence, our whole past vibrates in their ready presence. Patience. The future stirs in the magic circle, wheels within wheels within wheels.

Do they also serve who only stand and wait? There is an exemplum in the stasis. To a country always in danger of floundering in its industry, *Godot* is a marvelous caution.

And with all its pretended antidrama, we know it is brazenly theatrical—an occasion for talent: the Noh, the pantomime, the music hall, the circus, the Greek messenger and the medieval angel; the play is a history of dramatic art. There is even the secret of the well-made play, Sardoodledom's ultimate question: Who is Godot? Will he come? But above all, there is Racine, the great dramatist of the closed system and the moral vacuum, salvaging exhausted *données*, illuminating what was at the beginning almost entirely known.

Someone cries, another weeps—by the sorcery of form Beckett defies the second law of thermodynamics. Energy is pumped back into the dead system by having it come back from the other side of the stage, crippled and much the worse for wear, crying pitiably for help, and then behaving like an ancient hero, wisdom having come from suffering: "Have you not done tormenting me with your accursed time! It's abominable! When! When! One day, is that not enough for you, one day he went dumb, one day I went blind, one day we'll go deaf, one day we were born, one day we shall die, the same day, the same second, is that not enough for you? (*Calmer.*) They give birth astride of a grave, the light gleams for an instant, then it's night once more. (*He jerks the rope.*) On!" (*Waiting for Godot*, page 57). In the great mystique of modern helplessness, Beckett's strange achievement is to provide us, exploring the rubble, with the most compelling theatrical image of the courage to be.

As character grows fabulous, so does nature—with the same paucity of means. The tree grows leaves, the moon appears in an instant. In this effect and in the knockabout farce, there are similarities to Brecht, who admired the play and wanted to write an answer. The difference: Brecht's moon is hung on a chain; Beckett's "bleeds" out of the sky. If Alienation means to be made strange, coercing you to look again at the familiar, salvaging it from history, Beckett is the most conspicuous dramatist of Alienation. It is another way of describing his subject.

In discovering a style, the effort was to extend the natural into the unnatural, to create the reality of illusion *and* the illusion of reality, to make the theatrical real and the real theatrical, to test the very limits of style and stage. Thus, the actors, who might be going through the routine motions of anxiety, as natural as possible, would move, almost without transition, into the shoulder-to-shoulder, face-front attitude of burlesque comedians. Or Gogo, wandering about the stage in irritation, would suddenly strike the proscenium and cry: "I'm hungry!" The motive was personal, the extension theatrical, the biological urge becoming the aesthetic question. The proscenium had, in our production, no "real" place in the "environment" presumably established by the scenery, but it was an immovable fact in the topography of the stage. It was part of the theatrical environment as a painter's studio is an environment for his painting. Our task in performance was to make such gestures believable moments of action, to reassert the oldest criterion of dramatic truth, to make the improbable probable.

Godot, indeed, gives the definitive turn to the idea of Alienation. A subterranean drama, appearing to care for nothing but its interior life, it searches the audience like a Geiger counter. No modern drama is more sensitively aware of the presence of an audience or its absence. There is this consciousness in its most delicate dying fall, when the actors are most intensely self-absorbed. Empathy is controlled with diabolic precision. The Chekhovian silences, the residue of aimless

261

doing, are measured as carefully as in Webern. It is then, in silence, that the whole emotive tapestry of the theatrical event can be *heard*. The music is the most artful polyphony. Listen to the awakened boredom, the very heartbeat of the audience in this superb threnody on desire, mortality, and Time:

> All the dead voices.
> They make a noise like wings.
> Like leaves.
> Like sand.
> Like leaves.
>   (*Silence.*)
> They all speak at once.
> Each one to itself.
>   (*Silence.*)
> Rather they whisper.
> They rustle.
> They murmur.
> They rustle.
>   (*Silence.*)
> What do they say?
> They talk about their lives.
> To have lived is not enough for them.
> They have to talk about it.
> To be dead is not enough for them.
> It is not sufficient.
>   (*Silence.*)
> They make a noise like feathers.
> Like leaves.
> Like ashes.
> Like leaves.
>
>   (*Waiting for Godot*, page 40).

I am talking of action-to-be-played. Gogo and Didi are like dully dressed bower-birds in what the ornithologists call a tight arena, absolutely attuned to each other but waiting for someone else. Here they are actually engaged in a competition of sound and image, two *performers* trying to top each other, while character disappears in the metabolism. If nobody comes, together they are (the word was said with a beautifully syllabified sibilance) *sufficient*, constituting a rhythm. The rhythm is their bower. And as they sit side by side, staring out into the dark auditorium, listening to nothing, who can avoid hearing more of himself, and thus becoming a participant in the drama?

"The air is full of our cries," loudest in silence. To live is to be dubious, the acting is a revelation, we are all exposed: "At me too someone is looking, of me too someone is saying...." The play within the play was never so poignant, so particular, in its quiet dignity.

For our company, in the midst of the Silent Generation, Beckett's silence was a considerable shock. And the actor, associating through his own anxieties, had to submit to the rhythm. If *Waiting for Godot* was another testament to the decay of language, it was no mere pantomime of impoverished rhetoric, a mere autotelic gabble of words, words, words. Beckett worked like an engraver or a diamond-cutter. And in the best classical French tradition, he was purifying the language of the tribe, by referring words back to things, by making things of words. Despairing of communication, some of us were getting our kicks from silence. Thus catatonic jazz, thus dope, thus Zen. I don't mean to simplify these phenomena of the period, but Beckett knows well how deceitful, and lazy, they can be. His personal addiction is to the hardest task. "It is all very well to keep silence, but one has also to consider the kind of silence one keeps." As Roger Blin has pointed out, Beckett is not only prudish, but "In daily life we are confronted with a positive personality; a man who has fought indignities."

If *Godot* was the most authentic revelation in our theater's history, it was some time before we could get to do it. By then it had become a cause célèbre in New York, when Michael Meyerberg asked the support of eighty thousand intellectuals to keep his production going. In San Francisco, we could parlay the notoriety into something of an event, but it was more than likely to be a hapless one. Even the actors were wary of the play. Others were revolted. Several weeks before it opened, a sense of disaster circulated around the company. Irving asked me whether I wanted to go ahead. This had nothing to do with rehearsals, where the rarity of the play mostly prevailed. The meaning was becoming plain below the level of meaning. If the play seemed at first sight appalling or remote (and we forget how remote it was a short time ago), it soon acquired the queer presence of the utterly familiar, the beauty of a manipulable thumb trying to undo a shoelace underwater.

Some of us became so engaged with the play that when one of the actors baited me at a company meeting until I dropped him from the cast, another one ran down the hall after him, pinned him to the wall, and shouted, "You bastard! It's like running a knife through a painting. You hear, it's a desecration!" We made a replacement, and in about a week I talked him through the play like a catechism, directing by hypnopedic suggestion. He is a Catholic and was suspicious of the play's despair, but no movie director ever had an actor who succumbed with such simple faith.

"On this soil of Europe, yes or no," André Malraux once put the question quite bluntly, "is man dead?" "No," Beckett answered in his novel *Watt*, "but very nearly so." If we were exempt from that question, *Godot* nevertheless broke through the hostility of our company and our audience. And there was a time when I was almost convinced that this very European play, written in French and translated into English by an expatriate Irishman, was by some miracle of cultural diffusion meant expressly for Americans. As a keynote to his book on *The Theater of the Absurd*, Martin Esslin has already described our experience with the production at San Quentin, where fashion could hardly have been the reason for the play's success. The word *Godot* has since become a clinical term at the prison, where a good portion of the inmates had, before our production, never seen a play of any kind. They knew nothing of the play's notoriety. Nor did it appeal only to their sense of confinement. As a teacher at the prison remarked, "They know what is meant by waiting . . . and they know if Godot finally came, he would only be a disappointment."[3] *Godot* was the very subtext of an "international style."

Though the San Quentin experience was, in the performance, almost surrealistic (I sat among the inmates, who tossed matches in the air), and in the response one of the purest we have ever had, it was a while later that I had occasion to define our own relationship to the play. In 1958, we were invited to represent the United States regional theater at the Brussels World's Fair, and we chose to play *Godot*. Prior to the trip abroad, we were to play six weeks in New York. I went there with the cast but returned to San Francisco after two weeks to start on another production. At the conclusion of the run the cast was to go on to Brussels without me.

Unlike the performance at San Quentin, the opening in New York was a terrible disappointment. To begin with, there were murmurs before our arrival about letting this pessimistic foreign play be performed as an American offering at the fair. The New York representatives of the State Department's Performing Arts Program, possibly rattled by newspaper criticism of our selection (adverse publicity makes everybody quaver in New York), didn't even show the courtesy of greeting us before we went abroad. Heat and humidity were high that summer; we felt the coolness. As for the performance, it began (I thought) with all the verve and precision that had been so triumphant in San Francisco and on other tours, but the audience seemed frozen too. Through the whole first act there was hardly an audible reaction to any one of the reliable lines or pieces of business that had enjoyed more than a year and a half of success in our own theater. Could San Francisco be *that* provincial? The actors nearly panicked, but by sheer doggedness they aroused some response in the second act. When I had gone backstage at intermission, one of them said, "We'll show the sons of bitches!"

The reviews were mixed, the talent of the actors couldn't be denied, and the houses were as good during those six weeks as anybody expected. But during my stay in New York no suggestions I could make, no dressing-room critique could restore full confidence and spirit. Maybe we had been playing it too long. In any case, the actors were going through the motions, showing mainly technical skill, and I left New York with misgivings about the appearance in Brussels, wondering too whether in our previous revivals and in rehearsals before the trip there hadn't been a mechanical set that I had hoped would disappear in the excitement and purpose of the tour.

About a week before their departure for Brussels, after they had been plagued by the snub and the heat, and then a State Department ban on our stage manager for unspecified reasons, I decided to write the actors a letter, in an effort to review the basic impulses of the production. The affair with the State Department had made the Brussels trip all the more meaningful, because we were now going under protest. After he was first informed of the ban, Irving (who was playing Lucky) and I exchanged long-distance calls and decided, after much legal counsel and because the choice of *Godot* was already an issue, that the strongest action we could take was not to refuse to go—we had the impression they would just as well have been rid of the play—but to go to the fair and make the production work, and to publish widely a denunciation of the ban. When the State Department—to which we showed the protest in advance, hoping they would change their minds—tried to persuade us against publishing it, saying it would be embarrassing to the Performing Arts Program at the fair, we said that if America wanted a good reputation abroad it ought to learn how to behave at home. To which we added: "We have no political character, except that we cannot abide political censorship of our work."

The protest was, indeed, picked up by the news services and the foreign papers, and when the company arrived in Brussels, there was a great deal of extra-aesthetic attention to the production. As for the eyebrow lifting over the choice of *Godot*, we had contended before that the risk was worth taking, that Europeans would prefer it to *J.B.* or *Carousel* and soda fountains, that the play was one of the seminal dramas of the postwar era, that Europeans would not only be interested in seeing an American company perform it, but they would be impressed that Americans could have some sense of the peculiar anxiety and dread underlying the European recovery.

Our view was confirmed. The performances were wonderfully applauded. The interpretation occasioned much discussion by theater people, who remarked especially on the Chaplinesque comedy of it. Moreover, it outdrew everything—we were told by the State Department—except Harry Belafonte and the jazz concerts. Since I do not believe the protest was responsible for that, let me not imply that my letter to the cast remade the performance. I quote from it at length now because neither my notes nor my production book will convey more immediately the directorial problem involved, the character of our work on the play, and the ultimate motives behind its original production. What the letter demonstrates is the degree to which *Godot* had provided us with a vocabulary for our own condition:

> . . . . At this distance I can hardly pretend to be an authority still on your performances. But I am restive with intuitions and would like as usual to have the last word—this time before you take off to Brussels. These are my considered reflections and my blessings. If they range beyond *Godot* itself, they may by indirections flush directions out.
>
> I was, not to begin too solemnly, disappointed by our reception in NY and by our initial response to it. The response was natural enough; pride only makes me wish it could have been otherwise. Perhaps that was impossible under the circumstances of heat, hostility, and what seems to be a proprietary interest in Beckett or a naïve contempt for him. But your disappointment had its fly open; it was profoundly on stage at most of the performances I saw, either in a sluggishness that verged on resignation, a caution unbecoming your talents, or a determination (admirable enough)

that made you strain to show the bastards when you weren't saving yourselves. You never quite showed them what I have seen, and I suppose the
most irritating result was not the intolerable comparisons . . . but the faint
praise and blind phrases that hurt all the more because they were kind.
You were not, we all agreed, so brilliantly received as in our richest fantasies. The fantasies were natural, too; something makes me wish they
could have been otherwise.

For I should like our work to be more pure, more selfless (hence deeper
to the Self), less deluded, and more durable. I don't think we have reached
the point yet in The Workshop where we are perfectly at home with this
grand conception of our vocation. But I hold these truths to be self-evident,
that neither fame nor fortune means as much as the personal integrity of
art and that to lose faith in the face of disapproval of what you have believed
to be good and true is not itself good and true. This happened, however
briefly. You were stricken. So was I. I hope you have recovered, because
you are not going to Brussels merely out of dedication to The Workshop
or to prove anything to the world. . . . I should like to believe you are going
to perform—as the word generically implies, to complete, to carry out to
the finish, to perfect, the action you have begun. . . . You are committed,
personally, each to yourselves. I should like us to reach that serenity in
our collective work, someday, when we are proving nothing to anybody,
even ourselves. Here we are. On the stage. We begin to act, for whoever
happens to be looking, but more, for the sake of the action itself. . . .

I used to think of our production as a Noh, an accomplishment, with
something ritualistic and devout about it. I don't mean to be sentimental;
I think you have all felt something of this yourself—and our audiences too.
. . . But there are dangers to devotion; you close your eyes. I think we have,
through negligence and necessity, and through intimacy, come to take the
play for granted and moved away from its nature.

Let me clarify this. Remember in our first discussion of the play a
drawing by Paul Klee that I showed you, of an Egyptiac-Negroid woman
with a rat growing out of her hair? The effect was grotesque and funny at
once. I said then that unless you grasp the play's morbidity (seriousness is
not the same thing), you'll never gain its humor. Intimacy has made the
play less strange and less repulsive, and whatever gain that may be in
catholicity of taste, it may be necessary to recall your first experience of it
to perform it again with maximum force. The performance needs a sense
of wonder. You have to be alive to the landscape of the play and its many
marvels, for it is an Odyssey of a kind, though it stands still. Its action is
a beautiful tension of buffoonery and gathering darkness, inevitable refrains
and seizures of truth, asceticism and acerbity, and a ruefully inadequate
humanity. I remember Gene [Roche] telling me before we left SF that
someone had told him that the play was not, when he saw it, serious enough,
and Gene defended it by saying that we saw the comedy in the play. We

did. But we saw much more. Only I think that Gene, with his alert and vivid sense of humor, slights, as we all have, the remorseless pessimism of Beckett. The drama, take it or leave it, offers very little in the way of salvation and you must, for the duration, live with the pittance it offers. Without accepting the next-to-nothingness that Beckett gives, you will never achieve the proper intensity of desperation. Didi and Gogo are incurable patients locked in an eternal Patience, sad, lonely, dreadful, without avail, two hands clasped in numbed fear and trembling:

> We are the hollow men
> We are the stuffed men
> Leaning together
> Headpiece filled with straw. Alas!
> Our dried voices, when
> We whisper together
> Are quiet and meaningless
> As wind in dry grass
> Or rats' feet over broken glass
> In our dry cellar
> Shape without form, shade without colour,
> Paralyzed force, gesture without motion....

Pozzo and Lucky are gesture with motion, motionless. Beckett's sense of the human condition, what makes it ironic and universal is not that they are trapped or condemned, but they are condemned to be free. Any way you look at it condemned sounds like damned, and you have a world with all the symptoms of original sin and neither cause nor recourse.

The rhythm and the meaning, the power and the glory, are in total surrender to this state of being; one's own optimism, negligence, or cosmic indifference cannot be imposed upon the plaintive and static anxiety of the play. And since the play was created so obviously with piety, like a stylistic prayer, you betray it by carelessness. And betray yourselves. In literature of this sort, precision is next to godliness....

I think you've had your fill of NY, but be sure you've had your fill on aesthetic grounds too. Ask yourself what you might have thought of your stay if you had been much better received. I am as much concerned about your return here as your stay in Brussels; each time I go back to NY I am more than ever convinced that with all our frustration and floundering, we know better what we are about, and that a theater worth the effort of decent artists cannot be built without vision....

I would eventually be qualifying my position as the devil's advocate, but it was that spirit of secret exultation that was even more wondrous in *Endgame*—in my opinion the most profound drama in the modern theater. It was also probably the most perfect production we have ever done at the Workshop.

Endgame is a play with a tenacious memory. One may understand more about it by contrasting it with *Godot*. For some the difference may be marginal, but in Beckett, a dramatist of the selvedge and salvage, the margins are immense. If the characters in *Godot* suffer from lapses of memory, that has certain disadvantages for behavior trying to place itself. Rational discourse depends on propositions that have gone before; you have to have something to refer to in order to proceed. All consecutive argument depends on memory and when, exasperated by an empty stomach, you refuse to be a historian, that's the end of consecutive argument.

Still, not being a historian has compensating advantages for behavior, which also likes to take its head. The lapses of memory are liberating. Unimpeded by custom, form, tradition, ceremony, canon, and code, all the restrictive appurtenances of the past, behavior becomes vital, improvisational, with a childlike sense of wonder, a thing unto itself. It is. A pebble in a shoe is a catastrophe, that carrot is really a carrot, never to be forgotten. Or so one thinks. Whatever one thinks, *Endgame* puts it to the test. The title taken from chess—the crucial, deadly terminus of the game—one has a sense of looking back through thousands of years of cultural history at almost every instant. One feels inside those gray walls, as amid the odalisque splendors of Stevens's *Sunday Morning*, the dark encroachment of old catastrophe. History dank and stagnant, ineliminable, the characters forget nothing. Thus, we have an intensification of the Hamletic condition, the maximum impediment of what Coleridge described as a "ratiocinative meditativeness." All motives present at once, moved equally in opposite directions, Clov can barely act. (There were times in rehearsals when Tom Rosqui, playing the role, nearly passed out by concentration to brain fever.) The choices are marginal; the stance is indifference; the effect is excruciating. We are in Artaud's Theater of Cruelty, at the dark root of the scream, unbearably humane. What is amazing about the play is its magnitude. Haunting the limits of endurance, it finds grandeur amid the trash, trivia, and excrement of living. More than any modern drama I know it creates explicitly that place where Yeats said love has pitched its mansion. And it does this by converting an enormous sense of loss into a retrospective vision, reaching back through the failure of a culture to its most splendid figures: Hamlet, Lear, Oedipus at Colonus, the enslaved Samson, eyeless at Gaza. This vision turns up in the acting out, affecting style. The characters are savagely solitary and dreadfully engaged, the engagement impacted by paralysis. In comparison, Didi and Gogo—having forgotten their history—live moment by moment improvising, as though time didn't exist, astonishingly active in a static scene. In *Endgame,* time is the measure and the plague. Every action seems the consequence of immaculate preparations mounting moment by moment through unnumbered years. Again patience, but fevered and fierce, moving by delayed reflex of the characters through stages of decantation, down corridors of hopeless end. And there is rage, rage, against the dying of the light.

At our first rehearsals, I kept emphasizing the savage dignity of the play and the great figures in the background. But in looking back through the grotesque image of the master Hamm, whom Clov attends with his rage for order, I had forgotten to mention another character, of whom I was reminded in the foyer of the Comédie-Française. There, encased in glass, is a large chair, its leather long worn—the chair in which Molière was supposed to have died while playing *The Imaginary Invalid.* (Biographers tell us he died after the performance, but the other is the kind of story that, if not entirely true, should be.) Now, if in some way the mind creates its world (nothing either good or bad but thinking makes it so), you can become sick by playing sick long enough. Blind and paralyzed in fact, Hamm is in this sense an Imaginary Invalid. He is given to an excess of that self-dramatization which mars and aggrandizes the Shakespearean hero; like Othello or Lear, he savors his grief and his role.

After the dread pertinacity of Clov's opening mime and the mournful cadence of his first lines, Hamm stirs and yawns under the bloody handkerchief that covers his face. In the production, we decided to meet head-on the problem of stasis in relation to time: The opening mime, before the ritual unveiling of Hamm, took anywhere from twelve to fifteen minutes without a word being spoken, with hardly a sound in fact. When Clov, after about ten minutes, opened the curtains of the small windows with a sudden jerk, the scraping of the curtain rings on a brass rod was a major "event." That one action was prepared by improvisations in which, at times, he took several minutes to pull the curtains apart. The single gesture was an expressive condensation of all the remembered effort. Since there was as much reason for not pulling as for pulling, by the logic of the play the action might have taken an eternity.

In this context, the stirring of Hamm was a "miracle"—and it was waited on as such. If Clov revealed the ashcans by some untraceable canon law, lifting the sheet like the cloth from a chalice, he folded Hamm's sheet with devotional care, painstakingly each fold, and the actual unveiling before that had all the grace of a matador in his moment of truth—the physical feat was to remove the cloth in one swift gesture, without disturbing by more than a dove's breath the handkerchief on Hamm's face. It was grueling for Clov. It seemed to be, for no reason, his duty. But the privilege of lifting the handkerchief itself—always a temptation to Clov—that was Hamm's own.

"*Very red face. Black glasses.*" Under the glasses, the blank eyes ("they've gone all white") like the hollow sockets of a pagan statue; the face red from congested blood, suppressed rage, and the intensest narcissism: "There's something dripping in my head. (*Pause.*) A heart, a heart in my head." If Didi and Gogo listen to the atmosphere and hear the pulse of the audience, Hamm bursts out at the audience and loses himself in his pulse. The actor takes his cues from the throb of his temple. Action: Listen to your life, damn you! The issue of subjectivity in the art of the actor comes to its dead end, vitally. He is his own object. (Or so he says, thinks):

Me—
(*he yawns*)
—to play.
(*He holds the handkerchief spread out before him.*)
Old stancher!
(*He takes off his glasses, wipes his eyes, his face, the glasses, puts them on again, folds the handkerchief and puts it back neatly in the breast-pocket of his dressing-gown. He clears his throat, joins the tips of his fingers.*)
Can there be misery—
(*he yawns*)
—loftier than mine? No doubt. Formerly. But now?
(*Pause.*)
My father?
(*Pause.*)
My mother?
(*Pause.*)
My . . . dog?
(*Pause.*)

Oh I am willing to believe they suffer as much as such creatures can suffer.
But does that mean their sufferings equal mine? No doubt.
(*Pause.*)
No, all is a—
(*he yawns*)
—bsolute. . . .

(*Endgame*, page 20)

And with that yawn, indifferent and cosmic, Hamm fractures the absolute. There is a sough of history in that joke, the crossbreeding of
satanic laugh and sonic boom. It is the somnolent zero of the Cartesian
abyss, the penultimate sigh of romantic irony. Can things be that bad?
It is to laugh, as they say. Beckett—and to a large extent Hamm—is
precisely aware of the possibility that the world may turn into his own
worst fears, if it is not that already.

In exploring the beauty, let us not minimize the gloom, the antarctic
frost of vast emotion. There is reason for withdrawing, and as our
production gathered devotees, I felt like Hamm, enraged by the ritual
performance of those who came to it for negative kicks, without the
discipline of Clov, who would not pull back the lids and look at the
eyes while Hamm was sleeping. The play is indeed forlorn, taking
place as it does—water out one window, land out the other—on the
cracked landscape of extinction. "Finished, it's finished, nearly finished, it must be nearly finished." Dread and desire, in contemplation
of the imminent "little heap, the impossible heap." (How does Clov
read the phrase "must be nearly finished"? Speculation or aspiration?
There are countless choices like that to be made. The actor may stress
the first and think the second.)

Endgame deals with "abstractions" of character (allotropic forms)
but abstractions attached to our nerve ends. Once again we are dealing
with man without a local habitation and a name, dispossessed and
deracinated, apart from the propriety, promise, and facile redemptions
of region, home, family, custom—which are not absent but cut down
to their stumps. Its memories of the past are, however laughable, full
of regret for its passing, and it reminds us of a heritage, worthy, but
next to impossible to sustain. The actor must be very aware of these
resonances, they must come to mean something to him.

In one facet of its being, a play like *Endgame* is so appalled at the
human condition, it can hardly speak. The compulsive talk, when it

occurs, is the distress signal of silence. The language of excommunication. Its view of the future is the whisper of the faintest perhaps. In this respect, it is the consummation of other dramatic visions of our century, from disparate sources: the final words of Mr. Kurtz in Conrad's *The Heart of Darkness*, "The horror, the horror"; the desperation of Willie Loman's "I've got no seeds in the ground"; the image of Mother Courage careening through the void of the empty stage, with its attendant feeling that "the world is dying out"; and the more genial despair of the early O'Casey, "The whole worl's . . . in a terr . . . ible state o' . . . chassis!" The parallels are endless, going back in nineteenth-century drama to, say, the old wives' tale of such a schizoid play as Buechner's *Wozzeck*, in which the universe is like an empty pot and "everyone was dead and there was no one left in the whole world."

It's an old story, no less truthful for its repetition but encouraged by its repetition (thinking makes it so). It's funny, but then it's no longer funny. Ubu mourns, and becomes Clov. The laughter turns elegiac, fading through the twilight of the gods. A friend of mine once objected to *Endgame* because "You can't call the characters on the telephone." True. But if you could, you'd only be talking to yourself. *Endgame* is the crisis of exhaustion playing itself out in the suburbs of hell. It has the eloquence of blood beneath the eyelids of the nearly dead. It comes out of the world of men and affairs like a scarcely audible bell out of the enshrouding fog—no less alarming for its remoteness. It is just such a story as Horatio might tell if he tried to fulfill the impossible burden placed on him by Hamlet in those exquisite dying lines: "Absent thee from felicity a while,/And in this harsh world draw thy breath in pain/To tell my story." How tell it? Where that story really took place, Horatio never was. To tell it, he'd have to re-enact the play, he'd have to *become* Hamlet. But wasn't it he who said, "'Twere to consider too curiously to consider so"? Failing to tell the story, he'd become Hamm.

In such a play, rehearsing visions of greatness around "the insane root," the magic is blacker than we might like; but you can't run away because where in the world would you go? No modern drama comes closer to making you feel what Socrates meant when he spoke of "a doctrine whispered in secret that man has no right to open the door and run away. . . ." There is no more poignant moment in our theater than when Clov, responding to Hamm's request for a kiss, says no; there is no braver moment than when Hamm discards his properties, his dog and his whistle, retaining only his stancher to support his self in defiance of nothingness. Yet, choosing estrangement, he is dependent in bristle and bone—and the play's black art awakens our will to survival by cutting us to the quick.

There was nothing more regenerative in our repertoire.

And this was also true of style. If *Godot* made us significantly aware of barriers to cross, with *Endgame* we made a decided leap. I am talking of the whole visceral life of performance, which was to a large extent prompted by the scenic idea. For it was with *Endgame* that the eye-opening blitz of modern art came most subtly and vividly into our theater.

We did a second production of *Godot* after we did *Endgame*. The first, designed by Robin Wagner, was enchantingly "seen," but it was more deliberately "symbolic," with the clean Gothic line of a romantic ballet. There was a huge black backdrop with raggedly-etched streaks of white and gray cloud. It was somber, but very handsome. There was even a certain luxury in the bare tree, bent like a willow (or a question mark), two low branches twisted into the shape of Rosicrucian crosses; or, since there was nothing exactly to be read, a pair of crossed fingers. Above two molded levels there was a hint of barbed wire strung from three stakes. They might have been telephone poles on an abandoned road; the perimeter of a junk yard; or a concentration camp; even, vaguely, a circus. The action, suited to the impeccable bleakness of the open spaces, broke out of deepest melancholy into dance: a gavotte of musing. If nothing were to be done, it could be done with the most meticulously orchestrated activity. *Endgame* was similarly orchestrated, but every move was made at great cost—and the reason could be read in the nonobjective surfaces of the walls. How they came to be the way they were is worth looking into, in view of all the current urgings for our theater to catch up with the discoveries of painting and sculpture. For there are dangers, particularly as the "antiform" of Beckett develops into a new Ashcan School, with ragtags of cadence and attitudes that are gratuitously worn, as though carrying by some willful assumption of feeling the burden of thousands of years of culture. With Beckett every discard is deeply felt. (I remember Roger Blin saying, after he dropped out of the role of Krapp, that he was tired of the absurd. Coming from him, the most relentlessly disaffiliated *régisseur* in the French theater, that was quite an admission. Beckett had worn him down. When I returned from France, I asked

Bob Symonds—who had been playing constantly in *Endgame*—how he felt. He said: "I feel terribly old.") Innocence having ended, however, some of our young artists try to sound as if they were born to a dying fall, prematurely ancient.

Axiom for absurdists: In art, even decay has to be earned.

Parody is the gamble made by Robert La Vigne, the painter who designed *Endgame*. His own "Black Art," a series of collages done after he had been with us for several years, owes a debt to assorted lions: Ubu, Beckett, Genet, and Cézanne. "I am the thief in the night," he wrote to me once with dark humor. "Beware my shifty voice."

Whatever La Vigne picks up in his wary passage through the night (during rehearsals of *Endgame* an amazing pile of junk accumulated in front of the stage), forage and style go—when he is in control—through the crucible of a fine sensibility. There is the liability of a lot of thrashing about, an impulse to desecrate, but La Vigne, with a French ancestry, has taste. Painting, he says, "is an old man's art." La Vigne himself is still young but has an instinct for the ages. And that is why I remembered him when the idea struck me for the scenic image of *Endgame*.

Beckett's stage direction calls for a *"Bare interior. Grey light."* (*Endgame*, page 1). Nevertheless, as in *Godot*, I wanted a landscape. We are beginning to realize that much abstract expressionism is fundamentally landscape painting, collage being its most urban manifestation. Beyond that, it attempts to put time into space. And I wanted a temporal landscape—a cultural geography, allusive, visual quotations from history, crepuscular, rhythmic, emblems of decay, bleedings, rot, scum, fragments shored up eloquently in the general ruin, blending into the nonobjective surfaces of gray walls. I took my clue from the Japanese Nō, which is a kind of dramatic collage, impacted with allusions remote beyond memory of its oldest connoisseurs—*Endgame* was of this nature. There was also Beckett's essay on Proust, in which he speaks of personality as a "retrospective hypothesis": "The individual is the seat of a constant process of decantation, decantation from the vessel containing the fluid of future time, sluggish, pale and monochrome, to the vessel containing the fluid of past time, agitated and multicoloured by the phenomena of its hours."[4]

So the walls, washed by the hours: the color of epochs coming back to gray. That's all to begin with: gray walls, and hardly a real object in sight. Only shapes: Hamm's shape under a sheet; the shape of ashcans under a sheet; Clov's stooped shape in the rear, barely discernible even as a shape. Bulk. Undifferentiated mass. Then more light. Two rectangles in the rear (the windows); the door; a patch on the wall (the picture turned in, waiting to be turned). The sheets removed: Hamm's stancher like a Veronica; the flutings of the ashcans, sulfated, like stumps of Corinthian columns, but ashcans. Collage was not only the principle of the scenery, it was also in the costumes and makeup. Clov, for instance, was virtually sealed into leather, as if preserving himself from whatever air was left, his face swollen red by concentration of his rage for order.

For all the implication that the drama takes place in the brain, the walls were rigidly squared, for chessplay and precise measurement, a graph in three dimensions—adjacent to a kitchen ten feet by ten feet by ten feet. Nevertheless: With a collage made of hundreds of nails, lace, paint, brocade, corrugations, glue, and grit, there was history for Hamm to look at (though he couldn't see) when Clov pushed him on his oriental journey amid these walls (the walls of the brain, the eyes of the mind) to the end that was hollow, hollow. It was a diffused, indecipherable sort of history, not easily read, but appropriate for such a journey (counterclockwise, like the movements of Krapp). When Clov finally brought him back to the dead center of the stage, gray light laving from above, one had the feeling they had gone through a rite of passage lasting untold years. It is near the end, as at the beginning. Something has taken its course. And it had a profound influence on the way we conceived our plays from that time on.

When, for instance, we revived *Godot* at our small theater, La Vigne did a new design. As we were discussing possibilities for the play, I happened to read an account of an underground nuclear test, in which the released megatons accelerated the process of mineral evolution, so that artificial jewels were imbedded in the ground. It was such a landscape I had in mind for the new production. The audience would be in the cave (our little theater has a low ceiling); the stage would look as if it were blown away from the end of the building by a blast. The whole landscape would be *man-made*. Junk would either be impacted in the ground, or look like it were growing out of it, like vegetation. The mound was a "found object," a gas tank rigged on a curved pipe; it looked like a toadstool. The entire floor (on which the audience looked down) was covered with foam rubber painted with black latex, so that the ground, tarred and tactile, would impede motion. The background was a collage of cloud forms and found objects, and the hole we cut in the front of the stage served numerous functions, a hiding place or a trap in an obstacle course. The floor of the stage was so inviting, like marrow, like mud, like pus, like the "bubos" which Artaud celebrates and children explore with their fingers, the bubos which appear "wherever the organism discharges either its internal rottenness or, according to the case, its life."

The floor led to one sequence where, after abusing the crippled Pozzo and trying out the names Cain and Abel, the tramps lay down to sleep, and all four actors became part of the total collage. Immobile. Time erased. The waiting reduced to inertness. Pre-totemic. (*Silence.*) Geologic birth. A setting for "the truthful precipitates of dreams. . . ." Then slowly the collage comes to life, motion festering in the inorganic, ontogeny recapitulating phylogeny. In their movements the actors rehearse both the natal cycle and the process of evolution: Didi crawling in and out of the hole, luxuriating in the landscape, a reptilian form; Pozzo twisting, flopping in agony, like a wounded mammoth; Gogo rolling into a fetus; and Lucky there, still, a fragile crustacean, his white hair like some sun-bleached fungus in the Encantadas. A preverbal poetry born of the death instinct, and the Plague; carrion man restored. The conscious waiting resumed in a rebirth of action marked by the completion of a game and the line: "Child's play."

It was in this production, too, that we did one of our first experiments with front curtains, in warfare with the proscenium (another Totem, with its own Double). Again the cue was taken from abstract expressionism, in which the painter's desire to escape the constricting boundaries of the frame is equivalent to the director's desire to escape from the proscenium stage. The painter "solved" his problem by widening the canvas so that the verticals and horizontals of the edges were out of his ken in the act of composition. He could work toward them, but they were, if he battled close in, no *a priori* imposition on his impulses— they were a periphery out of immediate sight. On the stage we were doing just that, working inside the box to lose sight of its limits. But once the director moves out of the frame and sits back in the auditorium, there is the Totem again. So, in our losing battle, we tried to violate it with a floating nonobjective form, with apertures—and when the lights came up on Gogo on his mound, he became part of a sculptured image. When the play began, the curtain jerked up once; no rise; then again; no rise, and then slid indifferently to the floor—a failure, disgraced. "Nothing to be done."

This action and the blitzed landscape were prepared for by a score of sound blocks by Morton Subotnick, electronic music composed directly on tape. The audience walked into this barrier of sound, this ambiance, as they entered the auditorium. They could not adapt to it because of its atonality and the accidental occurrence of its sequences, until, like a disarticulated Pied Piper, it led them directly into the play. Or so was the intention. For although I think this worked, and the revival was much applauded, there was, for me, a failure of harmony in the production. It lacked the "completion" of *Endgame*. One of the hazards of collage is its prodigality—the difficulty of resolve in the art of waste. In La Vigne, while it releases fantasy (loot and lust making for restorations), it also encourages a natural equivocation. Though one never knows when a theatrical composition is finished, you can feel when it is unfinished (I do not mean under-rehearsed). And so far as the scenic investiture went, it suffered from a desire for total mastery that, in principle, doesn't give a damn—by which I mean the collage, however permanently built, is a tribute to impermanence. It isn't quite a Happening, but doesn't know why it shouldn't be. In *Endgame* the possibilities were limited by the walls.

As for the acting and directing, it might have been submitted to a more ruthless scourge, in keeping with the landscape. The pocks should have secreted entirely new ghosts. I don't mean that it wasn't a compelling production, only that it depended somewhat too much on findings from the first; and the balletic motion of the original sometimes stumbled on the more cluttered stage. At the same time some of the exploration induced by the new environment tortured some of the old rhythms out of shape. When we played at the Seattle fair in the summer of 1962, we returned—because of the larger playhouse—to the old set, and the actors felt liberated by greater space. There may have been one additional factor: By the time of the revival, we had become accommodated to Beckett, exhilarated, possessive, dilatory over the nuances. I was also intensely engaged in the effort to find our own hieroglyph—a theatrical style that would stretch every action to the limits of the credible. The *mise en scène* was becoming a more powerful motive force in my own work; and I was talking then—conditioned by our production of *Lear*—about "risking the baroque."

NOTES

1. Samuel Beckett, *Waiting for Godot* (New York: Grove Press, 1956), 8. References in the text are to this edition.
2. Samuel Beckett, *Endgame* (New York: Grove Press, 1958), 18. References in the text are to this edition.
3. Following our appearance there, the inmates formed their own drama workshop and, after a year or so of preparation on other plays, have performed both *Godot* and *Endgame* themselves. They have since put out a commemorative edition of the prison newspaper containing reviews, commentary, and letters on our presentation of *Godot*.
4. Samuel Beckett, *Proust* (New York: Grove Press, 1970), 4-5.

WALTER D. ASMUS

Beckett Directs
"Godot"

Beckett is coming to Berlin to direct *Waiting for Godot*. He is no stranger at the Schiller Theater: after *Endgame*, *Krapp's Last Tape*, and *Happy Days*, this is his fourth visit as a director. He also took part in the rehearsals of *Godot* ten years ago, and it was then that he met the actors Bollman, Wigger, and Herm. Bollman and he had also worked together on *Endgame*.

Rehearsal conditions are ideal: from 28 December to 8 March, mornings only, mostly on stage. Everybody taking part in the production brings enormous sympathy and respect toward Beckett—to such an extent that this will be inevitably, though not obtrusively, reflected in the working process. But he is not only respected as an authority, as a competent interpreter of his own script; more than that the working relationship with him is characterized by caution, attention, concessions, and openness—criteria for attitudes to set free his own attitude. On this basis, everybody tries not to disturb, but to strengthen the tacit mutual trust and to do their job with the highest possible degree of understanding and appreciation toward Beckett. As the weeks go by, there is a strong and at the same time a very vivid and dynamic structure to the group, interchangeable relationships evolving. Beckett's immaculate German is characterized by a typical idiomatic exactness that seems to influence the tone of all taking part. The language gains generally a slight overemphasis, expressive of care and consciousness. As a result of this linguistic precision, most misunderstandings are resolved from the beginning. The everyday colloquial tone ensures a strange, unauthoritarian accent, unusual in the theater.

Should misunderstandings still arise, if only through chance mishearings, everybody, even if only taking part indirectly, is willing to help and clear them up. This atmosphere of constant, concentrated alertness, and the pleasure in following up processes, in which each individual might not always be directly involved, is a further result of the "unauthoritarian" working relationship. People who meet and work with Beckett inevitably seem to end up admiring him.

The rehearsals are carried out in a rather conventional way: After a relatively fast read-through of the script, the detailed work follows with increasing intensity. Content is not being discussed, only (if necessary) situations are cleared up, and with that explanations about the characters given. The great precision of the work and the striving to keep the form as tight as possible are fascinating in themselves. So the necessity to investigate the content of the play is being pushed to the background for the time being (which, of course, has also got something to do with Beckett's well-known aversion to "explaining" his play).

Beckett subjects his own script constantly to critical control in the most amazing and sympathetic way. He is also open to suggestions any time, and he even asks for them. He is not at all interested in carrying out a rigid concept but aims for the best possible interpretation of his script.

Should uncertainty occur, he is ready with a new suggestion the next day, always precise and thought through—even if it does not always work immediately. So it happens that before the second full rehearsal, there is a two-page cut to be discussed, because the scenic transformation remained unsatisfactory. The high degree of consciousness and self-control does not strike the actors as making them performing animals—indeed, they consciously accept it, intensify it, and build on it.

Friday 27 December 1974

Technical rehearsal. Matias, Beckett's designer, talks with the technical director about the stage design, on the stage. I am standing with Beckett at the footlights. He takes off his dark glasses and asks me whether we can rehearse today. No, the technical rehearsal will certainly take too long—added to which we have not asked the actors to come in yet. I pass him one of the scripts, which has been typed up and duplicated after his alterations. He seats himself immediately at a table, and is not distracted by the noise of the building gang on the stage. He is comparing the two scripts page by page, following each line with his pen. A picture of isolated relaxation.

As the chief of the costume department comes up to talk to him, he stands up to explain details about the costumes from the designs. Vladimir is going to wear striped trousers, which fit him, with a black jacket, which is too small for him: The jacket belonged originally to Estragon. Estragon, on the other hand, wears black trousers, which fit him, with a striped jacket, which is too big for him: It originally belonged to Vladimir. In this way, the differing physiques of the two actors, Bollman and Wigger, become part of the whole conceptual consideration. Similarly, Lucky's shoes are the same color as Pozzo's hat, his checked waistcoat matches Pozzo's checked trousers, as his gray trousers do Pozzo's gray jacket.

About Estragon and Vladimir, Beckett says: "Estragon is on the ground, he belongs to the stone. Vladimir is light, he is oriented towards the sky. He belongs to the tree." Beckett speaks very little. He asks me when I started working at the theater, and what did I do before that? There are long pauses between fragments of conversation as we watch the carpenters work on the stage.

When I ask him how he would like the first rehearsals to be, he reacts almost excitedly. No, the stage is not going to be free until 2 January. Is the rehearsal stage as large as this one? It is very important, because of the distance between stone and tree. We will have to be able to create at least almost the same distance, and we are using a raked stage, too.

Are we going to start with the first act up to the Pozzo-Lucky scene tomorrow? I ask him. No, he would like to start off with Lucky's monologue.

Estragon and Vladimir are going to join us at noon. In the meantime, the rake has been built. The carpenters are still experimenting with the moon—the same moon as the one used ten years ago when *Godot* was last played at the Schiller-Theater, partly with Beckett's help. Wigger comes and greets Beckett warmly: "I am very much looking forward to the work." Other members of the company are coming to shake his hand and are seemingly pleased to see him again. Beckett returns the cordiality.

Saturday 28 December 1974

10:00 A.M. on the rehearsal stage: The slope is there, the stone is marked by a small wooden box, a blooming apple tree presents itself Chekhov-fashion.

Almost abruptly, Beckett starts to talk about Lucky's monologue. It is not as difficult as it may seem, he says. We are going to divide it into three parts and the second part is going to be divided again into two sections. The first part is about the indifference of heaven, about divine apathy. This part ends with, "but not so fast. . . ." The second part starts off with "considering what is more" and is about man, who is shrinking—about man, who is dwindling. Not only the dwindling is important here, but the shrinking, too. These two points represent the two undersections of the second part. The theme of the third part is "the earth abode of stones" and starts with "considering what is more, much more grave." Beckett is very concerned to be exact in his explanations and to repeat certain ideas, underlining them with short gestures while we are looking for them and marking them.

Herm would like to know, how should he deal with the end of the monologue? Beckett explains that the different elements, belonging to the first three sections, are returning here, at the end. He compares these with a cadence in music: "The threads and themes are being gathered together. The monologue's theme is: to shrink on an impossible earth under an indifferent heaven."

Herm starts to read. Beckett stops him, to undertake some alterations in the script. Instead of *von der anthropopopopometrischen Akakakakademie*, it should read *von der Akakakakademie der Anthropopopometrie* (as it stands originally in the English version). The alteration is purely for rhythmical reasons. Herm repeats the line several times. Beckett insists on an exact, rhythmical rendering and reads each syllable with him, underlining it with gestures.

Herm carries on reading. Beckett stops him again and starts reading the lines together with the actor: ". . . that man in short, that man in brief in spite of the strides of alimentation and defecation is seen to waste and pine. . . ." He stresses the word *Mensch* (man) making the *sch* into a long, hissing sound. "'Dwindle': that is the climax," he says.

In the next section "the earth abode of stones" is the most important,

Beckett points out. The earth is good only for stones. Herm: "I looked up the meaning of Apathie, Athambie, Aphasie: *Gleichgültigkeit, Unerschrockenheit,* and *Sprachlosigkeit.*"

Beckett: "Yes, that is right. It concerns a god who turns himself in all directions at the same time. Lucky wants to say 'Quaquaquaquaversalis,' but he can't bring it out. He says instead only 'quaquaquaqua.'"

Herm: "I have looked them up, the names you use. Peterman was a cartographer."

Beckett: "It is all about stones, about the world of stones."

Herm: "Peterman exists."

"I haven't thought of that," says Beckett. "And Steinweg, the name means nothing."

Herm: "Belcher, that one was a navigator...."

Beckett interrupts him, excited and with delight: "No, Belcher, that is the opposite of Fartov, English to fart. And Belcher, to belch." With one blow the mysticism about Beckettian names is destroyed.

Beckett once again returns to the ideas he thinks most important. He scans "to shrink and dwin-dle," making a prophetic and threatening gesture with his finger. "To shrink and dwindle..." will cause bewilderment for the public: but at this point everything will be absolutely clear—for Lucky. Lucky's thinking isn't as good as it used to be: "He even used to think prettily once," say Pozzo. Herm could play it that way, watching Pozzo from time to time. And the two others, too. He is not talking simply to himself, he is not completely on his own, says Beckett.

Herm: "But he kind of refuses first, he doesn't like the idea of thinking."

Beckett: "He would like to amuse Pozzo. Pozzo would like to get rid of him, but if he finds Lucky touching, he might keep him. Lucky would like to be successful."

Herm: "He gives Estragon once, a long look. What do you mean to say with this long look?"

Beckett: "It's a kind of look you can't explain in a few words. There is a lot in that look. Lucky wants the piece of bone, of course. Estragon, too. That is a confrontation, a meeting of two very poor people."

Herm: "Something like solidarity, is that in it, too?"

Beckett: "Yes, there are so many things in his head. Recognizing the other one's situation, that is very important—but also some pride, that he is free to dispose of the bones, as opposed to Estragon. But Lucky does not forget either. The kick in the shin should be interpreted as Lucky's revenge for the fact that Estragon took the bone."

Beckett Interprets Lines for the Actors

Beckett carries on with his explanation of the play. It should be done very simply, without long passages, to give confusion shape, he says, a shape through repetition, repetition of themes—not only themes in the script, but also themes of the body. When at the beginning Estragon is asleep leaning on the stone, that is a theme that repeats itself a few times. There are fixed points of waiting, in which everything stands completely still, in which silence threatens to swallow everything up. Then the action starts again.

Wigger: "But in spite of everything, it is at odd moments quite a cheerful game."

Beckett: "Yes, of course, but that should be done very accurately. The splitting up of Vladimir and Estragon is such a point: They are, in fact, inseparable."

Wigger: "Like a rubber band, they come together time after time."

Beckett: "The principle is: They have to come together step by step."

Beckett walks on the stage, his eyes fixed on the ground, and shows the movement as he speaks Estragon's lines: "You had something to say to me?... You're angry?... Forgive me.... Come, Didi. Give me your hand...."

With each sentence, Beckett makes a step toward the imaginary partner. Always a step, then the sentence. Beckett calls this a step-by-step approach, a physical theme, which comes up five, six, or seven times and has got to be done very accurately. This is the balletic side of the story. Lucky falls twice, and this mustn't be done realistically, but very cleanly.

Wigger: "Does that mean that there is no naturalism left whatsoever?"

Beckett demonstrates: He goes down on his knees and, his arms first upward then stretching forward, lets himself slide on the ground.

Wigger: "But how can one prevent the loss of all human consideration, how can one prevent it from becoming sterile?"

Beckett: "It is a game, everything is a game. When all four of them are lying on the ground, that cannot be handled naturalistically. That

285

has got to be done artificially, balletically. Otherwise, everything becomes an imitation, an imitation of reality."

Wigger: "Are you implying a certain dryness?"

Beckett stands up. "It should become clear and transparent, not dry. It is a game in order to survive."

Beckett in Dialogue with Actors

Beckett continues to make associations with the play: He is very concerned to find clues and to share them with the others.

Beckett: "*Relaxation* is a word of Estragon's. It is his dream, to be able to keep calm. Vladimir is more animated. *Jupiter's son* is wrong: Atlas was not Jupiter's, but Japethos' son."

Wigger: "And no one noticed this in all these years!" (Much laughter.)

Beckett does not like to speak generally about the play. We undertake a discussion of the play, dividing it into different parts. In the first act, there are six parts, in the second, five. They are going to be called A1 to A6 and B1 to B5. Everybody makes the divisions in their scripts. The waiting points (which are not necessarily in accordance with the divisions of the script) are also fixed.

Right at the very beginning, there is an alteration. Estragon is sitting on the stone. Vladimir is standing in the shade near the tree, hard to see. Here is the first waiting point. This is quite an important alteration, that both characters are on stage right from the beginning—as also at the beginning of the second act. But the stage direction in script still says, "*Estragon, sitting on a low mound, is trying to take off his boot. . . . Enter Vladimir.*" But now Bollman and Wigger are sitting next to each other, reading the script continuously till the scene between Pozzo and Lucky. After that the blocking starts. Beckett is on the stage and demonstrates each move exactly on cue, while he speaks the lines, which he knows by heart.

Bollman and Wigger repeat the movements and make notes in their scripts. What Beckett described just now as an approach is becoming clear: Vladimir approaches step-by-step from behind the tree, which stands at the back of the stage to the right. Estragon is sitting on the stone in the front to the left. Vladimir is constantly in motion; Estragon sticks to his stone. The reason for dividing the acts is becoming clear: A2 starts when Estragon stands up and gets moving. With an almost frightening concentration and willpower, A1 and A2 are gone over with absolute precision until the scene with Pozzo and Lucky. The uncompromising attitude with which Beckett returned to the script time after time in the earlier conversation is now transformed into practice.

The Regie Book

In a red hardbound volume of checked paper, a book has been created about another book: a metabook. Written in black ink in English in 105 pages, there are detailed directions concerning the whole play.

Pages 2 to 53 contain the scenic arrangements. The right-hand page is mostly used for a written description, while the left hand page is used for sketches or is left blank for corrections or additional notes. The divisions follow those of parts A1 to A6 in the first act and parts B1 to B5 in the second. Each move, each section, is provided with the relevant cue of the German script, underlined each time.

The second part of the book is classified by themes: Lucky's movements; Estragon's feet; Estragon's sleep; the whip; Vladimir, Estragon, and the tree; examination of location (with sketches); doubt—confusions; come, let's go; help; what did I just say; heaven; sleep; to remember; step-by-step approach.

Added to each of the thematic cues are the relevant lines or situations or (as in the case of Lucky's monologue) descriptions or explanations concerning meaning. Both parts are diagonally connected too: In the second, thematic part, there are references to where to find the relevant lines of the first part, and vice versa.

Beckett compiled this regie-book before he came to Berlin. It has to be understood as his attempt to give a scenic outline—a structure—to a play that has been regarded as "not visualized." This is surprising: When one reads the script it appears to be a *non plus ultra* of exactness and form.

When Beckett made the attempt—sitting at his desk—to visualize his play, he knew, of course, why he always left the left-hand page in the regie-book blank. The practice on the stage during the rehearsals led—even if only occasionally—to corrections. Without these additions (in red) the regie-book is now no longer complete. The classification by themes reveals the structure of the production: Although under each heading there is an enumeration of all the places where the theme

287

comes, up it cannot be regarded as a mere catalog. For—and this can be followed through in the diagonal connections—in the blocking and in the construction of the dialogues there is a structure of repetitions, variations, similarities, parallels, of echoes and accumulated references, and these are realized in the production as concrete structure and form.

Tuesday 18 January 1975

The actors are on the stage. It is the usual relaxed starting ritual. While they are still chatting, Beckett walks up and down the stage, his eyes fixed on the ground, glancing at them from time to time. He is concentrating entirely on the coming scene. According to an agreement the day before, the rehearsal starts with Estragon's line "Sweet mother earth," where they are all lying on the ground in the second act. The actors take up their positions of their own accord; the transition from joking and chatting to concentrated rehearsal work happens naturally, almost without a break. The subjective, private attitudes of the actors and the play as a subject of work are correlating in such a way that it produces an atmosphere of "relaxed tension," which could also be described as an occupation of pleasure.

Bollman, Wigger, and Raddatz are lying on the ground. Herm is marked by a rolled-out carpet. It is not essential for him to lie there all the time, Beckett has said. The scene begins. Pozzo creeps away; Estragon and Vladimir are calling him. As they get up, there is an interruption. This structure has been fixed for quite a while, but Beckett would like to tighten it once again. The getting up at the beginning should be done in a normal way, but after that the movements should be slowed down. Bollman and Wigger synchronize once again the gestures between themselves. Then they come halfway up with a slight jerk, whereby they support themselves with their hands (they are lying next to each other), each of them in turn getting up first to the side, then to the back, moving up almost in slow motion and turning toward each other. After a short break, there follows a slow, graceful gesture with both arms, and Estragon's line, "Child's play." Vladimir accentuates his "Simple question of will-power" by performing the well-known obscene gesture with his right arm. Beckett calls this process "balletlike." Through this formal precision is the meaning both canceled and evident at the same time.

288

Actors Tease Beckett

Before the second run-through, the following occurs. Bollman, pretending to be serious, says to Herm, who is standing at the footlights watching, "Come here at once and lie down. What are you standing around for?"

Wigger (taking the point): "I can't rehearse like that...."

Herm also reacts to the game: "But Mr. Beckett has said—"

Bollman: "Will you come here at once? What are you getting paid for?"

Beckett smiles somewhat insecurely and watches Herm getting into his lying position. Bollman and Wigger are thrashing Herm on the behind with a pretended childish seriousness. Beckett gets the point and laughs at the echoing of a similar situation in the play:

ESTRAGON: And suppose, we gave him a good beating, the two of us?

VLADIMIR: You mean, if we fell on him in his sleep?

ESTRAGON: Yes.

VLADIMIR: That seems a good idea all right.

What Bollman and Wigger are carrying out privately, they perform in the context of the play, through a whole range of emotions—joyful, childish, naïve and sadistic—yet at the same time with a thrilling, funny kind of anticipation.

The getting up is repeated, and then Vladimir's and Estragon's "staggering" is tidied up. On the turn after Pozzo's question "What is it like?" Beckett has some doubts and would like to cut it. He is very much concerned with tightening the action at this point. They try it without the 360-degree turn.

"What do you think?" Beckett asks.

Herm: "I think it is good to have some motion at this point."

I agree too: "I find that Estragon's line 'Some diversion!' comes out much more strongly after the movement." We stick to the turn for the time being.

Starting with "Sweet mother earth," the scene is being played in context until the exit of Pozzo and Lucky. When Estragon and Vladimir—all lying on the ground—shout, "Pozzo," Beckett slips in a small alteration. Instead of speaking all the time toward the back, toward

289

Pozzo, Estragon should say his "We might try him with other names" directly to Vladimir. There is thus a small intimate moment of conspiracy created at this point, which is reminiscent of similar moments throughout the play.

After a short break for cigarettes, we take the whole section from the entrance of Pozzo and Lucky until the end of the play. Beckett is sitting in the auditorium at his desk with his cigarillo, watching anxiously the "conspiracy scene" between Estragon and Vladimir shortly after the start. He throws something in from time to time but without interrupting the action: "Glance toward Pozzo"; "Both on the top of your toes"—reminding them of things agreed beforehand.

The end of the play: Estragon's trousers are duly falling down. There is loud laughter from the auditorium. Beckett laughs too. Bollman's undershirt has been altered. It now reaches to his calves. It is of pink material, which has been added to but not yet sewn on properly. Bollman stands there looking like a rather unhappy old woman.

Beckett is very pleased with Wigger's monologue shortly before the entrance of the boy. Wigger looks very relaxed, very intense, listening inwardly, and makes only very brief glances around him. The key to this point in action is silence. After the break all scenes starting from Pozzo's entrance to the end of the play are rehearsed again. Beckett sits downstairs making notes. Short corrections are made: "The 'walk' of Estragon and Vladimir should be taken through without stopping; the tiger should 'rush' more in Vladimir's description. After 'Who farted?' jump further back. The pulling up of trousers should only be indicated."

Bollman tries. He is holding his trousers at his belly with his right hand, his pink shirt hanging out on the side. He makes a deplorable but touching picture.

Translated by Ria Julian

RUBY COHN

Beckett Directs: "Endgame" and "Krapp's Last Tape"

"For me theater is first of all a relaxation from work on fiction. We are dealing with a definite space and with people in this space. That's relaxing."
"Directing too?"
Beckett laughs: "No, not very. It's exhausting."

Beckett's involvement with theater has increased with the years. The main product of that affair is twenty-one extant plays, excluding the several abandoned fragments. The byproduct of that affair is intense attention to performance of those scripts, beginning with the lost *Kid*. Written in French in 1931, while Beckett was a graduate student at Trinity College, Dublin, the play is a parody of Corneille's *Le Cid*, mocking the unity of time. Twenty-four-year-old Beckett played Don Diègue, the aged father of the Kid, in period costume but a bowler hat. The play had only two performances and did not inspire Beckett to continue with theater. Five years later, asked by a friend to help her with a play, Beckett "began to hang around on the fringes of various dramatic groups in Dublin."[1] Other than the aborted *Human Wishes*, however, he was still not inspired to continue with theater. Ten years later, in 1947, *Eleuthéria* bears witness to his familiarity with problem plays, simultaneous sets, Pirandellian quips.

Affiliation with performance, however, came only with attendance at Roger Blin's 1952 rehearsals of *En attendant Godot*, whose premiere was 5 January 1953. Although accounts differ as to the extent of that affiliation, it seems clear that Beckett's grasp of staging was swift. By the late 1950s and early 1960s his advice was often sought for staging his plays, and his performance concepts dominate several productions directed by others, notably the London *Endgame* and *Krapp* of 1958, a Paris 1961 *Godot* and 1964 *Comédie*, a Paris-London *Endgame* of

291

1964, and the Royal Court *Godot* of 1964. Beckett's independent directing of his own plays began in 1965, although the first piece to bear his name as director was the 1966 Stuttgart telecast of *Eh Joe*. By 1962 he had enunciated his director's guidelines in a conversation with Charles Marowitz:

> Producers don't seem to have any sense of form in movement. The kind of form one finds in music, for instance, where themes keep recurring. When in a text, actions are repeated, they ought to be made unusual the first time, so that when they happen again—in exactly the same way—an audience will recognize them from before.[2]

Aside from those in Beckett's own plays, it is rare to find actions repeated "in exactly the same way," but they do recur in Robert Pinget's *Hypothèse*, and perhaps that is why Beckett undertook to direct it. He refuses to claim directorial credit, admitting only to helping actor Pierre Chabert "since there was no one else."[3]

As a student in Paris in 1963, Chabert played Krapp with sufficient rhythm to interest the musical Mrs. Beckett, who attended the performance. She suggested to Pinget that Chabert should perform his *Hypothèse*, another one-character play. The little-known author Pinget and the unknown actor Chabert began sporadically to rehearse, and Pinget brought Beckett to an early run-through. After brooding on what he saw, Beckett told Chabert that he would like to think about the performance. When Beckett next called Chabert, he had reconceived the production in his mind's eye.

The Hypothesis resembles *Krapp's Last Tape* in that a writer-protagonist reacts to another aspect of himself—Krapp to his tape and Mortin to films of his face. As the live Krapp moves physically between his table and an offstage room, Mortin moves physically between a bookcase, a stove, and his table on which are a glass of water and a manuscript. Unlike Krapp, Mortin never leaves the stage, for he is delivering a speech—the contents of the manuscript—to an audience in the actual theater. That speech is about a writer and *his* manuscript, which is hypothetically at the bottom of a well. "Mortin's struggle with this hypothesis by means of a series of pseudo-logical and delirious conclusions [imperfectly recalled and recited] . . . parallels the predicament of the imaginary author in the manuscript."[4]

In the light of Beckett's subsequent directing practice, his guidance of Chabert seems inevitable. But his decision to cut about one-third of Pinget's text, with the author's consent, was unpredictable. Since Chabert's face had already been filmed for the five movie sequences, Beckett accepted this fact and occupied himself with palpable theater. He moved the room's furnishings to dramatize the table, and he located the stove downstage right, the bookcase upstage left, thus creating three distinct areas but leaving the back wall as a free screen for the film. On the newly centered table lay the manuscript in an enormous pile of loose pages. Most important was Beckett's almost Stanislavskian spine for the play-author's relation to his manuscript: in Chabert's words, "a visceral relation." Whenever Mortin left his table, he took manuscript pages, which he dropped as he recited his text. Pages were soon strewn over the floor, functioning visually and also audibly, as Mortin-Chabert rustle-walked on the leaves of manuscript. By the end of the play, as three enlarged film images of Mortin shouted out his inadequacies, Pinget had his author throw the manuscript into the stove. Discourse broken, he slowly removed his clothes, and his staccato phrases closed the play. In Beckett's direction Mortin had only one page left to throw into the stove, which clacked shut sharply upon it. Pinget's final phrases were severely cut, so that the author seemed consumed with the remains of his manuscript. Although Chabert gave only three performances, the notices were so good that *L'Hypothèse* was included in 1966 on a Beckett-Ionesco-Pinget program at the Odéon Theater, where Beckett helped the late Jean-Marie Serreau direct *Comédie* and especially *Va et Vient*. A few months later Beckett staged his own production of *Va et Vient* on a different program in the same theater.[5]

Beckett's titles give us clues to the main action, and so with *Come and Go*.[6] Not actually sounded in the brief text, the titular phrase describes the physical actions of the three women on stage. When the bright lights come up, three women—Flo, Vi, Ru—are seated on an invisible bench, facing the audience, each clasping her bare hands in her own lap. Once speech begins, pattern reigns; once movement begins, pattern reigns. During the course of the brief play, each woman in turn *goes* out of the bright center light and *comes* back into it. Each woman utters short speeches, punctuated by her exit and reentrance. As each woman in turn disappears into darkness, one of the remaining two whispers into the other's ear, with ostentatious gesture.

The recipient of the inaudible message, with equally ostentatious gesture, exclaims, "Oh!" Then she asks whether the absent one is aware of her fate. The teller of the secret invokes deity in a fervent hope for the absent victim's ignorance. Finally, having gone into darkness and come back into visibility, the three women sit together again in the light, bare hands again clasped, but each hand clasps another's. The discrete individuals of the opening tableau are linked by their hands in the closing tableau, in a chain traditionally associated with harmony.

Beckett's text specifies "dull" colors for the three women's garments, and it only hints at their turn-of-the-century appearance in Serreau's production, long coats cloaking them from shoulder to ankle, and broad-brimmed hats shading their faces. Visually, they evoked Chekhov's three sisters rather than Macbeth's witches or Lear's daughters. The whispered destiny insinuates a hint of the three Fates, and not until the final tableau does a mannered pose recall the three Graces. The "dramaticule" leads to Flo's final line: "I can feel the rings," but Beckett's scenic direction stipulates: *"No rings apparent."* This is the play's second contradiction, for Ru reminisces about "Holding hands ... that way" before the three women touch hands.

When the three women sit together in the light, they recall their bright schoolgirl dreams of love. When one glides into the dark, however, the remaining pair share the knowledge of her doom. Their choral "Oh!"'s (changed in French translation to "Misère." "Malheur." "Miséricorde.") punctuate the secret each pair shares about a third. Choral chant and dance, offstage doom and onstage courage—this is minimal Greek tragedy. Both protagonists and chorus, the three women look the same at the beginning and at the end of the "dramaticule." However, they are seated in a new order as they clasp one another's hands in a stylized pose. Flo at right holds two left hands, and it is she who imagines feeling the ambiguously symbolic rings, but all three actually feel the mortal flesh of other human hands—ungloved and vulnerable to the light.

In the first French production Ru wore violet and Vi rose; Flo was in soft yellow, as specified in the text. Embellishing the text's description, broad-brimmed hats sported fruit, flowers, and feathers—perishable adornments. At rest, the three women suggested deities of vegetation; in motion, however, they were neither bird nor bloom, but softly gliding phantoms, feet invisible under the long coats.

A few months later, Beckett mounted his own production at the same Paris theater. The garments were muted to three shades of gray;

the broad hats and long coats were stripped of ornament: the women exuded a mineral quality. Beckett slowed the playing time from three to seven minutes, so that each gesture seemed wrested from stillness. When Flo finally announced that she felt the rings, their putative absence was at once the climax and conclusion of the drama that had spiraled slowly around an absent center. Since the bench was invisible, the three women were seated in a void. Each of them spoke unheard words, and one of them mentioned unseen rings, those rimmed holes. Not unlike a Mallarmé poem, this *Come and Go* drained away coming, going, listening and speaking, into a final harmony. As a Mallarmé poem resides in words about a void, Beckett's dramaticule, under his direction, resides in a worded rondo about a void, rendered almost palpable through strict pattern.

It was with this theater training that Beckett embarked on full directorial responsibility for the Berlin staging of his *Endgame* (1967), *Krapp's Last Tape* (1969), *Happy Days* (1971), *Waiting for Godot* (1975), *Footfalls* and *That Time* (1976), and *Play* (1978), along with sporadic stints in Paris and London. Although he has had other offers to direct, he has appreciated the distance from his plays provided by the German translations of Elmar Tophoven.

By 1978 Beckett had all but forgotten his French 1965 production of *Come and Go* when he undertook to advise Walter Asmus in a German version.[7] Aside from making minor phrasal changes, Beckett reassigned a few lines for stricter balance. When the three women are together on stage, they speak Vi-Flo, Flo-Ru, Ru-Vi, finally circling back to Vi-Flo. The opening speaker of these trio-couplets is always the one to leave, and the closing speaker is always the one to confide the secret. For that confidence new hand movements were choreographed. At each shocked reaction to the unheard secret, the listener brings a bare hand to her throat, while the speaker holds a bare hand to her lips. In synchrony the two hands slowly return to their respective laps. At the final joining of hands Vi in the center reaches out and up (breast high) for the outer hand of each neighbor. After a beat the neighbors clasp their inner hands, all hands high. Then slowly the three pair of hands fall to laps and rest there for a beat before Flo speaks of the invisible rings and the whole still image fades to darkness. In the words of Beckett's notebook, "Hands taken in air at top of gesture sink gently plumb together."

For production in Berlin, Beckett approached all his plays in the same basic way: (1) meticulous examination of Tophoven's German translation and subsequent correction toward his own English version (since Tophoven translates from the French); (2) intense visualization of the play in theater space—what Beckett calls "trying to see"; (3) commitment of the revised German text to memory (including stage directions); (4) composition of a director's notebook, to which he does not refer during actual rehearsals (his rediscovery of his own texts is remarkable)—for example, that it is always the center woman of three who opens speech in *Come and Go*, that glass is contained in several Winnie props of *Happy Days*, that there are twenty-one pleas for help in *Godot*, that the B-voice of *That Time* sketches a scene already conveyed by a verse of Hölderlin); (5) transmission of design ideas to his friend Matias, who does a first rending while they are still in Paris. Only when these steps are completed does Beckett arrive in West Berlin, where the plays are precast.

At Beckett's first meeting with the actors in a play, he never speaks *about* the play but plunges right into it. Work on scenes begins at once, and Beckett shakes his head at questions that stray from concrete performance. On the other hand, no practical detail is too small for his attention. Sitting or standing, he seems poised to spring to the stage. Early in rehearsals he requests permission to interrupt the actors, and this is always granted. The spoken text must be not only letter perfect, but punctuation perfect; he will stop an actor who elides a comma pause. Yet he rarely interrupts the early run-throughs, and he deliberately absents himself from a late rehearsal or two, so that the actors may feel freer in their final discoveries. Although Beckett arrives at the Schiller Theater with the production complete in his mind's eye, he usually makes minor changes during rehearsal.

Beckett chose to begin his German directing career (which he did not anticipate as a career) with *Endgame*, his preferred play. While still in Paris, he perused the German text with translator Tophoven, who has described their collaboration:

> Through constant work together, through tightening where this was possible, through expansion where the stage demanded it, through late discoveries and introduction of new assonance and harmony, through elimination of Gallicisms that had been overlooked, through prevention of undesirable associations and removal of phonetic difficulties, an improved German version appeared, which will be the basis for a new edition of *Endgame*.[8]

(This new edition has been published only in volume 1 of the 1976 Suhrkamp collected works of Beckett. Postproduction texts have not been published in English.)

In this eschatological play Beckett's slim director's notebook is limited to staging matters.[9] For rehearsal purposes he divided *Endgame* into sixteen scenes:

1. Clov's dumbshow and first soliloquy
2. Hamm's awakening, first soliloquy and first dialogue with Clov
3. The Nagg-Nell dialogue
4. The excited Hamm-Clov dialogue, with Hamm's first turn around the room, ending on Clov's sigh: "If I could kill him..."
5. Clov's comic business with ladder and telescope
6. Hamm's troubled questioning of Clov, climaxed by the burlesque flea scene
7. The Hamm-Clov dialogue, ending with the ironic mirror image of the toy-dog episode
8. Clov's rebellion, giving way to Hamm's story of the madman and subsiding in the alarm-clock scene
9. Hamm's story of the beggar
10. The prayer, ending with Nagg's curse
11. The play within the play of Hamm and Clov; Hamm's continuation of his story
12. The second round of the wheelchair
13. The Hamm-Clov dialogue leading to
14. Hamm's "role"
15. Clov's emancipation, ending with his monologue and exit
16. Hamm's final soliloquy (pages 42-43)

Concerned with the physical rather than the metaphysical, Beckett's director's notebook focuses on mobile Clov. A diagram delineates the path of his "thinking" walk, and another diagram traces his "winding up" walk. Carefully noted and numbered are Clov's sixteen entrances and exits, his twenty-six stops and starts, his nine repetitions of "There are no more..." and his ten repetitions of "I'll leave you" (in German).

Beckett's *Endgame* plays the ending of a world, and his set alerts us to that ending process. The original French describes the set as an interior without furnishings, and Beckett translated this as "Bare interior."[10] However, his Berlin stage set was spare rather than bare. High curtained windows, one on each side wall, face earth and sea—

what remains of nature. Turned inconspicuously to the foot of the left wall is a picture—what remains of art. Downstage left are two touching ashbins covered by a sheet—what remains of an older generation. In the center is an armchair covered by a sheet—what remains of the prime of life. After the opening tableau, action begins with Clov's removal of the sheets. (The notebook calls it an "unveiling.") What is unveiled is a family—ordinary in its memories, attachments, and quarrels but extraordinary since it is the last of the human race. The words *finish* and *end* punctuate the dialogue. Both Hamm and Clov utter the words of Christ on the cross: "It is finished."

Biblical echoes abound. The names Nagg and Hamm pun on Noah and Ham of Genesis, who are also survivors of a world catastrophe, safe in their shelter. Hamm and Clov use the apocalyptic imagery of the biblical book of Revelation—light and dark, earth and sea, life and death, beginning and end—although they experience no revelations. Hamm's chronicle is set on Christmas Eve, and Hamm's final soliloquy distorts scriptural phrases. However, Beckett does not place an actual Bible on stage, as in an earlier version of the play.

Beckett conveys endlessness through the grain-of-time theme, which apparently contradicts the ending theme. Hamm and Clov fear and wish an end, but the drama plays through an endless ending process. Toward the end of the play Hamm ruminates: "Moment upon moment, pattering down like the millet grains of . . . (*hesitates*) . . . that old Greek, and all life long you wait for that to mount up to a life" (*Endgame*, page 70). "That old Greek," whose name Beckett actually forgot, might have been any anti-empirical philosopher of the Megarian or Eleatic schools. Having forgotten the name when writing, however, Beckett later mentioned Zeno to his cast.

It was the playing theme that Beckett pointed up in directing. The title and stage tableaux hint at a chess game, and yet this was never more than a hint, as opposed to the weight assigned the game by critics. Hamm's whistle is the residue of more active games, and the word *discard* summons cards. In spite of Hamm's age, he calls for a toy dog; even his chronicle shows gamesmanship, and the whole play is a game in which Hamm initiates play with rhythm, pattern, spirit.

At the first rehearsal Beckett told his cast, "Here the only interest of the play is as dramatic material." (page 38). Only when rehearsals were well under way did he answer questions about the biblical flood and the Eleatic philosophers. He explained to Hamm-Schröder:

Hamm is king in this chess game that is lost from the start. He knows from the start that he is making loud, senseless moves. That he will not get anywhere at all with the gaff. Now at the last he makes a few more senseless moves, as only a bad player would; a good one would have given up long ago. He is only trying to postpone the inevitable end. Each of his motions is one of the last useless moves that delay the end. He is a bad player. (*Materialien*, page 83)

He's a bad player because he's a good performer—the show must go on. As Beckett admitted in another rehearsal: "Hamm says No to nothingness." (*Materialien*, page 75)

Hamm expressed that *No* under Beckett's meticulous direction. Of the month's rehearsal time, Beckett spent about half the period on individual roles and half on harmonizing the whole. Midway during the rehearsal period, after the actors knew the book, Beckett held a rehearsal for tone, pitch, rhythm. Especially in the last two weeks, he tended to comment in musical terms—legato, andante, piano, scherzo, and a rare fortissimo. Often he spoke of "*reine Spiel*," pure play.

Early in the rehearsal period he told Hamm-Schröder and Clov-Bollmann, "From the first exchange between the two, maximum hostility must be played. Your war is the nucleus of the play." (*Materialien*, page 40) And he defined the basis of their conflict: "Clov has only one wish, to get back into his kitchen, that must always be evident, just like Hamm's constant effort to stop him. This tension is an essential motif for playing." (*Materialien*, page 66) Beckett compared the Hamm-Clov relationship to a marriage—*nec tecum nec sine te*.

To all four actors Beckett declared, "There are no accidents in *Endgame*; everything is built on analogy and repetition." (page 54) Analogy and repetition supply the symmetry in this one-act play—two couples, two windows, two sheets, two ashbins. Such pairs nourish paired motions. In the opening mime Clov is similarly clumsy at each window. He draws each window-curtain with the same jangle, away from the audience. He removes each sheet with the same jerky motion, and he does not fold the sheets as specified in the text, but drags them to his kitchen. He lifts each ashbin cover with the same clatter. In Hamm's opening and closing soliloquies he folds and unfolds hs handkerchief with the same four limited, symmetrical movements. Nagg and Nell emerge from their respective ashbins, lids raised to precisely the same height; they never turn their heads, and they rarely blink their eyes. Nagg lifts his hand identically to rap twice on Nell's lid, and Hamm makes a similar gesture when he knocks at the hollow back wall. In Hamm's recollection of the painter-engraver, he points toward the earth-window after speaking of corn, and he makes a mirror gesture toward the sea-window after mentioning the herring-fleet. Hamm looks down at the beggar of his story as he looks down at the toy dog. Clov and dog, both lame, stand similarly, Clov supporting the dog. At each window Clov looks through the telescope in the same way. Clov lifts Nell's bin-cover, then Nagg's bin cover, to ascertain whether they are dead. In the final tableau of *Endgame* the four characters occupy the same position as in the opening tableau, props on the floor. During a late rehearsal, Beckett wondered whether there wasn't too much symmetry, but he kept it all.

In Beckett's *Endgame* text different characters speak the same old words, but more often they repeat their own words, and Beckett wanted such repetitions spoken identically. Often he asked actors to eliminate expression— *"Ein-tö-nig."* He increased echoes in the German text, changing all Clov's threats to go to, "I'll leave you." He drilled Clov-Bollmann to achieve lightness for frequent: "There are no more. . . ." To two different Clov questions, Hamm replies: "Less." Beckett didn't care whether the word was spoken dispiritedly or euphorically, but it must be repeated in the same tone. Aware of his verbal doublets, Beckett added some to the German text. He reinforced the double "Father" of Hamm's last soliloquy with a double "Clov," as well as earlier inserting a double "Nell" from Nagg. Nevertheless, Beckett did not want the play's end to mirror the beginning absolutely. He rejected Hamm-Schröder's suggestion that Clov re-cover him with the sheet: "Between the beginning and the end lies the small difference that lies precisely between beginning and end." (*Materialien*, page 75)

Nell declares: "Nothing is funnier than unhappiness." Beckett finds that the most important line in the play, and in Berlin he directed to display the fun of unhappiness. In Clov's mime he wanted small gestures, soft voice, and swift rhythms. *Leicht, locker,* and *schnell* were his recurrent injunctions, so that the few violent moments were striking. Although he paced the play quickly, he asked the actors for disjunction between gesture and word: first they were to assume an attitude and then speak the lines. The macabre humor of the effect was disturbing as though they *could* not move and speak simultaneously.

Hamm and Nagg are virtuoso performers in *Endgame*, and Beckett desired each of them to find three different voices; Hamm is narrator, protagonist, and beggar of his chronicle; Nagg is narrator, tailor, and client of his story, but both also criticize their own performances—a fourth voice. Nagg and Nell, caged in their bins, are comically romantic; when they strain to kiss, they can barely move. Since Clov alone is mobile, Beckett directed his movements to be both painful and funny, instructing him, "You should never run slowly; that's very dangerous for the play." (*Materialien*, page 87) Clov always takes eight steps from the door to Hamm's chair, where his normal position is an apelike stance. Bent over, he stumbles when he passes in front of Hamm, momentarily obscuring all but the toque. On his rare occasions of passion, Clov straightens up and flings out his left arm. When he speaks to Nagg or Nell in the ashbins, his own head disappears into the bins. In the parallel phrases beginning "Sometimes I wonder if I'm in my right mind" and "Sometimes I wonder if I'm in my right senses," Clov speaks the beginning with verve and the end with sadness. After trying the opposite, Beckett found it funnier that Clov react sadly to being as lucid as before, as intelligent as ever. At the play's end, a hatted Clov carries a gray-green coat in his right hand, and in his left a valise, raincoat, and umbrella—poor preparation for the desert outside. Partly because Clov alone is mobile, and mainly because of Bollmann's comic gift, he was the funniest character in the Berlin *Endgame*. His full face contradicts the asceticism implied in the text, and his roundness belies his bent stance and angular movements. His infectious laughter lightened the gray play's start, and his silence darkened the end.

Almost pathetically, Beckett warned his actors, "Pathos is the death of the piece." (*Materialien*, page 45) And yet his direction admitted pathos. Toward the end of the play, Beckett's notebook reads tersely, "Clov entrance 16 while Hamm trying to move chair. Stands near door watching Hamm. Turns head aside on first *Clov*. Back after *gut* and motionless till end." Clov-Bollmann did remain motionless, but he was under visible strain, forcing himself not to participate in the ending action. To Hamm-Schröder's question whether Hamm covers himself to die, Beckett replied, "No, only so he is better able to keep himself quiet." At the last Hamm-Schröder covers his face with his handkerchief-stancher, drops his hands to armrests—"Speak no more." Beckett commented, "The voice comes out of the silence and moves back into the silence." (*Materialien*, page 98)

In Matias's set the ashbins were gray-black, and their color blended into the lighter gray walls of the rectangular shelter. Gray curtains shaded small rectangular windows cut into the side-walls. Hamm wore dark gray and Clov light gray. Hamm's dark embroidered toque was a gift from Sean O'Casey to Beckett through Jack MacGowran. Hamm's foot rug was lightly striped at the base, and his chair wheels were as small as those of roller skates. The red-and-white faces of the published text were monochromed to gray-white, and the handkerchief lost its bloodstains. Cold light shone on door, chair, and ashbins—invariant throughout. In homage to the German philosopher Schopenhauer, who loved his poodle, the toy dog became a ragged, almost black, almost lifesize poodle. And that poodle is emblematic of the production— philosophy concealed, artifice patent, injury risible, since "Nothing is funnier than unhappiness."

After the intricate cross-relationships and complex repetitive texture of *Endgame*, directing *Krapp's Last Tape*[11] might seem like child's play. It will be recalled that Beckett wrote the one-character piece in English for actor Pat Magee, who was first directed by Donald McWhinnie. In 1958 in London Beckett worked closely with actor and director. The three of them played hard and then pub-crawled, but there was no pub crawling in 1969 in Berlin, where Krapp's role went to ponderous Martin Held.

James Knowlson has discussed the complex symbolism of *Krapp's Last Tape*, succinctly summarized in Beckett's Director's Notebook:

> Krapp decrees physical (ethical) incompatibility of light (Spiritual) and dark (Sensual) only when he intuits possibility of their reconciliation as rational-irrational. He turns from fact of anti-mind alien to mind to thought of anti-mind constituent of mind.[12]

Despite this esoteric and symbolic background, the surface of *Krapp's Last Tape* is realistic, but Beckett's director's notebook dwells on realistic and nonrealistic detail.

Unlike the *Endgame* notebook, that for *Krapp* does not divide the play into rehearsal scenes. Instead, Beckett lists twenty-seven matters needing directorial attention, from the metaphysical "1. *Choix-hasard*" (choice-guess) to the very physical "27. *Endgültig Werkstatt*" (final [Schiller] Werkstatt [version]) Beckett calculates that Krapp has been recording for forty-five years, since there are nine boxes, each containing five spools of tape. The notebook designates the tape recorder as a masturbatory agent, and Beckett instructed Held to hold the box erotically. His separation of speech from motion, introduced into *Come and Go* and *Endgame*, becomes the fulcrum of performance: "Play therefore composed of two approximately equal parts, listening-immobility and nonlistening-motion." For the *écoute* (listening) Beckett began rehearsals with a provisional tape of thirty-nine-year-old Krapp, but this was replaced.

Beckett wished abrupt and vivid disjunction between still listening and agitated nonlistening. Toward this end, he amplified his stage directions and simplified his stage picture. He eliminated Krapp's clown makeup and endowed him with worn-out rather than farcical clothes. Krapp's table was clean at the start, and Beckett excised the comic business with keys and envelope, but he introduced fumbling rheumatic fingers. He suggested to Held a moving "rest" gesture; Krapp hugs himself shivering. Realistically, an old man seeks warmth; symbolically, Krapp loves himself.

Because of Beckett's stage simplification, we more easily grasp similarities between the young and the old Krapp. Action begins when Krapp peers shortsightedly at his large silver watch, and it proves to be time for his banana. After two bananas are eaten on stage, Krapp on tape mentions three. The man who has stepped from his spotlighted circle into darkness and back listens to a tape announcing that he loves to return from darkness to himself, Krapp. And yet, Krapp-Held looks in astonishment at the tape recorder when he hears the voice say: "Me. (*pause*) Krapp." For Krapp as for Rimbaud, "*Je est un autre*" ("I is another").

Separating speech from motion, Beckett moved Krapp toward pathos, although the effect in *Endgame* was lugubriously comic. In the opening mime Krapp makes clumsy comic gestures, but it is a rheumatic old man who makes them, and it is a lonely old man who personifies tapes as "little rascal" and "little scoundrel." Whenever Krapp-Held rises from the table, he leans heavily on both hands. Whenever Krapp walks away from the table, he crosses in front and to the right; he fears the darkness at his left. His love-hate relation with objects is comic, for pathos is a greater danger to *Krapp's Last Tape* than to *Endgame*. Beckett dissolved pathos by beating time for Krapp-Held's nonverbal and comic noises—wheezing, walking, turning pages, drinking, and even slamming objects on his table.

When taped speech fills the theater, Krapp listens motionless, comic gestures spent. His head is bent at an angle of 45 degrees, his left hand caresses the tape recorder, and the fingers of his right hand sometimes drum impatiently. Unrecorded in Beckett's notebook is the frequent ternary rhythm evident in performance. Krapp listens to three main events; there are three breaks in the equinox account and three in the "Farewell to Love." At the play's beginning Krapp walks three times out of his spotlight into darkness and back. He disappears through his backstage curtain three times—for his ledger, pile of tapes, and tape recorder, the increased weight of the objects revealed by increased fatigue. In the later action Beckett changed the three backstage exits to offstage drinking, search for a dictionary, offstage drinking and search for a microphone. Krapp consults his watch three times; he moves the tape ahead three times and back three times. After he records, he looks at the machine three times before he wrenches off his last tape.

Within this ternary pattern Krapp shows emotional variety—his lubricity on peeling a banana, his impatience with a younger self, his contained grief at his mother's death, his boast to a whore, his extrapolation of a novel, his fear of dark at his left, his inability to sustain love, which he perhaps regrets when he plays and replays the "Farewell to Love." Krapp-Held squinted when he tremulously spoke of eyes—in the words of the notebook, *"ein Traumgefressener Mensch"* ("A man consumed by dreams").

With improved vision of his own (after operations to remove cataracts), Beckett returned to *Krapp* in 1975—in his French translation, to accompany the French premiere of *Not I* at the Petit d'Orsay. Ten years after *L'Hypothèse* Beckett and Chabert again worked together on a one-character play. In Paris as in Berlin, the central image remained a Krapp who was "one body with the machine."[13] As in *L'Hypothèse* Beckett divided the small stage into areas: the central table (place of reverie) and the backstage alcove (place of practicality).

Because of Chabert's relative youth, Beckett dressed him in a frayed dressing gown to hide his tall frame, a toque to hide his abundant hair, and black half gloves that evoke premonitions of death. Pale and thin, Krapp-Chabert shivered with an old man's cold, and his myopic eyes seemed intent on piercing the dark. He stretched to listen so as to compensate for his deafness, one hand curled round the recorder handle. Immobile, he sucked at his cheeks, leaving his mouth open. Tall, he bumped the overhead light when he rose from the table, and the light continued to move while he listened, still, to the "moves" of the "Farewell to Love."

Musically trained, Chabert readily responded to Beckett's sonata breakdown of the dialogue into b-A(b)-A-B-a, A being the taped voice, B the live voice, and small letters standing for short duration. Much of the brief (three-week) rehearsal period was devoted to the B-voice, sharp and staccato in b and (b), but rhythmically varied in B; the high-pitched quaver of the conventional stage old man was especially to be avoided. In both A and B, Beckett wished counterpoint between objectivity and self-disgust or between objectivity and fascination with a woman or a word.

In Paris Beckett revised key scenes of both nonlistening and listening. When Krapp goes backstage to drink, he leaves a curtain open, so that his guzzling shadow is seen in a long light rectangle, projected from a Chinese lantern on a screen. This space is sharply different from the dream-memory space of Krapp's table. Thus, Krapp versus his past is theatricalized audibly as Krapp versus his taped voice; visually as a shrunken actual Krapp versus his enlarged shadow. In the three playbacks of the love scene, Krapp listens first with bowed head, then with his face on the table, and finally, after a long look over his left shoulder into darkness, with stony erectness. Krapp-Chabert's last playback of "Farewell to Love" is clarified as his stoic farewell to life as well. After the stage lights go out, the tape-recorder light continues to glow—a small *memento mori*.

A little over two years later, in 1977, Beckett found himself directing an English *Krapp* in Berlin's Akademie der Künste, as a favor to his friend Rick Cluchey. Despite two previous productions, he made extensive director's notes, which have been published in the San Quentin Drama Workshop Program and in Bethanien Center Publications. His headings summarize the areas of his concern: "Tape Montage, Costume, Props [a long list], Lighting, Opening, *Hain* ["friend Death" in a poem by Matthias Claudius], Drinks, Song, Microphone, End." Visual details were carried over from the Paris production—a dressing gown, modified banana business, enlarged shadow of drinking, erect posture at the end as at the beginning.

This time Beckett divided the play into four rehearsal scenes: (1) Beginning to ledger note: "Farewell to—love"); (2) "Thirty-nine to-day . . ." to "A girl in a shabby green coat. . . . No?" (with "Connaught" replaced by "Kerry" and the hymn cut); (3) "When I look back—" to preparations for recording. (Watch business is cut. Looking up "viduity" in the dictionary, near-sighted Krapp first reads "vicar" and "vicious."); (4) From the newly introduced "Fanny" before "Just been listening..." to the end. ("One pound...doubt" disappears. "Finger and thumb" replaces "a kick in the crutch," and "dozed away" replaces "went to sleep.")

In contrast to Held's erotic recorder, Cluchey's is both friend and enemy, alternately caressed and cursed. Even more sharply than earlier, the Akademie *Krapp* points up opposites: stillness-movement, silence-noise, dark-light, black-white. As a corollary to such polarity, Beckett had Cluchey emphasize the "or"s in the "viduity" definition.

Beckett never spoke to the Workshop members of the symbolic genesis of the play, but they worried together in the inadequately equipped Akademie about nuances of light and sound. To the ternary rhythms of the earlier productions Beckett added long still "brood"s after the words "Incomparable," "crystolite," and "side by side." He sought tonal interest for the often-repeated phrase "Ah well," which had nearly become the play's title. Live Krapp's "Be again, be again" was to sound like the churchbells of his youth. Clinging to rhythm in the face of death, Krapp-Cluchey was sometimes rehearsed with Beckett beating time—for the little rushes of seven steps to and from the table, for the longer series of thirteen steps to and from the alcove, for the offstage drinking sounds (clink of bottle against glass, bottle down, drink, glass down, cough-sigh), and for the long *Hain* (sudden stiffening, slow head turn to left, hold, slow return to right, resume tape). Although the American group knew little German, they prattled glibly of the *Hain*, unaware that it derived from the Matthias Claudius poem. Seeking the precise shuffle sound he wanted from Krapp's run-walk, Beckett gave Cluchey his own worn slippers. In the last week (of nearly four) of rehearsals Beckett changed Krapp-Cluchey's listening position, right hand embracing the recorder, left hand behind it, head angled about 60 degrees to the table. Under a conical dunce-cap light, the metallic rotating tape was reflected on Cluchey's left cheek—a kind of shadow pulse. San Quentin technical men Hauptle and Thorpe conferred on how to eliminate it, but Beckett told them softly, "I love it."

NOTES

1. Deirdre Bair, *Samuel Beckett* (New York: Harcourt Brace Jovanovich, 1978), 236.
2. Charles Marowitz, "Paris Log," *Encore* (March 1962), 44.
3. Information on *L'Hypothèse*, which I did not see, comes from Pierre Chabert's letter to me of 20 July 1978 and from transcripts of his interview with Dougald McMillan.
4. For a more detailed account of Beckett's staging of *L'Hypothèse* see Martha Fehsenfeld and Dougald McMillan, *Beckett at Work in the Theatre* (London: Calder, 1986). I can repeat this for almost any production I describe, and I am most grateful to them for allowing me to read the manuscript of their work, enabling me to minimize overlap in our two studies.
5. Beckett's memory and mine are at odds on this version, since he credits Serreau with direction. Alec Reid, *All I Can Manage, More Than I Could* (New York: Grove Press, Inc., 1968), 93, credits Serreau with directing the French premiere. Breon Mitchell, *"Come and Go," Modern Drama* (September 1976): 252, credits Beckett but erroneously sets the production in the Odéon Theatre's Petite Salle. (Mitchell's manuscript study is invaluable.) Bair, *Beckett*, leaves the director vague and mistakenly states *Come and Go* to be a translation of *Va et Vient*.
6. Samuel Beckett, *Come and Go*, in *The Collected Shorter Plays of Samuel Beckett* (New York: Grove Press, 1984), 191-97.
7. Beckett insists that he was merely a consultant on the Berlin *Come and Go*, but Walter Asmus told me that joint discussion governed the production.
8. Michael Haerdter, *Materialien zu Becketts 'Endspiel'* (Frankfurt: Suhrkamp, 1968), 127. Page numbers in parentheses refer to this book. This fine account is the main source of my information about *Endgame* rehearsals, upon which I drew in my *Back to Beckett* (Princeton, N.J.: Princeton University Press, 1973). I thank Princeton University Press for permission to quote that account.
9. See Fehsenfeld and McMillan, *Beckett at Work in the Theatre*, for fuller details.
10. Samuel Beckett, *Endgame* (New York: Grove Press, Inc., 1958), 1. Page numbers refer to this edition.
11. Beckett, *Krapp's Last Tape*, in *Collected Shorter Plays*, 53-63.
12. Cf. James Knowlson, "Krapp's Last Tape," *Journal of Beckett Studies* (Winter 1976): 50-65.
13. Pierre Chabert, "Beckett as Director," *Gambit* (28):62.

S. E. GONTARSKI

Literary Allusions in
"Happy Days"

Discussing *Godot* with Beckett, Colin Duckworth asked, "Is a Christian interpretation of the play justified?" Beckett responded, "Yes, Christianity is a mythology with which I am perfectly familiar. So naturally I use it."[1] The response is something of an understatement, for Beckett's corpus is saturated with Christian mythology and variations on its ideology. He is as tied to Christian thought as Lucky is to Pozzo, as obsessed with Christian dogma and its implications as was Joyce. Maria Jolas suggests, "Like Joyce he is also a Christ-haunted man. . . ."[2] And little wonder. Born 13 April 1906. Friday the thirteenth. Good Friday the thirteenth. On the 606th anniversary of Dante's descent into Hell. A persistent theme of Beckett's is divine caprice, the arbitrary nature of salvation, a theme that haunts his plays like the ghost of King Hamlet. In *Godot*, one of Estragon's feet is comfortable, one in pain; one of his feet is saved, one damned. Beckett is fond of quoting a sentence from Augustine (ostensibly for its shape): "Do not despair; one of the thieves was saved. Do not presume; one of the thieves was damned."[3] The sentence indeed has a fine shape and balance, but it imposes shape on chaos. The symmetry of the sentence veils the horror of arbitrary salvation, a frequent torment for Beckett's characters. What are the reasons that one thief was saved, one damned? What had they done or said? Why is the story treated in only one of the four gospels? What is the reason for God's refusal of Cain's gift, his acceptance of Abel's? Was Cain somehow forewarned that God expected his chosen to remain nomadic shepherds and not farm the land? Had He something against sodbusters? The questions suggest the failure of a covenant of benevolence, the failure of love and order. Beckett's characters are hounded by the inconsistencies of systems that have dominated the western world at least since Christ. Moran may be speaking directly for Beckett as he ponders: "Certain questions of a theological nature preoccupied me strangely."⁴

Beckett is, of course, preoccupied with mythologies other than Christian, and their promise, their pretense to order haunts him as well. His works exude the mythos and ethos of western civilization. In his first important essay, "Dante... Bruno. Vico.. Joyce," a defense of Joyce's *Work in Progress*, Beckett placed Joyce in a developing western, intellectual tradition by comparing him to the three Italian writers. Beckett's characters often appear to exist in isolation, but they play their roles against a backdrop made from the shattered traditions of western man. In *Molloy*, for instance, Beckett continues the variegated development of the epic form, most recently manipulated by Joyce. *Molloy*, however, is still another development, a contrapuntal epic, played fugally—two epic journeys. It is also a parody of the novel itself, a middle-class form that developed with Richardson and Defoe, and that, under the guise of verisimilitude, has carried on an orgy with things, objects, portable possessions, the stuff of middle-class lives. As Hugh Kenner observes, somewhat hyperbolically, "The trilogy is, among other things, a compendious abstract of all the novels that have ever been written, reduced to their most general terms."⁵ And philosophical systems are not spared. Beckett's *oeuvre* echoes and reechoes of the inconsistencies western philosophical traditions from Zeno and Pythagoras to Wittgenstein and Sartre. His characters are invariably either committed to systems that fail, that must fail, or haunted by the failure of systems. They are fascinated and befuddled by the problems of Eleatic paradoxes, the Pythagorean incommensurability of side and diagonal, Cartesian bifurcation, phenomenology, logical positivism, and existentialism.⁶

The tradition within which Beckett works, however, includes not only western man's literary forms and philosophical systems, but popular culture as well. The title of *Happy Days* invokes the cheery toast and the popular song, "Happy Days Are Here Again," while the ending suggests the French proverb, "Everything ends with a song."

The mythological reality with which Beckett works is then a complicated patchwork worth careful scrutiny. The mythic peregrinations of Odysseus provided Joyce with a framework for *Ulysses*. The single myth was for Joyce both skeleton and foil and was used virtually allegorically. As Eliot saw in 1923, Joyce manipulated "a continuous

parallel between contemporaneity and antiquity." The Odyssian myth
was for Joyce a "way of controlling, of ordering, of giving shape."⁷ In
his most allegorical works, Beckett too wove his tale around a single
myth, not so much to order and control as to universalize and ironize.
Myth is never for Beckett a skeleton on which to hang his narrative
flesh. During the thirty-odd seconds of "Breath," Beckett has hardly
time for a single allusion, the Biblical version of creation: "And the
Lord God formed man . . . and breathed into his nostrils the breath of
life" (Genesis 2:7). Naturally, twentieth-century philosophers were not
the first to contemplate the paradoxical nature and absurdity of existence; neither were they the first to devise images of perpetual agony.
Beckett draws freely on Greek and early Christian images of torment.
From Dante, Beckett borrows the image of the indolent Belacqua. And
without being direct allegories, "Act Without Words, I" calls to mind
the frustrations of Tantalus, "Act Without Words, II," Sisyphus (di-
varicated). Such myths are not a framework, but the mythic echoes
help equate the daily frustrations of modern man with those torments
devised by our fathers, the Greeks and early Christians, to punish the
sinners, the defiant, the vain, and the slothful. In Beckett's vision, of
course, the justice of punishment is removed, and Everyman suffers.
And the mythic echoes emphasize the repetitive nature of experience,
for Beckett a convenient means of illustrating his cyclical view of history.

Beckett's use of a single myth is, however, rare. Even Joyce realized
that too close an allegorical pattern may be restrictive ultimately. "I
may have oversystematized *Ulysses*,"⁸ he confessed. The Verticalist
manifesto, "Poetry is Vertical," 1932 (and Verticalism is the one literary
movement to which Beckett has allowed his name to be linked, albeit
loosely), contains a rejection of Eliot's appeal for a return to classicism.
The manifesto proclaims, "We are against the renewal of the classical
ideal." But again, Beckett's ties with the Verticalists were slight, and
as he himself had warned in 1929, "The danger is in the neatness of
identifications." The manifesto, however, goes on to proclaim an interest in a new mythic reality, as opposed, evidently, to a classically
mythic reality: "The synthesis of a true collectivism is made possible
by a community of spirits who aim at the construction of a new mythological reality."⁹ Although Beckett has evidently not been much
interested in "a community of spirits," his composition of *Happy Days*
reveals a continuing interest in "a new mythological reality" formed

from fragments of great western traditions shattered or decaying. The mythic reality is not an allegorical rendering. We see, instead, the backdrop of western thought in jagged fragments, like a collage of found objects, the draff of Winnie's education.

The fragmented mythic pattern parallels the way in which Beckett presents the background of his characters through their minced and quasi-objectified autobiographies. Each of Beckett's works, in a Miltonic echo, is a rendering of paradise lost, or more precisely, of paradise denied. And the pervasive myth is a composite, a montage of western culture, which, like the Bible specifically, is a hope unbloomed. It is painfully obvious, for instance, that the Lord does not uphold "all that fall." The particular literary allusions in *Happy Days* take on a mythic quality as they reverberate throughout the play.

Creation of the cultural montage is an integral part of the making, the shaping of *Happy Days*. The collection of literary allusions Winnie tries to recall is part of her old style, part of her attempt to maintain order. The tendency of Winnie to reach back into her school-days literature was part of Beckett's design as early as the first full holograph (H-1). As she realizes that her lipstick is running out, Beckett notes: "Lips. First words of famous line—transitoriness of all things—Bible possibly..." (first typescript [TS-1], page 3). After an exchange based on a *Cymbeline* quotation, Winnie's sense of estrangement is reflected in her quoting Cordelia after her disinheritance. The earliest use of allusion appears local, however, a parallel to Winnie's immediate condition. As the play grows, a more complicated pattern of allusion develops. Fragments of literary quotations are added throughout the play's composition, allusions in which themes and a pattern of imagery are surprisingly consistent. And literary references only obliquely suggested in early drafts are emphasized, clarified, and restated as the play develops. Throughout, Winnie recalls fragments of the old culture without fully understanding the ironies in the contrast with her present condition. And the growing number of allusions is not only part of Beckett's attempt to universalize Winnie's struggle, but an ironic commentary on a school girl's intellectual tradition—her references are not, after all, as esoteric as Watt's or Murphy's. Winnie's allusions are interwoven with her other habits and add to her ability to go on. Allusions are used, notes Lawrence Harvey, "in a ... closely integrated ... fabric ... in his later ... writings—in *Happy Days*, for example."[10]

Few critics, however, have paid close attention to the pattern of literary allusions in *Happy Days*, often assuming that identifying the quotations is sufficient, an indication that the speaker is another of Beckett's scholar-tramps. But even the identification has been incomplete and occasionally misleading. Ruby Cohn's identification of the phrase the "old style" with Dante, however, is a significant contribution to our understanding of the complexity of Beckett's literary allusions in *Happy Days*: "Winnie's 'old style' is implicitly contrasted with Dante's *dolce stil nuovo*; she even utters the phrase 'sweet old style.' Dante's *dolce stil nuovo* ushered in the vigorous literature of the Renaissance, but by the time of *Happy Days* that Renaissance has become a weary decadence." And she identifies most (but not all) of Winnie's quotations, arguing that they have a function in the immediate situation, to "emphasize the *un*happiness of the human condition," and a more general purpose: the "literary echoes" along with Winnie's other ritualized activities ("the inventory of possessions, the repetitive refrains, the constant doubts and denials") are part of her "attempts to fill the void of existence."[11] And so they are. Yet, they are more. The quotations do not all point to human woe. One quotation evokes a nineteenth-century, romantic, hedonistic ideal. Winnie's "paradise enow" is an allusion to Edward FitzGerald's translation of *The Rubáiyát of Omar Khayyám*. Another, "damask" cheek is a reference to Shakespeare's *Twelfth Night*, a comedy of mistaken identities firmly rooted in the *Commedia dell'Arte*. And certainly the duet from *The Merry Widow* reflects more joy than despair. Ihab Hassan complicates matters by suggesting that the play contains a reference to the *Song of Songs*,[12] but Hassan does not specify the allusion, and to date it has defied precise identification. We may guess that perhaps Hassan considers Winnie's song to be a parody of the wedding song, but such an association is tenuous.

The allusions, then, function on a broader level than additional aids to Winnie's adaptation or as a means of establishing a somber mood. They are also a crucial adjunct of the play's central irony. The snippets of quotations are designed to function most effectively when they call to mind the broader context of the work alluded to. As Winnie recites her classroom exercises to fill time and check her own physical deterioration, the cumulative weight of the quotations, as they reverberate and are orchestrated throughout the play, form Beckett's mythic pattern. As John Fletcher suggests, Beckett's examination of man's contemporary predicament "is structured in the form of myth."[13] The examples of Beckett's use of Dante's *dolce stil nuovo*, the endlessness of Winnie's Eleatic burial, the addition of the fragment from the Lesser Doxology, "World without end, amen," and the pervasiveness of images of fundamental changelessness under the sun and human vanity (echoing Ecclesiastes) demonstrate the ways in which fragments of Christian mythology and western intellectual tradition help provide a mythic backdrop for the play.

Fortunately, Beckett has taken the trouble to note in the margin of the final typescript the exact references to most of the literary fragments Winnie recalls. Clearly, Beckett intended these references to be an integral part of the play, since in his preproduction correspondence with Alan Schneider he carefully prepared a list of Winnie's literary references for the director, a list that, incidentally, includes one more quotation than Beckett's notes in the final typescript. He also suggested to Schneider that as Winnie's personality deteriorates, the quality of the literature to which she alludes also declines, a point Professor Cohn echoes: In Act II, "She actually quotes from such sentimental versifiers as Charles Wolfe, rather than from the great poets of the English language."[14] The judgment is at least open to question, since in Act II Winnie also quotes from Milton, Keats, Shakespeare, and Yeats, as well as Wolfe, but Beckett's literary judgments may be less in question here than the importance he seems to attach to the quotations.

The first direct literary allusion Winnie makes is to *Hamlet*: "Woe woe is me ... to see what I see."[15] It is Ophelia's recognition of Hamlet's madness, his deterioration: "O, what a noble mind is here o'erthrown! ... O, woe is me, to have seen what I have seen, see what I see" (*Hamlet*, 3.1). The reference was added late in the play's development in a verso note to the fifth full version of the play and provides the core of a curious and parodic comparison. Hamlet was virtually immobilized by his problems. He would have preferred not to act, to crawl instead into a cave and enjoy Willie's "Belacqua bliss." Winnie, buried in her problem, Time, and Willie, immobilized, are analogues of Hamlet, who himself might have uttered Winnie's line "What a curse, mobility!" (page 46). And Willie, like Hamlet, has also been unable to take his own life; as Winnie recalls: "Remember Brownie, Willie? ... Remember how you used to keep on at me to take it away from you? Take it away, Winnie, take it away, before I put myself out of my misery" (page 33). This reference to Willie's suicide temptation is also added late in the play's composition to balance and anticipate Willie's final struggle toward the revolver.

For Hamlet, order and stability have collapsed, but the collapse is temporary. In Hamlet's world human action still mattered; it affected the events of men. Willie's and Winnie's chaos is permanent, and Beckett's two immobilized characters yearn for oblivion, but their actions are inconsequential. Winnie admires Willie's ability to sleep: "sleep for ever ... marvellous gift ... wish I had it" (page 10). The phrase echoes Hamlet's "To die: to sleep;/No more; and by a sleep to say we end/The heartache and the thousand natural shocks/That flesh is heir to" (*Hamlet*, 3.1). Ironically, Winnie makes certain that Willie's sleep is only temporary: she wakes him at the opening of the play and keeps Brownie from him.

Moreover, Hamlet's "Oh that this too, too solid flesh would melt," is echoed twice by Winnie: "and wait for the day to come ... the happy day to come when flesh melts at so many degrees" (page 18); and again, "Shall I myself not melt perhaps in the end, or burn, oh I do not mean necessarily burst into flames, no just little by little be charred to a black cinder, all this ... visible flesh" (page 38). And in another allusion to *Hamlet*, Winnie's inability to act is dramatized through the impossibility of singing when one desires: "How often I have said ... Sing now, Winnie, sing your song ... and did not. Could not. ... No, like the thrush, or the bird of dawning ..." (page 40). The allusion was included in the first full holograph, and Beckett identifies it specifically in the marginalia to his final typescript: "Some say that ever 'gainst that season comes/Wherein our Savior's birth is celebrated,/The bird of dawning singeth all night long;/And then, they say ... The nights are wholesome ..." (*Hamlet*, 1.1). But Winnie's world contains no seasons, no night in which the bird might sing. And Marcellus's remark suggests that the bird's song is a signal of the celebration of the birth, the coming of the savior and the withdrawal of the restless shades. Winnie's inability to sing is then appropriate. The savior is not coming; in fact, the reference to the bird of dawning is followed by Winnie's strange feeling that someone is watching her, that is, the ghosts are abroad. When she finally does sing, at the end of the play, Willie is struggling toward the revolver, in a parody, a travesty of salvation which itself fails. If Willie is in any way a savior, he is like Mr. Rooney in *All That Fall*, who "saved" the little boy from life by pushing him from a moving train. Mr. Rooney, however, seems to have succeeded in his role as savior. Willie not. And finally, Winnie's "I call to the eye of the mind" suggests Hamlet's vision of his father, "In my mind's eye, Horatio." Although the last quotation does call to mind *Hamlet*, Beckett identifies it as a reference to the opening song of Yeats's "At the Hawk's Well."

Winnie then, at the very beginning of the play echoing Ophelia, calls our attention to the deterioration of a man, of men, once noble. Vestiges persist. Willie defines hog, clears up a grammatical point about hair, identifies the emmet's eggs. These are chivalrous touches like returning the parasol that slipped from Winnie's grasp early in the play. Willie was evidently once a great admirer of Winnie, and, if we use the admittedly slight evidence of his moustache as a link, Willie is Mr. Johnson, or Johnston, or Johnstone, who, as Winnie described him, had a "very bushy moustache." In Beckett's revision of the Johnston episode, moreover, he was careful to retain some reference to the moustache, but others were cut to decrease an overt connection. In the early version of the episode, Winnie reveals that Johnston's moustache "vanquished my scruples" (H-1). In the same version Winnie complains about being tired of the sight of the revolver. Willie mistakenly thinks Winnie is referring to him. She allays his fears as follows: "Oh not you, Edward, not you, who could ever weary of the sight of you ... Your moustache alone ..." And at one time Beckett contemplated making Willie's moustache much more conspicuous than it finally is: "B moustache visible on both sides of head." At the end of the play, when we finally see Willie full-face, we note he wears a "Very long bushy white Battle of Britain moustache," which he then proceeds to smooth like a villain of melodrama threatening the innocent, defenseless heroine (page 61).

Happy Days abounds with echoes of *Hamlet*. We see that the Prince's struggle against state and self has in the long run been futile; the forces of chaos and disorder have won. The ideals of the Renaissance, its hopes for art and science, its faith in man himself, ideals ushered in with Dante's *dolce stil nuovo* and developed by Shakespeare, have for modern man "become a weary decadence," useless and futile, as ineffective an aid to man as the Christianity suggested by Winnie's early prayers.

Winnie's next two quotations focus on her vanity. As she is concerned with her lips, she quotes Milton: "O fleeting joys/Of Paradise, dear bought with lasting woes" (*Paradise Lost*, 10.741-742). The allusion to the misery of existence is obvious, and Beckett used the quotation as a replacement for his earlier thought to represent "the transitoriness of all things" with a biblical allusion. Shortly thereafter, Winnie quotes Romeo as he discovered the drugged Juliet: "Ensign crimson.... Pale flag" (page 15). During the rehearsals of *Glückliche Tage*, Beckett told his actors that "Ensign crimson" is life, and "Pale flag," death.[16] Of course Juliet too is entombed at this point and, like Winnie, buried *alive* in a state between life and death. And as Romeo reminds us in this speech, "How oft when men are at the point of death/Have they been merry!" (5.3). *Romeo and Juliet* details a frustrated love, a love destroyed at least in part by forces beyond man, by something innocently called circumstance. As Shakespeare informs us in the prologue, these are "A pair of star-cross'd lovers." The failure of love is evident throughout *Happy Days*, but especially in Winnie's unconscious parody of the marriage vows, which omits all reference to love: "I would obey you instantly, as I have always done, honored and obeyed" (page 36). As the echoes of Shakespeare's tragedy reverberate through *Happy Days*, we are reminded that a consistent pattern of disaster runs through the affairs of men. Winnie's next quotation provides a variation on the love theme; this from Shakespeare's romance *Cymbeline*, a part of a funeral dirge sung by Imogen's lost brothers, who believe Imogen is dead. She, like Juliet, is also drugged. Although the end for Imogen and her husband, Posthumus Leonatus, is happier than Romeo's and Juliet's, the bulk of *Cymbeline* recounts a love frustrated by sinister forces.

Thomas Gray's use of landscape to set the mood of a poem, his brooding on death and sorrow make him a particularly apt poet for Beckett (and Winnie) to quote, and her "laughing wild amid severest woe" (page 31) is an allusion to Gray's "Ode on a Distant Prospect of Eton College": "And moody Madness laughing wild/Amid severest woe." Gray's longing is for the innocence and ignorance of youth: "Alas regardless of their doom,/The little victims play!/No sense have they of ills to come,/Nor care beyond today." The lines suggest Beckett's description of Winnie's conception of Time, her existence only in the present. As he notes in his director's notebook, "Her time experience incomprehensible transport from one inextricable present to the next, those past unremembered, those to come inconceivable." It is a child's sense of time. The present moment is, was and will be.

"And should one day the earth cover my breasts, then I shall never have seen my breasts..." (page 38).

The entire mood of Gray's "Ode" reflects Beckett's view of tragedy, virtually a synonym for human existence, life: "To each his suffering: all are men,/Condemned alike to groan." And Gray's solution to the oppression of knowing, understanding, seeing, is also Winnie's: "Thought would destroy their paradise./No more; where ignorance is bliss/'Tis folly to be wise." It is Ecclesiastes again: "For in much wisdom is much grief: and he that increaseth knowledge increaseth sorrow" (1:18).

The mood suggested by Winnie's allusions shifts abruptly as she evokes another vision of paradise, this from Edward FitzGerald's translation of *The Rubáiyát of Omar Khayyám*. Though virtually unnoticed at the time of its publication, FitzGerald's translation of the Persian mathematician and astronomer's epigrammatic collection of poems gained a tremendous popularity among the late Victorians. It appealed to a growing epicurean revival, a reaction from the dour Victorian gospel of work. The poem suggests as an alternative to the oppression of social striving, a decadent hedonism. It is also another echo of the theme Beckett suggested in an earlier version of *Happy Days*, "the transitoriness of all things." "The Worldly Hope men set their Hearts upon/Turns Ashes—or it prospers; and anon,/Like Snow upon the Desert's dusty Face,/Lighting a little hour or two—is gone" (*Rubáiyát*, 16). The theme is again close to Ecclesiastes: "How dieth the wise man? As the fool."

The *Rubáiyát* suggests that given man's transitory state, given the fact of deterioration, the most he can hope for is a temporary pleasure of the senses: "A Book of Verses underneath the Bough,/A Jug of Wine, a Loaf of Bread—and Thou/Beside me singing in the Wilderness—/Ah, Wilderness were Paradise enow" (*Rubáiyít*, 12). Through the seven full versions of *Happy Days*, Beckett had used, either mistakenly or as an intentional misquotation, the line, "Happiness enow" (altered from "enough for my happiness" in the first holograph), changing it only in an autograph emendation in the fourth typescript to "Paradise enow." Evidently (and unfortunately) the typesetter missed the correction, as did Beckett reading proof, and the allusion was printed incorrectly in the first edition. It has subsequently been corrected and the allusion to the *Rubáiyát* clarified, the parody of

Khayyám's idyllic vision sharpened. For Winnie is denied even this brief interlude of pleasure. She has no shade under a bough. The wilderness is within, and frightening. And the lover's song is Willie's harsh, guttural response to the music box, a parody. If Winnie's plight had earlier served to parody Christian idealism and Renaissance humanism, it now parodies the epicurean alternative—worldly pleasure.

The allusion to the *Rubáiyát* is followed quickly by Winnie's reference to Browning's "Paracelsus": "I say confusedly what comes uppermost" ("Paracelsus," 3.372). The reference was evidently important to Beckett, for he noted the quotation early in his notebook, and, as with the FitzGerald quotation, Beckett's revisions clarify the reference. The earliest version of the Browning allusion made no specific reference to the poet. Browning's name was first included in the holograph version to help the reader identify the allusion and establish the ironies surrounding the confusion of the poet with what is perhaps the brand name of the revolver and even, perhaps, the benevolent, elfin spirits. The quotation suggests not only the possible failure of gravity (an occurrence as unnatural as Paracelsus's rejection of love), a theme Winnie develops shortly thereafter, but also the failure of human love. Paracelsus not only rejected authority and the traditional means of learning, but also human love in his pursuit of knowledge. He had none of Aprile's sensitivity toward people, art, and nature.

An additional irony, whether intentional or not, results from the close coupling of FitzGerald and Browning, especially when one of the themes connecting the allusions is the failure of love. On the death of Mrs. Browning, FitzGerald had written a friend, "Mrs. Browning's death is rather a relief to me, I must say: no more *Aurora Leighs*, thank God!" Needless to say, Browning's response in "To Edward Fitz-Gerald" was bitter.[17]

Act 2 opens with a reference to Milton: "Hail, holy light" (*Paradise Lost*, 3.1). The quotation continues the light-shade imagery; as Milton reminds us, "God is light," and light is eternal: "never but in the unapproached light/Dwelt from eternity." But the celebration of the eternity of light is a sharp contrast to the reality of Winnie's condition. What Winnie needs, in point of fact, is not a rhapsody on the divinity of light, but shade, relief from oppressive reality. The disjunction between the ideal and real is further developed in the next allusion to Keats's "Ode to a Nightingale," "beechen green." The song of the

318

nightingale is an intoxicant that draws Keats's narrator from the woe of reality to the ideal of the imagination, but within the poem the narrator himself recognizes the disjunction, and the portion of the poem Winnie quotes refers to the idyllic abode of the bird that contrasts sharply to her own environment. The bird sings in the shade; Winnie is forced to suffer in the sun.

The Keats quotation re-sounds earlier images and themes. As with other allusions, Beckett clarified the Keats reference in revision. The earliest appearance was simply a reference to "Shade." The revision to "beechen green" not only sharpened the allusion to Keats, but strengthened the connection to Winnie's earlier amorous encounter, the Charlie Hunter episode, which also occurred "in the back garden at Borough Green, under the horse-beech" (pages 15-16). And the horse beech itself was revised from horse chestnut. Also, the Johnston episode takes place in "The shadows deepening among the rafters" (page 16). Moreover, the nightingale is a thrush, the bird Winnie earlier coupled with "the bird of dawning." They would both signal the arrival of the savior, or at very least, salvation. The alternative to harsh reality is the idyllic grove of beechen green and the song of a bird reflecting a cosmic order, a celestial harmony, and perhaps an amorous interlude. But Winnie's world has only a parody of celestial music, Willie's spontaneous outburst. Nature is dead. She lives in the harsh light of day, in what Beckett has called in his notebook "Eternal sun" and intimates that "tender is the night" and longs for "the wholesomeness of night." Finally, Keats's poem echoes the ignorance-is-bliss theme: "Where but to think is to be full of sorrow." Winnie picks up the theme soon after the Keats allusion: "not to know, not to know for sure, great mercy, all I ask" (page 51).

The Keats reference is followed shortly thereafter by an allusion to the Shakespearean comedy, *Twelfth Night*. The title of Shakespeare's play alone resounds with ironies for Winnie. Twelfth Night is the night of the Epiphany, Christ's manifestation to the Magi. Winnie is Viola, yet disguised as Cesario, hinting of the strength of her love for the Duke: "She never told her love,/But let concealment like a worm i'th' 'bud/Feed on her damask cheek" (2.4.110-112). Viola's stoic restraint stands in sharp contrast to Winnie's ignorance, but Winnie too withholds her overt protestation of love until the very end of the play, when she sings the Waltz Duet from *The Merry Widow*. The reunion

319

of the lovers at the end of *Happy Days*, however, is a travesty of love. And Viola's image of grief is also appropriate for Winnie: "She sat like Patience on a monument,/Smiling at grief" (2.4.114-115).

Winnie's reference to *Twelfth Night* contains another interesting dimension. Throughout Shakespeare's play runs an undercurrent of nostalgia for the good old days, for that merry old England represented by Sir Toby Belch, and in other Shakespearian plays by Falstaff. They are vestiges of medieval castle life now out of place, a nuisance in a Tudor country house. Winnie follows her *Twelfth Night* allusion with a recollection of her old style, an idyllic, romantic interlude: "The sunshade you gave me ... that day ... that day ... the lake ... the reeds" (page 53). The memory is for Winnie, as it was for Krapp, an ideal, a recollection of a time when retreat from the sun was possible. The word *sunshade* itself is a composite of the play's conflicting images, sun and shade. Part of Winnie's old style was the ability, the freedom, to withdraw from the oppressive sun: "I speak of when I was not yet caught—in this way—and had my legs and had the use of my legs, and could seek out a shady place, like you, when I was tired of the sun..." (page 38). Beckett himself took pains in his production to remove all shadows on the stage.[18]

The theme of love frustrated, the images of sun, song, shade, and change are further orchestrated in Winnie's allusion to a rather obscure Irish poet, Charles Wolfe. The allusion provides the only concrete suggestion we have of Winnie's ancestry: The poem is a minor, sentimental piece, one perhaps an Irish schoolgirl might read as a student, "Go! Forget me." Winnie (mis)quotes the opening stanza:

> Go! forget me, why should sorrow
>   O'er that brow a shadow fling?
> Go! Forget me—and to-morrow
>   Brightly smile, and sweetly sing.
> Smile—though I shall not be near thee;
> Sing—though I shall never hear thee.
>   May thy soul with pleasure shine,
>   Lasting as the gloom of mine.

Hardly a classic. But her citing it as such reinforces our skepticism about Winnie's sensitivity and awareness. Willie is apparently gone. The quotation is Winnie's sentimental, self-pitying farewell to Willie, who now will never hear her sing. Ironically, the departure of the lover in Wolfe's poem brings on the night, but even this consequence of the failure of love is denied Winnie.

Almost immediately after the Wolfe quotation, Winnie begins a play within a play, complete with dialogue: the Shower-Cooker story again. Winnie opens this play in the manner of another Irishman, Yeats. The allusion is to the opening of "At the Hawk's Well" and is sung: "I call to the eye of the mind." It is another attempt to escape reality via the imagination. Yeats invites the audience's imagination to supply the props and scenery for the play, as well as some of the preliminary action, a man climbing a hill. The man climbing the hill will shortly be Willie. Perhaps we have crossed the line between reality and imagination. Perhaps Winnie created Willie climbing toward her, dressed in the old style. Winnie's savior may be a figment of her imagination.

The allusion to Yeats reemphasizes the disjunction between the ideal and the real which is the core of Hamlet's problem as well as that of Keats's narrator. Yeats's life-long pursuit of universal order, of harmony between the imagination and reality, a harmony epitomized by the dancer in whose image artist and work of art fuse, serves as an ironic contrast to the disjunction, permanent and irreparable, between Winnie and Willie. Even the Unnamable comes closer to Yeatsian harmony than this couple: "... I still the teller and the told" (*Three Novels*, page 310).

Winnie's final direct literary allusion is to Robert Herrick's "To the Virgins, to Make Much of Time," a poem also alluded to by the Unnamable: "For me to gather while I may" (*Three Novels*, page 350). As Willie reappears Winnie asks, "Where are the flowers?" The pattern of Beckett's revisions of the Herrick quotation differs from the others. The earlier version was closer to Herrick's "Gather ye rosebuds while ye may." Earlier, Winnie said: "All you need now is the rose in your button-hole." The final allusion to flowers is vaguer and would have been difficult to identify, if not impossible, had Beckett himself not done so in his final typescript. With the allusion clear, however, the image of Willie's coming to gather his rosebud is grotesquely comic, as well as another example of Winnie's incorrect assessment of Willie's quest.

Other of Herrick's images parallel the pattern Beckett established in *Happy Days*. Herrick's time "a-flying" and "The glorious lamp of heaven, the sun" again serve as ironic contrasts to Winnie's plight, where youth is lost and time has virtually ceased. Herrick could, after all, take "Delight in Disorder." His solution to the transitoriness of youth is similar to that in the *Rubáiyát*, a hedonistic solution impossible for Winnie, who "having lost but once her prime ... may forever tarry." Forever!

As the literary allusions build over the course of the play, as they echo each other, as images are repeated and gain an accumulated weight, we realize that the imaginative treatment of life (the province traditionally of literature), the order and hopes of literature are as mythologically unreal, as irrelevant to the human condition as the elaborate structure of divine, cosmic order devised by the Greeks. The hope provided by literature and the imagination is unfounded, a hope irreconcilable with reality. Literary and humanistic failures parallel the failure of religion to meet the needs of man. And although the Biblical allusions in *Happy Days* are not identified by Beckett or signaled by Winnie, they nonetheless saturate the play. In addition to using echoes of Ecclesiastes, the parody of Christ's "When two are gathered in my name," the ridicule of Genesis around which Beckett built the slight "Breath" and also used in *Happy Days* (that is, "the nostrils ... breath of life," page 52), Beckett invites parallels to Psalm 40 in *Happy Days*. The opening of the psalm, in fact, provided the central situation of *Godot* some twelve years earlier:

> I waited patiently for the Lord; and he inclined unto me, and heard my cry. He brought me up also out of an horrible pit, out of the miry clay, and set my feet upon a rock, and established my goings. And he hath put a new song in my mouth.... Withhold not thou thy tender mercies from me, O Lord; let the loving kindness and thy truth continually preserve me. (Psalm 40:1-3,11)

Again, from the same psalm that provided Beckett with the title for *All That Fall*: "The Lord is good to all: and his tender mercies are over all his works" (Psalm 145:9). And from Isaiah, the hope that the failure of mercy is only temporary:

> For the Lord hath called thee as a woman forsaken and grieved in spirit, and a wife of youth, when thou wast refused, saith thy God.
> For a small moment have I forsaken thee; but with great mercies will I gather thee. In a little wrath I hid my face from thee for a moment; but with everlasting kindness will I have mercy on thee, saith the Lord thy Redeemer. (Isaiah, 54:6-8)

Of Beckett's early working titles, three, *Great Mercies, Tender Mercies, Many Mercies*, would have signaled the direct biblical allusions; perhaps the signal would have been too strong for Beckett. Unlike Mr. and Mrs. Rooney, who can laugh at the promise of the psalms, Winnie continues to hope and believe as she sinks into her pit. Although many of the literary works from which Winnie quotes focus on the failure of human love, the disjunction between the promise of the psalms and Winnie's plight suggests something of the failure of divine love. Each quotation marches past Winnie as the Unnamable's characters, his lies, march before him, and each quotation is ridiculed by the desperation of Winnie's plight. But the audience sees the ridicule, not Winnie. The dramatic irony is intense in *Happy Days* precisely because Winnie retains her optimism, her faith, and is unaware of the contrast between the way in which things are and the way in which she thinks they are.

The pattern of literary allusions and echoes in *Happy Days* is complex. The themes of the failure of love, the misery of the human condition, the transitoriness of all things, the disjunction between the real and ideal, the misery of awareness, have been carefully reinforced in Winnie's literary allusions and reverberate throughout the play like a constant drumbeat. The word *mercy* itself becomes a refrain, like *happy*. And in Beckett's selection of quotations and obliquer references virtually every historical epoch is represented: pre-Christian Greek philosophies, the blind religiosity and Christian idealism of the Middle Ages, Renaissance humanism, eighteenth-century rationalism, and nineteenth-century romanticism. The philosophies, literature, and religion of western man comprise the fragmented mythology against which Winnie fails and suffers, and like a jeweler's foil, mythology highlights the suffering.

NOTES

1. Colin Duckworth, *Angels of Darkness* (New York: Barnes & Noble, Inc., 1972), 18.
2. Maria Jolas, "A Bloomlein for Sam," *Beckett at 60: A Festschrift* (London: Calder and Boyars, 1967), 16.
3. Harold Hobson, "Samuel Beckett: Dramatist of the Year," *International Theatre Annual, No. 1* (New York: Citadel Press, 1956), 153.
4. Samuel Beckett, *Malone Dies*, in *Three novels by Samuel Beckett* (New York: Grove Press, 1965), 166.

5. Hugh Kenner, *Samuel Beckett: A Critical Study*, 2nd edition (Berkeley: University of California Press, 1968), 63. See also 67-70, et passim.

6. See especially David H. Hesla, *The Shape of Chaos: An Interpretation of the Art of Samuel Beckett* (Minneapolis: University of Minnesota Press, 1971).

7. T. S. Eliot, "Myth and Literary Classicism," in Richard Ellmann and Charles Feidelson, Jr., eds., *The Modern Tradition* (New York: Oxford University Press, 1965), 681.

8. Richard Ellmann, *James Joyce* (New York: Oxford University Press, 1959), 715.

9. "Poetry is Vertical," *transition*, 21 (March 1932): 148-149. The manifesto is signed by Hans Arp, Samuel Beckett, Carl Einstein, Eugene Jolas, Thomas McGreevy, Georges Pelorson, Theo Rutra, James J. Sweeney, Ronald Symond.

10. Lawrence E. Harvey, *Samuel Beckett: Poet & Critic* (Princeton, N.J.: Princeton University Press, 1970), 423.

11. Ruby Cohn, *Samuel Beckett: The Comic Gamut* (New Brunswick, N.J.: Rutgers University Press, 1962), 252-255.

12. Ihab Hassan, *The Literature of Silence: Henry Miller and Samuel Beckett* (New York: Alfred A. Knopf, 1967), 196.

13. John Fletcher, "The Arrival of *Godot*," *The Modern Language Review*, 64 (January 1969):38.

14. Ruby Cohn, *Samuel Beckett*, 255-56.

15. Samuel Beckett, *Happy Days* (New York: Grove Press, 1961), 10. References in the text are to this edition.

16. Ruby Cohn, "Beckett Directs *Happy Days*," *Performance*, I, 2 (April 1972): 115.

17. M. H. Abrams et al., eds., *The Norton Anthology of English Literature*, II (New York: W. W. Norton & Co., 1968), 1007n.

18. Ruby Cohn, "Beckett Directs *Happy Days*," 117.

PAUL LAWLEY

Counterpoint, Absence, and the Medium in Beckett's "Not I"

"The medium of drama," asserted Ezra Pound, "is not words but persons moving about on a stage using words."[1] Pound stated a truism, but one sometimes forgotten by critics of Beckett's plays. This omission is perhaps not surprising. After all, "persons *moving about* on a stage" are few and far between in his plays, especially in the "microscopic" dramas of the 1970s. And are the beings in these plays "persons" anyway? It is all too easy to feel that the static stage picture emancipates the text, licensing the critic to consider the play as a dramatic poem-in-prose. In a holograph note written in 1976 during the composition of *That Time* (in which we see on the stage only a disembodied head hanging in the air), Beckett himself wrote: "To the objection visual component too small, out of all proportion with aural, answer: make it smaller on the principle that less is more."[2] In this essay, I want to concentrate on *Not I* (1972) and to demonstrate that, in this play, much less than the whole body is made to yield more dramatic interest than a whole body ordinarily does. For in *Not I*, it is precisely the extraordinary nature of the "visual component" that encourages the fertile interaction between this single disembodied mouth and the text it pours forth. Beckett conspires with his medium to make less more.

There are several interesting individual essays on *Not I*,[3] but the fullest and most authoritative account is James Knowlson's in *Frescoes of the Skull*. Knowlson's remarks on the stage image and on the language of the play are thorough and satisfying in themselves, but he only hints at the way visual and aural elements might interact. I take one of those hints as my starting point. Knowlson writes: "Speaking of the image of Mouth, the drama critic of *The Times* wrote that 'in isolation it could be any bodily orifice.'⁴ And certainly Beckett displayed no trace of displeasure as, watching the BBC television version, he realized that Mouth had the appearance of a large, gaping vagina."⁵ If we consider in detail the opening of the play, we can understand why Beckett should not be displeased by the strong televisual suggestion.

For ten seconds we hear a voice *"unintelligible behind curtain,"* and as the curtain rises we see the *"Stage in darkness but for* MOUTH, *upstage audience right, about 8 feet above stage level, faintly lit from close-up and below. . . ."* The text begins with an account of conception and birth:

> MOUTH . . . out . . . into this world . . . this world . . . tiny little thing . . . before its time . . . in a godfor- . . . what? . . . girl? . . . yes . . . tiny little girl . . . into this . . . out into this . . . before her time . . . godforsaken hole called . . . called . . . no matter . . . parents unknown . . . unheard of . . . he having vanished . . . thin air . . . no sooner buttoned up his breeches . . . she similarly . . . eight months later . . . almost to the tick . . . so no love . . . spared that . . . no love such as normally vented on the . . . speechless infant . . . in the home . . . no . . . nor indeed for that matter any of any kind . . . no love of any kind . . . at any subsequent stage. . . .⁶

"It is clear," writes Hersh Zeifman, "that the Mouth's monologue is subject to some kind of corrective process, internal or external, and it seems to me that the Auditor [*'downstage audience left, tall standing figure, sex undeterminable, enveloped from head to foot in loose black djellaba, with hood . . . facing diagonally across stage intent on* MOUTH . . .' page 14] comes to represent, for the audience, the visual symbol of that corrective process—the attempt to make the Mouth admit the truth about herself—as well as being a witness to its failure."⁷ It is the Auditor's silent quibbling that emphasizes the suggestiveness of the text. We are looking at a mouth, just that. "Out," it says, "into this world." But this world is not just *the* world, but the world of *this* particular theater; and the Mouth is *out* of its body, a "tiny little thing." We are given time to register the suggestion that the tiny little thing is the mouth we are looking at; then comes the inevitable silent query and correction: "tiny little *girl*." Phrases are recapitulated until we come to "godforsaken *hole*.." "An ambiguous reference to the vagina and/or Croker's Acres [where 'she' lives] . . ."⁸ note the editors of the *Student's Guide*. But the reference is surely *trivial* (as James Joyce might have said): the godforsaken hole is also the one we are looking at, "called . . . no matter." That is what a hole is: no matter. The parents are negatives, "unknown...unheard of...he having vanished," like Mouth's own body, into "thin air" (the absence of the preposition prompts us to relate the thin air into which the father disappeared to the thin air now around Mouth). "Buttoned up his breeches" alludes to another hole: the fly. The tick of time suggests the Mouth's own activity, nervous to say the least. The love She is spared is that "such as normally vented": the oddness of the last word (wrath is normally "vented," and, in Beckett, "pent" too[9]) makes us relate the absent love to the words Mouth can now justly be said to be "venting." Likewise, Mouth's furious venting of words calls forth the etymology of "infant" and thus underlines the tautology of "speechless infant": an eerie phrase in a play that is jammed with speech and that centers on a breaking of silence. The No Matter speaks again of matter in "nor indeed for that matter any of any kind," and the "subsequent stage" returns us to "this world" of the theater.

To continue such commentary would be tiresome. What I have tried to establish, by taking for granted the story Mouth is telling about the conception, birth and upbringing of a little girl (She, not I), and by concentrating on the effects created by the peculiar mode of progression, is the interplay or counterpoint between two dramatic dimensions: that of the text, in which we are told the story of She, and that of the stage image. The text offers us something about someone else that happened at some other time, but the stage image is, as it were, magnetic: It is unignorable, attracting the text to itself and thus insisting upon a present-tense dimension to the story. The text hovers in panic between a past other, of which and of whom it can safely talk, and a present self (hopelessly fragmented though that is), which it must continue to deny: Not I. The counterpoint between stage and text enacts the play's fundamental conflict: between the need to deny the imperfect self and to maintain, even in agony, a fictional other, and the wish for an oblivion that would come with the acknowledgment of the fragmented self.

The *Times* critic quoted by Knowlson had noticed an effect that is of central importance to the play. In addition to the Mouth-as-vagina (*dentata?*) that occurs at the opening of the play and is overwhelmingly evident throughout the television version,[10] Knowlson notes that "the wild stream of words is expressly linked by Mouth with excremental discharge...":[11] "...sudden urge to...tell...then rush out stop the first she saw...nearest lavatory...start pouring it out...steady

stream . . . mad stuff . . . half the vowels wrong . . . no one could follow . . ." (page 22). Mouth-as-eye (even though Mouth is Not Eye) is
strongly suggested. She searches in the field: ". . . a few steps then stop
. . . stare into space . . . then on . . . a few more . . . stop and stare again
. . . so on . . . drifting around . . ." (page 15). The halting rhythm of the
speech here reflects the rhythm of the search, so that the stares become
the silences and the Mouth an eye, one that does indeed drift, disembodied. After the "change" there is ". . . no part of her moving . . . that
she could feel . . . just the eyelids . . . presumably . . . on and off . . . shut
out the light . . . reflex they call it . . . no feeling of any kind . . . but the
lids . . . even best of times . . . who feels them? . . . opening . . . shutting
. . . all that moisture . . ." (page 17). The mechanics of the eye find their
visual referent in the mouth we are looking at: the lids are the lips,
which we see shutting out the light, opening, and shutting again, and
the saliva is the moisture. The eye we cannot see might even be turned
into the ear we cannot see: ". . . she fixing with her eye . . . a distant
bell . . . as she hastened towards it . . . fixing it with her eye . . ." (page
17).

Although the eye cannot be considered simply as an orifice, it does
occasionally function as one. We are alerted to this function when
Mouth describes a scene from "her" past:

> . . . drifting around . . . day after day . . . or that time she cried . . . the one
> time she could remember . . . since she was a baby . . . must have cried as a
> baby . . . perhaps not . . . not essential to life . . . just the birth cry to get her
> going . . . breathing . . . then no more till this . . . old hag already . . . sitting
> staring at her hand . . . where was it? . . . Croker's Acres . . . one evening on
> the way home . . . home! . . . a little mound in Croker's Acres . . . dusk . . .
> sitting staring at her hand . . . there in her lap . . . palm upward . . . suddenly
> saw it wet . . . the palm . . . tears presumably . . . hers presumably . . . no one
> else for miles . . . no sound . . . just the tears . . . sat and watched them dry
> . . . all over in a second. . . . (page 20)

In this passage crying links mouth and eye. We pass from crying as a
sound—the *vagitus*—to crying as silent weeping. In "pouring . . . out"
her "steady stream" of words Mouth tells of dropping tears, and the
stage-text counterpoint works to suggest that Mouth is shedding its
words like tears. The poignancy of the passage is of course as much a
result of the contrast between the verbal torrent of the stage situation
and the vast silence of the narrated event, as of the parallelism I have

tried to indicate; but then this is why we must speak of "counterpoint" and not just "parallelism." The scene is one of acknowledgment: Mouth tells how She came to acknowledge the tears as her own; yet Mouth will not acknowledge her own words or the self (She) that they create. The play of likeness and unlikeness can take place only in the pronominal space between She and I which is as important to the success of the drama as it is to the continuing existence (if that is the word) of Mouth.

So when Knowlson says that "Mouth speaks of a face moving and of eyelids opening and closing and of tears being shed; but of all this we see nothing,"[12] he is of course right, but his comment misses the stage-text counterpoint that follows from the "magnetic" power of the central image: the capacity of Mouth to draw commonplace images and expressions into its orbit and to endow them with a new, disturbing life. Phrases like "in point of fact" (page 17) and "on the point" (page 18) are themselves probed when we hear them spoken by something that is itself, in the theater, a point of light and almost the sole focus of our attention. Likewise, the Mouth speaks of the beam as "ferreting around" (page 21); "the spotlight does not," asserts Knowlson. But Beckett is surely disturbing the cliché: To drive rabbits out and into the nets, ferrets are put into their *holes*. Whatever else Mouth is, it is a godforsaken hole. And in the absence of a real self on the stage, Mouth's commonplace phrases "bring herself" (page 17), "found herself" (page 15), and "to say for herself" (page 21) gain fresh point.

A further consideration of the way stage-text counterpoint reactivates cliché and commonplace can, I think, lead us to the heart of Beckett's achievement in *Not I*. We have looked at two of the specific episodes that Mouth recalls (or invents?) in its outpourings—the conception and birth, and the silent weeping at Croker's Acres—and we have noted how the counterpoint allows us to see them as elaborate metaphors of the stage situation that confronts us. The other two isolable episodes work in a similar way, though each of these draws on an idea familiar from Beckett's previous works. The silent She stocking up at the supermarket with her "old black shopping bag" reminds us of Winnie in *Happy Days*, cherishing the contents of her bag (*"capacious black bag, shopping variety"*[13]) as she cherishes her words because they are her means of survival ("how she survived!" page 18). The courtroom scene in which the silent She is unable to plead recalls the "setting" of *Texts for Nothing*, 5: "that obscure assize where to be is to be guilty."[14]

I want to consider certain verbal details in these two scenes. To begin with the supermarket scene:

> ...even shopping...out shopping...busy shopping centre...supermart ...just hand in the list...with the bag...old black shopping bag...then stand there waiting...any length of time...middle of the throng...motionless...staring into space...mouth half open as usual...till it was back in her hand...the bag back in her hand...then pay and go...not so much as good-bye...how she survived! (page 18)

The adjustment "the *bag* back in her hand" directs attention to a strange effect: "mouth half open as usual...till it was back in her hand" gives us a momentary surrealistic image, as does the earlier "just hand in the list," where the verb "hand" feels briefly like a noun. It is as though She is shopping for the missing parts of Mouth's body.

A similar effect is felt in the courtroom scene:

> ...that time in court...what had she to say for herself...guilty or not guilty...stand up woman...speak up woman...stood there staring into space...mouth half open as usual...waiting to be led away...glad of the hand on her arm.... (page 21)

Not her *own* "hand on her arm," of course, but momentarily it feels as though this is the sense of the phrase. Such effects are, I want to argue, calculated. They go with other suggestions of physical dislocation and dismemberment which are thrown off by clichés that have been galvanized by the physical fragmentation implied in the stage image. "Some flaw in her make-up" (page 17) is meant as a comment on her moral nature, but the makeup we think of is not only moral. The hint in "the whole being...*hanging* on its words..." (page 19, my emphasis) is strengthened by a correction: "...and now this stream ...not catching the half of it...not the *quarter*..." (page 18, my emphasis). No drawing, but hanging and quartering—the punishment of and for being. (This may seem absurdly far-fetched, but why else was "not the quarter" added?) At the very end of the play, "back in the field" and "face in the grass" (both page 22) suggest equally bizarre dislocations and quarterings. In this context, when we hear "off-hand" (page 16), we do indeed think of a hand off. At Croker's Acres that hand turns up "there in her lap" (page 20), as though dislocated. Throughout the play, the fragmentary discourse throws up a fragmented body, the image of the fragmentary self.

Such effects highlight not just particular parts of the body, but physical posture generally. At Croker's Acres She sits; at the Supermarket and in the courtroom She stands. In the latter case, standing up is more than just a physical posture. "Guilty or not guilty . . . stand up woman . . . speak up woman. . . ." She has to "stand up for herself," which would mean telling a truth, the Truth: ". . . something she had to tell . . . could that be it? . . . something that would tell . . . how it was . . . how she—. . . what? . . . had been? . . . yes . . . something that would tell how it had been . . . how she had lived . . . lived on and on . . . guilty or not. . ." (page 21). What She must "stand up" for is the truth of being, the form of words which would release her from her pensum. Yet that truth is something Mouth wants to avoid: the saying of "I." The desire to avoid it is insisted upon, again in physical terms, by a climactic pun:[15]

> . . . she did not know . . . what position she was in . . . imagine! . . . what position she was in! . . . whether standing . . . or sitting . . . but the brain—. . . what? . . . kneeling? . . . yes . . . whether standing . . . or sitting . . . or kneeling . . . or lying. . . . (page 15)[16]

The Auditor insists upon the "lying," for the whole of the monologue, insofar as it is a denial—"Not I"—is a lie, a refusal to acknowledge the fragmentary nature of the self.

We have noted the ways in which the episodes of the conception and birth, the shopping expedition, the weeping at Croker's Acres, and the ordeal in the courtroom all parallel the stage situation. However, we must acknowledge again that the most obvious points are those of contrast. In all the episodes She is speechless, and in three of them She stares, in two of them her "mouth half open as usual." The Mouth which tells us this cannot stop speaking, cannot stare and cannot hold itself half open. It is a function rather than a being, a conduit through which pour the words which testify to being. Thus it cannot be silent, "half open" or otherwise, *and* embody a presence as the narrated She can, for in itself it is a no-thing, a "no matter," an absence. It is the Mouth as an *emblem of absence*[17] of which, ultimately, the stage-text counterpoint makes us so acutely aware. What enables Beckett to renovate clichés involving the body, by bringing particular textual details up against a single stage image, is the absence of the body from that image. Every example of counterpoint we have noted depends, finally, upon this absence. If we bear this in mind, we can understand the special poignancy in the verbs which Mouth uses to describe its (and her) continuing endeavor: she must *"piece* it together" (page 20), *"pick it up"* (page 22) and *"make* sense of it" (page 20), while *"dragging* up the past" (page 20), *"grabbing* at the straw" (page 20), *"straining* to hear" (page 20) yet "not *catching* the half of it" (page 18); perhaps she will *"hit* on it in the end" (page 22, my emphases). It is as though Mouth were attempting to reassemble its scattered, absent body.[18]

I took as my starting point a dictum about the medium of drama, and I think it is clear that the effects I have examined could have been achieved only in that medium. Pound's "persons moving about on a stage" are important to this play because they are felt absences. Yet in presenting us with an emblem of absence, Beckett's exploitation of his medium in *Not I* must involve a creative contradiction of its very nature, for as Alain Robbe-Grillet has said, the stage is the "privileged resort of presence": "The essential thing about a character in a play is that he is 'on the scene': *there.*"[19] Robbe-Grillet contends that Beckett's achievement is the realization of absence in the medium of presence. *Not I* seems to me to confirm this contention with great visceral power,[20] "embodying" in its "mouth on fire" (page 19) the central paradox of Beckett's drama. Such an imagination of absence creates, for a little time, a new kind of presence.

NOTES

1. Ezra Pound, as quoted in Christopher Ricks, "The Tragedies of Webster, Tourneur and Middleton: Symbols, Imagery and Conventions," in Christopher Ricks, ed., *English Drama to 1710* (London: Barris & Jenkins Ltd., 1971), 313.

2. Reading University Library MS 1639, as quoted in James Knowlson and John Pilling, *Frescoes of the Skull: The Later Prose and Drama of Samuel Beckett* (New York: Grove Press, 1980), 219.

3. E.g., Enoch Brater, "The 'I' in Beckett's *Not I,*" *Twentieth Century Literature*, 20 (July 1974):189-200, and "Dada, Surrealism and the Genesis of *Not I,*" *Modern Drama*, 18 (March 1975):49-59; Hersh Zeifman, "Being and Non-Being: Samuel Beckett's *Not I,*" *Modern Drama*, 19 (March 1976): 35-46; and S. E. Gontarski, "Beckett's Voice Crying in the Wilderness, from 'Kilcool' to *Not I,*" *Papers of the Bibliographical Society of America*, 74 (January 1980):27-48.

4. Knowlson quotes Irving Wardle from the *London Times*, 17 January 1973 (Knowlson and Pilling, *Frescoes*, 235, n. 13).

5. Knowlson and Pilling, *Frescoes*, 200.

6. Samuel Beckett, *Not I*, in *Ends and Odds: Plays and Sketches* (New York: Grove Press, 1976), 14. *Not I* is reprinted (pp. 14-23) as one of the "ends." All references, cited parenthetically in the text, are to this edition.

7. Zeifman, *Being*, 45, n. 4.

8. Beryl S. Fletcher, John Fletcher, Barry Smith, and Walter Bachem, *A Student's Guide to the Plays of Samuel Beckett* (London: Faber and Faber Ltd., 1978), 199.

9. "No, with me all was slow, and then these flashes, or gushes, vent the pent, that was one of those things I used to say, over and over, as I went along, vent the pent, vent the pent" (Samuel Beckett, "From an Abandoned Work," in *First Love and Other Shorts* (New York: Grove Press, 1974), 42.

10. "Beckett had nothing to do with filming, was skeptical about its feasibility, but finally was so captivated by it that he pronounced the telecast more effective than the stage play" (Ruby Cohn, *Just Play: Beckett's Theater* [Princeton, 1980], 213). The Auditor, whom Beckett seems always to have regarded as a problematic element in the theater, was eliminated altogether from the television version.

11. Knowlson and Pilling, *Frescoes*, 200.

12. Ibid., 206; comment on "the spotlight" below, 205.

13. Samuel Beckett, *Happy Days* (New York: Grove Press, 1961), 7.

14. Samuel Beckett, "Texts for Nothing," in *Stories and Texts for Nothing* (New York: Grove Press, 1967), 95.

15. For an illuminating general discussion of the lie/lie pun, see Christopher Ricks, "Lies," *Critical Inquiry*, 2 (Autumn 1975):121-42. Beckett is briefly considered on 140-41.

16. Enoch Brater remarks: "Like the 'she' of Mouth's monologue, we have no idea what position Mouth or 'she' is in—whether standing, or sitting, or kneeling. We see merely 'whole body like gone.'" This image is taken to exemplify "our annoying situation as members of the audience" ("The 'I' in Beckett's *Not I*," 199).

17. The counterpoint to Mouth as absence/hole is the description of She "wandering in a field . . . looking aimlessly for cowslips . . . to make a ball . . ." (page 13). We may recall that in *Krapp's Last Tape*, the black ball that Krapp remembers having given to a white dog just at the crucial moment (for him) of his mother's death comes to represent, on the tape, the life he *might* have had, the solid self that went to the dog(s): "In the end I held it out to him and he took it in his mouth, gently, gently. A small, old, black, hard, solid rubber ball. (*Pause.*) I shall feel it, in my hand, until my dying day. (*Pause.*) I might have kept it. (*Pause.*) But I gave it to the dog." (Samuel Beckett, *Krapp's Last Tape*, in *Krapp's Last Tape and Embers* [in *The Collected Shorter Plays of Samuel Beckett*, (New York: Grove Press, 1984), 60].) A ball, even a ball of cowslips, is the opposite of a hole—a nonhole ("He took it in his mouth").

18. For the re-membering Mouth as dismembered Orpheus, see Katherine Kelly, "The Orphic Mouth in *Not I*," *Journal of Beckett Studies*, 6, Autumn 1980: 73-80.

19. Alain Robbe-Grillet, "Samuel Beckett, or 'Presence' in the Theatre," trans.

Barbara Bray, from *Pour un nouveau roman* (Paris, 1963); reprinted in Martin Essling, ed., *Samuel Beckett: A Collection of Critical Essays* (Englewood Cliffs, N.J., 1965), 115, 108.

20. "I am not unduly concerned with intelligibility," Beckett wrote to Jessica Tandy, who gave the first American performances. "I hope the piece may work on the nerves of the audience, not on its intellect" (quoted in Brater, "Dada, Surrealism, and the Genesis of *Not I*," 53). The intelligibility of the text when performed is of course crucial to my own argument; yet the counterpoint I examine depends largely upon the *merging* of text and stage image that will happen naturally, I suggest, at a fast performance tempo. In other words, the actuality of theatrical performance is built into the play's structure. What is "intelligible" in the theater cannot be defined simply as that which works on the intellect of the audience. The nerves-intellect duality in Beckett's statement is a necessary, even vital, one for the performer to keep in mind, but the pronouncement does not, it seems to me, do justice to the audience's experience of the play in either its theatrical or its televisual incarnation. "Nervous" and "intellectual" effects are surely not mutually exclusive: Counterpoint, we might say, works upon the nervous intellect, or upon the intellectual nerves.

WALTER D. ASMUS

Rehearsal Notes for the German Premiere of Beckett's "That Time" and "Footfalls"

The rehearsals began on 1 September 1976, and the premiere was on 1 October 1976. The rehearsals were in the morning between 10:00 A.M. and 2:00 P.M., about half the time being devoted each day to each piece. Beckett had already staged both pieces in London early in the same year. In London he had worked with Billie Whitelaw in *Footfalls*. They knew one another very well, and right from the start the rehearsals had gone ahead in an atmosphere of mutual understanding and intuitive sympathy. In Berlin, Beckett was confronted with an actress whom he didn't know in the part of May, an actress whose work in the theater was based on the search for realistic, concrete motivations and who was not willing or not able automatically to work in an intuitively structural way. The rehearsals therefore evolved in an atmosphere of productive questioning on the part of the actress and of respect on the part of Beckett for the striving of a very talented actress to perfect her role by constantly seeking, in her own way, for access to the characteristics of the "strange, mysterious" figure of May.

This process of tense concentration, which took place under constant reciprocal esteem, in an atmosphere of unfeigned effort, resulted in an exciting production. It is therefore not surprising that the greater part of these notes is devoted to this process. The fragmentary diary character has been kept purposely, because I think that in this way the most essential characteristics of the course of the rehearsals are reproduced most faithfully. More emphasis has been placed on recording remarks and observations that are important for their content and also on the difficulties of the production rather than on an apparently smooth course to a definite goal. May became quite naturally a dominant, central figure such as corresponds to the reality of the text.

Footfalls

MONDAY, 30 AUGUST 1976

Beckett comes to the theater around 9:30 A.M. He has arrived the day before in Berlin and wants—one is accustomed to this from him—to begin work as quickly and purposefully as possible. The part of the mother is not yet cast. The choice is between two actresses whom Beckett will meet later in the morning. In the meantime, there is a discussion in the studio with the technical director and the chief lighting technician. Beckett describes precisely the rhythm of the lights in both pieces. In *Footfalls*, the unit of time should be seven seconds each time; in *That Time*, ten seconds. The bell at the beginning of *Footfalls* dies away in seven seconds; then the light comes up during seven seconds and one can see May walking. At the end of the three parts, the light fades out each time inside seven seconds, the bell dies away in seven seconds, and the light comes on again in seven seconds. At the end of the third part, the light comes on again after the bell, lights up the empty strip for seven seconds, and then fades out. In each part, the light will be somewhat darker than in the preceding one. Therefore it is darkest when the strip is lit up without May at the very end. Correspondingly, the bell gets slightly softer each time.

In *That Time* the light comes on for ten seconds, remains quite bright for ten seconds, and then fades correspondingly to a darker level, which leaves the head of the man in twilight.

After this introductory technical explanation, accompanied all the time by new modifications of the exact description, the meeting with the two actresses for the mother's role takes place. Both read the part of the mother, and a short conversation follows. The choice is obviously unpleasant to him; he calls it discreetly "a little embarrassing."

Immediately after this he is introduced to the actress for the part of May, Hildegard Schmahl (called H in the following). She is in her mid-thirties and has already played many big parts at the Schiller-Theater. She is a rather introverted, sensitive, meditative, and serious person who, in the last few years, has increasingly turned toward the enlightened, politically motivated theater.

A slight embarrassment ensues. H says she has difficulties with the text. "I don't understand the play." Beckett emphasizes the importance of the footsteps. The walking up and down is the central image, he says. This was his basic conception of the play. The text, the words, were only built up around this picture.

"But how is the figure of May to be understood, then?"

Only hesitantly does Beckett take up this challenge to give more detailed information about the play. In the thirties, he says, C. G. Jung, the psychologist, once gave a lecture in London and told of a female patient who was being treated by him. Jung said he wasn't able to help this patient and for this, according to Beckett, he gave an astonishing explanation. This girl wasn't *living*. She existed but didn't actually live. According to Beckett, this story had impressed him very much at the time.

TUESDAY, 31 AUGUST 1976

The rehearsal takes place in the Studio, a little theater with about 150 seats, which are raked steeply as in an arena. The strip is about six feet away from the first row of seats and stretches from right to left over about two-thirds of the whole width of the stage, which is thirty-three feet.

Beckett explains the walking again. It begins on the right with the right foot, on the left with the left, each time nine steps from right to left and back again. He demonstrates this.

There is a technical run-through of part 1, which goes very quickly, since the stage directions in the text can mostly be followed.

After the longish passage beginning with "Straighten your pillows?" H asks: "Does she do that every day?"

"Yes, that is routine."

H: "Without feeling?"

"Yes routine." The bedpan can express some feeling, that is, warmth, he says.

The first section is read and Beckett points out that the tempo should not be too slow. The dialogue should flow and should have only a few, quite definite pauses—which means that the pauses indicated in the text, with a few exceptions, are relatively short.

In this first part there is the only conversation between the mother and May, which, however, should be fairly neutral. When, for example, May asks, "Were you asleep?" that is not so much an interested question as a routine statement.

337

In part 2 the mother speaks of the daughter, in the third part, the daughter of the mother, in a way that is exactly parallel. "One must sense the similarities of both narratives. Not so much from the text as from the style, from the way that the text is spoken." Beckett explains to the mother why she interrupts herself in the sentence, "In the old home, the same where she"—(*pause*) and then continues "the same where she began." She was going to say, "the same where she was *born*," but that is wrong, she hasn't been born. She just began. "It began. There is a difference. She was never born." There is the connection with the Jung story. A life, which didn't begin as a life but which was just there, as a thing.

H: "The conversation between mother and daughter has something very practical and normal—it has nothing lyrical about it?"

"Yes, while May is speaking she is perhaps thinking of something quite different; perhaps she is occupied with her story," Beckett says. "The position of the body will help to find the right voice." Beckett demonstrates the stance: the arms crossed, with the hands clasping the shoulders in front. "When you walk, you slump together; when you speak, you straighten up a bit." And the steps? "If the play is full of repetitions, then it is because of these life-long stretches of walking. That is the center of the play; everything else is secondary."

"Is the posture supposed to express fear?"

"No, not fear. It expresses that May is there exclusively for herself. She is isolated. The costume will look like a ghost costume. It is described in the play: 'Tattered . . . A tangle of tatters . . . A faint tangle of pale grey tatters.' It is the costume of a ghost."

WEDNESDAY, I SEPTEMBER 1976

The formal technical course of the play is made more precise. The walking should be like a metronome; one length must be measured in exactly nine seconds. The fade-out at the end of part 1 begins with the third step from the left, so that it is dark after the ninth step, that is, in seven seconds. The mother speaks her text at the end of part 1 on certain definite steps of May's. The first *May* comes on the fourth step while May is walking from right to left, the second *May* on the eighth step. May says her "Yes, Mother" on the fourth step when she is walking from left to right, and on the sixth step of the same stretch, the mother begins with, "Will you never have done?" The sentence ends immediately before the turn. During the next length (from right to left) the mother begins on the second step with, "Will you never have done revolving it all?" and ends before the turn on the left.

Referring to the mother, Beckett points out that for her a most dramatic story begins with "Till one night...she called her mother and said..." That was the turning point for mother and daughter.

H asks about a translation detail: "Why is South Door translated by '*Nordpforte*' (North Door)?"

"That is a correction," says Beckett. "South Door is too warm. North Door is colder. You feel cold—the whole time, in the way you hold your body too. Everything is frost and night."

THURSDAY, 2 SEPTEMBER 1976

Part 3. Beckett says that "Sequel" was first translated by "*Epilog*" (epilogue), but he found "*Folge*" (continuation) better. In the English it is a pun: *Sequel = seek well.*

The voice in the third part could be a bit more alive than in the first. "One can suppose that she has written down everything which she has invented up to this, that she will one day find a reader for her story—therefore the address to the reader ('Mrs. Winter, whom the reader will remember...'). Words are as food for this poor girl," Beckett says. "They are her best friends." She is a most strange being, and that must be absorbed into the tone—just like her enjoyment of modeling the words, of their sound. Everything depended on the dramatic effect.

Beckett reads out individual passages. "Amen" to be spoken as two syllables. The walking will be slower in the third part. Just as the light from part 1 to part 3 becomes constantly darker, the tone quieter, so the walking gets slower. When she begins to walk, there's a small hesitation, as though she is unsure if she should walk or not. H doesn't know the text by heart yet. Beckett says with the exact posture and the memorized text the inner relationship to the role will also come. She has difficulties in reproducing what Beckett demonstrates and what he tries to get across. "I can't do it mechanically; I must understand it first and then think."

At the end of the rehearsals, Beckett already in his coat, he again points out the similarity between daughter and mother: "The daughter only knows the voice of the mother." One can recognize the similarity between the two from the sentences in their narratives, from the expression. The strange voice of the daughter comes from the mother. The

Not enough in the mother's story must sound just like the *Not there?* of Mrs. W in Amy's story, for example. These parallelisms are extremely important for the understanding of the play, he says.

FRIDAY, 3 SEPTEMBER 1976

Run-through. Too much color. Quite still. No movements with the head, and the eyes open, fixed. The voice is too normal and healthy, is Beckett's criticism of May. "Monotone, without color, very distant. You are composing. It is not a story, but an improvisation. You are looking for the words, you correct yourself constantly. You are in the church with the girl. The voice is the voice of an epilogue. At the end it can't go any farther. It is just at an end."

SATURDAY, 4 SEPTEMBER 1976

Technical Details. "Will you not try to snatch a little sleep?" should begin only with May's third step and end immediately before her turn on the right. May's posture is still not quite right. When she walks she is bent over, when she stands she straightens up slightly. "Slip into the walking. She is on her way before one has grasped the fact that she has begun to move." The hands should be visible in both directions. The costume designer thinks May is in fact an old woman. "No, she is ageless. One could go very far toward making the costume quite unrealistic, unreal. It could, however, also be an old dressing gown, worked like a cobweb."

Run-through. Beckett proposes to differentiate the mother-daughter voice in the narratives, in order to create a further analogy. May's voice is gray, becoming rigid, quite small and slow.

MONDAY, 6 SEPTEMBER 1976

Beckett shows a photo of Billie Whitelaw in the London production. He demonstrates her posture. The left hand at her neck, the right arm crossed over the left and the right hand clasping her left shoulder. The posture should reinforce the tension. The fingers grip the arm rigidly.

Part 1 is already going much better. It is still too slow, however. The speeches are now following basically on from one another, apart from individual pauses. Still May is not satisfied with her tone. "It is a terrible singsong now. When you do it," she says to Beckett, "each tone sounds like a real conversation."

"Yes, the tone is hard to hit off," he says. It must sound as though May were standing on the sidelines, not as though she were in the midst of it. Beckett demonstrates. The tone must be colder. A monotone but not without tension. H says: "No, each word spoken must also have its meaning; it shouldn't just be a monotone...."

In the second part May should move her lips twice during the mother's text, as though she were murmuring something to herself, from "she has not been out since girlhood" until the interruption in the sentence "... the same where she—(*pause*)" and then again from "... till one night, while still little more than a child" until "May: Not enough." Each time at the end of the lip movements she drops her head and closes her eyes for a moment. Beckett asks to have the lip movements timed—they should be roughly the same length, and in fact one is 22 seconds and the other 24 seconds.

In the course of the third part Beckett interrupts: "That is not right yet." From the beginning, it should be much more mysterious.

H: "A whisper?"

"Yes, it could be, if it is audible."

Above all, it is important that the narrative shouldn't be too flowing and matter-of-course. It shouldn't give the impression of something already written down. May is inventing her story while she is speaking. She is creating and seeing it gradually before her. It is an invention from beginning to end. The picture emerges gradually with hesitation, uncertainty—details are always being added....

And his final comment: "A very small play, but a lot of problems concerning precision."

TUESDAY, 7 SEPTEMBER 1976

Before the rehearsal, Beckett explains an idea for the end of the play. In order to avoid the impression that the piece was over with the second-last fade-out, a vertical strip of light should be visible in the background, which could give the impression that the light was falling through the crack of a door. Then it would add a vertical accent to the horizontal light on the strip that would remain lit after each part. At the very end of the play, the empty strip will be faded out first, then, after seven seconds, the vertical strip of light. In this way, the aesthetic aspect and a technical necessity will be combined.

Slyly, Beckett adds: "Then they will know when it is the end—I hope."

The problem lies still in the third part, especially from the Mrs. Winter story on.

"How can I make this story fit together, it keeps falling apart on me?" H's eyes are watering from strained gazing. She is in despair.

Beckett again demonstrates and explains: the gaze to the front, into emptiness. Sometimes it looks as though H were looking at someone. "That is not right. By every means try to keep the tension...."

H: "I can't get it any better at the moment. But I understand it more all the time. I think I can do it. Can I just ask something quite simple? How is it that when you speak the text it gets more and more tense and exciting, when the story always slips away from me?"

Beckett's explanation: That comes because she is not enough "for herself." She is too much in the concrete space of the theater, not absolutely enough concentrated on May, in this figure. A psychological explanation lies perhaps in the fact that with her story May speaks her last words, she has turned everything to and fro, this is now her epilogue—but for Beckett, that is not so important; more important is the absolute encapsulation of the figure in itself.

WEDNESDAY, 8 SEPTEMBER 1976

Beckett sits right at the top in the last row. Run-through. The acoustics turn out to be a problem. A lot cannot be understood. "It?" spoken with a question-mark is a difficult problem, says Beckett. He has tried it, can't do it either. He tries it. "You *can* do it," calls H. She is bathed in sweat from the exertion of her narrative. "I am still too over-tense." The position of her hands is corrected. During each stretch of her walk one hand must be clearly seen.

THURSDAY, 9 SEPTEMBER 1976

H interrupts herself again during the Mrs. W story. "I can't go on." She tries it again. Tears run over her face: "I don't want to make it unpleasant for you. I'm not crying... it's just the tension inside, in my head. My God, what torture...."

Beckett turns to the mother; the microphone is tried. The voice is still too breathy.

Here is the danger for Charlotte Joeres, the actress playing the mother. She has a tendency toward a loving, lyrical tremolo in her voice and is therefore in danger of giving the figure a soft, pathetic element. She, too, must try for more coldness of expression.

Then part 3 again. "Faint, but by no means invisible," etc.: colder. In the Mrs. Winter story: "The daughter speaks slower than the mother." The whole should not be too sad; it should under no circumstances sound tragic.

SATURDAY, 11 SEPTEMBER 1976

H tries out a modified walk and does it for Beckett. An animal, "tigerish" walk along imaginary bars. The turn is accomplished as though before an invisible wall: a slight raising of the head and a scarcely perceptible jerk back of the body as though before an obstacle. Beckett is skeptical. Is it perhaps too realistic in intention? The strip is covered with wooden boards; the shoes make a light sound—too light. Beckett proposes a slight hesitation before each turn, as though she didn't know exactly whether she should go on.

THURSDAY, 16 SEPTEMBER 1976

H is still not satisfied. "How is it that I can't get it?"

Beckett finds her too soft. "Sometimes you have it, then it gets lost again." He speaks the text, doggedly, almost maliciously, uncompromisingly. "When you feel yourself too far away from the right tone, you have already failed. You are looking in your acting for the right *tone*, that is fatal. You are acting in too healthy a way.... Try gradually, while you speak the words, to see the whole inwardly. It has a visionary character... it is an image which develops gradually. When you begin to narrate the story, you don't yet know the end.... It is too easily narrated.

"I will leave you alone for a few days."

TUESDAY, 21 SEPTEMBER 1976

H has been to a psychiatric clinic and has had discussions there with a doctor about female patients who suffer from obsessions. She promises herself a more concrete approach to her part from this. During the run-through, she again breaks off during the Mrs. Winter story: too long-drawn-out. No tension.

WEDNESDAY, 22 SEPTEMBER 1976

The best run-through so far. The Mrs. W story takes shape. It narrates something. It's taut and logical and exciting, cold and uncompromising. Everyone is relieved.

343

On Beckett

"That was not your strongest performance," says Beckett after the run-through. In the Mrs. Winter story the two voices are again tried out: the mother and Amy. H sharply spits out "Mrs. W" and "Amy" each time as the name of each speaker, as though she wanted to play one name off against the other, as though they should bounce off each other. The argument between Mrs. W and Amy can be still quicker. It ends with the sentence "The love of God..." which, with pauses, hesitatingly, is almost sung and so dissolves the tension of the preceding passage.

MONDAY, 27 SEPTEMBER 1976

The lighting transitions are tested. May gets a little spotlight on her face at the wheeling points, it is added only when she stands still. The crack of light at the back is about a third of an inch wide and about five feet high, quite straight and bare. The stage is hung with black velvet, and the strip is steeply lit from the front to mark its boundaries clearly. The difference in atmosphere between the three parts turns out to be a difficult business. The light should be as weak as possible without becoming unbearably dark.

H breaks off again at the beginning of the Mrs. W story. A general feeling of helplessness. She says she just has to work on by herself. Beckett suggests that he go. Perhaps he is pushing her into a false conception of achievement, he says. H rehearses on until 4:30 P.M. We again discuss the problem of concentration, that is, what Beckett terms the "being for herself" of May and the visionary development of the story. The constant modifications in the text must emerge jumpily, violently, sudden formations of associations that form a chain of thought.

In trying to produce the images from the inside, H has strongly tended up to now to emphasize the words with more or less unconscious movements of the body, especially of the head. Here lay the basic gesture of a natural way of speaking that softened the story and allowed no artificiality to appear. H tries to hold her body quite stiffly, to avoid every small movement. An artificial immovability develops; a tauter articulation takes over the soft, agreeable modulation. A concentrated creation of art does indeed emerge, a cold, stiff, encapsulated being; the "being for itself" of the figure comes across.

344

The Stage

The so-called first principal rehearsal, Ruby Cohn and an audience from the theater are there. Even from the first sounds, one senses that H is on the right track. Nothing soft, nothing that is not binding, nothing accidental in her way of speaking. A great coldness and tautness without sentiment. May stands independent of her surroundings as a concentrated bundle on the strip of light. No superfluous movement distracts; the tension communicates itself to the observer; one is drawn into the undertow of her story—the concentration is passed on and challenges the observer to an absolute concentration. Beckett is satisfied with the result. "You have found the trick," is his comment.

Some of those present misunderstand the strip of light in the background as a mistake—as though the velvet curtain had been left slightly open by accident.

Experiments with the strip of light: It is placed diagonally, to the left, to the right. Beckett suggests jokingly that it be made into a cross; then it can't be a mistake. Finally it is decided to make it a foot longer.

The second principal rehearsal on the next day and the dress rehearsal go very well. The whole room is hung with black velvet in order to force the attention of the audience absolutely on the illuminated strip.

That Time

TUESDAY, 31 AUGUST 1976

Beckett defines first of all the function of the three loudspeakers. They are supposed to make the transition from one story to another clear. It is the same voice but the stories are taking place at different levels of time. The voices flow without serious interruption into one another and are differentiated only by the position of the loudspeakers on the left, in the middle, and on the right of the eight-foot-high platform on which the man is sitting. The B story has to do with the young man, the C story is the story of the old man, and the A story is that of the man in middle age. From a great distance he hears the voice he has today, says Beckett.

Klaus Herm reads. Beckett speaks the text from memory with him, only moving his lips, breaking in at times to correct. Herm tries to construct images from the content, makes breaks, reads for the sense.

Beckett interrupts after the first A story. It should be spoken quite quickly, he says. Since Herm can't physically manage to speak it without pauses, he should make pauses where it is necessary, which would then be cut out by the sound engineer. At the end of part 1 the voice gets quieter from "to keep the void from pouring in." With "the shroud" the light will come on for ten seconds (later this is changed to fifteen seconds), stays for ten seconds very bright, and then fades in the same space of time back to the original twilight level. Part 2 begins quietly, "Like a car drawing up, a machine." The play consists of three parts in which the speeches A B C are each present four times in a different order. In the following the speeches will be denoted as A1, A2, B1, B2, C1, C2, etc.

WEDNESDAY, 1 SEPTEMBER 1976

The rehearsal begins between Beckett and Herm with quotations from the text. They throw the ball to each other with visible delight. Key words like "when was that?" "after this," "after that," are accentuated and stretched out with joy—at the end of each speech somewhat slower, at the end of the twelfth speech slowest of all. The first recording is made of part 1.

THURSDAY, 2 SEPTEMBER 1976

The pauses in the text are not yet cut out precisely enough; one can still sense them. The new beginning also seems to differ too much from the last preceding word; it is too loud and strong. The loudspeakers are placed too far apart and are moved to a maximum distance of roughly eighteen feet apart. In the sound studio another recording is made, and the pauses are cut out immediately. Between A, B, C there must be a transition without interruption, as for example in music from A minor to C major, Beckett says; a flow without beginning and end, without very much being emphasized or pointed up.

FRIDAY, 3 SEPTEMBER 1976

The B story is the most emotional; the C story, however, is cold, almost cynical. There is still the problem of the uninterrupted flow of the text. Herm would like to make still more pauses, which would then be cut out. Beckett demonstrates the speaking himself: Flat, inaudibly breathing, murmuring, dreamy, without any noticeable interruption, he goes through a whole speech without stopping. In order to acquire the flow of the text both of them go through the whole passages with imploring gestures. If one could get by without cuts, keeping the same tempo constantly, that would be best....

Beckett comments in C7 that the text here is a difficult place for the audience: "... The old rounds trying to wangle you into *it*," whereby he emphasizes the *it*. That is a story of depersonalization—seeing oneself as an object. In A8 "the passers pausing to gape," that is from the Bible, he says.

Herm: "Yes, from St. Luke's gospel."

Beckett: "I looked it up, but I didn't find it. Aha, Luke."

SATURDAY, 4 SEPTEMBER 1976

Herm tries to read with small pauses for breath. This turns out not to be practicable. There are too many, and a staccato impression results, not the desired legato.

Part 2, B5. Beckett insists on a small pause after "muttering (:) that time..."

B6. Beckett accentuates the parallelism in the order of the speeches where individual units begin with an emphasized *never*; *always*; *never*; *no*; *always*; *no*, culminating in the key word *vows* at the end, which should be spoken with a lot of "tenderness."

A series whose individual members are separated by small pauses can be found in C7: "... till the words dried up and the head dried up and the legs dried up...."

B8. A further small series: "no stir or sound only faintly the leaves in the little wood behind or the ears or the bent or the reeds..."

This rhythmical rendering of the text goes into the recording.

THURSDAY, 9 SEPTEMBER 1976

The recording of the second part is unsatisfactory. The new beginnings after the pause are still too strong and loud. Through this, unmotivated accents are created, and the flow of the text is ruined. A new method is tried: Herm reads up to a certain point, makes a pause, and begins again with the text a few words before the stop, so that with the first words an acoustic balance has already been achieved. The overlapping turns out, when we hear it, to be practicable. A very good smoothness in the text results.

347

Beckett reminds Herm to remember the ritardando at the end of parts 1, 2, and 3. Above all, at the very end a dramatic effect should be achieved: "will it go on again."

WEDNESDAY, 5 SEPTEMBER 1976

Herm reads part 3.

Beckett finds it too chopped up and too little flowing. He demonstrates. At the end of the last speeches in the B A C series, Beckett misses the emotion. It should not be sentimental, but he has the impression that Herm is too occupied with technique, with breathing, etc. There is too little feeling in it. Perhaps it would be an interesting exercise to read it once with too much feeling. It could always be reduced afterward.

THURSDAY, 16 SEPTEMBER 1976

Beckett comments on the silence after each of the three parts: In these moments the man comes back to the present. While he was listening to his voice he was in the past. During the listening everything is closed. In the silence he is startled to find himself in the present; everything is open. It is not decided whether he opens his eyes and the voice stops for that reason or whether the voice stops and therefore he opens his eyes.

The recording of the previous day seems to him to be too even and lacking in tension.

Herm suggests making a new one immediately. Beckett is agreeable but strangely uneasy. Finally he says, half jokingly, he can't bear the text any more—he is completely impregnated with it. We make the recording without him.

TUESDAY, 21 SEPTEMBER 1976

At the playback of the recording Beckett is visibly bored with it. He finds the text too long. It is his mistake, he says, to have been so fixated on the flow. It becomes too monotonous. How would a recording be in which the text is spoken quite normally, with breaths?

Herm tries it over a microphone; it doesn't sound bad.

WEDNESDAY, 22 SEPTEMBER 1976

The recording that has been spoken for the "sense" is running. It is unbearably long. Beckett twists nervously. The recording is thirty minutes long, eight minutes longer than usual. The text loses all tension, gets at the same time a false significance.

The "flow" is the right way. A new recording with pauses cut out is very good. It gains a tempo that forces one to concentrate when listening, simultaneously a power of suggestion that pulls one into the story, structured by the highly dramatic moments of the silence, in which the white-haired head in the black surroundings begins to sway and the wide-open eyes provide a picture of fixed horror.

The text flows without being monotonous, and its images are present in the round without a long-winded narrative resulting. All the chopping and changing has produced the best possible result.

Translated by Helen Watanabe

JAMES KNOWLSON

"Footfalls"

Beckett began to write the short play *Footfalls* in Berlin on 2 March 1975,[1] a little less than a week before the opening night of his now famous production of *Warten auf Godot* at the Schiller-Theater. The first manuscript draft consists of only two and a half pages. This includes most of the opening dialogue between the old mother and her daughter (who was called Mary in the first draft), together with an early version of the mother's monologue, which is very different from that printed in the published text. By autumn the Royal Court Theatre's plans for a Beckett seventieth birthday season for the coming April and May in London were well advanced. These plans included an evening of "shorts," for which *That Time* was already written. With this in mind, Beckett returned to work on his earlier draft of a play written especially with the actress Billie Whitelaw in mind. On 1 October[2] he added a "sequel" (called then an appendix) to what he had already written, recast the mother's speech later that month, and then worked almost continuously on the play in Paris until early November, when he felt sufficiently satisfied to announce that it was completed,[3] although it was to be modified later in several minor respects in the course of the three productions Beckett has directed.

Two alternative titles, *Footfalls* and *It All*, were assigned to the first version, but *Footfalls* soon emerged as the right one: Beckett insists that the image of the woman pacing relentlessly up and down is central to the play. "This was [my] basic conception," Beckett commented. "The text, the words were only built up around this picture. . . . If the play is full of repetitions, then it is because of these life-long stretches of walking. That is the center of the play; everything else is secondary."[4] The woman, renamed May, a diminutive, of course, of Mary, but with an added ironic suggestion of spring (and yet another of Beckett's characters with the M siglum), paces up and down across the stage in nine[5] "clearly audible rhythmic" steps (page 42), revolving "it all" in her mind. Her pacing punctuates, or accompanies, the words in each of the three sections or stages of the play in which she appears. Moments of frozen immobility alternate with this pacing and an intricate interplay of movement and speech is envisaged from the earliest stage. But what is also clear from the manuscripts is that this central, and only visible, pacing figure, itself dimly lit, was conceived from the outset in relation to the surrounding darkness; it was also accompanied by another essential element in the drama, the mother's voice emanating from the darkness. In other words, the play was visualized in terms of a composite and specifically theatrical image: sound and silence, repeated movement and total stillness, faint—and steadily diminishing—light and complete darkness supplying the various contrasting elements that were to be organized into a miniature and delicate drama that appears every bit as mysterious as the strange spectral figure of May herself.

After the premiere in London in May 1976, many critics confessed themselves intellectually baffled by this elusive little play. Yet in one sense, the feeling of bewilderment helped at least to focus critical attention upon some of the features of the play that are most crucial to its dramatic impact: the shocking image of the woman, May, dressed in a worn gray tattered trailing wrap, her face skeletal, her hair gray and disheveled, her bony hands clasped tightly across her body, grasping her shoulders in a gesture of isolation and distress; the remorseless nature of the slow, rhythmic pacing; the subtle interplay of light and darkness; the different voice levels, that of the mother coming from the back of the stage and amplified, that of the daughter coming from the front of the stage and live; the gradual fading away of the chimes, the light, and the footfalls and, finally, the disappearance of the ghostly presence of May herself; and the stark patterning of verbal echoes in the mother's account of the daughter's strange life and in the story recounted later by the daughter.

Everything in the writing, and in the London production directed by Beckett, seems, in fact, to have been shaped to evoke feelings of distress, of strangeness and mystery, a sense of inexplicable seeking and yet the distillation of absence and loss. This does not, of course, mean that elements of the play that might, at first, have appeared tantalizingly obscure do not later fall into much sharper and clearer focus. What it does mean is that, for many spectators, the play could succeed in the theater at a level that involved the senses and the emo-

351

tions rather more than it did the intellect. In fact, the reason inevitably seeks for explanations for this unusual phenomenon, as the sight, sounds, and rhythms of a woman's determined pacing are revealed. Yet only enough information is offered to add to the resonance of the image and not enough to destroy the sense of mystery that pervades the entire play.

The pacing, although never really explained, acquires, nonetheless, a strange form of justification. Partly this arises from its very obsessional quality and partly from the mother's own words, which present May's solitary pacing as representing the externalization of an inner anguish. So as well as pacing out the eternal round of time, May appears to be seeking to resolve something that cannot ultimately be resolved. For the enigmatic "it all" that she constantly revolves in her "poor mind" is linked quite clearly to her own life in particular, to the point when "it all" began, and to life in general. Beckett explained to Charlotte Joeres, the actress who played the part of the mother at the Schiller-Theater Werkstatt in 1976, that she interrupts herself in the sentence "'In the old home, the same where she—(*Pause*)' and continues 'The same where she began' because she was going to say '. . . the same where she was *born*.' But that is wrong, she hasn't been born. She just began. It began. There is a difference. She was never born."[6] In *All That Fall* (1957), Mrs. Rooney recounted how she once attended a lecture given by one of those "new mind doctors":

> I remember his telling us the story of a little girl, very strange and unhappy in her ways, and how he treated her unsuccessfully over a period of years and was finally obliged to give up her case. He could find nothing wrong with her, he said. The only thing wrong with her as far as he could see was that she was dying. . . . The trouble with her was that she had never really been born.[7]

This story derives from a lecture given by the psychologist C. G. Jung, in the mid-thirties, that Beckett attended while he was staying in London.[8] It should be remembered that Beckett had a slight personal link with Jung, in that James Joyce's daughter, Lucia (who was in love with Beckett), was Jung's patient at the end of 1934.[9] May in *Footfalls* is Beckett's own poignant re-creation of a girl who had never really been born, isolated and permanently absent, "as though May were standing on the side-lines,"[10] distant and totally encapsulated within herself.

And yet immured as she is within herself, at times May can and does speak. Indeed, just as her pacing expresses her own inner torment, so, as for Mouth in *Not I*, words become her means of attempting to tell obliquely "how it was." The words that she invents, however, in the third part of the play, evoke only a double representation of her own pseudo-existence—the strange life of an unhappy girl who had never really been. For she appears first in the fiction, as the ghost whose "semblance" we see pacing in front of us, "a faint tangle of pale grey tatters," (page 47); then again, in the final story, she materializes as yet another image of herself, in the shape of Amy (appropriately enough an anagram of her own name, but also, in the normal English pronunciation "ay-me" or in French "ami"), who was unable to observe the strange, ghostly figure walking in the church at Evensong, because she too was "not there."

Repetition, parallels, and balance evidently play a crucial part in this play. The pacing persists throughout, relating a concrete, dramatic reality—which may itself be that of a ghostly nonexistence—both to the woman's past life as it is recounted by her mother and to the phantom presence that may be seen walking in the transept of the church. Similarly, each part ends with a reiteration of the daughter's obsessional concern with revolving, or telling, "it all." The third part repeats exactly the words that conclude the opening dialogue, but both voices now issue from the mouth of the same woman. The Amy of the story has replaced May, but she repeats the same words spoken earlier by the mother and daughter.

It is worth looking in a little more detail at the various phases of the play's development in order to see what effects such repetitions and parallels achieve. In the first tableau, the opening words of the play, the repeated "Mother," summon a voice out of the darkness, as if May were herself conjuring a ghost back from the past. And the voice answers from the darkness, as if this were indeed true. But the mother also seems able to relate to the stage presence of her daughter, counting the steps as she paces and responding to her questions like an aged relative whose present sufferings might conceivably be alleviated. For the subject of the dialogue is a precise evocation of human concern. May's questions suggesting both realistic actions and objects for the easing of suffering. The scene is, in fact, clearly that of a "dying mother" and is referred to as such by Beckett in a manuscript note.[11] But what could easily have been full of human pathos becomes more neutral, less stark and harrowing, yet more mysterious, because of its ritualistic quality and strange fusion of past and present time. Repetition and balance play, then, an important part in shaping a liturgy of suffering in which not only age and illness are evoked, but as the following extract reveals, life itself is indicated as a Passion to be lived through and wished away:

M. What age am I now?

V. And I? (*Pause. No louder.*) And I?

M. Ninety.

V. So much?

M. Eighty-nine, ninety.

V. I had you late. (*Pause.*) In life.(*Pause.*) Forgive me again. (*Pause. No louder.*) Forgive me again.

M. What age am I now?

V. In your forties.

M. So little?

V. I'm afraid so.

(page 44)

The mother's monologue that makes up the second section seems to be addressed to the watching audience ("But let us watch her move, in silence," (page 45) and is unheard by the daughter, with whom she now has no contact. In Beckett's own German and French productions, May whispers or mouths words to herself, illustrating the mother's answer to her own question "Does she still sleep?... Still speak? Yes, some nights she does, when she fancies none can hear" (page 46). The exact status of the voice and its invisible owner remains mysteriously ambiguous. It bears witness to the strange presence that we too observe. But it is the voice of a ghost, seeing but herself unseen. The mother's voice has its own idiosyncrasies of vocabulary and phrasing, which are later adopted by the daughter in the "sequel." The mother also poses some of the questions that the spectator may be asking: "Where is she, it may be asked," "But this, this, when did this begin?" "Does she still sleep, it may be asked" (page 46). But the answers are more likely to deepen the mystery than to solve it. We learn from the mother, for instance, that the place in which she is seen pacing up and down is the old home, that the strip upon which she walks was once a carpeted pile, and that when she sleeps, "she bows her poor head against the wall and snatches a little sleep," (page 46). It is disconcerting to realize, then, that May sleeps on her feet facing the wall, which is the front of the stage and through which we observe her. In this way, the invisible fourth wall of the naturalistic theater takes on a new and most unusual dimension. As the time sequence is uncertain in the first part, so, in this second part, the physical location too becomes dubious and mysterious.

The principal "event" of this section represents a development in the strange biography being recounted, and it clearly came as a surprise to the mother, who is at once here narrator and biographer. For suddenly, the daughter had announced that the motion of her pacing was in itself not enough and that she needed to *hear* the sound made by her feet on the floor. The carpet has not therefore simply been worn away as a result of her pacing, as one might at first have surmised. It had been expressly removed to allow the evidence of her own pacing to be heard. No explanation for this request is offered. It is simply described as a crying need.

The third part of the play consists of May's "epilogue," partly composed already but for the most part invented as she goes along. Before this, however, she adds a "sequel" to her mother's account, in which an undefined "she" (presumably herself, the "I" being as unacceptable to her as it was to Mouth in *Not I*) returns to haunt the church, slipping through a locked door and standing stark still or pacing up and down, as we have seen May doing throughout the play. Only the absence or presence of sound seems in fact to differentiate her account of what occurred in the church from what we have witnessed of her own behavior. Yet even sound, which in the theatrical sense is real and audible, is at another level uncertain and unverifiable: "No sound. (*Pause.*) None at least to be heard" (page 47), which is echoed by a phrase in the poem "Neither," written some time after *Footfalls* (indeed during the Berlin rehearsals of the play), "unheard footfalls only sound."[12]

In this third stage of the play, the ghost walks in the church, "up and down, up and down, his poor arm" (page 46). The manuscripts and typescripts of the play reveal quite clearly how this particular image developed. Entering the church by the south door (which became the north door in performance and in the collected volume, *Ends and Odds*, Beckett commenting that south gave too warm an idea, for "Everything is frost and night"[13]), in the first manuscript, the figure paced up and down "the corresponding transept." This becomes in the first typescript the "corresponding arm"—the church being built, of course, in the shape of Christ crucified on the cross—which, in typescript 2A, is again changed to "his poor arm."[14] The change not only introduces a further element of mystery but it confers a sense of human pathos on the passage, and if the allusion is picked up, it also adds a religious dimension to the suffering evoked in the text.

May goes on to invent a story in which the only two characters are again a mother, Mrs. Winter, and her daughter, Amy. The chief common link between this story and May's own biography is that the girl, Amy (called Emily in the first drafts), also claimed not to have been there, when the strange apparition had been observed by her mother during Evensong. But there are other parallels between the two sections. The question "What do you mean, Amy?" (page 48), for instance, picks up the earlier "What do you mean, May?" (page 45), and expressions like "the child's given name" appears in both parts, as well as the verb *fancy* used to mean "suppose" by both mother and daughter. In performance, it was also found that phrases like "Not enough?" and "Not there?" could be spoken so as to sound like direct echoes from the previous section. The technique of handling dialogue in narration is also similar in both cases, the name of the character speaking being given on every occasion.

But what is the purpose of such intricate parallelism? First, the dominant verbal repetitions clearly echo the revolving motions of the woman whom we see in front of us. The form of the play, therefore, becomes that of a series of circular revolutions, moving from one phase of absence to another, gradually fading away into less and less sharp definition and moving toward silence, stillness, and deepening darkness. There are, in fact, four stages to the play, the fourth consisting of an empty stage, on which there is "no trace of May" (page 49). By reading through the earlier drafts, which are looser, less taut, and less meticulously shaped than the finished text, it is also possible to see how much more compelling the play becomes as a result of these parallels and echoes, which confer aesthetic pleasure, as well as lending wider resonance to the play.

For every element in *Footfalls* is part of a total choreography of sound, light, and movement. As Walter Asmus's production notes show, Beckett was anxious as a director to make the lighting and sound levels as much a part of the formal patterning as was the verbal text. So the chimes of the bell that separate and frame each section died away in seven seconds, and the light came up and faded away also in seven seconds; the light and the bell become respectively dimmer and softer as the play proceeded. There is no doubt that in all of Beckett's work as a playwright and as a director, what has been called the echo principle is merely part of a way of conceiving of the text rather like a musical score, in which phrases, notes, and rhythms are picked up and restated, sometimes in the same form, sometimes with variations, whether slight or intricate. It matters relatively little whether these echoes are consciously perceived by the spectator. They register unconsciously and confer shape and strength on a work that inevitably appears lacking in the interest derived from conventional narrative or delineation of character.

In *Footfalls*, however, the many parallels and repetitions, together with the analogies that exist between mother and daughter in both the drama and the story set into the drama, serve also to create a play in which we can never be quite sure of what we are looking at or to what we are listening. We realize, perhaps only after the play has ended, that we may have been watching a ghost telling a tale of a ghost (herself), who fails to be observed by someone else (her fictional alter ego) because she in turn was not really there. So Beckett's ghost story, which probably has its roots in a fusion of the image of a woman pacing (perhaps, it has been suggested in Deirdre Bair's biography, Beckett's own mother)[15] and the account of Jung's girl patient who "had never really been born," assumes the form of a complex set of variations on appearance and dramatic reality. For since, as we have seen, even the mother's voice may be a voice in the mind of a ghost, everything may be regarded as illusion in this little play. And yet it is an exceptional achievement on Beckett's part to have made the strange amalgam of absence and suffering created by these various levels of ghostly representation seem so tangibly real.

It might appear, as with the protagonist of *That Time*, that with May, Beckett was presenting an extreme case that could possess little general significance. And yet, although the play begins with a specific and very human mother-daughter relationship and appears to narrow down to focus upon one woman, in fact its echoes reverberate much more widely. For May, though virtually absent from life herself, seems in her constant pacing to be both sharpening and questioning its pain and its suffering. This apparent paradox is achieved by the repetition of phrases such as "your poor lips," "your poor mind" (page 44) and the more resonant "his poor arm" (page 46), but also by the force of a stark statement like "She would halt, as one frozen by some shudder

357

of the mind" (page 46). Perhaps more crucial in this respect, however, is the evocation of the expanded version of the closing prayer of Evensong, taken from the second book of Corinthians, chapter thirteen, "The love of God, and the fellowship of the Holy Ghost, be with us all, now and for evermore. Amen." In the London production, the final *amen* was pronounced as two syllables, "ah-men," just as the earlier *sequel* had been pronounced "seek well." In this way the play absorbs into itself much wider associations. There are, in fact, signs that, in the course of writing the play, Beckett developed the figure of May as a tormented soul, in the world but not of it, suffering every day from "some shudder of the mind." For the association with religion and with Christ's Calvary are in no way accidental. The pacing along "his poor arm" has already been mentioned, but the game of "lacrosse" is adopted for the religious association of the pun and, when translated into French, the game became significantly *"ce jeu du ciel et de l'enfer."*[16]

Among human beings, May is exceptional in Beckett's terms only in the undiluted concentration of the "rounds" of her distress. Seven or nine, the figure is uneven, as she paces out the days of the week or the months of gestation, after which, in Beckett's stern vision, suffering is handed on from mother to daughter. If Jung's girl patient has haunted Beckett for so long, it is because she epitomized for him a permanent sense of existence by proxy, of being absent from true being. And if, in discussing May's posture in the course of directing the play in Berlin, Beckett used a term with strongly Sartrean associations, "being for itself," it is, I think, not only because this expressed admirably the girl's isolation, but because it also focused upon a constant feature of life on "this old muckball" (Krapp's Last Tape).[17] But with this "an intuition of a presence, embryonic, undeveloped, of a self that might have been but never got born."[18] The *être manqué* is not, then, simply May but Man in general.

NOTES

1. Holograph manuscript, Reading University Library (R.U.L.) MS 1552/1. First page dated 2 March 1975.
2. Holograph manuscript, R.U.L. MS 1552/1; the second page is dated 1 October 1975. The second draft of the mother's monologue is dated 25 October 1975.
3. Letter to James Knowlson, dated 7 November 1975.

4. Walter D. Asmus, "Rehearsal Notes for the German Premiere of Beckett's *That Time* and *Footfalls* at the Schiller-Theater Werkstatt, Berlin (Directed by Beckett)," *Journal of Beckett Studies* (2, Summer 1977), 83, 85. Reprinted in this volume.

5. In *Footfalls* (London: Faber and Faber, 1976), May paces seven steps across the stage, but this was corrected in the Royal Court performance to nine steps, to give greater width. The Faber text was set before the production in May 1976. In *Ends and Odds* (London: Faber and Faber, 1977), the text is amended to nine, although an error has crept in on page 33, where the steps are mistakenly left as seven. In the French premiere of *Pas*, with Delphine Seyrig as May, at the Théâtre d'Orsay (11 April 1978), nine steps were also adopted. The text closest to Beckett's intention is in *Ends and Odds* (New York: Grove Press, 1976); references are to this edition. For an analysis of the textual variants of *Footfalls* see S. E. Gontarski, "Text and Pre-Text of Samuel Beckett's *Footfalls*," *The Papers of the Bibliographical Society of America*, 76 (1983): 191-95.

6. Asmus, "Rehearsal Notes," 83–84. In the first typescripts, reference is made to "a general practitioner named Haddon. Long past his best" for whom her birth was "his last mess" (R.U.L. MS 1552/2).

7. Beckett, *All That Fall*, in *Collected Shorter Plays* (New York: Grove Press, 1984), 35–36.

8. Asmus, "Rehearsal Notes," 83–84.

9. See R. Ellmann, *James Joyce* (New York: Oxford University Press, 1959), 689–93.

10. Asmus, "Rehearsal Notes," 87.

11. R.U.L. MS 1552/1.

12. "Neither" was written to be set to music by Morton Feldman in September-October 1976. Beckett terms it a "text." It is published in the *Journal of Beckett Studies* (4).

13. Asmus, "Rehearsal Notes," 85.

14. Typescript 2 is R.U.L. MS 1552/3 and 2A is R.U.L. MS 1552/4.

15. Deirdre Bair, *Samuel Beckett: A Biography* (New York: Harcourt Brace Jovanovich, 1978), 10–11.

16. *Pas suivi de quatre esquisses* (Paris: Les Editions de Minuit, 1978), 11.

17. Beckett, *Krapp's Last Tape*, in *Collected Shorter Plays* (New York: Grove Press, 1984), 62.

18. L. Harvey, *Samuel Beckett, Poet and Critic* (Princeton: Princeton University Press, 1970), 247.

MARTIN ESSLIN

Samuel Beckett and the Art of Radio[1]

Samuel Beckett's work for radio is a highly significant part of his *oeuvre* and far less fully discussed in the mounting literature on Beckett than his other output, far less readily available, also, in performance, which alone can bring out its full flavor. But beyond that, Beckett's experience with broadcasting, and above all radio, has played a significant and little-known part in his development as an artist.

It has become a kind of cliché of the Beckett literature that the BBC commissioned radio plays from Beckett. Even the cover of the first American publication of *All That Fall* and *Embers* in the Grove Press paperback *Krapp's Last Tape and Other Dramatic Pieces* (1960) baldly states: "Two radio plays commissioned by the BBC's Third Programme." Beckett himself has always strenuously denied that he writes plays on commission from anyone. And the truth is that he was, indeed, never commissioned by the BBC to write anything. The real story of the genesis of these radio plays is far more complex and interesting.

The first communication between Beckett and the BBC goes back to the period before his rise to fame as the author of *Waiting for Godot*. On 1 June, 1952, Beckett sent P. H. Newby (then a talks producer, later to become controller of the Third Programme, and later still, director of programs for radio) the text of *Cascando*. The brief note from Beckett stands forlorn and unexplained in the file. Clearly this was not the radio play of that title, but the poem. Mr. Newby assumes that he had heard about Beckett's poetry from someone familiar with the Paris scene—possibly Christopher Logue—and asked him to send some of his poetry. Nothing seems to have come of this first contact.

It was only after the success of *Waiting for Godot* that inquiries were made about the play early in 1953 and, indeed, steps were taken to secure the rights to translate the play. On 6 August 1953, the BBC

360

was informed that the author insisted on making his own translation. When a copy of this arrived, the producer who had been enthusiastic about the Paris production (let him remain mercifully nameless) found the translation not as good as the original. He felt that perhaps it might be made workable if the author was willing to allow improvements to be written into it. But alas, he added in a final memorandum (dated 24 May 1954), Beckett's Paris publisher had assured him that the author was *"un sauvage"* and quite unwilling to listen to reason. Nevertheless, after the success of the London performance, another producer, Raymond Raikes, warmly urged that it should be preserved for posterity by being recorded and broadcast. By 6 December 1955 the rights to broadcast the performance had been obtained, though, for some reason now impossible to ascertain, nothing came of the project.

Through all this argument and agitation Beckett's name had become familiar within the Drama Department and the Third Programme team, and John Morris (then controller of the Third Programme) was very eager to broadcast something by him. In June 1956, he heard rumors of a new play to be performed in Marseilles and asked the Paris representative of the BBC, Cecilia Reeves, to make inquiries. She wrote to Morris on 21 June 1956:

> I have written to Beckett asking if he would write a piece for Third and if he would let us have the text of *La Fin du Jeu* [*sic*—either that was the title at that stage or Miss Reeves had misremembered it]. He is, as you know, an elusive character and spending much of his time outside Paris and our mutual contact Desmond Ryan has already gone South. He has however reacted amiably to the suggestion that his mime piece *Soif* [clearly the original title of *Acte sans paroles I*], also to be given at Marseilles, should be considered for television, so I imagine that his former, rather hostile, attitude to radio in general is improving.

The head of television drama, Michael Barry, must have met Beckett in Paris shortly afterward to discuss the television broadcast of the mime play, for on 4 July 1956, Cecilia Reeves's assistant wrote to the head of radio drama:

> This is just to confirm what Mr. Barry has already told you that Beckett is agreeable, in principle, to writing a radio play for Third and that he will discuss the idea in more detail with Miss Reeves when she comes back. He says, however, that he has never written anything for radio before and will probably need a little persuasion from Miss Reeves before he actually starts working on it. As regards the play which is to be produced at Mar-

361

seilles next month, Beckett has not yet finished writing it and is not yet sure about its title which is at present *Fin de Partie*. He will certainly let us have the text later on.

On the same day Beckett wrote to Miss Reeves, who was on leave in England, that he had had an idea that might or might not lead to something. Within a week John Morris wrote to Beckett to tell him how excited he was to hear of this and suggested that he might meet him for lunch in Paris to discuss this and other ideas. The lunch duly took place on 18 July 1956, and John Morris wrote on the same day to the Head of Radio Drama, Val Gielgud:

> I saw Samuel Beckett in Paris this morning. He is extremely keen to write an original work for the Third Programme and has, indeed, already done the first few pages of it. I got the impression that he has a very sound idea of the problems of writing for radio and I expect something pretty good. He says his output is unpredictable. Sometimes he works slowly, at others very fast, but he does not wish to be tied down to any definite date.... The play which was to have been done at the Marseilles festival has now been cancelled because of some sort of muddle with the organizers.... He has promised the Third Programme the first chance to do an English translation as soon as the French stage production is fixed up.

Beckett sent John Morris the finished manuscript of *All That Fall* on 27 September, 1956. So only just over two and a half months had elapsed between the date at which Beckett first mentioned the idea and the actual completion of the play. In a brief note accompanying the manuscript Beckett stated that the play might well call for a special quality of *bruitage* and that if necessary he would let him have further details. Morris expressed his delight with the play and asked for a note on the special *bruitage*. On 18 October, Beckett replied that he found it difficult to put his ideas about the sound effects on paper and suggested that it might be best for him to meet the *bruiteur*. By return of post, on the following day, Morris responded with the news that "Donald McWhinnie who will be producing *All That Fall* is going to be in Paris for a week from Monday next, 22nd October. I think it would be very useful for you to meet him since I know he would like to discuss with you personally a number of production points." And so started the immensely fruitful relationship between Donald McWhinnie (then assistant head of the radio drama department, and one of the great pioneers of the art of radio) and Samuel Beckett.

The play was scheduled for the third week in January 1957. Donald

McWhinnie, having discussed the production with Beckett and finding that their ideas closely agreed, got down to work. On 28 November, Beckett wrote supplying the only amendment: in the very first line of dialogue he changed the phrase that originally ran "all alone in that old crazy house" to "all alone in that ruinous old house." He later informed McWhinnie that the opening of *Fin de partie* was now planned for 15 January at the Théâtre de l'Oeuvre and that he would therefore be unable to attend the rehearsals and recording of *All That Fall* in London between 2 and 6 January.

In his reply (13 December 1956) McWhinnie expressed his regret at this decision and informed Beckett that he had decided to have all the animal noises in the script recorded by humans. He also asked for a short contribution (from five to five hundred words) for the BBC's program periodical, *Radio Times*. Beckett politely declined on his customary ground that he was incapable of writing about his own work. Nor could he see the point of having the animal noises imitated by humans. The opening of his play at the Oeuvre having been postponed, he had thought of coming to London for the production. But he had decided against it because he felt that he might be a hindrance rather than a help in the studio.

McWhinnie wrote to explain his ideas about the animal noises:

> I am sorry to disturb you about the animals. Of course we have realistic recordings, but the difficulty is that it is almost impossible to obtain the right sort of timing and balance with realistic effects. By using good mimics I think we can get real style and shape into the thing. The other factor is that existing recordings are very familiar to our listeners and I do feel that without being extreme we need, in this particular case, to get away from standard realism. As far as we have got, I am very pleased with the results of this experiment; but, of course, if it should not prove right, when we have put the whole thing together, we shall have to think again.

This was on the eve of the start of rehearsals with the actors. The experiments with sound effects had been going on for some time, mainly late into the evening in drama studios vacated by their daytime users. The sound technician principally involved was Desmond Briscoe, a radio enthusiast of immense inventiveness and imagination. Beckett's script demanded a degree of stylized realism hitherto unheard of in radio drama, and new methods had to be found to extract the various sounds needed (both animal and mechanical—footsteps, cars, bicycle wheels, the train, the cart) from the simple naturalism of the

363

hundreds of records in the BBC's effects library. Briscoe (and his gramophone operator, Norman Baines) had to invent ways and means to remove these sounds from the purely realistic sphere. They did so by treating them electronically: slowing down, speeding up, adding echo, fragmenting them by cutting them into segments, and putting them together in new ways. These experiments, and the discoveries made as they evolved, led directly to the establishment of the BBC's Radiophonic Workshop. Beckett and *All That Fall* thus directly contributed to one of the most important technical advances in the art of radio (and the technique, and indeed technology, of radio in Britain).

The first broadcast of *All That Fall* took place on 13 January 1957. In a letter dated 14 December 1956 (although it was clearly written on 14 January 1957, the day after the broadcast) Beckett sent McWhinnie a hearty "*bien travaillé*." The reception of the BBC's Third Programme wavelength in France had been very poor, but he had heard enough to realize that the two principals, Mary O'Farrell and J. G. Devlin, had given excellent performances, although the latter had sounded somewhat perfunctory at times. Beckett had greatly liked the laughter with which they greeted the text of the sermon (the line from the psalms that gives the play its title). But he still had not thought the animal noises quite right.

Donald McWhinnie has supplied a very convincing justification for the solution of the problem of the animal noises in his excellent and detailed account of the production process of *All That Fall* in his book *The Art of Radio*.[2] Recordings of actual animal sounds could never have been blended into the stylized convention of the play. The atmosphere and acoustics of the circumstances under which they were made inevitably cling to such recordings and would have punctured the enclosed, subjective universe of *All That Fall*.

Yet it is remarkable to what extent Beckett had, in his first attempt at a radio play, intuitively grasped the specific qualities and capabilities of the medium and how brilliantly he had seized those aspects of radio that were most germane to his own thematic and formal preoccupations.

Thematically, *All That Fall* clearly links up with Beckett's last previous work in English, *Watt*. The cast of seedy genteel Irish types, the provincial milieu, even the railway station clearly belong to the same world. But whereas *Watt* is still narrated in a clinically cool objective manner, the action of *All That Fall* is experienced by the listener subjectively from Maddy Rooney's point of view. It is precisely the nature of the radio medium that makes possible the fusion of an external dramatic action (as distinct from the wholly internalized monologues of the narrative trilogy that followed *Watt*) with its refraction and distortion in the mirror of a wholly subjective experience. In radio the dramatic action is directly placed in the listener's mind and imagination. The microphone becomes the listener's own ears. And these ears can be directed either to the outside world or inward to pick up an internal monologue; indeed, they can enable the listener to experience the external world *subjectively* with the ears of the character in the play.

Through the use of acoustic perspectives the radio writer and director can clearly convey to the listener with *whose* ears, from which subjective viewpoint, he is witnessing the action and, indeed, inside whose mind he is supposed to be. Thus, by the use of stylized and distorted sounds, radio can create a subjective reality halfway between the objective events experienced and their subjective reflection within the mind of the character who experiences them—halfway between waking consciousness and dreamlike states, halfway between fact and fantasy, even hallucination. Just as the subject experiencing such states finds it difficult to decide whether his experience is reality or fantasy, so the radio dramatist can keep the listener in a similar state of uncertainty. In *All That Fall*, Maddy Rooney's progress towards Boghill Station has a nightmare quality; it might indeed be a bad dream. Eventually, by various subtle means, the author establishes that we are in the mind of a character to whom objective reality itself is a kind of perpetual nightmare.

Only radio among all dramatic media can create this kind of effect, this peculiar kind of dramatic suspense. Unlike a visual medium, which supplies a multitude of descriptive elements in each instantaneous picture, radio—like music—exists in the temporal dimension alone and must build its picture in a linear manner, adding one descriptive element after another. Information gradually emerges, can be withheld and then dramatically revealed.

Almost as a centerpiece to the nightmarish sequences of *All That Fall*, we are made aware of the objective reality of the place we are in and, indeed, made to see it objectively, albeit through Maddy Rooney's eyes. "The hills, the plain, the racecourse with its miles and miles of white rails and three red stands, the pretty little wayside station, even you yourselves, yes, I mean it, and over all the clouding blue, I see it all, I stand here and see it all with eyes . . . through eyes . . . oh, if you had my eyes . . . you would understand." For, far from being a blind medium (as stressed by Marshall McLuhan), radio is an intensely visual medium. The nature of man's consciousness and sensory apparatus is predominantly visual, and inevitably compels him to think and imagine in visual images. Information that reaches him through other senses is instantly converted into visual terms. And aural experiences, which include the immense richness of language as well as musical and natural sound, are the most effective means of triggering visual images. These images, moreover, being generated by each individual listener, have the advantage of being completely satisfying to him. There is no danger that the image seen will fall short of what he may have expected—as it often does in the theater or on the screen.

Another aspect of the sound medium grasped by Beckett was its need for strict formal patterning. Because they are totally immaterial, aural art forms are in danger of becoming amorphous and demand great clarity of structure and pattern. Rhythm and rhyme, strophic forms, the patterning of music in movements, all these are devices designed to impose form on the formless. Not only is *All That Fall* very closely a three-movement structure (Maddy Rooney's anabasis, her wait at the station, her and Dan's katabasis), but it has also a very complex pattern of small-scale rhythms—the footsteps of the anabasis, the doubled footsteps and the thumping of Dan's stick in the katabasis, the rhythmic panting, etc. (That rhythmic and recurrent panting also became a feature of Beckett's *Comment c'est.*) *All That Fall* was acclaimed as a radio masterpiece; it received an enormous amount of critical attention and has established itself as one of the classics of radio drama. . . . The play has been translated and broadcast in many languages. It was filmed for television in France, but Beckett is supposed to have disliked the transfer of the play to another medium. When Laurence Olivier and Kenneth Tynan attempted to persuade him to allow them to mount a stage production in the British National Theatre, Beckett refused.

The tremendous success of *All That Fall* spurred the BBC to urge Beckett to write more for radio. After meeting him in February 1957, shortly after the first broadcast of the play, McWhinnie reported that radio had obviously captured Beckett's imagination. But he was preoccupied with the plans for the stage production of *Fin de partie*, which had run into all sorts of difficulties in Paris. As it happened, the first performance of the play (in the original French) took place in London at the Royal Court Theatre, and the BBC obtained permission to broadcast it. Michael Bakewell (one of the radio drama department's most gifted young directors) undertook the task of overseeing the transfer of the production to radio; it was broadcast on 2 May 1957.

In the same month, Beckett, who had been thinking of writing a work for radio in collaboration with his cousin, the composer John Beckett, wrote to McWhinnie that he could not foresee any chance of writing an original piece for radio for a long time to come; he suggested instead that John Beckett might be asked to compose music to accompany a solo reading from one of his prose works. He was thinking of a section of *Molloy*, "from the shore to the ditch," the final section of part I.

This idea was eagerly accepted, and John Beckett commissioned to write the music (which eventually turned out to be for a small ensemble of nine players). To read the part of Molloy, McWhinnie cast Patrick Magee, one of the group of superb Irish actors he had assembled for *All That Fall* (Magee had played Mr. Slocum; Jack MacGowran, later to become the second of Beckett's preferred interpreters, played Tommy, the porter at Boghill Station). In November, shortly before the recording of *Molloy*, Beckett suggested another reading, of a passage from an unfinished novel, originally referred to in the BBC's records as *The Meditation*. The broadcasts of these two readings took place within the same week: *Molloy* (which ran to 59 minutes, 14 seconds) on 10 December and the meditation, now retitled *From an Abandoned Work* (23 minutes, 30 seconds) on 14 December 1957.

These readings by Magee were immensely effective and successful, not least with Beckett himself, who had found an ideal interpreter. One of the consequences of this success was that George Devine, who was planning the English-language premiere of *Endgame* at the Royal Court, suggested to Beckett early in 1958 that he should write a stage monologue for Magee to go with the performance of *Endgame* (just as the original French performance of the play had been linked with *Acte sans paroles I*).

Beckett mentioned in a letter to McWhinnie (26 February 1958) that he had indeed had an idea for a stage monologue for Magee and in March informed him that he had written the piece, which involved the use of a tape recorder; he asked McWhinnie to send him operating instructions for such a machine, for he had to be sure how it worked.

367

Thus *Krapp's Last Tape* owes its existence both to Beckett's discovery of the fascinations of tape recording in the wake of the production of *All That Fall* (the reception of its second broadcast had been even worse than the first, so the tapes were sent to Beckett) and to his discovery of Magee as an ideal embodiment of characters like Molloy. Yet this play, directly inspired by Beckett's contacts with radio, is by its very nature incapable of being performed on radio. The effect of the play depends, above all, on the counterpoint of the powerful visual image of a man listening to his own recorded voice with his reactions to his past personality registering on his features. On radio it would be difficult to differentiate Krapp's recorded voice from his unrecorded utterance: Both would be on tape, and to distort the recorded voice would be unrealistic, since tape recording only slightly distorts human speech.

The success of Magee's readings from *Molloy* and *From an Abandoned Work* led to further readings—from *Malone Dies* (with music by John Beckett; read by Magee; duration 1 hour, 11 minutes, 38 seconds) on 18 June 1958; and from *The Unnamable* (also with music by John Beckett and read by Magee; duration 1 hour, 51 seconds) on 19 January 1959.

The beginning of 1959 brought the completion of Beckett's long-awaited second original play for radio. Copyright clearance for this as yet untitled manuscript was requested on 13 February 1959. On a later memorandum a suggested title, *Ebb*, was penciled in. By April the title had definitely become *Embers*. It was in rehearsal from 19 to 23 June 1959, under Donald McWhinnie's direction; Jack MacGowran was cast as Henry; Patrick Magee doubled the parts of the Music and Riding Masters. The first broadcast took place on 24 June.

In *Embers* Beckett has moved further away from objective reality, closer to radio's unique ability to present an inner, wholly subjective reality. The background—a background of sound, the sea, Henry's boots on the shingle—is still real, but the voices are all internal: Henry's internal monologue as he tries unsuccessfully to conjure up his dead father's presence, and later the voices of his wife and daughter and her instructors, which materialize in his memory. Apart from the basic situation, the images of an old man sitting by the sea, all the visual images built up are internal. They are all the more intense for that: like the strange, haunting scene of the two old men standing by the dying fire in the dead of night, arguing about something that never becomes wholly explicit, except that it involves an injection or a shot of drugs.

If *Embers*, although its action is confined to the inner reality within its protagonist's mind, still retained the external reality of his situation within a real framework, that is, on the seashore, Beckett's next two radio plays shed even that last tenuous link with the outside world.

Words and Music finally realized Beckett's long-cherished intention of collaboration on an original work with John Beckett. The decision to put this plan into practice is mentioned in a memorandum from Michael Bakewell to me (I had succeeded Donald McWhinnie as assistant head of the radio drama department) dated 20 February 1961. The completed manuscript of the play was in the hands of the BBC by the beginning of December. It was first broadcast on 13 November 1962.

Beckett's preoccupation with the process of human consciousness as an incessant verbal flow (on which the whole of his Trilogy as well as *Texts for Nothing* was based) here found its logical culmination, and one only radio could provide. For after all, human consciousness—the self's awareness of its own existence—does consist not *only* of a constant stream of language. It has a nonverbal component as well, the parallel and no less unbroken stream of wordless consciousness of being, made up of body sensations, inner tensions, the awareness of body temperature, aches, pains, the throbbings of the flow of one's own blood: These are the multiple facets of nonverbal consciousness summed up in the overall concept of emotion. In the arts, as perhaps Schopenhauer first showed, this stream of nonverbal life-awareness, of life force or *will*, is the subject matter of *music*, which portrays and represents the ebb and flow of the emotions. To give an adequate representation of the Beckettian exploration of the self's experience of itself, music had to be added to the verbal stream of consciousness. This is precisely what Beckett attempts in two of his later radio plays.

There are three characters in *Words and Music*: a Lord and Master, called Croak, and his two servants, Words (or Joe) and Music (or Bob), the court poet and court musician in his lordly household. In Beckett's Trilogy, the self is split into a listener and a voice telling that listener stories. In this radio play the listener, Croak, commands one of his servants to regale him with a verbal, the other with a musical (that is, emotional), stream of consciousness. He sets them themes on which to improvise, and if they fail to please, he silences them by thumping them on the head with his club.

The movement of the play, after unsuccessful improvisations on the themes of Sloth, Love, and Age, converges on the evocation of the features of a beloved woman—on Croak's command to his servants to improvise on Face. At one point Croak exclaims: "Lily!" Here words and music merge into song. Words' shocked exclamation: "My Lord!" the sound of the master's club, which slips from his hand, and the shuffling away of slippered feet indicate that the memory of fleeting fulfillment, "one glimpse of the wellhead," has silenced Croak in total despair of fulfillment. The play ends with Words' attempts to make Music repeat the statement about the wellhead again and again. The last sound is a deep sigh from Words.

This short play (it ran for 27 minutes, 30 seconds) has appeared in book form; but so totally radiogenic is its very nature that the printed page cannot represent it. It exists only in sound—in radio or perhaps as a recording—for the third character, Music, in every way of equal importance with the other two, is of necessity absent on the printed page.

Cascando was an even shorter play than *Words and Music*. Beckett's work for radio echoes the tendency of all his other works to get progressively more concise—the BBC's production barely exceeded 21 minutes in duration. It was written in French in collaboration with the Rumanian composer Marcel Mihailovici—whose opera based on *Krapp's Last Tape* Beckett had greatly liked—with the French radio and Süddeutscher Rundfunk (Stuttgart) in mind. The French text reached the BBC in June 1962, but Beckett's translation took some time to be completed; there were also fairly lengthy negotiations to obtain the tape of the music as performed in Stuttgart, so that the first broadcast of *Cascando* in English (it had been transmitted in French by ORTF on 13 October 1963) did not take place until 6 October 1964. Donald McWhinnie directed the play as guest producer.

Here again we have three characters—the Opener, a Voice that is heard when he opens one door or channel of his consciousness, and Music, which emerges if he opens the other. Occasionally he opens both (doors? channels? he never specifies what it is that he opens), and then music accompanies the Voice. The Voice tells a story about the pursuit of an elusive character called Maunu in the French, Woburn in the English version (Mau-nu has suggestions of evil-born, evil-naked; Woburn of born in woe, or burning in torment). The play ends at a point where Maunu-Woburn has almost been caught; yet whether he will slip away again remains uncertain in a final silence. As in *Embers*, the action takes place in the vicinity of water. The Opener, who repeatedly mentions that people say that it is all happening in his head, might be seen as analogous to Henry, who felt compelled to tell himself stories, to keep on talking all the time.

And here again the music supplies a new element, the nonverbal stream of consciousness that the Opener can evoke either by itself or in unison with the verbal flow of the Voice. The outside world is again absent, except for the repeated statement by the Opener that for him it is May....

Besides Beckett's four original radio plays, the canon also contains a translation by him that clearly displays his great skill as a translator and is also truly creative. This is the translation of Robert Pinget's radio play *La Manivelle—The Old Tune....* This translation had its first broadcast in the Third Programme on 23 August 1960.

Apart from works specially written for radio, the BBC has broadcast a number of Beckett's stage works. *Waiting for Godot* finally reached the listeners of the Third Programme on 27 April 1960, more than seven years after it had first been suggested.... *Endgame*, which had been discussed with Beckett since the very first contacts between him and John Morris in 1956, did not get a broadcast in English till 2 May 1962 (Donald Wolfit played Hamm). This delay was partly due to scruples about the supposedly blasphemous line "The bastard, he doesn't exist."

One of the most interesting experiments in transferring a stage play by Beckett to the radio medium, and one that revealed the workings of Beckett's mind most clearly, was the broadcast of *Play*. The BBC's experimental group of radio actors and directors, the Rothwell Group, undertook (under the leadership of a young producer, Bennett Maxwell) to find a sound equivalent for the light beam, which directs the utterance of the three characters whose heads protrude from their urns. Maxwell had the idea that it would be possible to replace the operation of that light by creating a continuum of sound—an endless loop of

371

tape of the three characters' voices saying "I," which would be abruptly interrupted each time one of the characters was jerked into speech by that mysterious beam of light. Beckett had categorically refused permission to broadcast *Play*, but he agreed to come and listen to a playback of this experimental production.

I remember that playback in my office very vividly. Beckett sat through the whole play with an enigmatic and inscrutable expression on his face. When it was over, he said, "I don't like it at all. You got it wrong."

He then proceeded to explain that the text fell into three parts: Chorus (all characters speaking simultaneously); Narration (in which the characters talk about the events that led to the catastrophe); and Meditation (in which they reflect on their state of being endlessly suspended in limbo). These three parts are repeated, and the play ends, as it began, with the Chorus. But, Beckett explained, there must be a clear progression by which each subsection is both faster and softer than the preceding one. If the speed of the first Chorus is 1 and its volume 1, then the speed of the first Narration must be 1 plus 5 percent and its volume 1 minus 5 percent. The speed of the following segment, the first Meditation, must then be (1 plus 5 percent) plus 5 percent, and its volume (1 minus 5 percent) minus 5 percent. The implication is quite clearly that any quantity, plus or minus, still has to be a finite quantity; however soft, however fast, the same text will go on *ad infinitum*, ever faster and ever softer without quite ceasing altogether.

Having expounded his suggested *modus operandi* Beckett had clearly become interested in the project. So when Bennett Maxwell and I asked him whether he would permit a broadcast provided we adhered to his prescription, he readily agreed and supplied us with another modification of the text that is not apparent in its published form. In the original production at the National Theatre in London, Beckett had not merely had the whole text repeated exactly as it had been spoken the first time around; he had supplied a new way of permutating the order in which each of the three characters spoke his text. Each character spoke the same lines in the same order *within his own text*, but the order in which he was called upon to speak was different. Beckett suggested that each character's part should be recorded separately in duplicate, and that these permutations of exactly the same words spoken in exactly the same way be achieved by cutting the tape together like the takes of a film.

This remarkable production of *Play* was first broadcast in the Third Programme on 11 October 1966.

The tradition of readings of nondramatic texts by Beckett was kept up throughout the 1960s. . . .

A reading that—so at least it seemed at the time—stood halfway between the mere delivery on the air of a text written for the printed page and a work that was specifically radiogenic was that of *Lessness*, Beckett's own translation of *Sans*.

Lessness is a text in which Beckett returned to his preoccupation with permutations of fixed verbal elements *ad infinitum*—a simulacrum of eternity itself, with time as an infinite combination of a finite number of basic elements. It started from six groups of statements, each containing ten sentences. The sentences within each of the six groups bear a distinct family likeness, being themselves variations on a single theme or image. Sentences from these six groups of ten—sixty in all—were then combined by Beckett at random in a given order and subdivided into paragraphs of varying lengths containing between three and seven sentences each. Having thus arrived at a random structure, Beckett then went through the process of combining the same sentences again, using the same method of finding a new sequence and paragraph structure by random selection. It is clear that the same process could be continued indefinitely; the barren landscape with the little upright human figure can literally stretch out to the end of time, or rather to its endlessness.

The suggestion that radio might be the means of making the very complex structure of this text more clearly visible came from Beckett himself via his London publisher, John Calder, who passed the structural key to the work to me. Calder and I went to Paris to discuss the production with Beckett. He read a passage of the text to me, clearly indicating the exact intervals between each sentence and the longer intervals between the paragraphs, and also specified that he wanted the voices to be distinguishable from each other although so unified in tone that they might be aspects of the same voice. As in the case of the radio production of *Play*, he wanted each group of sentences to be recorded separately by their speaker, so that the final production would consist of exactly the same sentences recombined in a different se-

373

quence by mechanical reproduction and editing, which would make it possible for the intervals of silence to be of exactly the same length, down to a tenth of a second.

For the production I tried to assemble a group of speakers whom I knew to be deeply sympathetic to Beckett's work: Nicol Williamson (who had given a breathtaking reading from *Texts for Nothing* at a Royal Court matinée some time before); Harold Pinter; Patrick Magee; Donal Donnelly; Denys Hawthorne; and Leonard Fenton. Once their recordings had been duplicated, cut up, and reassembled in their correct sequence, a strangely musical structure almost miraculously emerged.

Alas, Beckett was deeply dissatisfied with the broadcast. He felt that the voices were far too strongly differentiated, that the reading seemed too slow (we had rigidly adhered to the tempo he himself had adopted when reading a sample to me) and thus too sentimental. With his usual kindness and courtesy he took the blame upon himself and confessed that the idea of using six different voices might have been a mistake. There is certainly a dilemma inherent in this concept, for in reproducing the work in German for Westdeutscher Rundfunk (Cologne) I tried to lessen the differentiation between the voices and to speed up the tempo—and the final result was far less effective than the original English version. But *Lessness* seems to me an ideal text for radio, which alone can bring out its daring structural conception. I feel that this structure can only be made manifest by having voices as differentiated as those in our original production, and that the idea that those voices emanate from a single consciousness (which I agree is crucial to the work) does not necessarily get lost by such differentiation. After all, the Opener and the Voice in *Cascando* are very strictly differentiated and yet remain clearly within one individual's head; and this is even more the case in *Words* and *Music*.

Be that as it may, the broadcast (25 February, 1971) of *Lessness* on Radio 3, as the Third Programme had been renamed, had a very considerable impact on listeners—a fact attested by the unusual volume and fervor of letters of appreciation.

On Beckett's seventieth birthday, 13 April, 1976, BBC Radio 3 broadcast the first performance of a further radio script by Beckett, *Rough for Radio*. Harold Pinter played the part of the Animator; Billie Whitelaw, the stenographer; and Patrick Magee, Fox.

Rough for Radio, which, as the title of the English version implies,

Beckett himself considers to be little more than a rough sketch, is nevertheless of very considerable interest for the light it throws on some of Beckett's recurring themes and preoccupations. The playlet, which in performance runs to about twenty minutes, is closely linked with *Words and Music* and *Cascando* as well as with an uncompleted play *Esquisse radiophonique*.

Esquisse radiophonique was published in the fifth issue of the bi-monthly review *Minuit*, the literary house organ of Beckett's Paris publishers, Editions de Minuit, in September 1973. Beckett himself dates it there as "vers 1962-63?"

Number 16 of *Minuit* (November 1975) contains the first publication of *Pochade radiophonique* ("pochade" means a skit or sketch, hence the title of the English version, *Rough* [that is, a rough sketch] *for Radio*). This is dated by Beckett "années 60?" In some of the publications of this text it appears as *Radio II*.

Like *Words and Music* (1962) and *Cascando* (1963), these two radio pieces are concerned with aspects of the process of artistic creation, with voices and streams of music emanating from more or less mysterious sources, and the dependence of the principal characters on these and their more or less successful attempts at achieving some sort of control over them.

Esquisse radiophonique (Beckett's own translation into English gives it the title *Radio I*, while the English version of *Pochade radiophonique* carries in the typescript of the translation the title *Radio II*)[3] presents us with a man (He) who is completely dependent on one stream of music and another of words, which go on unceasingly but are made audible by turning two knobs of an apparatus reminiscent of a radio set. These voices are *live (en direct)*; the use of technical language from the world of radio is significant. The sketch opens with the man being visited by a woman (She), who assumes that she has been asked to come to listen to these sounds, though the man insists that he never asks anyone to come and that he merely "suffered [her] to come" because he "meets [his] debts" (page 107). The woman listens to the stream of music that emanates from the apparatus when one of the knobs is turned; she is surprised to find this music seems to be made by more than one instrument? person?—this remains unclear. In the French version her question as to the number of those involved is answered by the man, "*Cinq ... six.*" In the English version he merely agrees that there are several but remains silent when asked, "How

375

many?" The source of the words, on the other hand, which become audible when the other knob is turned, is a solitary one. When the woman expresses her surprise that the speaker of the words is all alone, the man replies, "When one is alone one is all alone" (page 108). When both knobs are turned at the same time the music and the words are heard simultaneously, but the two streams of sound nevertheless are, as the woman observes, not together. Nor, as the man adds, can they see or hear each other. Asked whether he likes these sounds, the man—who never leaves the place because he has to listen to them—replies, "It's a need" (*j'en ai besoin*) (page 109).

The woman leaves. The man telephones his doctor in a panic, disclosing incidentally that his name is Macgillicuddy. Finding the doctor absent, he insists to the doctor's secretary that the matter is extremely urgent. And when, after several abortive calls, the doctor finally rings back to inquire what has happened, the man discloses in tones of extreme distress that the sounds are not only getting fainter, as though they were "ending," but they are also coming "together." It seems that the doctor's answer (which we do not hear, since he is on the other end of the telephone line) indicates that this coming together of the two sources is connected with their dying, as "last gasps" are "all alike" (page 111). The doctor then, it seems, puts the receiver down. As music and voice are audibly failing, the telephone rings again, and it seems that the doctor's secretary is informing the man that the doctor cannot come to see him as he has been called to two urgent confinements, one of them a breech birth (*par le siège*). The doctor, it seems, cannot come before "tomorrow . . . noon." The sounds from the apparatus become feebler and feebler and finally cease altogether. The man is heard to whisper, "Tomorrow . . . noon" (page 111).

The structure of the play, its central image, and its narrative line are fully developed. What is missing in the text is the stream of words emerging from the apparatus. This is indicated merely by a row of dots. When the play was first published, the composer Humphrey Searle, who was eager to write the musical part, suggested to the BBC that we should ask Beckett to translate it into English and to complete it. At first Beckett agreed, for he was interested in collaborating with Searle; but after some months he informed me that he felt unable to proceed. When the manuscripts of both radio sketches reached me at the beginning of 1976, I felt that the play might nevertheless be produced without a text for the voice because it might be possible to treat it as no more than a faint mumbled murmur. But Beckett did not find this suggestion acceptable.

Shortly after *Pochade radiophonique* had appeared in the November 1975 number of *Minuit*, I wrote to Beckett to ask if there was an English version of the play and whether he would agree to our producing it. He referred me to his London publisher, Faber & Faber, who had typescripts of the translations of both of the hitherto untranslated radio pieces, and agreed to a production of *Pochade radiophonique*. At that stage both pieces merely had the titles *Radio I* and *Radio II*. Because the BBC's four national radio networks are labeled Radios 1, 2, 3, and 4, it would clearly have been very confusing if Radio 3 (the network on which most of Beckett's work is broadcast) had transmitted a play called Radio II. I therefore asked Beckett whether we could not call the play *Sketch* or *Skit for Radio*. He rechristened it *Rough for Radio* (published as *Rough for Radio II*).

The image of the play is that of a room containing a hooded, gagged, and blindfolded figure called Fox (in both the French and the English versions). Three other characters come to visit Fox bent on the task of extracting from him a monologue—or stream of words—to be written down. The leader of this group is called the Animator. He is accompanied by a woman stenographer and a mute figure, Dick, equipped with a whip (a bull's pizzle) and hence something like a professional torturer.

After hood, blindfold, and gag are removed from Fox and some earplugs taken out of his ears, the Animator asks the stenographer to read out the "report of yesterday's results" (page 116), from which it appears that "these dicta, like all those communicated to date ... are totally inacceptable" (page 116) and, indeed, that the outlook for future results seems equally hopeless. The stenographer is then asked to read out "the exhortations," which consist of a number of points: that mere animal cries must not be recorded; that the transcript must be strictly literal; and that the subject must be completely neutralized when not in session. As the stenographer proceeds to read out a fourth point, she is stopped by the Animator, who has heard enough, and so we are denied knowledge of what that fourth point, or any further points, might contain. The stenographer then reads out the end of the previous day's text. This refers to an episode in which the speaker, Fox, has been washing and drying a mole he seems to have rescued in the dead of winter, after which he took the animal, with its little heart still beating, out into the blizzard and back into its chamber.

After the stenographer has shed her overalls because of the heat and glare in the room, which greatly arouses the Animator ("Ah, were I but ... forty years younger!" page 117), and after Dick has wielded his whip on Fox's body, Fox begins to utter fragments of a monologue, interrupted by comments from the Animator and the stenographer. Fox's text is a kind of parody of the typical Beckettian interior monologue. From time to time Fox, whose vitality is low, falters and has to be recalled to his duty by the Animator's impatiently knocking on his desk with his ruler and by threats of Dick's whip. Fox's monologue deals with a past life ("Live I did," page 117) and his leavetaking from the changing seasons ("such summers missed, such winters," page 119). But he breaks down weeping when he mentions his brother, his old twin, inside him: "my brother inside me, my old twin, ah to be he and he—but no, no no. (*Pause.*) No. No. (*Silence. Ruler*) Me get up me go on, what a hope, it was he, for hunger. Have yourself opened, Maud would say, opened up, it's nothing, I'll give him suck if he's still alive, ah but no, no no (*Pause*) No no" (page 119). The mention of a woman's name, which seems to be the first instance of Fox actually naming any other character, excites the Animator: "And of a sudden, in the same sentence, a woman with Christian name to boot, and a brother. I ask you!" (page 120). It seems to the Animator that they might be near their goal. He urges Dick to beat Fox into further utterance. But Fox merely screams, "Let me out! Peter out in the stones!" (page 121). As so often before, Fox "has gone off again" (page 122). The Animator adjures Fox to change his subject matter, to get away from rocks and rodents. "Of course we do not know, any more than you, what exactly it is we are after, what sign or set of words" (page 122). He goes so far as to beg Fox to bring someone into the story, "even though it is not true!" (page 122). This suggestion horrifies the stenographer.

Fox has fallen silent. As the whip no longer works, the Animator orders the stenographer to kiss him "till it bleeds! Kiss it white! ... Suck his gullet!" (page 122). Fox reacts with a howl and faints away.

There is clearly no more to be got during this session. The Animator feels that the mention of a woman might be "something at last." But when the stenographer reads the passage back to him, the Animator asks her not to omit some words. She assures him that she has omitted nothing. In spite of this—correct—assurance, the Animator orders her to insert the words "between two kisses" after the mention of Maud, thus giving the passage a spicier, erotic flavor. At this evidence of the Animator's cheating, the stenographer bursts into tears. The play ends with the Animator's consoling her, "Don't cry, Miss, dry your pretty eyes and smile at me. Tomorrow, who knows, we may be free" (page 124).

Both the *Esquisse* and the *Pochade* are *"radiophonique"* in a double sense. They are not only written for radio, but they also make use of radio in their imagery. In the *Esquisse* sounds and words emerge from an apparatus reminiscent of the equipment of a radio studio; and they come into the apparatus *live*, that is, from somewhere like a radio studio in another, perhaps subterranean, region, a situation that frequently occurs in radio buildings, of which Beckett knows a fair number. In the *Pochade* the Animator with his ruler and stenographer and additional acolyte reproduces the team of producer, secretary, and technician that Beckett must have encountered in his contacts with production teams at the BBC or the French radio. (In French *animateur* is a term used for a radio or television producer.)

That radio and its techniques have a fascination for Beckett is clear. And so are the reasons for that fascination: Voices emerging from the depths, from unseen and mysterious sources, play an immense part in Beckett's imagination—the storytellers of the Trilogy, the murmured voice of *Texts for Nothing*, Krapp's tape-recorded reminiscences, the three points from which the old man's voice emerges in *That Time*, the compulsive voice breaking out of the mouth in *Not I*, to mention merely the most obvious instances.

That *Esquisse radiophonique* and *Pochade radiophonique* are intimately related to *Words and Music* and *Cascando* and are indeed in the nature of preliminary sketches for them, seems to me fairly evident. The *Esquisse*, however, is much closer to both of these than the *Pochade*. In *Words and Music* and *Cascando* we encounter the same duality of the inner sounds: a strand of music, which seems to me to represent the nonverbal, nonarticulated component of human consciousness, the flow of the emotions themselves, and a strand of words, an endless interior monologue. When I once asked Beckett about his method of work, he replied that, having attained a state of concentration, he

379

merely listened to the voice emerging from the depths, which he then tried to take down; afterward he would apply his critical and shaping intelligence to the material thus obtained.

There is—and this is a frequent theme of Beckett's writings—a deep tension between his conviction that ultimately all artistic endeavor is futile and his deep need, even compulsion, to listen to his inner voice and to shape its utterance. Hence, on the one hand, the Opener's (in *Cascando*) and the Animator's (in *Rough for Radio*) hopes that one day, perhaps soon, the voice will cease and the objective of the quest be reached and, on the other, the man's alarm (in *Radio I*) that the voice and the music are ending. He has become a slave to both, cannot leave his listening post because they are continuous, and yet, as he confesses, they have become a need, a necessity for him. In *Cascando* the coming together of words and music "as though they had joined arms" is felt by the Opener (who can open both sources without having to operate knobs, the technical *accidentia* having been shed as the subject was being refined and developed) as a blessing, a sign that the quest will cease and the sounds end in silence; in the *Esquisse* their ending puts him into a panic. The woman of the *Esquisse* has disappeared in *Cascando*. Her role is a mysterious one. At first sign, it might seem that she is merely there to provoke a demonstration and explanation of the phenomenon by the man. Yet in a brief passage during the man's telephone conversation with his doctor there is a hint that her visit might be causally connected with the dying away of the voices: "who? ...but she's left me...ah for God's sake...haven't they all left me? ...did you not know that?...all left me" (page 110).

In *Words and Music* the source of the music and of the words is not, as in the *Esquisse* transmitted by mechanical means; here we are in a kind of medieval setting of a lord and his two jesters, Joe (Words) and Bob (Music). But here, too, at the climax words and music come together, and they do so in evoking the memory of a woman, a lost love. And the final silence ensues as a result of the quest having led to at least a degree of satisfaction, a longing fulfilled, a desire accomplished. It is surely not without significance that what appears as an alarming and disastrous development in the *Esquisse*—the coming together and cessation of the streams of sounds—is seen as a fulfillment of sorts both in *Words and Music* and in *Cascando*, which, being finished works, clearly represent a later stage of the development of the idea.

The *Pochade* varies the same theme from a slightly different and even more deeply despairing viewpoint. Here the voice (Fox surely equals *Vox*) is a somewhat comic character; his utterances are parodies of the style and subject matter of the more serious voices in Beckett's *oeuvre*. Moreover, Fox's vitality is extremely low; he "goes off" again and again, and when savagely whipped by Dick, his cries of pain are faint, a sign that he has barely enough vitality even to scream out under savage torture. He responds equally feebly to the stenographer's disrobing (which excites even the Animator, who by implication is a very old man—he wishes he were forty years younger so as to be able to consummate his desire for the stenographer!) and faints away when she kisses him. The situation portrayed in the *Pochade*, therefore, is far removed from that of those of Beckett's works in which we see the artist as victim of a never ending torrent of inner voices; here we have an artist who is still under the compulsion of extracting something from his inner voice, who is still hoping that one day the right word will be said which will bring release, but who is faced with a sluggish, sleepy, and feeble creative core. Hence he—the Animator, the conscious, critical part of the artist's mind—falls victim to the temptation to cheat and to insert material that is not a genuine product of his inner voice into the finished text. The *Pochade* is a truly tragicomic work, for the more parodistic, the more feeble, the more comic Fox's utterances become, the more tragic is the Animator's position: He, after all, is bound to go on with his weary task until something of significance has been extracted from Fox. He is Ixion tied to a creaking, faulty wheel which increases his suffering.

If we see *Rough for Radio* as a monodrama about the artistic process in which each of the characters represents one aspect of the artist's mind, we must regard the Animator as the critical faculty trying to shape the utterances of the voice that emerges from the subconscious, while the stenographer is the recording faculty and, also, in her distress about the spurious sentence the Animator inserts in the text, the artist's conscience; Dick, the torturer, is the artist's determination to stimulate his subconscious by suffering; the stenographer's disrobing and kissing of Fox represents analogous attempts to stimulate the subconscious by erotic fantasies.

If this view of the meaning of *Rough for Radio* is correct, it must surely be regarded as one of the clearest, least "encoded" statements of Beckett's view of the artistic process or, at least, his own process of creation. He himself regards the work as unfinished, no more than a rough sketch, and felt, having heard the production, that it had "not come off." He put the blame—with his customary kindness and courtesy—on the script and thus on himself, although he felt that the production, which made the Animator and his team start briskly and become more weary and discouraged as time went on, should already have started at a high degree of weariness and despair. Yet the very roughness of the work gives it its special importance: Although it may be more schematic, less refined, by dint of that very circumstance, by representing an early stage of the creative process, it allows us to see structures and methods of Beckett's technique with greater clarity, just as the first outline of a novel or the rough sketch for a painting gives us insights into the skeleton of the finished work, which, in its completed state, is hidden by the flesh and blood around it. Here the allegory is still very obvious in its rough state; in more completed works that allegorical skeleton has been concealed and refined into a far subtler organic image so that the one-to-one correspondence of allegory has become the complex allusiveness of metaphor. Croak, the lord in *Words and Music* who commands Joe and Bob to perform for him, is a far more distanced, less obvious, far more poetic concept than the Animator, who whips his bound and gagged subconscious into producing a text; but the image of the Animator having Fox whipped, by being more open and more mechanical, is clearer than Croak's mysterious pursuit.

Even the process of literary allusion, so beloved by Beckett, is far more openly displayed in *Rough for Radio*. When Fox sheds a tear, the Animator asks the stenographer whether she is familiar with the works of Sterne; and when she replies that she is not, he supplies the allusion: "I may be quite wrong, but I seem to remember, there somewhere, a tear an angel comes to catch as it falls. Yes, I seem to remember ... admittedly he was grandchild to an archbishop" (pages 119–20). And at another point in the play, when Fox talks about his having lived in the past, the Animator asks the stenographer whether she is familiar with "Purgatory ... of the divine Florentine." And being told that she has "merely flipped through the Inferno," he informs her that, strangely, in the Purgatory the souls all sigh, "I was, I was. It's like a knell. Strange, is it not?" The stenographer asks why that should be strange. The Animator replies, "Why, one would rather have expected I shall be. No?" (page 118).

Technically, the greatest difficulty presented by *Rough for Radio* lies in the presence of the mute character, Dick, whose only sign of life in radio is the sound of the effort he makes when cracking his whip, followed, when he actually strikes rather than merely threatening to do so, by the impact of the bull's pizzle on Fox's flesh. Curiously enough, this difficulty would disappear if the play were performed on a stage. And indeed with its unity of place and time *Rough for Radio* would be fairly easy to produce on the stage. This is another indication of the rough state of the work. *Cascando*, which contains, in a far more refined state, many of the elements roughly present here, being more abstract in its subtlety and perfection, is essentially radiophonic. By comparison *Rough for Radio* is, if not naturalistic, at least far more earthbound, far more material, more palpable in its concept. The stage play *Catastrophe* is clearly a development of *Rough for Radio*.

The four radio pieces revolving around voices and sounds are, in any case, among Beckett's most personal and revealing works. Here he deals with his own experience of the creative process both as a quest for fulfillment and release and as a form of compulsion and slavery. In *Rough for Radio* his basic concept of splitting the consciousness into distinct portions and making them into characters in a metaphorical monodrama of the mind in conflict with itself is most clearly displayed. Here we have, I feel, the key for an understanding of much that is mysterious and difficult in Beckett's other works...

Beckett's profound understanding of the highly technical electronic media springs ultimately, I think, from the meticulous craftsmanship that forms his basic attitude to his work. His contributions to the production process are always characterized by humility toward the technical side of the work, combined with a respect for the craftsmanship involved, which seems to derive from an approach similar to that of the medieval craftsmen who regarded accurate workmanship as a form of religious worship. There is an intimate connection between the highest reaches of intuitive insight (inspiration in its truest sense, the inner voice) and the need for complete mastery of the techniques—of whatever order they may be—through which that inspiration is shaped, ordered, and communicated to listeners, readers, audiences. That combination of inspiration and craftsmanship characterizes the work of a true master.

NOTES

1. A longer version of this article, "Beckett and the Art of Broadcasting," originally appeared in *Encounter* (September 1975), reprinted in *Mediations: Essays on Brecht, Beckett, and the Media* (New York: Grove Press, 1982).
2. Donald McWhinnie, *The Art of Radio* (London: Faber, 1969), 133-51.
3. Both are included in Samuel Beckett, *The Collected Shorter Plays of Samuel Beckett* (New York: Grove Press, 1984) as *Rough for Radio I* and *II*. References are to this edition.

ENOCH BRATER

Light, Sound, Movement, and Action in Beckett's "Rockaby"

Rockaby, which had its world premiere performance in Buffalo, New York, on 8 April 1981, continues Beckett's recent preoccupation with a small-scale play written specifically for a prerecorded voice in conflict with live stage action. A strange mixture of the carefully controlled and the spontaneous, the drama, whose sole protagonist is a woman dressed in black and whose only scenery is a rocking chair, restricts its subject matter and directs our attention instead to the formal elements of the play as performance. Light, sound, movement, and action therefore must be understood within the context established by this deliberately circumscribed stage space, an acting area in which a single image is expressed, explored, and advanced. Clear, articulate, definite, and precise, the visual impact becomes progressively haunting in its lonely simplicity. Simultaneously remote yet urgent in its personal appeal, a human shape is transfixed by the strong and pitiless light of a cold lunar glare. Much is made out of almost nothing.

What *Rockaby* gives up in breadth it makes up in fineness. The closely valued harmonics in the interplay of all that is visual and verbal, the use of light, the rocking of a chair that is controlled mechanically, the function of movement to emotionalize meaning, and the incorporation of electronics in the form of a magnetic recording tape are developed tactfully and richly. Beckett has employed elements of this strategy before, most notably in the two plays immediately preceding *Rockaby*—*That Time* and *Footfalls*. Yet the technique crafted here has its roots much earlier in his repertory. As far back as *All That Fall*, the radio play written in 1956 "to come out of the dark,"[1] Beckett experimented with the purity of sound as something uniquely recorded, an art, as the Italian futurist Marinetti predicted, that will imitate electricity. Beckett was in Paris when *All That Fall* was broadcast on BBC. Across the English Channel, he could hear it only poorly. He then wrote to the BBC Radio Drama Division in London asking for a tape of the show. This was soon followed by another letter requesting an instruction manual on how to operate a tape recorder.[2] The rest is familiar history: *Krapp's Last Tape* had its primary inspiration in a situation not so much romantic as it was mechanical and technological.

Although in *Krapp's Last Tape* Beckett had found a practical stage device for demonstrating the past's effect on the present as well as the present's commentary on the past, he did not in that work concern himself with the physical materialization of the inner voice central to so much of his writing. It is not until another play for radio, *Embers*, and especially his work for television, plays like *Eh Joe* and more recently *Ghost Trio* and *... but the clouds ...*, that inner voices achieve electronic audibility in performance. Yet the voices we hear in these media, typically (though not always) signified by a dynamic switch in gender, are clearly not the protagonist's own. In radio and television Beckett's characters are usually obsessed by voices heard as indentifiably "other."[3] It is only in Beckett's new work for the theater that voice and protagonist finally become one.

In order to understand what is new in *Rockaby* some additional distinctions must be made. In *Footfalls*, a play, like *Rockaby*, that features a female protagonist, May engages in a formalized duet with her mother's voice (another *m*-"other" = "mother"), even though the dramatic development of this work consists in demonstrating how these two voices come to resemble each other. In *That Time*, on the other hand, an *"old white face"* hears but does not seem likely to control voices A, B, and C, which are, as the stage directions indicate, *"his own coming from both sides and above."*[4] Unlike May, a "faint, though by no means invisible" "tangle" of "pale grey" "tatters,"[5] a head suspended in space is by no means a complete human figure, surrealistic overtones and relationships to *Not I* notwithstanding. And unlike May, the fragmentary and disembodied Listener of *That Time* does not talk, though he is, of course, a heavy breather. Beckett's late style in the theater is, therefore, a limited yet surprisingly changing one. Within the narrow and austere range he sets for himself, there is in fact some variety. He does not repeat himself in *Rockaby*. The woman seated in this rocking chair not only listens along with us to her own inner voice, but summons it to start up again and joins with it to recite in a series of highly patterned voice-overs. The play thus offers us a new dramatic solution to what remained only momentarily accessible in Beckett's earlier works. *Rockaby*, then, displays both the assurance and the increasing harmony of what is for Beckett not only a new theatrical concept, but a pervasive artistic preoccupation.

In *Rockaby* what looks, at first glance, like a radical simplification of style turns out on further acquaintance to be a new and deeper complexity. The play is never quite as easy or accessible as it seems to be on our first encounter in the theater. It harbors depths that cannot be quickly encompassed. In the world premiere production directed at the Center Theatre in Buffalo by Alan Schneider as part of A Samuel Beckett Celebration sponsored by the University-Wide Program in the Arts and the Department of Theatre and Dance, SUNY/Buffalo, its running time was only 14 minutes, 50 seconds; yet this play for W (" = *Woman in chair*") and V (" = *Her recorded voice*")[6] can in fact be divided into four acts, each of which begins with the stage direction "*long pause*." The four long pauses are critical. They remind us that for Beckett the dramatic image is the primary thing. The degree of radical concentration and intensity achieved in the pictorial constituents of this theater style is meant to be studied, scrutinized, and finally assimilated during each break in the action. In this short script enormous attention is given to visual detail, for in this play the image commands attention, something we will be forced to come back to again and again.

Let us consider this image more carefully. Earlier I said that in *Rockaby* the rocking chair was the only scenery. But that is not really the case, for in Beckett's late theater style it is not really possible to talk about scenery in the usual sense. *Rockaby* makes us conscious that darkness, grays and blacks, shades, and other gradations of sheerly theatrical light can be "scenery" too. What initially appears to be monochromatic is, on closer inspection, not really monochromatic at all. For light and color in *Rockaby* appear soft and faded but never dull. A "subdued" light uncovers the chair. The rest of this stage is "dark." A "subdued spot" rests on the face "constant throughout, unaffected by successive fades" (page 273). Beckett in fact makes us see the same figure in different artificial lights, offering us an ever-shifting series of perspectives from which to encounter the image anew. At the opening fade-up the stage directions are "first spot on face alone. Long pause. Then light on chair" (page 273). At the close of the play the movement is reversed. For his final fade-out Beckett specifies "first chair, long pause with spot on face alone" (page 273). Throughout the play other gradations of light are similarly meant to shift and vary, sometimes even to sparkle and gleam as the rocking chair is made to sway "to and fro." So insistent was this rocking in the original production that the actress, Billie Whitelaw, never had her feet rest on the stage floor for one moment during the entire production.

When there is speech in this play, the face is "slightly swaying in and out of light" (page 273). For movement in *Rockaby* is soon accompanied by the sound of a human voice, the woman's own: "whom else"? And this spectacle of light, sound, and movement also features color, or more precisely, shades. The "pale wood" of the chair is "highly polished to gleam when rocking." The woman's unkempt hair is "grey." Her face and hands are "white." Fabric and texture are selected and designed along the same lines for maximum visual stimulation. As worn by this draped and seated figure, the clothes appear in this shifting light as ever-changed and ever-changing. As the published stage directions read, the "lacy high-necked evening gown" is "black." At those moments during the rock when we see it in full light, we realize for the first time that it sports "long sleeves." But this is no three-dimensional *Whistler's Mother*. Beckett's seated figure is kinetic: "Jet sequin . . . glitter when rocking." And then the baroque detail: "Incongruous frivolous head-dress set askew with extravagant trimmings to catch light when rocking" (page 273). In the original Buffalo production, later seen at LaMama E.T.C. in New York,[7] the hat worn by Billie Whitelaw even had a touch of Irish green. To introduce "Jet sequins" and the kind of flamboyant "head-dress" associated with the Winnie of *Happy Days* into the stark visual landscape established by this play is profoundly and unexpectedly luxurious. In the presence of such somber light it seems like an act of free sensuality, almost heroic.

Sound in this work can be similarly triumphal. For in *Rockaby* Beckett has written a performance poem in the shape of a play, a lyrical drama in which the language we hear not only offers us the background exposition for the image we see, but describes it neatly and precisely as well:

so in the end
close of a long day
went down
in the end went down
down the steep stair
let down the blind and down
right down
into the old rocker
mother rocker
where mother sat
all the years
all in black
best black
sat and rocked
rocked
till her end came
in the end came. . . . (page 280)

A striking visual metaphor materializes before our very eyes as a poem comes to (stage) life. A visual image created by words is therefore something far more substantial in *Rockaby* than the term metaphor usually implies. For in this play we watch a verbal metaphor become concrete and palpable. In a word, it has become real. Sound therefore structures sight in *Rockaby*, just as sight skewers sound. Coming to us in the shape of words, sound provides the proper context for the dynamic image we see; the image we see provides the appropriate context for the haunting rhythms we hear.[8] The coincidence of all that is audible and visible is perhaps even more carefully structured than this, for there is in this play more than one source of sound competing for our attention. Although the largest part of what we hear is recorded, that little that is recited live has been clearly calculated to sustain maximum dramatic tension. In each of the four "acts" of *Rockaby* it is the "live" voice that gets the "recorded" one going. Demanding and then intoning "More" a little more softly each time, the woman's "live" voice has the mantic power to set not only poetry in motion, but rocking chair as well. And it is this same "live" voice that creates *Rockaby*'s most arresting dramatic action. The voice-overs of "time she stopped," heard a little more softly each of the seven times the phrase is intoned, as well as the echoes of "living soul" (page 278) and the one that ends the piece, "rock her off" (page 282), call attention to these lines by

389

giving them psychological texturing and an emotional tenderness that greatly humanizes their meaning. For a few isolated moments of stage time we are back to the pyrotechnics of *Krapp's Last Tape*. In that play Beckett had already shown himself capable of having his hero extract a broad range of emotional response by similarly interfering with a tape. Though Krapp's interruptions are far more mechanical, the special effects he achieves in this way are the same—especially when lips move and no sounds come.[9]

In *Rockaby* the sounds come, and when they do so they form heard melodies that create an additional poetic drama of their own. The almost linear progression in the narrative spoken by the recorded voice contrasts with the back-and-forth motion of the chair on which the actress is seated. The figure, however, never really changes; only our perception of it does as we build up the image through the steady accumulation of expository facts offered by the narrative. A story develops from scene to scene. And as it does so the figure "moves" gradually inward. Here Beckett's verbal artistry is at its height, the lyrical opportunity he has been waiting for: *Rockaby* is Beckett's first play in which the language is not merely poetic, but a poem complete in itself. A limited lexicon is printed not as prose dialogue with the highly poetic rhythms we remember from *That Time* or *Footfalls*, but as a more traditional modern poem whose words move "to and fro," "high and low," to imitate the gentle sway of a rocking chair in graceful motion. Hard phonemes match the back-and-forth rhythm of the chair's rock: "stop her eyes/rock her off/rock her off" (page 282). Each line of printed text thus coincides with one complete revolution made by the rocking chair's arc-shaped course. "All sides" of this verbal orbit move back and forth: Lines are rotated, made to formulate new allegiances with other words, then recombined in a different way before reassuming the original shape in which we first encountered them. Out of the cradle endlessly rocking, it is the language of the play that is always in full swing.

The pattern is easy to identify and even easier to hear. Acts 1 and 3 begin with the same four lines and will end in the same voiced-over couplet:

> till in the end
> the day came
> in the end came
> close of a long day.... (pages 275, 278)

time she stopped
time she stopped. . . . (pages 277, 279)

Acts 2 and 4 have been similarly designed to open with another patterned repetition, one that, moreover, cunningly reshuffles the words
we have already heard before in a slightly different permutation:

so in the end
close of a long day. . . . (pages 276, 281)

But here Beckett breaks the symmetry in order to signal the proper
poetic closure of this play. While the second act concludes with the
somber intonation of "another living soul/one other living soul" (page
278), the final words of the piece offer us a surprise ending as unan-
ticipated as the jet sequins and the flamboyant headdress we have
already noticed as foregrounded accessories to this woman's black costume:

saying to herself
no
done with that
the rocker
those arms at last
saying to the rocker
rock her off
stop her eyes
fuck life
stop her eyes
rock her off
rock her off (page 282)

This denouement needs no punctuation. The words have stopped. The
rocking chair comes to rest. There is stage silence. There is also stage
stillness. In the slow fade-out of the chair, the lights of a spot, like
sudden stigmata, momentarily isolate the head, now "slowly inclined"
(page 273) to resemble—if not become—the narrative's "head fallen"
(page 280). The poem's performance is at an end.

In *Rockaby* Beckett therefore uses recorded sound to achieve a very
spectacular stage effect. In this short play the special sound of a recorded voice becomes the true voice of feeling, the voice of lyric poetry.
Yet its eerie tone, modulated but always metallic, is never entirely
human. It is only the conflict between what we hear and what we see,
the interplay between the "live" voice and its recorded counterpart,

that makes the poetry not only lyrical, but dramatic. In *Rockaby* a woman seated on stage slowly becomes the image created by her own inner voice in a Yeatsian extravaganza in which man, in this case woman, is literally nothing until she is united with her own image. But as the stage lights darken, as the head slowly falls (in Billie Whitelaw's performance with an uncanny girlish look in apparent death), no soul claps hands and sings. This performance poem relies instead on the mechanics of sound, light, and movement for the skillful coordination of its most impressive stage action. Electronics, for example, will also be called upon to produce still another element crucial to the atmosphere of this work, the echo, that gradual diminution of sound that ends each act and parallels the play's fading light and slowing motion. The echo effect is in this context an especially dynamic one, for here *la voix humaine* literally turns inhuman as, through amplification, it reverberates in our ears through live theater space. With each contraction of sound, light, and movement, however, the audience's "famished eyes" gradually focus on an image free of all nonessentials. For each loss in *Rockaby* progressively validates the purity of Beckett's condensed image. With every softening sound, every fading light, every decrease in stage movement, the image unexpectedly expands as we study in production its simplicity and authenticity. Technology wears a human face, the face, if not of tragedy, then of dramatic poetry. The performance, moreover, *is* the poem. Language art and theater art have finally become one.

NOTES

1. Samuel Beckett, as quoted in Alec Reid, *All I Can Manage, More Than I Could: An Approach to the Plays of Samuel Beckett* (Dublin, 1968), 68.
2. Martin Esslin, "Samuel Beckett and the Art of Broadcasting," in *Mediations: Essays on Brecht, Beckett, and the Media* (New York: Grove Press, 1982), 134. Reprinted in this volume.
3. *...but the clouds...* offers us an interesting variation of this technique. In this television play the voice we hear belongs to the man we see; yet his own obsession is with the voice of the woman whose image we see momentarily— and then only subliminally. The man we see "mouths" her words, the final lines from Yeats's *The Tower*, in an arresting voice-over.
4. Samuel Beckett, Note, *That Time*, in *The Collected Shorter Plays of Samuel Beckett* (New York: Grove Press, 1984), 228.
5. Samuel Beckett, *Footfalls*, in *Collected Shorter Plays*, 242.

6. Samuel Beckett, *Rockaby*, in *Collected Shorter Plays*, 275. Subsequent references appear in the text.

7. The dates for this production were as follows: 8, 9, 10, 11 April (Buffalo); 13, 14, 15 April (New York City); 17 April (SUNY College at Purchase).

8. For a discussion of the coincidence of the visual and audible in Beckett's plays immediately preceding *Rockaby*, see Ruby Cohn on "theatereality" in *Just Play* (Princeton, N.J., 1980), 30-31, 273.

9. See Samuel Beckett, *Krapp's Last Tape*, in *Collected Shorter Plays*, 63.

PIERRE ASTIER

Beckett's "Ohio Impromptu": A View from the Isle of Swans

In an interview given the same day he had staged the premiere of *Ohio Impromptu* at Ohio State University, Alan Schneider remarked, "I think the title is sort of interesting. I believe it is Beckett's first 'place' name. And I think there's a bit of a joke in it."[1] Does the joke—if there is a joke—refer to the word *Ohio* or to the word *impromptu* or to both? As far as the word *impromptu* is concerned, and to the extent that etymologically it means "on the spot," there is undoubtedly a joke in the title. As we shall see and as Schneider and others knew, it took Beckett a long time to complete this so-called impromptu. If there is also a joke in the use of the place name, it could only be because the play has nothing to do with the state of Ohio—unless, as some prefer to think, this name is not Beckett's joke but a pleasant gesture toward the organizers of the Beckett symposium at Ohio State University.

I agree that it would be perfectly in keeping with Beckett's sense of generosity to make such a gesture, or with his sense of humor to call this play *Impromptu* through the ironic use of antiphrasis and *Ohio Impromptu* just for the fun of it. Nevertheless, I concur with those who spontaneously associated the term *impromptu* with a certain type of artistic creation, musical or literary, that is *en principe* improvised but actually composed or written carefully to give the *feeling* of improvisation: on the one hand, like the impromptus of Schubert, Schumann, Chopin, Fauré, or others; and on the other, like Molière's *Impromptu de Versailles* (1663), Giraudoux's *Impromptu de Paris* (1937), and Ionesco's *Impromptu de l'Alma* (1955). In other words, I think that *Ohio Impromptu* not only is like a musical impromptu[2] (as far as the composition of the story within the play is concerned), but is truly, as a play, a theatrical impromptu.

394

Through its very title, *Ohio Impromptu* shares a feature with the other three dramatic impromptus: the name of the location where it was first performed.[3] It also shares two other characteristics: It is short, very short indeed; and it is, up to a point, comical. Finally, all previous impromptus have in common two other features, one apparently lacking in Beckett's play, while the other is most certainly there, although perhaps not as obvious. First, the missing link: Whereas Molière, Giraudoux, and Ionesco used their respective impromptus to defend their own theater aesthetics through explicit and virulently satirical attacks against their respective critics, Beckett does not seem to defend anything or attack anyone in this impromptu.[4] Second, the meta-theatrical dimension: Previous impromptus all deal to a large extent with problems of play acting or play writing through the acting or the writing of a play that turns out to be the very one performed before our eyes. So it is with *Ohio Impromptu* but with two marked differences. The work within the play is not a play, but a story read from a book. Moreover, this story ends with events the audience can witness on stage at the end of the play; yet it also seems timeless. Read aloud now by a character in the play, it is concerned with a certain "sad tale" once read aloud by another character (the visitor in the book story), a "sad tale" of which we know nothing except that it is a repetition of the repetition of a repetition, and so on ad infinitum, of the same old "sad tale." The story we hear might refer to the relatively recent past of the characters in the play, but the "sad tale" to which it is linked refers to a past so absolutely remote that it might well go back to the very origin of time itself.[5]

In consideration of the fact that the work within the play is not a play but a story, it has been argued that the difficulties of playwriting usually encountered and raised in such impromptus are those of fiction writing in Beckett's play.[6] Well, yes and no, because the difficulties of play writing have been not only an important factor in the making of *Ohio Impromptu*, but an integral part of this impromptu made specifically *for* Ohio, the place name in the title. The following brief historical background of the play should convince anyone that if this work is an impromptu in the sense of improvisation, it is so only because it was written on request.

That request was sent to Beckett in early February 1980 by S. E. Gontarski. One month later,[7] Beckett answered that, although "unfitted . . . to write to request," he would do his best to have something for the Ohio symposium. In May 1980 several people in Paris mentioned that Beckett was, indeed, working on a play "for Ohio." According to some, it was probably "another monologue," and according to others, probably a "new mime" requiring from four to five actors. Beckett himself told Gontarski that yes, he was onto "something," but he could not say what. In June[8] Beckett reaffirmed his promise to write a "short piece" for the symposium but warned that he was "by no means certain" that he would succeed, adding: "I thought I was onto something, but it has petered out. I'll try again." Four months later, in October,[9] he wrote again to say that he had "failed so far to write a short piece" for the symposium but that he would try again by mid-November, after being rid of some "current prose" he was "struggling to finish." At that point, Beckett was actually so unsure of being able to succeed that he closed his note by saying that should he fail again, we might want to consider "one of the theater fragments"[10] presently "under investigation by Alan Schneider in San Diego." Two months later, however, around mid-December, Beckett wrote that a play for Ohio was finished, and finally a typescript of *Ohio Impromptu* arrived in the mail.

All in all, and on and off, Beckett spent some ten months working on this play, which is a rather long time for an "improvised" impromptu. In fact, the present text of *Ohio Impromptu* is not only the last of at least four versions, but the byproduct (I think) of Beckett's earliest attempt to write "something for Ohio," that "something" which was thought back in May 1980 to be either another monologue or a new mime. Most likely, the "new mime" eventually became *Quad*, which premiered 8 October 1981 on German television. And I have reason to believe that the "monologue" is that "something" which "petered out" sometime between May and June and which Beckett— kindly and also, it seems, deliberately—attached to the three versions (one holograph and two typescripts) that preceded the final one.[11] This *"faux départ"* reads as follows:

I am out on leave. Thrown out on leave.
Back to time, they said, for 24 hours.
Oh my God, I said, not that.
Slip on this shroud, they said, lest you
catch your death of cold again.
Certainly not, I said.
This cap, they said, for your [death's-head] skull.

396

Definitely not, I said.
The New World outlet, they said, in the State
of Ohio. We cannot be more precise.
Pause.
Proceed straight to [Lima] the nearest campus, they said, and
address them.
[Address] whom? I said.
The students, they said, and the professors.
Oh my God, I said, not that.
Do not overstay your leave, they said, if
you do not wish it to be extended.
Pause.
What am I to say? I said.
Be yourself, they said, stay
yourself.
Myself? I said. What are you insinuating?
[Yourself before, they said.]
Pause.
[And after.]
Pause.
[Not during? I said.]

Whatever it may be worth, this broken piece of monologue fits very well into what would eventually become *Ohio Impromptu*, for it undoubtedly contains a number of elements that, however transformed, find their ways into the play:

1. The decidedly *comic vein* in which the fragment is written remains visible in the final version. It runs openly through the first version, where Reader interrupts his reading not only when Listener knocks on the table but also, of his own volition, when he takes a sip now and then, blows his nose, or refills his empty glass. These Krapp-like idiosyncrasies totally disappear from the second version on. But there remains, throughout and almost unchanged, at least one such comical pause: Having read the phrase "After so long a lapse that as if never been,"[12] Reader stops, "looks closer," and utters a "Yes" of disbelief. In the first version the only difference is that he also grumbles a "Hm" of disapproval after repeating it, but in both cases it is evident that Reader is shocked not so much by the primitive syntax (he has read similar phrases before) as by his discovery in the text of such an unexpected and perfect alexandrine.

2. The *reluctance* of the character—a ghost feeling no more pain in

397

the eventless, timeless, and spaceless world of the dead—to be forced back into action, into time and space, into the world of the living, is refracted in *Ohio Impromptu* through Reader's way of reading the book. Whereas Listener seems completely engrossed in *what* the story is about, Reader's interest seems limited to *how* it is written. Otherwise, he keeps on reading passively, mechanically stopping when Listener, his master, knocks on the table, calmly repeating the passage and proceeding when he hears the second knock. His indifference to the story itself even becomes comical as he reaches a passage particularly charged with emotion, realizes that a sentence is cut off at the end of the bottom line, and takes his time to turn the page and read on: "White nights again his portion. As when his heart was young. No sleep no braving sleep till—[*turns page*]—dawn of day" (page 286).

3. The *apprehension* of the ghost on being ordered to go back not only to the world of the living, but specifically to the New World, to some far away and unknown places with such strange names as *Lima* or *Ohio*, is reflected by the fearfulness of the character in the story upon his decision to move to an "unfamiliar room" in an "unfamiliar scene" on the "far bank" (page 285).

4. The *frustration* of the ghost when instructed to address a group of academics to whom he feels he has nothing to say—in the New World and within a twenty-four-hour deadline—also has a parallel in the play. The story character feels anguish upon realizing that his "last attempt to obtain relief" (page 285) on that "far bank" has only led him to a completely hopeless situation, forced him into an extreme corner from which he can no longer escape: "Could he not now turn back? Acknowledge his error and return to where they were once so long alone together . . . no. What he had done alone could not be undone" (page 286). In "this extremity his old terror of night laid hold on him again" (page 286), until one night and thereafter occasionally he is visited by a man who reads him a "sad tale" to comfort him. This reading indeed brings him some comfort, more at any rate than the ghost receives from the two little notes of solace added to his order for detail duty: Namely, that the New World is not a trap but an "outlet" and that he should not worry about what to say over there, because all he will have to do is to be and stay himself.

5. Whether the ghost might have found the *relief* thus hinted at by

his masters we shall never know, because like the opening of a *Mission Impossible* venture, the script did, indeed, self-destruct right after the initial instructions were given. But we do know that although the story character finds comfort in the company of his visitor—with whom he even grows "to be as one (soul)"[13]— he never obtains the true relief for which he had "once half hoped" (page 285). Failure on his part, however, guaranteed success for his creator. As I shall now show, while such relief is not to be found *in* the play, the play itself, *Ohio Impromptu*, provided through its very achievement the relief for which Beckett had been longing.

To think that the play has nothing to do with its title is to forget that both have at least one thing in common: place names. One of these, "Ohio," occurs in the title (and can be explained otherwise as normal for a theatrical impromptu), and three appear in the play or rather in the story within the play. The three place names in the play are: *Isle of Swans, old world,* and *Latin Quarter.* We can add a fourth, since what is called "far bank" in the third and fourth versions and "other bank" in the second was called "right bank" in the first, thus evoking immediately (along with *Latin Quarter*) the city of Paris, located of course in the "old world," in Europe. Altogether, then, we have five names, four of which designate *actual* places. Inasmuch as these "actual" places are elements of a narrative fiction, they can also be considered *fictional.* Fictional, that is, but not *fictitious.* Now, what about the "Isle of Swans"? Fictional it is, of course, but is it only fictitious?

At first glance, Isle of Swans does look and sound fictitious, because it seems to owe its very existence to a mere symbol—and, for that matter, to a too obvious symbol: that good ol' swan-song symbol, here underscoring the fact that although the "sad tale" could go on being told forever, the story to which it is linked has come to an end. This being the end of the story—as it is written in the book and especially *as* it is written in its last pages[14]—would indicate that the days of fiction and/or poetry writing are over. Furthermore, since that story, while read aloud by Reader, becomes the play itself, it would seem that the days of play writing are also over, except perhaps as shown in the closing mute scene, for some new mimes, some new "acts without words." However, this fictional Isle of Swans, with its swan-song symbol as big as a billboard, is not merely fictitious—because there is an

Isle of Swans. Actually, there are at least two,[15] spatially close to each other in the Seine in Paris, although temporally very far from each other because one of them, located upstream in relation to the other, no longer exists.[16]

The Isle of Swans that no longer exists was originally called Ile Maquerelle, that is, Whore's Island, and was used by Parisians not only as an adult playground (which its name implied) but as pasture land for heifers and cows. In striking contrast with this original and long-gone Isle of Swans is the one that exists now. Located downstream in relation to the other, between the pont de Passy and the pont de Grenelle (both linking the avenue du President Kennedy on the right bank and the quai de Grenelle on the left bank), it was artificially created in 1825. Actually, then, it is not a true island, and its official designation is not even "Ile" but "Allée des Cygnes," the term *Allée* referring usually to a tree-lined path in a garden, a park or other public places. Most Parisians, however, continue to call it Ile des Cygnes, and in this case both terms *île* and *allée* are proper, because the whole surface of this long and very narrow isle—or rather islet—is entirely occupied, from one end to the other, by such an *allée*.

Although few Parisians have ever set foot on it, they have all seen—especially from the windows of the *métro aérien* (elevated subway) that passes over its upstream tip—its one and only tourist attraction standing high at the end of the *allée*, at the downstream extremity of the islet: a much reduced but still quite imposing replica of one of Frédéric Auguste Bartholdi's most famous works, the Statue of Liberty.[17] In other words, unless totally blind, nobody could ever miss it—nobody, that is, except the character in the story within the play who, looking out from the single window of his single room on the far (right) bank, can see only that "downstream extremity of the Isle of Swans" (page 285) but not the statue that *is* there and who, in his daily slow walks on the islet itself, always pauses at the very place where it is supposed to stand without ever noticing it. As far as he is concerned, and to say the least, this replica of Liberty Enlightening the World does not seem to shed much light upon the tiny bit of land on which it is built. But its very absence in the story, as obvious as the presence of the swan-song symbol, does indeed illuminate the play.

If we consider that what is fiction for us, reader or writer, is reality for the characters in the fiction and that the only symbols to be found by us in the real world are those which we put in it—thus creating a new kind of reality, both real and symbolic, that is metaphorical—it follows that if a fiction writer does not put a symbol in the "real" world of his characters, the latter's reality cannot be metaphorical but must be only and plainly real. And so it is for the character in this story within the play: *His* Isle of Swans, deprived by Beckett of its replica of the Statue of Liberty—symbol of a free New World—loses its metaphorical value. For the character it is real and nothing but that: a geographically intermediate location between his familiar left bank and the unfamiliar right bank, a nice place where, at the downstream extremity, he can even find some comfort "dwelling" as he does—before retracing "his slow steps" (page 286)—on the receding stream of the Seine. But for him even the sight of the river, with its two arms reunited in "joyous eddies" (after it has been slit in the middle by the islet's upstream tip), is just a natural phenomenon. He does not see in it any symbol of division and reunion, as we do immediately and all the more because we, as Beckett's readers, are already so used to water symbolism in his works. That is why the character also cannot find on his Isle of Swans the relief for which he had hoped: His Isle of Swans, without its statue symbolizing freedom—and, *lato sensu*, self-liberation—cannot provide him with the "outlet" he needs to free himself from his feelings of frustration. Always wrapped up in his "long black coat" (page 286) and always hidden in his "Latin Quarter hat" (page 286), he remains a hopeless prisoner of his "old world" thoughts, unable ever to open his mind to a "new world" of ideas.[18] But where he fails, and precisely because he fails in his search for relief, Beckett succeeds, because nobody has removed from his reality the Statue of Liberty at the downstream extremity of the Isle of Swans. It is therefore in this artificial islet with its artificial statue, geographically but also symbolically equidistant from Beckett's familiar Left Bank (associated through its ancient quai de Grenelle with the Old World), and from what seems to him a strange, quasi-foreign Right Bank (associated through its modern avenue du President Kennedy with the New World), that Beckett found at last the "artifice" he needed to fulfill his promise of a play *for Ohio*, a new play in which his old "sad tale" could be "a last time told" by him (page 288).

A new metaphor for the repetition of that original "sad tale"—through an endless series of subsequent stories—the Statue of Liberty on the Isle of Swans in the middle of the Seine in Paris is a replica of the original Statue of Liberty on Bedloe's Island in the middle of New

York Harbor; the former is in its turn duplicated by the two characters at the end of the story within the play, sitting "as though turned to stone" (page 288), and again by two more replicas of these replicas at the end of the play itself, Reader and Listener, gazing at each other over the same end of the table, "*Unblinking. Expressionless.*" (page 288), thus blindly mirroring each other—like the Statue of Liberty in the New World facing eastward, across the ocean, its westward-facing replica in the Old World—in a double perspective of infinite nothingness.

And yet, from that very nothingness something has emerged in the play: At the end of the long white bare table there is the book that we may assume to be "filled" with all the texts that were ever conceived under the "black wide-brimmed hat,"[19] the latest and largest of those "thinking headgears" once made famous by Lucky and Vladimir but now emptied of its thinking power and resting on top of the same table, discarded once and for all, perhaps, by its last owners (presumably Listener and Reader at a time when both the sensitive artist and the sensible critic were one and the same thinker). All the texts filling the book would thus constitute a writer's lifework, a whole *oeuvre* representing in this case, I think, that of Beckett himself in the form of a make-believe compilation of all his writings so far. The compilation would therefore include in its very last pages a last "little something" that Beckett had promised to write for the symposium at Ohio State University, a "little something" appropriately called *Ohio Impromptu* that was finally brought to completion, thus bridging at last the frustrating gap of silence between the "What am I to say?" of the ghost at the beginning of the aborted monologue and the "Nothing is left to tell" (page 288) of Reader upon closing the book at the end of the play.

NOTES

1. Nancy Gilson, "Director describes 25 years of work with Samuel Beckett," *Columbus Citizen-Journal*, 9 May 1981, 8.
2. An analysis of the play as such was made, convincingly, by S. E. Gontarski in "The world premiere of *Ohio Impromptu*, directed by Alan Schneider at Columbus, Ohio," *Journal of Beckett Studies* (8, Autumn 1982), 133–36.
3. Ionesco's impromptu was premiered at the Studio des Champs-Elysées, in Paris, close to the *Place* and the *Pont de l'Alma*.
4. Could it be that Beckett, who in *Waiting for Godot* had Estragon shout at

Vladimir the ultimate insult—"Crritic!"—now has no critic to attack or, if he has any, does not care?

5. Or, at least, to the time when Beckett began pondering the nature of time, as in *Whoroscope* and his essay on Proust.

6. See Ruby Cohn, "Beckett's Theater Resonance," in Morris Beja, S. E. Gontarski, Pierre Astier, eds., *Samuel Beckett: Humanistic Perspectives* (Columbus, Ohio, 1983).

7. Letter to S. E. Gontarski, dated Paris, 2 March 1980.

8. Letter to S. E. Gontarski, dated Paris, 6 June 1980.

9. Letter to S. E. Gontarski, dated Paris, 26 October 1980.

10. That is, *Theater I* and *II* in *Ends and Odds* (or *Rough for Theater I* and *II* in *The Collected Shorter Works*).

11. All these documents are now published as an appendix to Beja, Gontarski, Astier, *Samuel Beckett: Humanistic Perspectives*.

12. Samuel Beckett, *Ohio Impromptu*, in *The Collected Shorter Plays of Samuel Beckett* (New York: Grove Press, 1984), 286. References in text are to this edition.

13. The final version, p. 287, reads only: "They grew to be as one." But in the second version we find: "They came to be as one soul"; and in the third one this is changed to: "They grew to be as one (soul)."

14. That is, the kind of poetic prose Beckett has developed from *How It Is* on.

15. There is, in fact, a third island so named in Paris that may also have played its part in Beckett's choice of place name. Located in the artificial lake of the Bois de Boulogne, it was used by Proust as the scene where Odette de Crécy, Swann's unfaithful mistress, begins to indulge in lesbianism and where later Marcel himself vainly dreams of "possessing" madame de Stermaria, his first love. See *A la Recherche du temps perdu* (Paris, 1954), I, *Du Côté de chez Swann*, 270, 365-69, and II, *Le Côté de Guermantes*, 383-86.

16. My sources of information on both Isles of Swans are primarily: *Paris et sa proche banlieue* (Paris, 1963), 11-12; *Guide de Paris mystérieux* (Paris, 1976), 283-284, 514; Jacques Hillairet, *Connaissance du vieux Paris—Rive gauche et les Iles* (Paris, 1954), 1-2; Jacques Hillairet, *Dictionnaire historique des rues de Paris* (Paris, 1963), I, 43, 406.

17. There exists in the Luxembourg Gardens, at the heart of the Latin Quarter, a second, much more reduced replica of that Statue of Liberty. It may also be worth mentioning that there is, on Place Denfert-Rochereau, just one block from where Beckett lives in Paris, a replica of another famous statue by Bartholdi, the *Lion de Belfort*, equally dedicated to the spirit of liberty.

18. His particular way of dressing might remind one of Joyce's favorite garb while he lived in Paris, in which case one might infer that Beckett, through his protagonist, is alluding here to his own frustrating efforts in the past to free himself from Joyce's power.

19. This hat was not mentioned as a prop until the third version, in whose typescript Beckett added it in his own handwriting. It thus seems to have occurred to him as a kind of afterthought, which does not preclude—but does not prove either—the possibility of its being the very same hat worn by the story protagonist. Actually, it could be, like the play characters themselves, just a replica.

"*Quad*" and "*Catastrophe*"

The 1980s marked Beckett's overt return to mime, a return that drew together several strands of his theatrical work: *Fin de partie*, *Krapp's Last Tape* and the mimes of the fifties, the aborted "J. M. Mime," which Beckett outlined in the sixties, and the *near* mimes of the sixties and seventies: *Film*, *Eh Joe*, *That Time* and *Footfalls*. Filmed for Suddeutscher Rundfunk under Beckett's direction and presented on 8 October 1981, the twenty-minute *Quad*, written in English, may be Beckett's most formal work, as geometrical and symmetrical as the title suggests. One, then two, then three, then four figures, each clad to disguise, in pastel djellabas, appear in succession to describe a quadrangle to a rapid, polyrhythmic, percussion beat, then depart in sequence. Each figure describes the entire quad, and so each travels the square and its two diagonals fifteen times, tracing the incommensurability of side and diagonal. In Beckett's most vivid image of postmodern literary theory and literal decentering, each abruptly avoids the center, located mid way along the hypotenuse of an isosceles right triangle, that is, along a "Matrix of surds" (*Murphy*, page 112). Beckett told Martha Fehsenfeld that as the figures approach the center, each makes a "jerky turn to his left as a diversion away from it." It may first appear that "they were avoiding one another, but gradually one realizes they were avoiding the center. There was something terrifying about it.... It was danger." In the published text, Beckett says of the center, "supposed a danger zone." The action at first has comic potential, as the characters (or moving objects) rush toward an apparent central collision, only to avoid same by abrupt sinistral turns. The pattern is repeated, from one to four, then back to none, in an oscillation that shatters whatever comic possibilities were established early on. The sequence is presented four times, each time beginning with a different figure in a different corner. The final effect is that of prescribed, determined, enforced motion, a dramatization of Winnie's epithet "What a curse, mobility."

With *Quad* Beckett again carried the creative process through rehearsals. The precise timing of the original piece proved difficult to achieve, and Beckett was on the verge of scrapping the teleplay in rehearsals as unworkable. Instead, the actors eventually mastered the discipline necessary to perform the intricate, rapid movement to Beckett's satisfaction. Then, after a chance remark by one of the technicians that *Quad* had also been taped in black and white, Beckett decided to redouble his effort and make a second version, *Quad II*, this in monochrome; with the percussion eliminated, the tempo of footsteps is a haunting monorhythm, and the figures' movements in the shorter *Quad II* are considerably diminished. "No color," as Beckett describes it, "all four in identical white gowns, no percussion, footsteps only sound." The second version was a masterstroke, a second act to dramatize the entropy of motion and yet reassert (near) symmetry. And since the figures always turn left, the pattern is dominantly helicoidal, that of Dante's damned.

Quad, however, is not Beckett's only venture at overtly staging geometry. The thought dates at least from 1963 or so, when he began "J. M. Mime" for Jack MacGowran. The pattern of composition in "J. M. Mime" was toward greater and greater complication, an impulse Beckett reversed for *Quad*. He enlarged the triangles and added sound, rhythm. Theme was reversed. Center was to be avoided, not sought, and the oppression of mobility was reinforced by sinister twists. The principal critical problem with *Quad* may be deciding whether it is finally a single mime or a pair of mimes, but the two work effectively with and against one another. Beckett's late decision to double his mime has led to yet another singular drama.

Catastrophe, another of Beckett's occasional pieces, premiered at the Festival d'Avignon as part of *Une nuit pour Vaclav Havel*, sponsored by the Association Internationale De Defense Des Artistes 21 July 1982; Beckett dedicated the work to the Czech playwright and political prisoner Havel. The use of the theatrical metaphor, however, carries less political import than the dedication might suggest, although in Alan Schneider's New York production the icon looked decidedly like those newspaper photographs of holocaust victims, or like one of Rodin's Burgesses of Calais. The Director (and there is doubtless some self-mockery in Beckett's depiction of this autocratic character) is working on the "final touches to the last scene" of some unspecified play (but clearly something out of Beckett). The question in both the play and the play within the play is how much to reveal with that final image. On the one hand, Director wants more exposure, hands out of pocket, black gown off. "Could do with more nudity," he suggests. The one point he insists on is that the face be hidden. "There's a trace of face," he complains. The conflict seems to be between revelation and concealment, as Director objects to "this craze for explicitation." To His Female Assistant's suggestion of showing Protagonist's face, Director snaps, "For God's sake! What next? Raise the head! Where do you think we are? In Patagonia? Raise his head!" But as in *Ohio Impromptu*, the ending image is played against these instructions: "P raises his head, fixes the audience." The closing image suggests political defiance as well as the uncontrollability of art, art's tendency to exhibit its own Will, to reveal perhaps more than the artist intended.

Catastrophe finally suggests that Beckett's vision has not mellowed with age. His estimate of the human condition is as unrelieved now as it was sixty years earlier. *Catastrophe* and *Quad* are virtually companion pieces, since they make complementary comments on that human condition. What a curse mobility! What a curse immobility! What a curse life! What a curse death! What is finally astonishing about these late plays as a whole is less their evidence that Beckett remains a potent, innovative artist (while disclaiming both attributes) and has maintained a consistent vision for nearly six decades but that he has remained so productive, so committed to art, not solely as personal solace or company but also as something worthy of human effort. What faith, what affirmation Beckett retains may reside in just such creative effort. In *The Birth of Tragedy* Nietzsche notes that "[Art] alone may transform these horrible reflections on the terror and absurdity of existence into representations with which man may live. These are the representations of the *sublime* as the artistic conquest of the awful, and the *comic* as the artistic release from the nausea of the absurd." That is also the gospel according to Sam Beckett—up to a point. A hometown revolution, two world wars, and an impending nuclear holocaust have not altered it.

CODA

Burroughs with
Beckett in
Berlin

Dinner with Susan Sontag and Maurice Girodias:
New York 1980

Bockris: Were you at that famous meeting with Beckett in Berlin?

Sontag: I was indeed. Why has it become a "famous meeting"?

Bockris: William has told me the story so many times and I was intrigued to see how accurate his account is.

Sontag: Beckett is probably the only person I ever really wanted to meet in the adult part of my life. I was very pleased to be in his presence. I felt and feel a general reverence for him.

Bockris: How long were you with him for?

Sontag: We were there for about [*turning inquisitively to William Burroughs*]...

Bockris: No, don't ask him. It's your account I want to hear.

Sontag: It seemed very long, too long. When you were with Beckett you felt you didn't really want to take up too much of his time, that he had better ways of using his time than being with us. It all started like this: We were staying in this picturesque hotel in Berlin, and Allen Ginsberg said, "We're going to see Beckett, c'mon," and I said, "Oh, William and you are going, I don't want to butt in," and he said, "No, c'mon, c'mon," and we went. We knocked on the door of this beautiful atelier with great double height ceilings, very white. This beautiful, very thin man who tilts forward when he stands answered the door. He was alone. Everything was very clean and bare and white. I actually had seen him the day before on the grounds of the theater of the

409

Akademie Der Kunst. Beckett comes to Berlin because he knows his privacy will be respected. He received us in a very courtly way, and we sat at a very big long table. He waited for us to talk. Allen was, as usual, very forthcoming and did a great deal of talking. He did manage to draw Beckett out asking him about Joyce. That was somehow deeply embarrassing to me. Then we talked about singing, and Beckett and Allen began to sing, while I was getting more and more embarrassed.

Bockris: Bill says Beckett made you feel as if you would be welcome to leave as soon as you could.

Sontag: He didn't actually throw us out.

Burroughs: Oh, the hell he didn't! See, I have an entirely different slant on the whole thing. In the first place, John Calder said, "Bring along some liquor," which we did. I know that Beckett considers other people different from him and he doesn't really like to see them. He's got nothing particular against them being there, it's just that there are limits to how long he can stand being with people. So I figured that about twenty minutes would be enough. Someone brought up the fact that my son was due for transplants, and Beckett talked about the problem of rejection, about which he'd read an article. I don't remember this singing episode at all. You see, Susan says it seemed long; it seemed to me extremely short. Soon after we got there, and the talk about transplants, everybody looked at their watch, and it was very obviously time to go. We'd only brought along a pint, and it had disappeared by that time.

Sontag: Allen said, "What was it like to be with Joyce? I understand Joyce had a beautiful voice and that he liked to sing." Allen did some kind of "Om," and Beckett said, "Yes, indeed he had a beautiful voice," and I kept thinking what a beautiful voice *he* had. I had seen Beckett before in a café in Paris, but I had never heard him speak and I was struck by the Irish accent. After more than half a century in France he has a very pure speech which is unmarked by living abroad. Beckett didn't seem in any way like someone who has lived most of his life in a country that was not the country of his original speech. He has a beautiful Irish musical voice. I don't remember that he made us feel we had to go, but I think we all felt we couldn't stay very long.

Burroughs: Everybody *knew* that they weren't supposed to stay very long. I think it was ten minutes after six that we got out of there.

Sontag: I know people who claim to feel extremely comfortable with Beckett.

Coda

Burroughs: I was at a previous meeting with him in Paris in 1959 in which there was quite a bit of antagonism between us.

Bockris: How did that happen?

Maurice Girodias: I had the idea to arrange a dinner between Burroughs and Beckett with myself as the host in the thirteenth-century cavernous cellars of my Brazilian nightclub. There were also a couple of lesbians, and Iris Owens, who is always very lively and quickwitted. Neither of them said a word the whole evening.

Burroughs: I'd evolved the cutups, which Beckett didn't approve of at all.

Sontag: Is he familiar with your work?

Burroughs: Oh yes. He gave me one of the greatest compliments that I ever heard. Someone asked him, "What do you think of Burroughs?" and he said—grudgingly—"Well, he's a writer."

Sontag: High praise indeed.

Burroughs: I esteemed it very highly. Someone who really knows about writing, or say about medicine says, "Well, he's a doctor. He gets in the operating room and he knows what he's doing."

Sontag: But at the same time you thought he was hostile to some of your procedures?

Burroughs: Yes, he was, and we talked about that very briefly when we first came in during the Berlin visit. He remembered perfectly the occasion.

Sontag: Do you think he reads much?

Burroughs: I would doubt it. Beckett is someone who needs no input as such. To me it's a very relaxed feeling to be around someone who doesn't need me for anything and wouldn't care if I died right there the next minute. Most people have to get themselves needed or noticed. I don't have that feeling at all. But there's no point in being there, because he has no desire or need to see people.

Bockris: How did you feel when you left that meeting?

Sontag: I was very glad I had seen him. I was more interested just to see what he looks like, if he was as good-looking as he is in photos.

Burroughs: He looked very well and in very good shape. Beckett is about seventy-five. He's very thin and his face looks quite youthful. It's really almost an Irish streetboy face. We got up and left, the visit had been, as I say, very cordial, decorous. . . .

Sontag: More decorous than cordial I would say. It was a weightless experience, because it's true, nothing happened.

Burroughs: Nothing happened at all.

Sontag: I remember that Allen was carrying on like a puppy. Beckett responded. He's curiously passive, and if someone had been very aggressive and pushy he probably would have responded to that, but if no one wants to do that he's not going to help it in any way, it's really up to you, isn't it?

Bockris: Do you think you'll ever see him again?

Sontag: No.

Bockris: Why not?

Sontag: Why?

Burroughs: There's no likelihood that I will ever see him again.

Sontag: It's interesting when you say that he doesn't need any input. That's true. There are no references in his work, nothing that appears from outside.

Burroughs: Because most writers do. For example, I get a lot from reading, I get a lot from newspapers, but with Beckett it's all inside, I don't think he needs that sort of thing at all.

Sontag: I wonder if he has many books. I would think not.

Burroughs: I didn't see any while we were there, but those of course were temporary quarters.

Sontag: People who are involved in books always manage, even on a trip, to accumulate some.

Burroughs: That's true. I saw no books.

Dinner with Fred Jordan: New York 1980

Jordan: You wrote a piece about the visit to Sam Beckett in Berlin.

Burroughs: I didn't write anything. This is getting to be the local Rashomon. Everyone has a completely different story.

Jordan: Sam was in Berlin at the time, rehearsing *Endgame* in German. John Calder was in Berlin at the same time, and I had lunch with John, Susan, and Allen. I think you were there too.

Burroughs: When Allen asked Susan bluntly if she was dying of cancer?

Jordan: Yes. Allen turned to Susan and said, "You've got cancer, right? How you doin'?" and she said, "Okay." "How's your love life?" "Very good," said Susan, "I'm getting more propositions than ever." John Calder wanted to meet me the next day at five. I told John that I couldn't because I was seeing Beckett. Allen then turned to me and said, "You're seeing Sam? Can I come along?" "Sure," I said, "why not?" And Susan said, "Oh, I've always wanted to see Beckett." "Come along," I said, and before we knew it there were six of us going to see Beckett. The following afternoon when Sam opened the door to all these people he looked a bit surprised. I remember Allen talking to him about whether Joyce wrote songs, and Sam's answer to be that he did. Allen asked Beckett, "Can you sing one for us?" Do you remember when he sang that song, which turned out to be an English version of a Schubert song?

Bockris: How long were you there?

Jordan: For an hour.

Burroughs: Do you remember anything else that Beckett said, or anyone said?

Jordan: Allen kept the conversation up with questions about Joyce. He then asked Beckett what he was doing in Berlin. Allen was the most active interlocutor, but it was getting darker and darker, and there was no light in the room.

Bockris: Why no light?

Jordan: There was a light, but Beckett didn't turn it on.

Burroughs: Quite a signal, I think. Do you remember any direct exchanges between Beckett and Susan Sontag?

Jordan: Afterward she said he was the sexiest man she had ever met. I don't remember any exchange between them.

Burroughs: I think this is a terribly interesting exercise. A number of people saw someone on a sort of momentous occasion and each has a different version of what happened.

Jordan: Do you remember how he was dressed?

Burroughs: He had on a turtleneck sweater, a very hard flat kind of tweed sports jacket, it looked thorn-resistant, not the furry kind, and some kind of slacks. On his feet I have an impression of sandals.

Jordan: Had you known him before you saw him in Berlin?

Burroughs: I met Beckett once in Girodias's restaurant in Paris.

Jordan: Was that the time when, apparently, you explained to Beckett the cut-up method and he responded by saying, "But . . . but that's plumbing, that's not writing!"

Burroughs: Oh, yes, he was quite upset by the whole thing. "You're using other people's words!" he said at one point. I said, "Well, the formula of one physicist is after all available to anybody in the profession." When I saw him in Berlin I reminded him that "I think we've met before, Mr. Beckett." And he said, "Yes, in Maurice Girodias's restaurant," and I said, "Yes, as a matter of fact I remember it very well." That was my opening exchange.

Bockris: Had the Paris meeting been standoffish, had the conversation dribbled to a close?

Burroughs: John said we were both really pretty much drunk at that point, so it just trailed off into amnesia....

NOTES ON
CONTRIBUTORS

Walter Asmus is a theater director in Germany and has acted as Beckett's assistant in several Schiller-Theater productions.

Pierre Astier is professor of twentieth-century French literature at Ohio State University. He is the author of *La crise du roman français et le Nouveau Réalisme: essai de synthèse sur les nouveaux romans* and of *Ecrivains français engagés: la génération littéraire de 1930*. He is also co-editor, with Morris Beja and S. E. Gontarski, of *Samuel Beckett: Humanistic Perspectives*.

Georges Bataille (1879-1962) was a French novelist, essayist, and founder of numerous journals, including *Critique* in 1946.

Tom Bishop is Florence Gould Professor of French at New York University, the author of *Pirandello and the French Theater* and co-editor with Raymond Federman of the Beckett *Cahiers de l'Herne*.

Maurice Blanchot is a French novelist and critic whose major critical work, *L'Espace littéraire* (1955) examines Mallarmé, Kafka, Rilke, and Hölderlin.

Herbert Blau is currently professor of English at the University of Wisconsin—Milwaukee, where he is also a senior fellow at the Center for 20th Century Studies. He was co-founder and co-director (with Jules Irving) of the Actor's Workshop of San Francisco and later co-director of the Repertory Theatre of Lincoln Center in New York. His book *The Impossible Theater* is about his earlier work. He is also the author of *Take up the Bodies: Theater at the Vanishing Point* and *Blooded Thought: Occasions of Theater*.

Roger Blin (1908-84) was a French theatrical director best known as the first to stage Beckett and Jean Genet.

Victor Bockris is the author of *Fighter, Poet, Prophet: The Poetry of Muhammed Ali* and *Nothing Happens: Photographs of Muhammed Ali and Andy Warhol* and editor of *With William Burroughs: A Report from the Bunker.*

Enoch Brater is associate professor of English and Theater at the University of Michigan and has written widely on modern drama and Samuel Beckett in particular. He is editor of *Beckett at 80/Beckett in Context* and the author of *Beyond Minimalism: Beckett's Late Style in the Theater.*

Ruby Cohn is professor of comparative drama at the University of California (Davis) and the author of many books and articles on modern drama, including *Dialogue in American Drama, Currents in American Drama, Modern Shakespeare Offshoots,* and on Beckett, *Samuel Beckett: The Comic Gamut, Back to Beckett,* and *Just Play: Beckett's Theater.*

J. E. Dearlove has written widely on Samuel Beckett and is the author of *Accommodating the Chaos: Samuel Beckett's Nonrelational Art.*

Martin Esslin is professor of drama at Stanford University and the author of many books on modern drama, including *Brecht: The Man and His Work*; *Harold Pinter*; *The Theater of the Absurd*; *Reflections: Essays on Modern Theater*; and *Mediations: Essays on Brecht, Beckett, and the Media.*

S. E. Gontarski is associate professor of English at the Georgia Institute of Technology and author of *Samuel Beckett's 'Happy Days': A Manuscript Study* and *The Intent of Undoing in Samuel Beckett's Dramatic Texts,* and with Pierre Astier and Morris Beja has edited *Samuel Beckett: Humanistic Perspectives.* He is currently editor of the *Journal of Beckett Studies* and editing Volume 2, *Endgame* and *Play,* of the Grove and Faber series *The Theatrical Notebooks of Samuel Beckett.*

Lawrence Harvey is emeritus professor of English at Dartmouth College and the author of *Samuel Beckett: Poet and Critic.*

Wolfgang Iser is professor of English and comparative literature at the University of Constance; among his works to be translated into English are *The Implied Reader: Patterns of Communication in Prose Fiction from Bunyan to Beckett* and *The Act of Reading: A Theory of Aesthetic Response.*

James Knowlson holds a personal professorship in French studies at the University of Reading, where he has also been appointed curator of the Beckett Archive. He is founder of the *Journal of Beckett Studies*, author of *Universal Language Schemes in Britain and France 1600-1800*; *Light and Darkness in the Theatre of Samuel Beckett*; and with John Pilling, *Frescoes of the Skull: The Later Prose and Drama of Samuel Beckett*. He has also edited *Samuel Beckett: An Exhibition* and a bilingual critical edition of *Happy Days*. Professor Knowlson is currently general editor of *The Theatrical Notebooks of Samuel Beckett*, to be published by Grove Press and by Faber and Faber in 1987.

Paul Lawley is tutor in the Department of English and Comparative Literary Studies at the University of Warwick and has published essays and reviews in the *Journal of Beckett Studies*, *Modern Drama*, *Theatre Journal*, and *Modern Language Review*.

Eric P. Levy is assistant professor of English at the University of British Columbia and the author of *Beckett and the Voice of Species*.

Jack MacGowran (1918-73) was an Irish-born actor who worked on numerous productions with Beckett.

Dougald McMillan is the author of *Transition: The History of a Literary Era 1927-1938*; he has edited with Edouard Morot-Sir and Howard Harper, *Samuel Beckett: The Art of Rhetoric* and with Martha Fehsenfeld he has co-authored/co-edited the forthcoming multivolume *Beckett at Work in the Theater*. He is currently editing volume 1, *Waiting for Godot*, in the series *The Theatrical Notebooks of Samuel Beckett*.

Marjorie Perloff is Professor of English and Comparative Literature at Stanford University and is the author of *Frank O'Hara: Poet among*

Painters and *The Poetics of Indeterminacy: Rimbaud to Cage.* She is currently working on a book about futurist poetics before World War I, especially the futurist ruptures between genres, between media, and between verse and prose.

John Pilling is reader at the University of Reading and author of *Samuel Beckett*; *Autobiography and Imagination: Studies in Self-scrutiny*; *A Reader's Guide to Fifty Modern European Poets*; and with James Knowlson, *Frescoes of the Skull: The Later Prose and Drama of Samuel Beckett.* He is also former editor of the *Journal of Beckett Studies.*

Rubin Rabinovitz is professor of English at the University of Colorado and author of *The Reaction against Experiment in the English Novel, 1950-1960*; *Iris Murdoch*; and *The Development of Samuel Beckett's Fiction.*

Richard Seaver was an editor and founder of *Merlin*, a literary journal in post World War II Paris and associate editor of *Evergreen Review.* He was publisher of Seaver Books and is currently president and publisher of Henry Holt and Company.

Alan Schneider (1917-84) was a Russian-born, Tony Award-winning American stage director of Samuel Beckett, Harold Pinter, Edward Albee, and Bertolt Brecht.

Richard Toscan is a professor of Drama at the University of Southern California. He is a playwright, and writes on nineteenth and twentieth century theater.

BOOKS BY SAMUEL BECKETT
Available from Grove Press

BOOKS ABOUT BECKETT AVAILABLE FROM GROVE PRESS